Monetary Policy in a Globalized Economy

'This is a unique collection of essays on monetary policy, banking and finance. I can think of no other book which presents such an authoritative account of recent developments in these fields, and their impact on growth with financial ability in India and abroad. What distinguishes this book is the hands-on experience of its author, Dr Rakesh Mohan, as a central banker, his extraordinary academic credentials, wide international experience and excellence as an economist. I strongly recommend this book to all those who are interested in India's potential as an emerging global economic power of the 21st century.'

—BIMAL JALAN, Former Governor, Reserve Bank of India; and Member of Parliament

'India's success in combining faster growth and low inflation should be of interest to every emerging market country. No one is better able than Rakesh Mohan to explain India's monetary policy and its relevance for the global economy.'

—MARTIN FELDSTEIN, George F. Baker Professor of Economics, Harvard University

'This collection of Rakesh Mohan's insightful articles provides a veritable, tour d' horizon of all the key issues in India's monetary or financial policy. The volume gives us an insider's account written with the knowledge of a professional and the detachment of a scholar. A must read for anyone interested in the monetary and financial aspects of India's reform.'

—MONTEK SINGH AHLUWALIA, Deputy Chairman, Planning Commission

'Rakesh Mohan is that rare economist who has been at the forefront of policy *making* throughout India's economic transformation while also leading the charge on the frontier of academic policy *writing*. The essays in this volume handsomely display his uncanny ability to combine the wisdom of a practitioner with the cutting-edge analysis of an economist. The essays are indispensable for anyone interested in learning how the transformation of the conduct of monetary policy has helped sustain India's growth miracle and what more must be done to further reform this important sector.'

—ARVIND PANAGARIYA, Professor of Economics and Jagdish Bhagwati Professor of Indian Political Economy, Columbia University

'Rakesh Mohan has shaped India's financial sector reforms and participated in formulating monetary and exchange rate policies during his term as Deputy Governor of the Reserve Bank of India. This volume is a collection of his speeches during his term. Not only do his speeches contain far more relevant data than other similar speeches, but they are also unique in their deep analytical content, reflecting his characteristic of analytical thinking that is rare among Indian civil servants. I found the entire volume, in particular the chapters on Indian financial reforms and monetary policy and challenges to monetary policy in a globalizing world, very thought provoking and full of policy insights. The introduction is a masterly survey of issues covered in the book. It is a must read for anyone interested in Indian monetary policy. I highly recommend the volume.'

—T.N. Srinivasan, Samuel C. Park Jr. Professor of Economics, Yale University

'Over the last two decades, the Reserve Bank of India has played a key role in propelling the Indian economy onto the world stage. Rakesh Mohan, Deputy Governor of the RBI, and a leading economist-practitioner, lucidly and convincingly explains how that was done—the monetary policy and financial structure choices that were made, and the challenges that remain. Read the book to better understand—under Rakesh Mohan's expert guidance—the surging Indian economy and key issues that will determine its future.'

—Stanley Fischer, Governor, Bank of Israel

'Rakesh Mohan's book is a valuable addition to the literature on monetary economics. The compulsions of global economy on the conduct of monetary policy is the main theme of the book. The various essays reveal not only scholarship but also a deep understanding of the working of the monetary and financial systems in the emerging economies. All the key concerns of monetary policy such as multiple objectives, nexus with fiscal policy and interaction with exchange rate management are adequately addressed. I warmly recommend the book to academics and policy makers.'

—C. Rangarajan, Former Governor, Reserve Bank of India; Former Chairman, Economic Advisory Council to the Prime Minister; and Member of Parliament

'Dr Rakesh Mohan's book provides unique, extraordinary, deep and timely insights into the complexities of monetary policy in a globalizing economy. The speeches bear the stamp of Dr Mohan's scholarship, association with wide-ranging areas of public policy for three decades, close involvement in central banking in India, and above all, the leading role played by him in multilateral bodies addressing these complex issues. The book narrates the art and science of the subject by one of the most successful and respected central bankers now.'

—Y. Venugopal Reddy, Former Governor, Reserve Bank of India

'Rakesh Mohan gives us an invaluable guide to a complex subject which is becoming increasingly relevant not only for policy makers and scholars but also for the private sector. He covers a great deal of technical ground in a rigorous yet understandable manner while addressing complex issues that have been at the core of policy debate in India for over two decades.'

—Isher Ahluwalia, Chairperson, Indian Council for Research on International Economic Relations

Monetary Policy in a Globalized Economy

A PRACTITIONER'S VIEW

Rakesh Mohan

OXFORD UNIVERSITY PRESS

OXFORD
UNIVERSITY PRESS

YMCA Library Building, Jai Singh Road, New Delhi 110 001

Oxford University Press is a department of the University of Oxford. It furthers the University's objective of excellence in research, scholarship, and education by publishing worldwide in

Oxford New York

Auckland Cape Town Dar es Salaam Hong Kong Karachi Kuala Lumpur Madrid Melbourne Mexico City Nairobi New Delhi Shanghai Taipei Toronto

With offices in

Argentina Austria Brazil Chile Czech Republic France Greece Guatemala Hungary Italy Japan Poland Portugal Singapore South Korea Switzerland Thailand Turkey Ukraine Vietnam

Published in India
by Oxford University Press, New Delhi

First published in 2009
Third impression 2010

ISBN-13: 978-019-569735-3
ISBN-10: 019-569735-9

Typeset in Bembo by Le Studio Graphique, Gurgaon 122 001
Printed in India at De Unique, New Delhi 110 018
Published by Oxford University Press
YMCA Library Building, Jai Singh Road, New Delhi 110 001

Contents

Tables, Figures, and Boxes

TABLES

FIGURES

BOXES

Preface

Issues related to the conduct of monetary and financial sector policies remain at the core of central banking and these are of particular interest to emerging and transition economies. These issues have acquired even greater interest since mid-2007 following the turmoil in the global financial markets and collapse of some major financial institutions. In this context, the Indian experience in the transition of its financial sector and conduct of monetary policy from a regime of extreme financial repression to that of an increasingly market-based system stands out in the global economy. The transition, which has been achieved over a relatively short period of less than two decades, has been associated with a distinct lowering of inflation and inflation expectations and acceleration of growth in an environment of macroeconomic and financial stability. The period has also been associated with financial deepening, efficiency and productivity gains in the domestic banking system, and growing depth and width of domestic financial markets.

I came to the Reserve Bank of India (RBI) in September 2002 as Deputy Governor with little background in the arcane world of monetary theory, monetary policy, or in the conduct of monetary policy operations. Unlike many other central banks today, the Reserve Bank is responsible for a number of functions in addition to monetary policy, which many central banks also performed traditionally but which have been hived off from some of them to varying degrees. The RBI is more like a traditional unified central bank and is the regulator and supervisor of the banking industry, of non-banking financial companies (NBFCs), and of primary dealers. It is also the debt manager of the government, guardian of its foreign exchange reserves, issuer of currency, manager of the payments system, and regulator of the foreign exchange market, of the government securities market, and of interest rate and other derivatives. Like other central banks, it has evolved over time and different functions have assumed greater relative importance in different periods. With this vast expanse of its functions, as Deputy Governor one gets a bird's eye view of the whole financial system and its intricate workings. From the monetary policy making point of view this is invaluable since one is able to observe the monetary transmission mechanism working in real time, along with its shortcomings that are inevitable in a rapidly developing, now middle income, country. The interaction of regulatory policy and practice with the operation of monetary policy has also been very useful to observe, which has also informed the actual practice of monetary policy in India. Thus, I have had the luxury of learning on the job, also perhaps innovating as we have gone along in the past five years, but I hope not at the country's expense!

This book reflects these various features of the Indian financial system, and the conduct and development of monetary policy since the early 1990s. The book represents a collection of my speeches and papers, and reflects my thinking as it has evolved, since 2002. Although this book bears my name as the author, and for which I take full responsibility, it really encompasses the collective work of the highly dedicated Reserve Bank staff.

I was inducted into the art of monetary policy making initially by the then Governor, Dr Bimal Jalan, and then put through my paces by his successor Dr Y. Venugopal Reddy over the last five years. Despite exhibiting vastly contrasting styles, a common penchant for pragmatism in monetary policy making can be described as their hallmark. This was particularly notable during a period in which considerable theoretical and policy making rigidity has crept into monetary policy globally. My own approach therefore reflects this overarching importance being given to the contextual environment that should inform monetary policy making. The underlying objectives of maintaining price stability and economic growth, along with financial stability must dominate, and theory and principles must be used as guidance for achieving these objectives. The adherence to any particular theory should not become an objective in itself.

The implementation of monetary policy is carried out through daily money market operations by all central banks. In our case, such operations also include forex market operations. Liquidity management is therefore rendered more complex with the objective of implementing the monetary policy stance and maintaining overall financial stability. This daily practice is an art in itself, and consistent innovation is the order of the day. I was inducted into this activity very skilfully and patiently by Usha Thorat and later Shyamala Gopinath (who are now my colleague Deputy Governors), as part of the internal Financial Markets Committee (FMC). I owe a deep debt of gratitude to them for keeping me on the straight and narrow, and generously giving me the benefit of their long experience and depth of expertise. The Adviser in charge of the Monetary Policy Department has a crucial role to play in monetary policy making, and also acts as the conscience keeper of the RBI, restraining the worst excesses of pragmatism that Governors and Deputy Governors might be prone to exhibit. D.V.S. Sastry, Deepak Mohanty, K. Kanagasbapathy, and Michael Patra have performed this role over the past five years and, in the process, have been excellent tutors for me. They have tolerated my ignorance with grace: my heartfelt thanks to them.

Speechmaking and communicating is an integral part of central bank functioning. Hence, these essays. It is not possible to produce this volume of writing and speechmaking without a host of ghost writers and advisers. I have had the benefit of constant discussions with my colleagues, spread across the various departments of the Reserve Bank and who have helped extensively in doing all the background work, research, where necessary, and in collating and analysing the vast data that exist in the vaults of the Reserve Bank. Specifically, I would like to express my sincere gratitude to Indranil Bhattacharyya, Abhiman Das, Saibal Ghosh, T. Gopinath, Sanjay Hansda, Meena Hemachandra, Asha P. Kannan, R. Kannan, Arun Vishnu Kumar, Sangeeta Misra, Michael Patra, R.K. Pattnaik, Mridul Saggar, Amitava Sardar, Charan Singh, Chandan Sinha, Indranil Sen Gupta, and Y.S.P. Thorat for their valuable assistance and inputs. Staff members of the Department of Economic Analysis and Policy (DEAP), in particular, are always the front line victims for the speeches of Governors and Deputy Governors. They usually go unheralded. I would like to express my deepest appreciation to all my colleagues in DEAP who are not recorded here.

The brunt of my speechmaking load fell on my Executive Assistants. I was inducted into the Reserve Bank by A. Prasad. He was ably succeeded by Partha Ray, and then by Muneesh Kapur. They have given me their unstinting help through thick and thin, in the day and at night, in India and abroad, in the office and in hotel rooms. Neither the speeches nor this book would have been possible without their help. My heartfelt thanks to each of them, and apologies to their families and friends for keeping them busy at all hours of the day or night over the past five years. A particular word of thanks to Muneesh Kapur for his laborious work in the actual production of this book, both substantive in terms of content, avoidance of repetition, updation of data, and also in proofreading.

My able secretaries Rajalakshmi Balasubramanian and Ashok Bathija have toiled away noiselessly all these years and put up with the innumerable drafts that each speech entailed. My heartfelt thanks for their unstinting, affectionate, and loyal support.

The family always comes at the end of such acknowledgements. My wife, Rasika, has been very happy that all the work entailed in preparing these speeches, and then the compilation of this book, kept me out of her hair in the evenings and on weekends, leaving her free to pursue her own art. My children, Tarini and Rasesh, were largely away at school or college during these years. However, they were always puzzled and curious about what it was that I was doing at my desk all the time.

For their cheerful forbearance and constant support, I dedicate this book to Tarini and Rasesh, especially to keep up the promise I made to them in my last book. However, in recognition of who have really done the work, they have to share this dedication with all the staff of the Reserve Bank.

I would like to express my sincere thanks to the following journals/ organizations for permission to re-print my following speeches in this collection: the Pakistan Institute for Development Economics for 'Reforms, Productivity, and Efficiency in Banking', published in the *Pakistan Development Review*, Volume 44, No. 4, Part 1 (2005); the National Institute of Bank Management for 'Evolution of Central Banking in India', published in *Prajnan*, Volume XXXV, No. 2, July–September 2006; and the *Economic and Political Weekly* for 'Agricultural Credit in India: Status, Issues, and Future Agenda', Volume 41, No. 11, March 2006.

Abbreviations

ACLF	Additional Collateralized Lending Facility
AFS	Available for Sale
AgRC	Agricultural Refinance Corporation
AIDIS	All-India Debt and Investment Survey
APMC	Agricultural Produce Marketing Committee
ARC	Asset Reconstruction Company
ARDC	Agricultural Refinance and Development Corporation
ATM	Automated Teller Machine
BIS	Bank for International Settlements
BoP	Balance-of-Payments
CAD	Current Account Deficit
CAMEL	Capital Adequacy, Asset Quality, Management, Earnings, and Liquidity
CAMELS	Capital Adequacy, Asset Quality, Management, Earnings, Liquidity, and Systems
CBLO	Collateralized Borrowing and Lending Obligations
CCIL	Clearing Corporation of India Ltd
CEO	Chief Executive Officer
CIB	Credit Information Bureau
CLF	Collateralized Lending Facility
CPI	Consumer Price Index
CRAR	Capital to Risk-Weighted Assets Ratio
CRR	Cash Reserve Ratio
DFHI	Discount and Finance House of India
DFI	Development Finance Institution
DI	Deposit Insurance
DICGC	Deposit Insurance and Credit Guarantee Corporation
DVP	Delivery Versus Payment
EBITD	Earnings Before Interest, Taxes, and Depreciation
ECB	European Central Bank
EME	Emerging Market Economy
EMS	European Monetary System

EMU	European Monetary Union
ESCB	European System of Central Banks
EU	European Union
FDI	Foreign Direct Investment
FERA	Foreign Exchange Regulation Act
FHC	Financial Holding Company
FII	Foreign Institutional Investor
FIR	Financial Inter-relations Ratio
FR	Finance Ratio
FRA	Forward Rate Agreement
FRBM	Fiscal Responsibility and Budget Management
FSA	Financial Services Authority
GATT	General Agreement on Tariffs and Trade
GDP	Gross Domestic Product
GNP	Gross National Product
HFT	Held for Trading
HTM	Held to Maturity
IAIS	International Association of Insurance Supervisors
IDBI	Industrial Development Bank of India
IDFC	Infrastructure Development Finance Company
IFCI	Industrial Finance Corporation of India
IFS	International Financial Statistics
IIBI	Industrial Investment Bank of India
IIP	Index of Industrial Production
ILAF	Interim Liquidity Adjustment Facility
IMD	India Millennium Deposit
IMF	International Monetary Fund
IMFC	International Monetary and Financial Committee
IOSCO	International Organization of Securities Commission
IR	Inter-relations Ratio
IRAC	Income Recognition and Asset Classification
IRDA	Insurance Regulatory and Development Authority
IRS	Interest Rate Swap
IT	Information Technology
KCC	Kisan Credit Card
LAB	Local Area Bank
LAF	Liquidity Adjustment Facility
LTCM	Long-term Capital Management
MICR	Magnetic Ink Character Recognition
MNB	Magyar Nemzeti Bank
MoU	Memorandum of Understanding
MSS	Market Stabilization Scheme

NABARD	National Bank for Agriculture and Rural Development
NBFC	Non-banking Financial Company
NDDB	National Dairy Development Board
NDS	Negotiated Dealing System
NDS-OM	Negotiated Dealing System-Order Matching
NEER	Nominal Effective Exchange Rate
NIM	Net Interest Margin
NIR	New Issue Ratio
NPA	Non-performing Asset
NPL	Non-performing Loan
NRI	Non-resident Indian
NSDP	Net State Domestic Product
OECD	Organisation for Economic Co-operation and Development
OeNB	Oesterreichische Nationalbank
OMO	Open Market Operation
OPEC	Organization of the Petroleum Exporting Countries
OTC	Over-the-Counter
PACS	Primary Agricultural Credit Society
PBC	People's Bank of China
PCA	Prompt Corrective Action
PD	Primary Dealer
PDO	Public Debt Office
PLR	Prime Lending Rates
PPI	Producer Price Index
PSB	Public Sector Bank
R&D	Research and Development
RBA	Reserve Bank of Australia
RBI	Reserve Bank of India
RBS	Risk-based Supervision
REER	Real Effective Exchange Rate
RFI	Rural Financial Institution
RIDF	Rural Infrastructure Development Fund
RRB	Regional Rural Bank
RTGS	Real-time Gross Settlement
SARFAESI	Securitization and Reconstruction of Financial Assets and Enforcement of Security Interest
SARS	Severe Acute Respiratory Syndrome
SBI	State Bank of India
SCB	Scheduled Commercial Bank
SCRA	Securities Contracts Regulation Act
SEBI	Securities and Exchange Board of India

SFC	State Financial Corporation
SHG	Self-help Group
SIDBI	Small Industries Development Bank of India
SLAF	Second Liquidity Adjustment Facility
SLR	Statutory Liquidity Ratio
SME	Small and Medium Enterprise
SSI	Small-scale Industries
TFP	Total Factor Productivity
UTI	Unit Trust of India
WEO	World Economic Outlook
WPI	Wholesale Price Index
WTI	West Texas Intermediate
WTO	World Trade Organization

1 Introduction

Interest in the conduct of monetary policy and in regulation and supervision of the financial sector has been unusually high globally over the past decade. The actions of central banks and of other regulatory authorities are now watched more closely than ever before. The unfolding of the present global financial and economic crisis has now brought the actions of central banks into the spotlight.

After the long interregnum caused by the two world wars, when international markets got disrupted in all spheres of activity, coordinated trade liberalization went through a tortuous journey through the second half of the twentieth century under the aegis of the General Agreement on Tariffs and Trade (GATT) and its successor, the World Trade Organization (WTO). As a consequence, by the late 1990s, after the Uruguay Round of the WTO, the international market for goods and services had become substantially liberalized, though trade in services has still some way to go. Corresponding financial liberalization had been slower but it gathered pace through the 1980s and 1990s, with increased opening of both the current and capital accounts, including in developing countries particularly in what are now known as emerging market economies (EMEs). Cross-border financial flows have increased accordingly to volumes never seen or even imagined hitherto. The advent of the information technology (IT) revolution has of course contributed to this transformation of financial flows and of the financial sector alike.

The changes that the financial sector went through during the 1980s and 1990s were also accompanied by a large number of banking and financial sector crises, covering about 100 countries over these two decades, both developed and developing, with the current crisis enveloping the largest advanced economies. Internationally, financial and monetary stability had been anchored by the gold standard in earlier eras, followed by fixed exchange rates based on the sterling anchor and then the US dollar anchor. The advent of floating exchange rates, free trade flows, and cross-border capital flows in the backdrop of growing deregulation and liberalization contributed to the financial instability during the 1980s and 1990s, and now in this decade. The search for a new anchor and the quest for price stability after the high global inflation of the 1960s and 1970s have led to this increased focus on monetary policy and the role and functioning of central banks: hence this popular interest in monetary policy over the past decade.

In fact 'the great inflation of the late 1970s gave way to an age of low, steady inflation thanks in large part to the skill with which central banks learnt to steer policy. The anchoring of inflationary expectations at moderate levels in turn combined with technological change and globalization to support strong steady economic growth...Central banks' success in controlling inflation has won them credibility as economic managers' (*The Economist*, 2007). This credibility was, however, put to a severe test by renewed inflationary pressures during 2008. Indeed, inflation in many countries was at its highest level over the past two decades.

Thus, economists, financial market participants, governments, the media, and members of the general public alike, all express great interest in the actions of central banks. It is now well accepted that, in this environment of generally enhanced credibility of central banks, it is important that the rationale and basis of their policy actions be well understood.

In our own case in India, the overarching economic reforms initiated in December 1991 have included the implementation of monetary policy and financial sector reforms over the whole period since then. Our financial sector was more controlled and repressed than even other EMEs, particularly through the 1970s and 1980s. Thus, our reforms have had a longer trajectory than in many other countries. One distinguishing feature of our trajectory is that financial stability has been successfully maintained despite repeated shocks, both international and domestic. Even in the ongoing global financial crisis, our banks continued to exhibit significant financial stability. It is thus important for us to understand the content of our monetary and financial sector policies as they have evolved over the reform period.

In the best tradition of central bankers, governors and deputy governors of the Reserve Bank of India (RBI) have maintained the convention of recording and documenting their speeches as they are delivered. I have also attempted to maintain this tradition, with two differences: many of my speeches contain more data than is usually done by central bankers, and some have been documented after the passage of some time subsequent to the delivery of the speech. The subject of each speech is clearly influenced by the forum in which it is delivered and the extant topics of contemporary interest. Hence, there is no necessary thematic connection or temporal sequence in the speeches. However, *post facto*, I have been able to group this selection into two themes: the evolution of banking and finance, followed by that of monetary policy and central banking. An underlying theme cutting across the speeches is that of monetary policy and financial sector reform being conducted in the context of increasing globalization, while fostering growth and maintaining price and financial stability in India.

Whereas all these speeches have been published in the *Reserve Bank of India Bulletin*, their availability in this form in one place should provide some understanding of the thinking that has gone on in the evolution of monetary and financial sector policies in these years. This issue has gained new importance in the light of the current financial turbulence that global financial markets have been going through since mid-2007.

BANKING AND FINANCE IN INDIA

Financial market reforms in emerging economies like India have to essentially focus on facilitating increased efficiency in overall financial intermediation while at the same time ensuring financial stability. While there may be some concern over the pace and sequencing of reforms in the financial sector vis-à-vis the real sector in India, a considerable distance has been traversed since 1991. The Indian financial sector has essentially been bank-based, and the funding of a substantial part of economic activity has depended on the efficient functioning of the banking system. With the successive nationalization of banks in 1969 and 1980, and the prevalence of credit rationing, administered interest rates, and overall financial repression, a good deal of reform activity in the 1990s was focused on banking reforms. The first set of chapters in this book therefore deals with the functioning of banks.

Reforms in the financial sector encompassed important issues such as ownership, corporate governance, regulatory and supervisory issues, and the like. The chapter 'Transforming Indian Banking: In Search of a Better Tomorrow' discusses important policy issues that were confronting the financial sector at the beginning of this decade, with ramifications for economic growth and for sustained profitability of the banking industry. First, although banks had started reducing their deposit as well as lending rates by the late 1990s in conjunction with moderation in inflation and corresponding lowering of inflationary expectations, the decline in the nominal lending rates was comparatively slower, thereby leading to some increase in real interest rates at that time. Second, the phenomenon of high lending rates was accentuated by segmentation in the credit market. In general, large corporates have been able to negotiate favourable rates with banks and have been able to bring down their overall interest costs. In addition, the large corporates also have the option of accessing international capital markets for funds through external commercial borrowings. The burden of adjustment has, therefore, fallen on small and medium enterprises (SMEs), which have limited access to funds. The high interest rates paid by SMEs may not always be in accordance with their risk profile. Third, in the context of development finance institutions (DFIs) converting themselves into banks, the future of long-term lending acquires great importance. Fourth, although there has been a significant improvement in the asset quality of banks in the past three to four years, this was not the case around the late 1990s when the absolute amounts of non-performing assets (NPAs) were a major drag on the performance of banks.

A particular feature of fiscal dominance in the 1970s and 1980s had been the increasing pre-emption of resources from the banks in terms of the elevated statutory liquidity ratio (SLR) reaching 38.5 per cent and the cash reserve ratio (CRR) reaching 15 per cent by the early 1990s. These ratios had been brought down to the then statutory minimum of 25 per cent in the case of SLR and to 9.75 per cent in the case of CRR by October 1997. It was expected that this reform would free up bank resources for lending to the private sector. However, it turned out that around the period 1998–2002, banks exhibited a marked preference for safe investment in government securities instead of pursuing their core activity of lending to the commercial sector. Such large investments in government securities, well beyond the statutory requirement, could be best characterized as 'narrow banking', or more popularly as 'lazy banking', which reflected dissipation of banking knowledge capital with regard to credit appraisals. There was a danger of the link between liquidity, credit, money, and economic activity being severed in the long run as a result of continued over-investment in government securities as a substitute for bank financing to the commercial sector.

Against this backdrop, this speech, delivered in December 2002, highlighted the need to work towards reducing the real lending rates of banks. Stress was laid on the need for the government and the RBI to make concerted efforts to remove certain structural rigidities, and for the banks to themselves improve their credit appraisal processes so that they could make their role as financial intermediaries more efficient. The chapter also draws attention to the need for an increased flow of credit to SMEs and also for creating an enabling environment for long-term financing. Reduction in NPA levels and improved risk management by banks would go a long way towards improving efficiency of banks for inculcating a sound credit culture in the economy.

Finance is a crucial ingredient for economic growth. In India, beginning in the 1950s, the industrial financing strategy was largely bank-based, centred around the government as the primary entrepreneur. Banks were expected to provide short-term working capital and DFIs longer-term funds (on the back of the government-guaranteed bonds and concessional RBI funding), with supplementary funding from the capital market. This model of industrial financing started crumbling by the mid-1990s in the wake of macroeconomic stabilization, structural reforms, and emergence of market-based interest rates in an increasingly opening economy. An impression that gained ground in the context of the industrial slowdown in the latter half of the 1990s was that bank finance for industry had gone down. The chapter titled 'Finance for Industrial Growth' examines whether financing was indeed a constraint on the growth process and, in particular, industrial growth during the industrial slowdown phase. A critical analysis revealed a different story: bank credit to industry (including small-scale industries, SSIs) and agriculture, together or individually, increased as a proportion of overall or respective sectoral gross domestic product (GDP). The increase in credit was, however, less than the size of SLR reduction. Banks' non-SLR investments also increased. Long-term financing by DFIs, however, declined with the drying up of concessional sources of financing. Following the stock market's exuberance in mid-1990s, the spurt in capital issues during 1993–6 could not be sustained.

At the same time the analysis suggests that, given banks' maturity profile of liabilities and assets, prevailing levels of fiscal deficit, and the associated supply of long-term government paper (SLR bonds), banks' ability to lend longer-term does seem to be limited. As the government securities market grows and the private placement market is regulated, the corporate bond market needs to be developed, enabling the mobilization of longer-term funds by the larger creditworthy corporates. However, only a small proportion of corporate borrowers can be financed by the capital market: those that can obtain adequate credit ratings and those that are large enough to issue bonds repeatedly. All the others would continue to depend on the banking system for financing their debt needs. This is particularly important in a developing economy where it is essential to foster entry by new entrepreneurs who can then provide competition to incumbents.

As it happens, the level of private saving in India is impressive by international standards and so there is no effective supply constraint on the availability of financial resources. The issue is to channelize these resources efficiently to foster investment and growth by way of knowledge-based banking, management of information, and, where feasible and necessary, securitization of corporate lending as the bond market develops. Banks (and FIs) could play an innovative role in project finance by way of longer-term credit enhancement, take-out financing, guarantees of corporate bonds, and marketization of a mix of loans. In view of the recent developments in international markets, however, financial innovation has to be guided by appropriate regulatory development along with enhancement of expertise among financial market participants, particularly in banks. Project finance is now facing competition from other avenues for long-term lending such as housing loans. Given the preference of retail investors in India to enter the equity markets directly rather than through intermediaries such as mutual funds, investors bear far more risks than in developed economies. Thus, there is a great potential to develop institutional intermediaries to tap these funds: mutual funds, insurance funds, pension funds, investment funds, and venture capital funds. Unlike equity markets, participation in bond markets, even in developed markets, is predominantly by financial institutions. Hence for bond markets to develop in India, it is essential to promote the expansion of institutional investors. Progress on this front will lead to greater supply of long-term funds and help in the development of the corporate bond markets. On the whole, while there is room for a greater role for the market in industrial financing, banking institutions will remain crucial in this area for the foreseeable future.

The Reserve Bank is unique among central banks in that it has a specific mandate in the RBI Act to promote agricultural lending. A good deal of banking development in India has been conditioned by the continuous need for improving the access of farmers to organized credit and to wean them away from money lenders. A perusal of banking history reveals that special committees have been appointed to look into the issue of agricultural credit almost every two to three years by the government or by the Reserve Bank ever since the early 1900s. Problems related to farm credit continue to receive special attention till today. The concern for food security, which guided the Green Revolution, led to a multi-layered 'supply-leading approach' to institutional development for agriculture credit. Rural cultivators' access to institutional credit has increased significantly over the years and the role of informal credit agencies including money lenders has declined, particularly following bank nationalization in 1969, spread of rural bank branches, and introduction of priority sector lending. It is only the recent 2001 All-India Debt and Investment Survey (AIDIS) that suggests that resort to informal credit channels has increased again, and this finding has led to a renewed policy focus on rural credit. But the results of this survey need to be analysed more closely, as argued in the Reserve Bank's *Report on Currency and Finance 2006–08*, before drawing any definitive inferences. During the 1980s and 1990s, commercial banks along with Regional Rural Banks (RRBs) became the main providers of rural credit. Though the overall flow of institutional credit has increased over the years, there are still several gaps: inadequate provision of credit to small and marginal farmers, paucity of medium- and long-term lending and limited deposit mobilization, heavy dependence on borrowed funds by major agricultural credit purveyors, and the existence of an antiquated legal framework alongwith outdated tenancy laws that are said to hamper credit flow. These issues are explored in the chapter 'Agricultural Credit in India: Status, Issues, and Future Agenda'.

While the share of agricultural credit in total credit, and particularly that of small farms, is declining in the wake of a declining share of agricultural GDP, it has been rising as a per cent of the value of agricultural inputs or outputs. The introduction of Kisan (Farmer) Credit Cards has probably aided the process in recent years. Long-term credit as a share of private investment has actually been rising in the 1990s. Thus, the agricultural credit effort did not slacken in the 1990s as is often believed. It is interesting to observe, however, that there are large regional differences in the performance of commercial banks in the delivery of agricultural credit. Expressed as a proportion of net state domestic product (NSDP), agricultural credit is found to be the highest in the southern states, followed by northern, central, eastern, and north-eastern regions.

It is generally believed that organized purveyors of credit, such as commercial banks, experience difficulty in extending agricultural credit because of the higher probability of loans turning into NPAs. It is found, however, that NPAs in agriculture, although higher proportionately than in the non-priority sector, are lower than NPAs in SSI and other priority sectors. Thus, agricultural lending may be more risky than lending for activities in non-priority sectors, but it does not appear as risky as is often believed. Banks therefore need to improve on their risk appraisal and risk management strategies in the agriculture sector: credit appraisal techniques need to be more information-based so that good credits can be better separated from those that could cause difficulty.

Since cooperatives continue to provide just under a half of rural credit, it is essential that they are revitalized and put on a sound business footing. Given the weaknesses of rural financial institutions (RFIs), much more attention is now being given to their strengthening. But this process is inherently difficult because it involves coordinated action by the Central Government, state governments, the Reserve Bank, National Bank for Agriculture and Rural Development (NABARD), and the cooperative institutions themselves. This is what is being attempted now.

As household expenditure on food is shrinking as a proportion of total expenditure, and that on cereals as a proportion of food expenditure, agricultural policy needs to shift its almost exclusive focus from foodgrains to the promotion of other food products and allied activities in pursuit of higher agricultural growth and employment. In the new growth areas of agriculture, the importance of post-harvest activities such as storage, transportation, processing, and marketing of non-cereal products increases which leads to greater links between agricultural diversification and rural industrialization. The success of this strategy depends on developing adequate infrastructural and other support systems, for example, rural roads and cold storage. As a result, credit needs of rural areas are expected to go up due to purchased-input-intensive and heterogeneous production cycles of the new areas of commercializing agriculture. This would also call for designing innovative schemes and products suited to differing nature of agri-business and supply chains for different products.

Accordingly, as the chapter argues, what is needed in agriculture now is a new mission akin to the Green Revolution. The difference now is that we need initiatives in a disaggregated manner in many different segments by region, agricultural products, and agro industry. Expert teams would have to be formed for each agro climate zone focusing on the relevant activities there. These teams can then design different packages that are suitable for each activity and region, just as an integrated package was devised for the Green Revolution. In the case of cereals, because of the broad homogeneity in their production process, a package could be designed on a national scale. The basic ingredients of each of these new packages can be similar: provision of technology inputs, infrastructure, extension services, arrangements for the supply of inputs, and the corresponding credit model.

Having addressed some key issues related to the delivery of credit to industry and agriculture, and banking developments in the 1990s, I now move to broader issues that need further thought and policy consideration. After the nationalization of banks in the 1960s and 1970s, almost 90 per cent of the banking system came to be owned by the Central Government by the early 1990s. A key ingredient of financial sector reforms was the re-introduction of private sector banks in the mid-1990s. This was aimed at fostering new competition into the banking system, which was expected to then lead to greater banking efficiency overall. The share of private sector banks in total assets of commercial banks is now approaching 20 per cent, and the second largest bank in the country is now a private sector bank. Other private sector banks are also growing much faster than public sector banks (PSBs): so their weight in the banking system can be expected to increase for the foreseeable future. As and when the country's political economy permits, there could also be the possibility of PSBs coming into the private sector as the share of government shareholding becomes less than 50 per cent. It is therefore of great importance that the governance and ownership of private sector banks is such that financial stability can continue to be maintained.

The issue of financial stability has received great attention in recent months internationally as financial turbulence in global markets has gathered force since mid-2007. It has also acquired growing explicit importance in the conduct of monetary and financial policies by the Reserve Bank in the past few years. In this context, the health of the banking system is critical. Banks are 'special', whether locally or foreign-owned, because they effectively act as trustees of public funds through their deposit-taking activities. Furthermore, by their very nature, banks have to be highly leveraged in order to be efficient intermediaries of financial resources. The lower the leverage, the higher would be the cost of funds to the borrowers. Thus owners of banks get access to the deployment of funds far in excess of their equity investments, typically by a factor of ten or thereabouts. Given banks' leveraging capacity, owners control huge public funds and, therefore, must be fit and proper as trustees. Moreover, banks form the lynch pins of the payments systems. The speed with which a bank under a run collapses is incomparable with any other organization. Failure, or even the threat of failure, of large banks/ financial institutions have an adverse impact not only on financial stability but can also lead to a significant contraction of real activity, as reinforced by the recent developments in the advanced economies. In a developing economy, there is also much less tolerance for downside risk among depositors, many of who place their life savings in banks. Hence from a moral, social, political, and human angle, the regulator has an onerous responsibility. In fact, it is because of this need for regulation of banks that many central banks were originally founded; it is ironic then that some of them have been relieved of their regulatory responsibilities in recent years. Against this backdrop, the chapter on 'Ownership and Governance in Private Sector Banks in India' explains the analytical foundations that underlie the Reserve Bank's policy on ownership and governance in private sector banks that were issued in February 2005. These guidelines were aimed at strengthening the Indian banking system and moving towards international best practices through a consultative process.

Given the high degree of leverage available to banks, and their role as trustees of public money, concentrated shareholding in banks poses significant risks of moral hazard and excessive economic concentration of power. Furthermore, control or ownership by those who have other significant commercial interests also poses serious issues of conflict of interest. Hence, diversification of ownership is desirable as is the need to ensure fit and proper status of owners and directors. At the same time, however, diversified ownership also poses other problems with respect to the pattern of corporate governance and professional management that is necessary to safeguard depositors' interests and to ensure systemic stability. The regulator/supervisor has to ensure that banks have adequate capital to cushion risks, follow prudent and transparent accounting practices, and are managed in accordance with the best practices for risk management. These issues assume added importance in view of the growing significance and share of private sector banks in the banking industry.

In most countries, an entity—individuals, non-banking financial companies (NBFCs), non-financial firms, or others—wishing to have shareholding beyond a 10 per cent threshold, directly or indirectly, are usually required to seek regulatory approval. Normally, there is no explicit cap on the maximum shareholding by a single entity. The regulators give approval on a case-to-case basis depending on, among others, sectoral impact of the transaction and the satisfaction of 'fit and proper' criteria for the acquirers. Crossholding amongst banks is also typically subject to regulatory approval and the threshold at times is lower than for non-bank entities.

Unlike many other countries, the banking laws in India, till 2004, did not provide for prior approval of the regulator for acquisition of significant ownership in banks—public sector or private sector. There was, therefore, a need for an articulation of policy in public interest and depositor's interest. In June 2004, the 'fit and proper' criteria for directors of private sector banks were spelt out by the RBI on the basis of qualification, expertise, track record, and integrity. In July 2004, banks/FIs were advised that they should not acquire fresh stake, if exceeding 5 per cent of investee bank's equity capital. The final guidelines set out a transparent road map for the existing investors to align their policies and for potential investors to make informed decisions. The intention of the policy was to ensure adequate capital and consolidation in the banking industry with the regulator being aware of the intention of existing and potential shareholders. These principles were made applicable to existing owners but in a non-disruptive and consultative fashion. Whereas there is no uniformity among different countries in the regulations governing bank ownership and governance, all countries have various regulatory provisions that banks have to observe. These issues assume added importance as a financial system undergoes transformation from a predominantly government-owned system to a more mixed one.

As I have already mentioned, the objective of the banking sector reforms in India initiated in the early 1990s was to promote a diversified, efficient, and competitive financial system that then helps to improve the allocative efficiency of resources through operational flexibility, improved financial viability, and institutional strengthening. Thus, whereas the efforts in the 1960s, 1970s, and 1980s were essentially devoted to financial deepening, the focus of reforms in the past decade and a half has been engendering greater efficiency and productivity in the banking system. What has then been the result of this reform process on the actual efficiency of the banking system? In the chapter 'Reforms, Productivity and Efficiency in Banking: The Indian Experience', I assess the impact of the various policy measures on the performance of the banking sector.

Analysis shows that, consequent to the reforms, there has been a consistent decline in the share of PSBs in total assets of commercial banks. The evidence of competitive pressure is well supported, for example, by the declining trend of Herfindahl's concentration index. Nonetheless, it is interesting to find that PSBs appear to have responded to the new challenges of competition, as reflected in the increase in the share of these banks in the overall profits of the banking sector. This suggests that, with operational flexibility, PSBs are competing relatively effectively with private sector and foreign banks. Improvements in efficiency of the banking system, as anticipated, are reflected, inter alia, in a reduction in operating expenditure, interest spread, and cost of intermediation in general. The decline in intermediation cost was facilitated by the large expenditures incurred in upgradation of IT and institution of 'core banking' solutions. Admittedly, intermediation costs of banks in India are still higher than those in developed banking markets. Evidence also supports distinctive improvements in productivity in the banking sector as reflected in substantial increases in indicators such as business per employee and profit per employee. Looking ahead, the challenge for the banks remains three-fold: acquiring the 'right' technology, deploying it optimally, and remaining cost-effective while delivering sustainable returns to shareholders. In effect, 'managing' technology so as to reap the maximum benefits remains a key challenge for the Indian banks.

Further ahead, as the chapter notes, and as I have noted in earlier chapters on agricultural credit and industrial financing, the emergence of new activities in the rural segment such as agri-clinics, contract farming, and rural housing have made rural lending and credit extension to SMEs a viable revenue proposition for banks. PSBs would need to devise imaginative ways of responding to the evolving challenges within the context of mixed ownership. Overall, as deregulation gathers momentum, commercial banks, across all categories, would need to devise imaginative ways of augmenting their incomes and more importantly their fee incomes so as to raise efficiency and productivity levels.

MONETARY POLICY AND CENTRAL BANKING

As already noted, till the early 1990s, the Indian financial sector could be described as a classic example of 'financial repression'. Monetary policy was subservient to the fisc. The financial system was characterized by extensive regulations such as administered interest rates, directed credit programmes, weak banking structure, lack of proper accounting and risk management systems, and lack of transparency in operations of major financial market participants. Such a system hindered efficient allocation of resources. Financial sector and monetary policy reforms, initiated in the early 1990s, attempted to overcome the weaknesses of the pre-reforms regime in order to enhance efficiency of resource allocation in the economy. The chapter 'Financial Sector Reforms and Monetary Policy: The Indian Experience' provides a broad overview of the whole reform experience since the early 1990s and the backdrop to the more detailed discussion of different aspects of monetary policy in subsequent chapters. Since the early 1990s, the Indian economy has achieved high growth in an environment of macroeconomic and financial stability. India's path of reforms has been different from most other EMEs: it has been a measured, gradual, cautious, well-sequenced, and steady process.

The basic emphasis of the Reserve Bank since the initiation of reforms has been to reduce market segmentation in the financial sector through increased inter-linkages between various segments of the financial market including the money market, government securities, and forex markets. Over the past few years, the process of monetary policy formulation has become relatively more articulate, consultative, and participative with external orientation, while the internal work processes have also been re-engineered. Reforms in the monetary policy framework were aimed at providing operational flexibility to the Reserve Bank in its conduct of monetary policy by relaxing the constraint imposed by passive monetization of the fisc. Given the critical role played by financial markets in the transmission mechanism, a number of initiatives have been taken to develop financial markets. Following the reforms, financial markets have now grown in size, depth, and activity paving the way for flexible use of indirect instruments by the Reserve Bank. Since stability in financial markets is critical for efficient price discovery, a liquidity management framework has been put in place for the facilitation of forex and money market transactions that result in price discovery sans excessive volatility. To aid this process, a liquidity adjustment facility (LAF) was introduced in June 2000 to manage daily liquidity in the money market.

An assessment of the banking sector shows that banks have experienced strong balance sheet growth in the post-reform period in an environment of operational flexibility. Significant improvement in capital adequacy and asset quality of banks is distinctly visible. It is noteworthy that this progress has been achieved alongwith the adoption of international best practices in prudential norms. Competitiveness and productivity gains have also been enabled by proactive technological deepening and flexible human resource management, while emphasizing social banking, namely, maintaining the wide reach of the banking system and directing credit towards important but disadvantaged sectors of society. Turning to an assessment of monetary policy, it has been largely successful in meeting its key objectives in the post-reforms period in terms of inflation control, while ensuring adequate availability of credit for productive sectors and ensuring financial stability. It is also noteworthy that monetary policy was successful in maintaining macroeconomic and financial stability, despite serious challenges posed by large and volatile capital flows.

A cross-country comparison of major EMEs that have adopted inflation targeting indicates that growth in India has been amongst the highest while inflation remains relatively low. Amongst the sample of G-20 and major Asian countries, growth in India during 2000–7 was the second highest after China. Inflation in India during the current decade has halved from that prevailing during the 1990s and was lower than many developing economies. Thus, the recent record of macroeconomic management in India is exemplary, even amongst the EMEs that target inflation. The challenge for monetary policy now is to reduce inflation further in the medium term towards international levels, while maintaining the momentum of high growth and preserving financial stability. Of course, inflation rose sharply during 2008 in India, as in many other economies, to intolerable levels. The upsurge in inflation reflected both supply and demand factors. Bringing down the inflation from these high levels and stabilizing inflation expectations, therefore, assumed the highest priority in the stance of monetary policy for the most part of 2008.

Although bank credit has witnessed significant expansion over the past three to four years, demand for bank credit is expected to remain strong in view of the higher growth path as well as relatively lower levels of credit penetration in the country. Banks, especially PSBs, will have to constantly innovate and look for new delivery mechanisms that economize on transaction costs and provide better access to the currently under-served sections, as well as new consumer demands and production demands of rural enterprises and of SMEs in urban areas. Second, fuller capital account openness will lead to a confrontation with the impossible trinity of simultaneous attainment of independent monetary policy, open capital account, and managed exchange rate. Emergence of financial conglomerates as well as enhanced presence of foreign banks over time in an environment of fuller capital account convertibility will pose additional challenges to the maintenance of financial stability. For Indian conglomerates to be competitive, and for them to grow to a semblance of international size, they will need continued improvement in clarity in regulatory approach. There is, as yet, no commonality in the financial structure of each conglomerate in India; in some the parent company is the banking company, whereas in others there is a mix of structure. It is in this context that the RBI has placed a discussion paper on the subject in public domain.

Third, a contemporary issue in central banking is the appropriate response of monetary policy to sharp asset price movements. It is in this context, and consistent with the multiple indicator approach adopted by the Reserve Bank, that monetary policy in India has consistently emphasized the need to be watchful about indications of rising aggregate demand embedded in consumer and business confidence, asset prices, corporate performance, the sizeable growth of reserve money and money supply, the rising trade and current account deficits, and, in particular, the quality of credit growth. In retrospect, this risk-sensitive approach served us well in containing aggregate demand pressures and second round effects during 2006–8 to an extent. Significantly, it also reinforced the growth momentum in the economy. As the economy is subjected to greater opening and financial integration with the rest of the world, the financial sector in all its aspects, as the chapter concludes, will need further considerable development, along with corresponding measures to continue regulatory modernization and strengthening. The overall objective of maintaining price stability in the context of economic growth and financial stability will remain.

A stylized fact of the current global economic environment is the growing degree of trade and financial integration amongst countries. Economic developments abroad have significantly higher impact on the domestic economy compared to the position a couple of decades back. Monetary policy is increasingly required to take into account not only domestic developments but also developments in the global economy and global financial markets. In a globalized environment of interdependent risks, monetary decisions have to be taken under heightened uncertainty. More than ever before, the choice of monetary arrangements depends on those made by other countries. These developments pose additional challenges for monetary management as discussed in the chapter 'Challenges to Monetary Policy in a Globalizing World'.

A notable development over the past couple of decades has been the achievement of low inflation, until the current upsurge, in almost all countries. Institutional changes in the conduct of monetary policy as also globalization, competition, productivity growth, and fiscal consolidation are believed to have contributed to the outcome. Concomitantly, volatility in GDP growth moderated in most G-7 countries, facilitated by rising shares of the services sector, better inventory management, financial innovations, fewer oil supply and price disruptions (until the current oil and food price shocks), and reduction in the material intensity of production. In the wake of globalization of trade and finance, the IT revolution, and erosion of traditional anchors of monetary policy, inflation targeting has emerged as orthodoxy.

Although the practice of inflation targeting is associated with a lowering of inflation over the period it has been in vogue, the jury is still out on the extent to which inflation targeting policies have actually contributed to the reduction in inflation that has occurred. Available empirical evidence does not suggest that inflation targeting improves economic performance. Furthermore, the relevance of a single inflation target for a large economy, in particular, can be debated. A certain amount of target flexibility and balancing of conflicting objectives are unavoidable in the real world, particularly in EMEs. Indeed, there is a growing sense that by the time the current phase of the global business cycle has run itself out, inflation targeting may not be seen to have stood the test of time. The simple principle of inflation targeting thus is also not so simple and poses problems for monetary policymaking in developing countries. As the recent episode of global financial market turmoil has revealed, even central banks with inflation targeting frameworks or price stability as the dominant objective have had to inject liquidity or ease monetary policy in order to maintain financial stability and support growth, notwithstanding persistent inflationary pressures.

An excessive fixation with short-run price stability could also neglect other signs of financial imbalances. Such imbalances can build up even when inflation is low—indeed, the continued expectation of macroeconomic and price stability can lead to exuberance, depress risk premiums, and induce excessive risk taking with adverse implications for future stability, as evidenced by the recent turmoil in financial markets—and hence monetary policy should have a slightly longer time horizon in terms of inflation, and also should focus on financial stability.

With growing external openness and liberalization over the past couple of decades or so, global capital flows to EMEs have increased significantly and these have profound implications for the conduct of monetary policy on a daily basis. Private capital flows to developing countries now vastly exceed official flows, as well as the current account deficits (CADs). With the tail of mobile capital accounts wagging the dog of balance-of-payments (BoP), it is the volume of capital flows—rather than real factors underlying trade competitiveness—that influence exchange rate and interest rates considerably, rendering some of the earlier guideposts of monetary policy formulation anachronistic. Given the experience with capital flows, corner solutions—a fixed peg à la the currency board without monetary policy independence or a freely floating exchange rate retaining discretionary monetary policy—are on the decline and intermediate regimes with country-specific features are observed to be favoured in most EMEs, for example, no target level of exchange rate, forex intervention to ensure orderly movements, and a combination of interest rate and exchange rate intervention during extreme market turbulence. For the majority of developing countries—who are typically labour-intensive export producers—exchange rate volatility can translate into large losses in the export sector particularly and in industry in general, which can then lead to generalized output and employment losses. Faced with loss of control over monetary aggregates, interest rates, and exchange rates, EMEs are resorting to a variety of instruments to manage the large capital flows.

Given the differences in their respective demographic profiles—relatively younger populations in EMEs and aging populations in advanced economies—capital flows to EMEs are likely to be enduring in the coming decades. At the same time, a key public policy challenge for the EMEs, especially in view of their underdeveloped infrastructure, is to ensure productive utilization of saving towards infrastructure development and urbanization.

Although inflation has been well contained over the past couple of decades, relapses in the trend towards globalization, deregulation, and benign fiscal policies could reverse the achievement of low inflation. Sharp increases in oil prices and, in particular, food prices, as were experienced during 2007 and the first half of 2008, run the risk of raising inflation and destabilizing inflationary expectations. Food prices are especially critical for EMEs, given their income levels and also the higher weight of such items in the price indices of EMEs. Reining in inflationary expectations requires clarity on price stability, effective communication, consistency in conduct of policy, and transparency in explaining actions. Policies to improve agricultural production will also be necessary to avoid episodes of sharp increases in food prices, as were observed over the past couple of years.

In a globalized world, it is thus not possible to formulate monetary policy independent of international developments. Continuous monitoring of financial markets, upgradation of technical skills at the central bank, flexibility, and eternal watchfulness hold the key to making monetary policy matter in the evolving global environment. Central banks need to take into account, among others, developments in the global economic situation, the international inflationary situation, interest rate situation, exchange rate movements, and capital movements while formulating monetary policy.

The issues posed above were brought into sharp focus in the international economy around 2005. A number of puzzling developments were observed, such as (a) the US dollar appreciating at that time despite increasing US twin deficits, (b) soaring oil prices accompanied by strong global growth, (c) long-term bond yields falling in the presence of Fed Fund rate hikes, (d) low consumer inflation in the presence of abundant liquidity and increasing asset prices, (e) strong global growth accompanied by slowdown in global saving and investment rates, and (f) the phenomenon of low inflation despite currency depreciation. These stylized facts posing puzzles for contemporary monetary policy at that point of time were flagged and explored for explanations towards designing appropriate policy responses in the chapter 'Some Apparent Puzzles for Contemporary Monetary Policy'.

In view of these monetary puzzles, as noted in the chapter, inflationary pressures could take more than the usual time to surface in conditions of low inflation. So, central banks need to recognize emerging financial imbalances by lengthening their policy horizons beyond the usual two-year framework. In view of the muted role of prices (exchange rate, interest rate, or commodity prices) as equilibrating mechanisms, central banks perhaps need to contribute to financial stability more through prudential regulation and supervision. There may also be a case for a return to more quantity-based instruments, either through micro actions by central banks or structural actions by the fiscal authorities. External imbalances need to be dealt with directly, rather than through increasingly ineffective exchange rate signals.

Given the need for financial stability alongside monetary stability, central banks need, as the chapter stresses, to be cautious before joining the recent trend of separating the monetary and supervisory authorities, particularly in view of the muted behavioural and market responses to the pricing channels of monetary policy. The availability of prudential instruments at the disposal of a central bank can better facilitate its twin task of maintaining monetary and financial stability. Indeed, developments in the UK in the context of the Northern Rock episode in 2007 brought to the fore the risk to financial stability that can emanate from coordination delays that can emerge in an environment of separation of banking regulation and supervision from the monetary authority.

In order to understand the current practices in central banking and monetary policymaking, it is instructive to review the evolution of central banking overall. Modern central banking is essentially a recent phenomenon in historical terms, as there were only about a dozen central banks in the world at the turn of the twentieth century. In contrast, at present, there are nearly 160 central banks. This is not surprising because the need for central banks obviously emerged as banking became more complex, while becoming an increasingly important part of the economy over time. There are a number of core reasons for the founding of central banks: to issue currency, to be a banker and lender to the government, to regulate and supervise banks and financial entities, and to serve as a lender-of-last-resort, as documented in the chapter 'Evolution of Central Banking in India'. What is interesting is that the role of central banks has undergone continuous change over the years in response to emerging changes in the overall economic landscape and to emerging needs in the specific domestic context of different countries. Hence, a great degree of variation is observed in the practice of monetary policy and central banking, both over time and across countries, historically and contemporaneously.

In India, the preamble to the RBI Act laid out the objectives as 'to regulate the issue of bank notes and the keeping of reserves with a view to securing monetary stability in India and generally to operate the currency and credit system of the country to its advantage'. Unusually, and unlike most central banks, the RBI, as noted earlier, was specifically entrusted with an important promotional role since its inception to finance agricultural operations and marketing of crops. A clear objective of the development role of the RBI was to raise the savings ratio to enable the higher investment necessary for growth, in the absence of efficient financial intermediation and of a well-developed capital market. The RBI also assisted the government in starting up several specialized financial institutions in the agricultural and industrial sectors, and to widen the facilities for term finance and for facilitating the institutionalization of savings. This even included the setting up of the first mutual fund in India, the Unit Trust of India (UTI). Specific responsibility for banking regulation and supervision came with the enactment of the Banking Regulation Act in the late 1940s.

The RBI is also the debt manager and banker to the Central Government statutorily and to the state governments by virtue of specific agreements with each of them. Thus, the Reserve Bank has a wide set of responsibilities now, wider than many central banks in the world. The effective loss of autonomy of the RBI that took place in earlier decades was not because of any conscious decision based on the currently prevalent thinking on the relationship between central banks and the government, but rather as a consequence of overall economic policy then prevailing, which gave the government a dominant role in the economy as a whole. Since 1991, following the economic reforms, the situation has witnessed far-reaching changes. The reforms have led to disinvestment in PSBs, encouraged the setting up of private sector banks, deregulation of interest rates, lowering of statutory ratios, cessation of automatic monetization, and implementation of current account convertibility. As excess foreign exchange inflows intensified in 2003–4, cooperation between the Reserve Bank and the Central Government resulted in a rare innovation designed to empower the RBI with new instruments for sterilization in the form of the Market Stabilization Scheme (MSS) that strengthened the Reserve Bank in pursuing its monetary policy objectives. In order to provide greater monetary policy flexibility to the RBI, the government introduced amendments to the RBI and Banking Regulation Acts in Parliament. These developments since 1991 indicate that the RBI already enjoys substantial autonomy in formulation of monetary policy.

As in other countries, the role of the Reserve Bank has evolved along with changes in the overall economic landscape. The RBI has, over the years, transformed itself continuously, functionally, and structurally, in response to the changing needs of the economy and government policies. During the years of administered interest rates and credit allocation, it assisted the government in these activities. When there was a need to set up new DFIs, it did so. Since the early 1990s, as the Indian economy has been liberalized in all its aspects, so has the Reserve Bank in its oversight of the financial sector and this has contributed to the development of financial markets. The practice of monetary policy has also evolved accordingly. Looking ahead, it will need to continue taking calibrated measures to strengthen the domestic banking and financial sector while ensuring greater financial inclusion. The RBI would need to further develop the financial markets to enhance the efficiency of the monetary transmission mechanism. Price stability and financial stability would continue to be of concern with expected increase in credit expansion and global integration.

A key task of central banks, without exception, is that of liquidity management. In fact, the implementation of monetary policy is conducted through monetary operations that modulate liquidity in the economy, and which directly affect the determination of short-term interest rates. What is interesting is that the conduct and mode of these operations is generally taken for granted. There is little discussion in the public domain of how these monetary operations are actually conducted by central banks. It is only in recent months that these operations have come into focus as the key central banks in major advanced economies had to conduct unprecedented monetary policy and liquidity management operations to manage the systemic strains in liquidity that have emerged since mid-2007.

In contrast to the current ongoing turmoil that has led to the sudden drying up of liquidity in both advanced economies and EMEs, the EMEs have over the past decade or so been largely characterized by excess liquidity in view of large capital flows. As a result, the conduct of monetary policy and management of liquidity in the context of large and volatile capital flows has proved to be difficult for many EMEs in recent years. Like other EMEs, monetary policy in India too has faced growing challenges in liquidity management from the significant increase and the volatility in capital flows. While capital flows appeared to be mean reverting till October 2002, there appears to have been a strong trend with wider oscillations subsequently. The Reserve Bank now has to cope with larger and more volatile capital flows than it had been faced with in about a decade from the onset of reforms. Large movements in government cash balances in the recent period have also posed challenges for domestic liquidity management. As discussed in the chapter 'Coping with Liquidity Management in India: A Practitioner's View', the changed scenario required appropriate policy responses. The evolving policy mix involved careful calibration that took into account diverse objectives of central banking, changes in the monetary policy framework and operating procedures, and widening of the set of instruments for liquidity management.

In view of the large capital flows, the problem for monetary management was two-fold. First, it had to distinguish implicitly between durable flows and transient flows. If capital flows are deemed to be durable, questions arise regarding the appropriate approach for determination of the exchange rate. If the flows are deemed to be semi-durable, essentially reflecting the business cycle, the task of monetary and liquidity management is to smoothen out their impact on the domestic economy, finding means to absorb liquidity in times of surplus and to inject it in times of deficit. Second, in the short term, daily, weekly, or monthly volatility in flows needs to be smoothened to minimize the effect on domestic overnight interest rates. In practice, ex ante, it is difficult to distinguish what is durable, what is semi-durable, and what is transient. Hence policy and practice effectively operate in an environment of uncertainty and a variety of instruments have to be used to manage liquidity in this fluid scenario.

The LAF, which was introduced in June 2000 in order to facilitate the shift from direct to indirect monetary policy instruments, has now emerged as the principal operating instrument of monetary policy. Although there is no targeting of point overnight interest rates, the LAF is designed to nudge overnight interest rates within a specified corridor, the difference between the fixed repo (injection) and reverse repo (absorption) rates. The LAF has had a pronounced favourable impact of lowering the volatility of short-term money market rates which had been much higher hitherto. Call rates have become largely bounded by the interest rate corridor after the introduction of the LAF, except for some very brief episodes of volatility.

Monetary management since mid-2002 has clearly focused on managing surplus liquidity. However, given that RBI had a finite stock of government securities, its ability to mop up large capital inflows indefinitely was therefore limited. In order to address these issues the Reserve Bank introduced the MSS in March 2004. The new instrument empowered the Reserve Bank to undertake liquidity absorption on a more enduring but still temporary basis. In the context of capital outflows in the second half of 2008, MSS redemptions and buybacks facilitated injection of liquidity into the system. The MSS has, thus, the flexibility to both inject and absorb liquidity, as warranted. The introduction of MSS has succeeded in restoring LAF to its intended function of daily liquidity management.

An important element in coping with liquidity management has been the smoothening behaviour of the central bank and the communication strategy. Markets are prepared with a careful communication on the stance of the monetary policy in the quarterly reviews. Policy communications have been backed by credible actions in accordance with stance to keep inflation in tight leash.

In spite of the relative success in liquidity management in India, several challenges remain ahead. First, absence of a vibrant term market, the illiquidity of a large set of securities, and limitations of corporate debt market continue to impede further refinements in liquidity management. Second, passive operations by the Reserve Bank in the market may be resulting in some market players not being proactive in their own liquidity management. Third, as the system moves to maintenance of SLR securities at the prescribed minimum levels, liquidity provision would become more difficult unless the instrument set is widened or the SLR is reduced. Fourth, there is an urgent need to bridge the institutional gap with minimal necessary changes so that market operations retain their efficiency. Finally, further improvements in liquidity management would substantially depend on our abilities to improve forecasting of liquidity in the system.

Although financial stability has always been of concern to the central banks, it has attracted more widespread specific attention in recent years, and has now achieved centrestage in the ongoing global financial crisis. However, there is no consensus on the definition of financial stability. Thus, unlike price stability, financial stability cannot be easily summarized into a single measure. Monitoring financial stability needs to encompass not only financial institutions and markets, but also the state of financial infrastructure. Integrity of the payment system is at the core of the financial system, and confidence in the use of money as a unit of account is essential to maintenance of financial stability. These are some of the issues addressed in the chapter 'Central Banks and Risk Management: Pursuing Financial Stability'.

Following the breakdown of the Bretton Woods system and loss of monetary anchor, there has been increasing quest for financial stability. By 1990s, open trade and capital accounts led to huge cross-border flows, which, coupled with deregulation, liberalization, and disintermediation, made financial systems more interconnected and prone to contagion risk. The sources of crises, which used to be one of the banking sector weaknesses, also became more varied. The Asian crisis as well as the 2008 financial crisis demonstrated that crises could also affect economies with sound fundamentals. In view of deficient international financial architecture, avoiding crises becomes ultimately a national responsibility. Central banks, traditionally mandated with the task of monetary and banking stability as also integrity of payments and settlement system, became the natural choice for the oversight of financial stability and, explicitly by legislation, in many countries. Following the transfer of supervisory responsibility outside, macro financial stability coupled with its communication has been the focus of many central banks.

Since the 1990s, the Indian economy has been subject to several shocks, both external and domestic. Unlike in the past, when such shocks had resulted in significant economic disruptions during this period, the Indian economy withstood these shocks well, with limited impact on the financial sector. The Reserve Bank's two-track approach to ensuring financial stability has helped in this process. First, monetary policy has helped in bringing down inflation and inflationary expectations. Second, the interconnected measures designed to develop financial markets, payment, and settlement systems and other financial infrastructure, along with further development of banking regulation and supervision, have all contributed to the maintenance of financial stability in India since the early 1990s. With regard to institutions, a Board for Financial Supervision was founded within the Reserve Bank in 1994 to upgrade its practice of financial supervision, and the degree of compliance with the Basel Core Principles has gradually improved. To induce better corporate governance, as noted earlier, guidelines on ownership and governance for banks have also been issued. Deposit insurance (DI) is mandatory and covers all banks. The RBI, rather than closing down insolvent banks, has preferred their merger with healthy banks in view of systemic concerns and in defence of small depositors. Given the multi-faceted nature of financial stability, the Ministry of Finance has constituted a High-Level Coordination Committee on Financial and Capital Markets to address policy gaps and overlaps. This arrangement is working smoothly and is contributing to the maintenance of financial stability in the economy.

Issues related to financial instability have been evident quite strikingly in recent months in a number of countries following the turmoil in the global financial markets in response to the sub-prime woes in the US. Although the problems originated in the US credit markets, they spread quite quickly to financial markets of other major advanced economies and, with some lags, those of EMEs. The sudden loss of liquidity and sharp increase in risk aversion forced central banks in a number of economies to inject massive liquidity, take unorthodox steps such as expanding the range of eligible collateral, enter into swap agreements with the US Federal Reserve, and also extending liquidity for longer maturities than is usually done by central banks. Further, they have reduced policy rates so as to stabilize financial markets and maintain overall macroeconomic and financial stability while attempting to safeguard economic growth. Governments in both advanced economies and EMEs have been forced to provide guarantees not only for bank deposits without limit but also for banks' other liabilities for an extended period to prevent run on banks and maintain financial stability. Risks to financial stability are expected to remain elevated in the coming years given the fast pace of deregulation, liberalization, openness, financial innovations, and introduction of complex instruments. The Indian financial system is not quarantined from global developments, but it remains robust, underpinned by the continued expansion of the Indian economy. The task is to remain alert, eschew harmful incentives, and adjust the regulatory environment for addressal of unforeseen contingency.

The concluding chapter 'Monetary and Financial Policy Responses to Global Imbalances' focuses on the issue of large global imbalances that has been debated at length since the beginning of this decade. Global imbalances in the international economic system refer to the large CADs of the US and correspondingly large surpluses in other regions, particularly in Asia. The concerns arise primarily over unsustainability of such imbalances and chances of disorderly adjustment hampering the global economy, in general. While the existence of global imbalances is well recognized, there are still no definite answers on its possible impact and what policy responses need to be considered. There is an emerging consensus that the US consumers cannot continue to support worldwide demand indefinitely and Asian EMEs and oil-exporting countries cannot continue financing these perpetually. Yet, there are differing views on the process of correction, its nature, pace, and consequences. In this context, any action for orderly medium-term resolution of global imbalances is a shared responsibility, and will bring greater benefit to members and the international community than actions taken individually. Key elements of an orderly global rebalancing which are generally advocated include increase in US savings, structural reforms in the Euro area and Japan, and exchange rate flexibility in EMEs. Furthermore, promoting efficient absorption of higher oil revenues in oil-exporting countries with strong macroeconomic policies should also be a key element of this correction mechanism.

Unlike in many of the Asian EMEs where current account surpluses have mainly contributed towards greater accumulation of reserves in these economies, in India reserve accumulation has been mainly due to large capital flows and the current account surplus had only a minimal role to play in this regard, for a few years. Thus, it is clear that India, as such, has not contributed towards enhancing global imbalances.

As regards the impact on India, as pointed out in the chapter, the effect of global imbalances could be indirect through a rise in domestic interest rates as a consequence of rise in international rates, which could increase the cost of incremental borrowings of the government. Moreover, if there are sharp fluctuations in interest rates and exchange rates on account of the adjustment process, corporates that have borrowed at variable rates would be subject to both exchange rate and interest rate risks. Furthermore, should there be any reversal of capital flows, asset prices could potentially decline. The most significant impact on banks' balance sheets, however, could be felt through their investment portfolio in government and other fixed income securities. To the extent a rise in international interest rates impacts the domestic interest rates, it would entail marked-to-market losses on the investment portfolios. Any disorderly unwinding of global imbalances is likely to have global ramifications and may affect the Indian economy indirectly. Any reversal of global capital flows from emerging and developing economies in the case of realignment of interest rates and slow investment growth on account of higher interest rates with the tightening of monetary policy stance by major central banks, as the chapter argues, remain the other downside risks. Of course, the current economic situation is diametrically opposite to the scenario that I had envisaged at the time when I spoke about this issue. The global economic situation has witnessed significant changes since mid-2007; growing signs of economic weaknesses have led to large cuts in key policy rates in the US and other economies as well. Nonetheless, the risk of capital outflows from EMEs has indeed fructified reflecting risk aversion to holding EME assets. Large capital outflows from EMEs in the second half of 2008 have led to sharp downward pressures on exchange rates and stock markets and on to real activity.

At the same time, it needs to be recognized that, during the last fifteen years, the opening up of the Indian economy has been accompanied with various measures to reform the financial sector, improve its fundamentals and create some built in measures to ensure financial stability. This approach has given the Indian economy enough resilience to withstand some major global risks. Indian growth prospects remain bright in the future and any significant correction to global imbalances via abrupt and sharp changes in exchange rates and international interest rates will be taken into account through appropriate policy responses.

The turmoil in international financial markets since late July 2007 and the increased uncertainty that financial markets are currently experiencing have brought issues relating to financial sector stability to the fore. In some ways, the recent developments are unprecedented in their occurrence and in terms of the emerging magnitude of financial sector losses. The sudden loss of confidence among traditional counterparties reflects extreme information asymmetry arising from the complex layering of risk diffusion and high leveraging, and the breakdown of risk assessment by reputed rating agencies and the like. The speed of contagion and the extensive involvement of large, reputed, and regulated financial institutions are indicative of regulatory shortcomings, which have then necessitated unconventional responses of central banks. All this has raised serious concerns relating to the ability and flexibility of national financial systems to withstand shocks emanating from such unusual developments. It has also spurred some reconsideration on certain aspects of monetary policy and of financial regulation, particularly as they relate to the maintenance of financial stability.

India has so far remained relatively insulated from these developments. Whereas this may be regarded by some as fortuitous, it is perhaps our nuanced approach to financial sector reform and development that has served us well; our approach has been marked by conscious gradualism with the implementation of coordinated and sequenced moves on several fronts that are predicated on the preparedness for change of the financial system in particular, and of the economy in general. We have also built in appropriate safeguards to ensure stability, while taking account of the prevailing governance standards, risk management systems, and incentive frameworks in financial institutions in the country.

While the overall policy approach has been able to mitigate the potential impact of the turmoil on domestic financial markets and the economy, with the increasing integration of the Indian economy and its financial markets with rest of the world, there is recognition that the country does face some downside risks from these international developments. As the Afterword, 'Global Financial Crisis and Key Risks: Impact on India and Asia', observes, the risks arise mainly from the potential reversal of capital flows on a sustained medium-term basis from the projected slowdown of the global economy, particularly in advanced economies, and from some elements of potential financial contagion. In India, the adverse effects have so far been mainly in the equity markets because of reversal of portfolio equity flows, and the concomitant effects on the domestic forex market and liquidity conditions. With external savings utilization low traditionally, between 1 and 2 per cent of GDP, and the sustained high domestic savings rate, the macroeconomic impact can be expected to be at the margin. The continued buoyancy of FDI suggests that confidence in Indian growth prospects remains healthy. As regards the domestic banking system, no direct impact on account of *direct exposure* to the sub-prime market is in evidence. However, stronger than anticipated slowdown in growth in advanced economies—indeed a contraction is expected in 2009—and the significant deceleration in world trade along with the reversal of capital outflows are expected to have some adverse impact, albeit temporary, on our growth prospects. But, compared to many other economies, our financial sector and real economy have exhibited remarkable resistance to the worsening external environment. The various pro-active steps being taken by the Reserve Bank and the government to boost aggregate demand in the face of external shocks should also help to minimize the impact on growth.

India has, thus, by-and-large been spared of global financial contagion due to the sub-prime turmoil for a variety of reasons noted. Financial stability in India has been achieved through perseverance of prudential policies which prevent institutions from excessive risk taking, and financial markets from becoming extremely volatile and turbulent.

Overall, these progressive but cautious policies have contributed to efficiency of the financial system while sustaining the growth momentum in an environment of macroeconomic and financial stability. The policy challenge is to continue to ensure financial stability in India during this period of international financial turbulence, while maintaining the momentum of high growth accompanied by price stability.

2 Transforming Indian Banking
In Search of a Better Tomorrow*

The significant transformation of the banking industry in India is clearly evident from the changes that have occurred in the financial markets, institutions and products. While deregulation has opened up new vistas for banks to augment revenues, it has entailed greater competition and consequently greater risks. Cross-border flows and entry of new products, particularly derivative instruments, have impacted significantly on the domestic banking sector, forcing banks to adjust the product mix, as also to effect rapid changes in their processes and operations in order to remain competitive to the globalised environment. These developments have facilitated greater choice for consumers, who have become more discerning and demanding compelling banks to offer a broader range of products through diverse distribution channels. The traditional face of banks as mere financial intermediaries has since altered and risk management has emerged as their defining attribute.

Report on Trend and Progress of Banking in India 2001–2, RBI.

Currently, the most important factor shaping the world is globalization. The benefits of globalization have been well documented and are being increasingly recognized. Integration of domestic markets with international financial markets has been facilitated by tremendous advancement in information and communications technology. But, such an environment has also meant that a problem in one country can sometimes adversely impact one or more countries instantaneously, even if they are fundamentally strong.

There is a growing realization that the ability of countries to conduct business across national borders and the ability to cope with the possible downside risks would depend, inter alia, on the soundness of the financial system. This has consequently meant the adoption of a strong and transparent, prudential, regulatory, supervisory, technological, and institutional framework in the financial sector on par with international best practices. All this necessitates a transformation: a transformation in the mindset, a transformation in the business processes, and finally, a transformation in

* Valedictory address at the Bank Economists' Conference 2002, at Bangalore on 29 December 2002.

knowledge management. This process is not a one shot affair; it needs to be appropriately phased in the least disruptive manner.

The banking and financial crises in recent years in emerging economies have demonstrated that, when things go wrong with the financial system, they can result in a severe economic downturn. Furthermore, banking crises often impose substantial costs on the exchequer, the incidence of which is ultimately borne by the taxpayer. The World Bank *Annual Report* (2002) has observed that the loss of US$ 1 trillion in banking crises in the 1980s and 1990s is equal to the total flow of official development assistance to developing countries from 1950s to the present date. As a consequence, the focus of financial market reform in many emerging economies has been towards increasing efficiency while at the same time ensuring stability in financial markets.

From this perspective, financial sector reforms are essential in order to avoid such costs. It is, therefore, not surprising that financial market reform is at the forefront of public policy debate in recent years. The burgeoning literature on endogenous growth theory has come to recognize the crucial role of sound financial markets in promoting rapid economic growth and ensuring financial stability. Indeed, it is by now widely documented that the structure of financial markets helps explain why some countries remain poor, while others grow richer. Financial sector reform, through the development of an efficient financial system, is thus perceived as a key element in raising countries out of their 'low level equilibrium trap'. As the World Bank *Annual Report* (2002) observes, 'a robust financial system is a precondition for a sound investment climate, growth and the reduction of poverty'.

Financial sector reforms were initiated in India a decade ago with a view to improving efficiency in the process of financial intermediation, enhancing the effectiveness in the conduct of monetary policy, and creating conditions for integration of the domestic financial sector with the global system. The first phase of reforms was guided by the recommendations of Narasimham Committee I. The approach was to ensure that 'the financial services industry operates on the basis of operational flexibility and functional autonomy with a view to enhancing efficiency, productivity, and profitability'. The second phase, guided by Narasimham Committee II, focused on strengthening the foundations of the banking system and bringing about structural improvements. While there may be some debate over the pace and sequencing of reforms in the financial sector vis-à-vis the real sector, we have traversed a considerable distance since 1991. Reforms in the financial sector and their beneficial impact have been well documented and I will not attempt to repeat them here.

I would, therefore, in this chapter like to sensitize the readers with certain important policy issues confronting the financial sector at the present juncture.

I believe they are critical in my opinion because they have important ramifications for economic growth and for sustained profitability of the banking industry. These issues are at the forefront of policy discussions on Indian banking and therefore need to be proactively addressed.

INTEREST RATE SCENARIO

The first important issue that I would like to highlight relates to interest rates.

As a result of interest rate deregulation, the interest rate structure of banks is competitively determined in the market, barring a few exceptions. A major factor that has influenced the trend in interest rates is the sustained decline in the inflation rate in the recent period. Notwithstanding year-to-year fluctuations, there has been a distinct downward drift in the inflation rate during the second half of the 1990s, which is now at around half the level as compared with the first half of the 1990s. Both the popular measures of inflation—the Wholesale Price Index (WPI) and the Consumer Price Index (CPI)—have shown a definite fall in the recent period. For example, the WPI on an average basis has declined from an average of about 10.5 per cent per annum between 1990–1 and 1995–6 to about 5 per cent per annum over the last five years. A similar trend can be observed with regard to the CPI for industrial workers. In the current year so far, inflation as measured by variations in WPI has remained benign around 3 per cent despite the adverse effect of drought and uncertainty on account of oil prices. As the inflation rate has decelerated, it has also had a positive impact on inflationary expectations. This is clearly reflected in the downward trend in nominal interest rates.

For instance, the overnight call money rate has fallen sharply from about 13 per cent in August 2000 to the current levels of 5.5 per cent. Similarly, the 91-day Treasury Bill rate declined from 10.5 per cent to 5.4 per cent and the 364-day Treasury Bill rate from 10.9 per cent to 5.6 per cent over the same period.

The long-term interest rates too have declined. The yield on ten-year government securities has declined from 11.5 per cent in August 2000 to the current levels of about 6.3 per cent. Similarly, interest rates on corporate paper have fallen significantly. For example, the interest rate on five-year AAA-rated corporate paper has declined from 12 per cent in August 2000 to about 6.7 per cent currently.

The banks have also reduced their deposit rates. The term deposit rates of PSBs over one year maturity have declined from a range of 8–10 per cent in August 2000 to 6–8 per cent now. This fall in the interest rates in the recent period has been in consonance with the monetary policy stance of a soft and a flexible interest rate regime. Despite the fall in deposit rates, depositors have received positive real interest rates of close to 2 per cent in the second half of the 1990s, which is much higher than the real return on deposits during the first half of the 1990s.

On the other hand, lending rates of banks have not come down as much. While banks have reduced their prime lending rates (PLRs) to some extent and are also extending sub-PLR loans, effective lending rates continue to remain high (Table 2.1 and Figure 2.1). It is estimated that the average lending rate of scheduled commercial banks (SCBs) has declined from a peak of about 17 per cent in 1995–6 to about 14 per cent by 2001–2. Hence, while nominal interest rates have come down, they have not fallen as much as the inflation rate. Consequently, the effective real lending rate continues to remain high. This development has adverse systemic implications, especially in a country like India where interest cost as a proportion of sales of corporates is much higher as compared to many emerging economies.

A cross-country comparison of interest rate trends during the 1990s provides some interesting insights (Table 2.2). The average inflation rate in all these countries has come down during the second half of that decade (1997–2001) as compared to the first half. In line with this, the average money market interest rates and government securities yields have also come down in real terms in most countries. On the lending side, however, prime rates in some countries have not shown similar falls in real interest rates (United Kingdom, Germany, Japan, Thailand, and Hungary). Thus, the Indian experience of sticky real lending rates is not unique. But, preliminary estimates do show a high correlation between government securities yields and real lending rate in Japan, India, and Germany during the 1990s as a whole. Hence, the downward rigidity in lending rates in India as compared with the government securities rates during the second half of the 1990s does seem more surprising in this context. It would seem that changes in inflationary expectations take a little longer to adjust than inflation rates themselves. It would be rational for interest rates to be related to inflationary expectations, and in particular, long-term interest rates. Therefore, bank economists have an important role of informing the management of appropriate inflationary expectations so that interest rates can be adjusted more systematically.

Understandably, there are certain rigidities in the overall interest rate structure in the economy that constrain banks from reducing their lending rates. These have been well documented in the earlier monetary and credit policy statements of the RBI. Subsequently, interest rates on small savings have also moved down and there is a commitment from the government to link these rates with market related rates. The recovery environment has also improved. A related issue pertains to transparency in lending rates. Especially after the introduction of sub-PLR lending by banks, the spreads between the minimum and maximum lending rates seem to have widened.

Table 2.1 Real Interest Rates

(per cent)

Year ended March	Weighted average lending rate of SCBs[a]	Weighted average interest rate of Central Government securities	Average cost of aggregate deposits of SCBs	Average cost of time deposits of SCBs	Inflation rate			Real interest rate		
					WPI	Manufactured products	CPI-IW	Borrowers	Central Government	Depositors
1	2	3	4	5	6	7	8	9 = (2 – 7)	10 = (3 – 6)	11 = (5 – 8)
1990–1	15.0	11.4	8.1	10.6	10.3	8.4	4.6	6.6	1.1	6.0
1991–2	16.5	11.8	7.1	9.1	13.7	11.3	13.5	5.2	–1.9	–4.4
1992–3	16.8	12.5	7.7	9.6	10.1	10.9	9.6	5.9	2.4	0.0
1993–4	16.5	12.6	6.9	8.7	8.4	7.8	7.5	8.7	4.2	1.2
1994–5	16.1	11.9	6.4	7.0	12.5	12.2	10.1	3.9	–0.6	–3.1
1995–6	17.1	13.8	6.9	8.5	8.1	8.6	10.2	8.5	5.7	–1.7
1996–7	16.9	13.7	7.6	9.4	4.6	2.1	9.4	14.8	9.1	0.0
1997–8	16.3	12.0	7.3	8.8	4.4	2.9	6.8	13.4	7.6	2.0
1998–9	15.5	11.9	7.4	8.9	5.9	4.4	13.1	11.1	6.0	–4.2
1999–2000	15.0	11.8	7.1	8.6	3.3	2.7	3.4	12.3	8.5	5.2
2000–1	14.3	11.0	6.8	8.1	7.2	3.3	3.8	11.0	3.8	4.3
2001–2	13.9	9.4	7.0[b]	8.3[b]	3.6	1.8	4.3	12.1	5.8	4.0

Contd

Table 2.1 Contd

(per cent)

Year ended March	Weighted average lending rate of SCBs[a]	Weighted average interest rate of Central Government securities	Average cost of aggregate deposits of SCBs	Average cost of time deposits of SCBs	Inflation rate			Real interest rate		
					WPI	Manufactured products	CPI-IW	Borrowers	Central Government	Depositors
1	2	3	4	5	6	7	8	9 = (2 – 7)	10 = (3 – 6)	11 = (5 – 8)
					Average					
1990–1 to 1995–6	16.3	12.3	7.2	8.9	10.5	9.9	10.4	6.5	1.8	–0.3
1996–7 to 2001–2	15.3	11.6	7.2	8.7	4.8	2.9	6.8	12.5	6.8	1.9

Notes: [a] Data are exclusive of RRBs and pertain to last Friday of March.
WPI: Wholesale Price Index; CPI-IW: Consumer Price Index-Industrial Workers.

Sources: 1. *Statistical Tables Relating to Banks*, RBI.
2. *Handbook of Statistics on Indian Economy*, RBI.

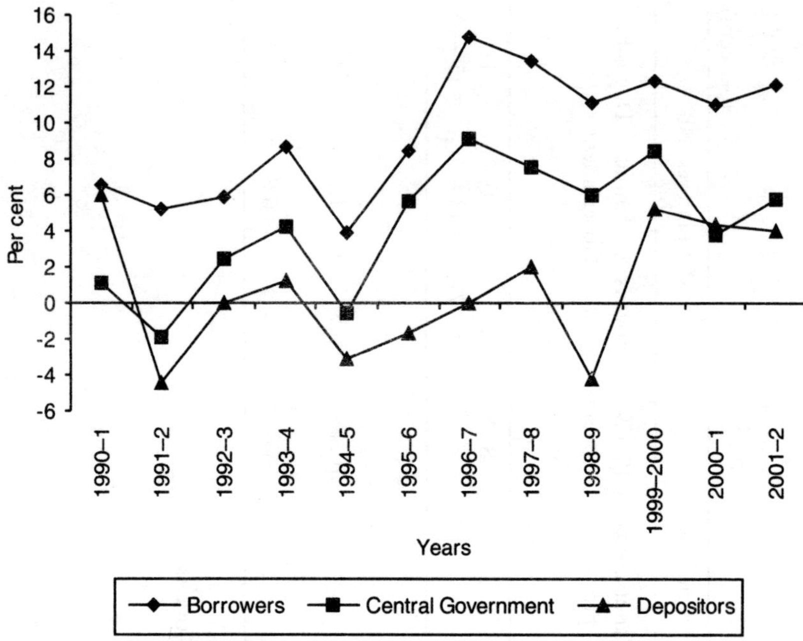

Figure 2.1 Real Interest Rates

Notes: For borrowers: weighted average lending rate – inflation rate of manufactured goods. For government: weighted average yield – WPI inflation rate. For depositors: average interest rate – CPI inflation rate.

Source: *International Financial Statistics* (*IFS*), International Monetary Fund (IMF).

The RBI is making efforts to publish on its website bank-wise information on the minimum and maximum lending rates. Our own internal exercises reveal that the concept of PLR may need to be reviewed in the current context. Perhaps, bank economists may like to study the international experience and come out with suggestions.

LENDING TO SMALL AND MEDIUM ENTERPRISES

The problem arising out of high lending rates gets accentuated due to segmentation in the credit market. The large corporates are able to negotiate fine rates with banks and are able to bring down their overall interest costs. In addition, the large corporates have the option of accessing the international capital markets for funds. The burden of adjustment has, therefore, fallen on SMEs, which have limited access to funds. The high interest rates paid by SMEs may not always be in accordance with their risk profile.

Table 2.2 Comparative Picture on International Real Interest Rates

(per cent)

Country and period average	Money market rate	Long-term government securities yield	Prime rate	Inflation rate	GDP growth
US					
1991–6	1.50	3.71	4.40	3.09	2.58
1997–2001	2.73	3.20	5.73	2.46	3.37
UK					
1991–6	4.05	5.30	4.25	3.25	1.92
1997–2001	3.40	2.77	3.46	2.57	2.76
Germany					
1991–6	3.63	4.09	9.04	2.85	3.20
1997–2001	1.99	3.17	7.75	1.57	1.75
Japan					
1991–6	2.00	2.78	3.57	1.16	1.74
1997–2001	0.09	1.40	2.07	0.13	0.69
Korea					
1991–6	7.50	7.21	3.16	5.99	7.35
1997–2001	4.79	5.85	6.74	3.82	4.31
Thailand					
1991–6	3.71	5.78	7.74	4.97	8.17
1997–2001	3.22	4.65	6.98	3.44	-0.20
China					
1991–6	–	–	–2.09	12.32	11.61
1997–2001	–	–	6.28	0.23	7.93
India					
1991–6	3.43	–	6.57	10.52	5.41
1997–2001	3.40	5.87	7.62	5.08	6.14
Hungary					
1991–6	–	–	5.11	25.04	–1.63
1997–2001	–	–	4.13	12.29	4.52

Source: *IFS*, November 2002.

It is clear that at present the Indian banking system is not fully equipped to promote small-scale enterprises around the country. The key issue is that banking institutions must be enabled to improve their credit assessment capabilities with regard to small-scale enterprises so that they can distinguish adequately between good and bad credit. Small-scale must not be equated with high risk. If the inflation rate is as low as 3 per cent and the interest rates charged to SMEs are much higher than normal good credit risk to large-sized industries, there is an implicit adverse selection in the credit appraisal process. Bank economists need to give focused attention to risk assessment to this sector so that there are no errors of high interest rate to low risk borrowers in the SME sector and vice versa.

The provision for Credit Information Bureaus (CIBs) and better exchange of information on credit risk between banks and financial institutions is also necessary to enable these institutions to recognize higher risk without excessive costs. Furthermore, the cost of credit assessment of SMEs can be reduced by a focused recognition of clusters of like SSIs that exist around the country. Such financial assistance programmes also need to be devised to provide assistance to those industries that are in the reserved list to enable them to expand and upgrade technology. This should be done both at the individual and group level. The focus of many such activities can be on the basis of industrial clusters so that economies of scale can be achieved both in financial assistance and in technology upgradation.

Very significant changes are also taking place in the agricultural sector. We can see the beginning of a much closer connection between primary producers, trade intermediaries, food processing entities, and eventual marketing of value-added products. With the share of unprocessed foods falling, the real growth area in the agricultural sector is in value added food products such as meat, poultry, fish vegetables, fruits, and the like. There is an accelerating move of consumers to basic processed foods. These trends need to be studied carefully so that supporting policy changes and investments can be made. Banks should explore the feasibility of expanding substantially lending to these activities.

Apart from adequate quantum of credit at an affordable price, there are issues relating to provision of high processing costs and the attendant cumbersome paper work. There are lessons to be learnt from the experience of the KCC Schemes and the Laghu Udhyami Credit Card Schemes to the agricultural and small entrepreneur borrowers. Surely, there is some scope for extending the benefits of hassle-free credit facilities through similar innovative methods to other borrowers requiring credit limits of over Rs 2 lakh also. It needs to be recognized that the SME sector has tremendous growth potential and accordingly pricing of loans to this sector should be at commensurate rates. Thus, there is need for realignment of interest rates among various segments of the financial market. As the financial market develops, ideally the interest rates on all types of debt instruments, both in the government and private sectors and in the credit market, should align in a relatively narrow band, reflecting realistic risk premia.

There have been some signals of industrial pick up during the last few months. For the four months from July to October 2002, on a point to point basis, the rise in index of industrial production (IIP) has been above 6 per cent. A major contribution to the high growth rates has been the manufacturing sector. In use-based classification also, the capital goods sector has registered impressive growth rates of over 15 per cent and 12 per cent in September and October 2002, respectively. Most (fourteen out of seventeen) industry groups in the index have shown positive growth rates. The increase in non-food credit of SCBs during the current financial year also appears to be commensurate with the IIP performance.

Nevertheless, banks have shown a marked preference for investments in government securities instead of pursuing their core activity of lending to commercial sector. At an aggregate level, the SLR holdings of banks are close to 39 per cent of their net demand and time liabilities as compared to the regulatory prescription of 25 per cent. Even strong commercial banks seem to be voluntarily adopting 'narrow banking' in a bid to minimize credit risk while increasing profitability. Such large investments in government securities well beyond the statutory requirement reflect dissipation of banking knowledge capital with regard to credit appraisals. The interest rate risk on investments in gilts need hardly be over emphasized. Further, the current focus of banks is bound to exact some heavy costs in terms of efficiency and credit availability. There is a danger of the link between liquidity, credit, money, and economic activity being severed in the long run as a result of continued over-investment in government securities as a substitute for bank financing to the commercial sector.

At a time when the industry is showing signs of pick up, banks should make efforts to increase commercial lending. The need of the hour is revival of the manufacturing sector and financing of the new slew of activities allied to agricultural lending. Of course, this would require focused attention through specialized branches, sound credit appraisals, adoption of sophisticated risk management techniques, and better information sharing. The legal environment has also improved with the passing of the new act to regulate securitization and reconstruction of financial assets and enforcement of security interest.

REVIVAL OF LONG-TERM FINANCING

The DFIs were set up in the 1950s to provide medium- and long-term finance to the private sector. Many of these institutions were sponsored by the government. DFIs were expected to resolve long-term credit shortages and to acquire and disseminate skills necessary to assess the creditworthiness of projects and banks. DFIs were traditionally dependent on concessional sources of financing, guaranteed by the government. On the asset side, they were predominantly engaged in term lending with banks financing working capital requirements. The post-reform period has altered the domain of the operations of DFIs both on the liabilities and assets sides. While DFIs started competing for funds at market rates of interest, their asset profile also shortened. On the other hand, banks have entered the domain of term lending. The current trend is of DFIs converting themselves into banks. In this context, the future of long-term lending acquires great importance.

Finance theory suggests that banks can play an important role in corporate financing, especially in situations of asymmetric information, principal-agent problems, design of incentive compatible contracts, and corporate governance issues. In their early stages of development, corporates are likely to rely on bank finance for working capital requirements. Bank financing is also likely to be predominant in an economy having a less-sophisticated legal framework. Considerations of lower transaction costs, efficient risk diversification, cost-effective assessment, monitoring, renegotiation, etc., are likely to make firms more reliant on bank finance than on market-based debt instruments.

International evidence on industrialized countries indicates that since the early 1970s, banks have played an important role in corporate financing. The benefits of a bank-based financial system vis-à-vis a market-based system were clearly noticeable particularly in the case of Japan, France, and Italy. During this period, bank financing was equally important in other industrialized and developing countries, although equity finance has gained momentum in recent years.

This is a challenging area as financing of long-term projects involves commitment of large funds over long periods with the concomitant asset liability mismatches. The shift from a fixed to a floating interest rate regime, development of corporate debt market, introduction of derivatives instruments and further enabling changes in the regulatory and legal environment are likely to increase long-term financing by banks. Banks would need to think in terms of setting up special wings for term lending, development of consortia and syndication, and co-operation in assessment of projects. These are areas for further exploration by bank economists.

NON-PERFORMING ASSETS (NPAs)

One of the main constraints to the above issues that I have raised is the level of NPAs. As of 31 March 2002, the gross NPAs of SCBs stood at Rs 71,000 crore, of which the NPAs of PSBs constituted Rs 57,000 crore.

The absolute amount of NPAs continues to be a major drag on the performance of banks. The large volume of NPAs reflects both an overhang of past dues and on-going problem of fresh accretion. As we move towards the international norm of ninety days for recognition of loan impairment, there may be a temporary increase in crystallization of NPAs in the banking sector. There is, therefore, a need to bring about improvements in credit administration and management of credit risk. In this context, the CIB should help in improving credit decisions by providing institutional mechanism for sharing of credit information on borrowers and potential borrowers among banks and financial institutions. The RBI modified the guidelines for compromise settlements of NPAs of the small sector to provide a simplified, non-discretionary, and non-discriminatory mechanism. Banks should work out processes for settlement procedures and expedite quick recovery of NPAs. The Securitization and Reconstruction of Financial Assets and Enforcement of Security Interest (SARFAESI) Act, 2002 should help in cleansing the balance sheet of banks by facilitating foreclosure. The constitution of an Asset Reconstruction Company (ARC) is another channel to remove NPAs from the balance sheets of banks through the processes of securitization of assets. The RBI has recently posted on its website the draft of the directions on prudential norms proposed to be issued by it to securitization companies/reconstruction companies.

RISK MANAGEMENT

In the current interest rate environment, banks are finding it more profitable to invest in government securities. In 2001–02, trading profits of PSBs more than doubled to Rs 5999 crore from Rs 2250 crore in 2000–1. The net profits of these banks during these two years were Rs 4317 crore and Rs 8301 crore, respectively, and this includes an additional Rs 1365 crore and Rs 1547 crore from forex operations. The RBI has been encouraging banks to be proactive in risk management. In this context, with a view to building up adequate reserves to guard against any possible reversal of interest rate environment in future, banks have been directed to maintain a certain level of Investment Fluctuation Reserve. The Reserve Bank is also taking a number of steps to develop further the derivatives market. As announced in the mid-term review of monetary policy for 2002–3, a Working Group has been set up with representatives from the market to enlarge the avenues of managing interest rate risks for banks and other financial intermediaries as well as corporates in the rupee derivatives market.

Recently, the Reserve Bank has issued a guidance note on market risk management. The guidance note delineates the minimum requirements for a bank including approval levels and requirements for any exceptions, deviations, or waivers. The note illustratively covers the responsibilities of risk management with regard to market risk management, the responsibilities of risk-taking unit, the responsibilities of market risk manager, risk identification, risk monitoring, funding and liquidity, models of risk analysis, and risk reporting.

In a rapidly changing business environment, no business can afford to remain static. It is well understood that risk-taking is an integral part of any business enterprise. It is important is that each bank needs to have in place the technical systems and management processes necessary to not only identify the risks associated with its activities, but also to effectively measure, monitor, and control them. If Indian banks are to compete globally, the time is opportune for them to institute sound and robust risk management practices.

SUMMARY

I have, in this chapter, highlighted the need to work towards reducing the real lending rates of banks. This would require concerted efforts on the part of the government and the RBI in respect of removing certain structural rigidities and by banks themselves through improving efficiency. I have also focused on the need to increase credit to SMEs and also look into aspects of creating an enabling environment for long-term financing. Reduction in NPA levels and appropriate risk management by banks would go a long way in improving efficiency of banks and inculcating a sound credit culture.

AFTERWORD

In Chapter 2, I had expressed concern on the banks' apparent preference during the period 1997–2002 to invest in government securities, far in excess of statutory requirements, rather than extending credit for productive activities. Subsequent events suggest that this behaviour of the banks could well have been rational. First, credit growth picked up sharply from 2003–4 onwards as overall economic conditions improved and significant corporate recovery took place after almost five years of subdued performance. Second, the nominal as well as real lending rates of banks softened significantly by 2004. (The lending rates hardened again in the subsequent period in tandem with the withdrawal of monetary accommodation that started in late 2004.) Third, NPAs of banks have seen a significant decline and net NPAs of banks are now close to 1 per cent of their net assets, despite the more stringent applicability of the 90-days norm for recognition of NPAs. Fourth, the Credit Information (Regulation) Act has been enacted which is expected to enable collection and sharing of credit histories and enhance flow of credit to the SMEs. Finally, the banking system appears to have been able to meet the long-term funding needs of the economy, thus filling the space vacated by the conversion of the DFIs into banks (the second major DFI also got converted into a bank in 2004). At the same time, a few of the concerns, which I expressed when this chapter was written, still remain. First, credit flow to the SMEs remains inadequate, despite some recent encouraging signs. Second, the banks' lending rates still do not appear to reflect risk profiles of the borrowers appropriately. Credit to the SMEs is still viewed as risky. There appears to be some element of opacity in lending practices in view of the substantial sub-PLR lending.

3 Finance for Industrial Growth*

Finance is a crucial ingredient for economic growth. In this chapter, I propose to examine the adequacy of the availability of finance for fuelling growth in the late 1990s, a period during which Indian economic growth has tended to slow down, particularly in the industrial sector. Although I am concerned with overall economic growth, my focus in this chapter is on the financing of industrial growth.

The way we think about the modes of financing industrial development has been changing over the years (Levine, 1997). The initial literature focused on the need to develop extensive financial systems that could tap savings and then channelize the funds so generated to a wide spectrum of industrial activities. It has been realized gradually that the mode of provision of industrial finance is as important for fostering industrial growth as is the quantum of funds. Cross-country experience suggests that economies that have mature financial systems for allocating funds efficiently among competing uses tend to grow faster. Well-functioning banks, financial institutions, and other financial intermediaries such as venture capital funds promote technological innovation and industrial growth by providing risk capital and funds to those entrepreneurs who have the highest probability of developing new products, production processes, and competitive production facilities (Rajan and Zingales, 2003). The Indian financial sector reforms of the 1990s, largely guided by the two excellent reports authored by M. Narasimham (Government of India, 1992 and 1998), have been designed to adapt the Indian financial system to the new realities of an open competitive economy in a globalizing world.

The key objective of India's economic reforms initiated in the early 1990s was to accelerate growth. The reform process of the 1990s did help to accelerate overall economic growth over that of the 1980s, but only marginally (RBI, 2003a). Real GDP grew at 5.9 per cent during the reform period (1992–3 to 2002–3), higher than that of 5.6 per cent in the pre-reform period

* Based on Mohan Kumaramangalam Memorial Lecture at the Administrative Staff College, Hyderabad, on 9 October 2003.

(1981–2 to 1990–1) (Table 3.1). Growth in both industry and agriculture has been slow after the initial burst in the 1990s, although growth in the tertiary sector has accelerated somewhat (Acharya, 2002).

Table 3.1 Sectoral Growth in the 1980s and 1990s

(per cent per year)

Sector	1981–2 to 1990–1	1992–3 to 2002–3	1994–7	1997–2002
Agriculture and allied activity	3.5	3.3	4.6	1.9
Industry	7.9	6.3	10.8	4.0
Manufacturing	7.6	6.7	12.2	3.8
Services	6.4	7.5	7.9	8.0
GDP	5.6	5.9	7.5	5.5

Source: Central Statistical Organisation.

In this background, I propose to examine if financing is now forming a constraint in the growth process. To do this, I will first review the alternative approaches to financing patterns as they exist in different countries and as they have evolved. I will then trace our own history and briefly review reforms in the financial sector in India. I will, thereafter, examine the performance of banks and financial institutions in recent periods. It is in this context that I propose to look into how the major contours of the financing pattern of Indian industries have changed over time. What are the key stylized facts of the financing of Indian industries? What has been the nature and dimension of changes that have occurred in the financing pattern in the recent period? Has Indian industry been credit-starved? Have the financial intermediaries done their task? I will finally put forward some ideas for discussion for further improvement of the financing system.

The rest of the chapter is formally structured as follows. As a perspective, the second section takes a look into the framework of corporate financing in India. The third and fourth sections delve into the pre-1990s and post-reform model of industrial finance in India. The fifth section is essentially futuristic in nature and discusses the options of long-term finance in India. Concluding observations are presented in the sixth section.

FRAMEWORK FOR CORPORATE FINANCING

To set the stage, let me start with the basic framework of corporate financing. Corporate entities raise capital from either (a) internal sources, essentially retained profits, or (b) external sources. External funds are accessed from sources outside the firm through the issue of equity capital and debt instruments. Equity capital can be raised from the firm's promoters or the capital market that taps institutional investors, mutual funds, and retail investors. Debt can be raised through floatation of corporate bonds or borrowing from banks and non-bank financial intermediaries. An important aspect of the growth process that has been widely discussed in recent times is the type of the financial system that is most conductive to growth. Seen from this standpoint, most of the systems of industrial finance in developed countries can be grouped into two clear systems. At one end is the Anglo-American model of market-based finance where financial markets play an important role and the role of the banking industry is much less emphasized. At the other extreme is the Continental/Japanese model of bank-based finance, in which savings flow to their productive uses predominantly through financial intermediaries such as banks and other financial institutions, and the capital market is less important for the raising of funds.

Most of the industrial financing systems have evolved endogenously from their own particular circumstances of economic history—and have their own success story to tell or otherwise. The market-based system is relatively impersonal because the sources of funds could actually be atomistic household savers, directly or indirectly through mutual funds, pension funds, or insurance funds. The bank-based systems are more relationship-based, because the lenders are few and large. At the risk of broad generalization, bank-based systems tend to be stronger in countries where governments have taken a direct role in industrial development, such as Germany, in the nineteenth century, and Japan, East Asia, South-East Asia, China and India, in the twentieth century.

The basic point of partition between the two systems is that in the one case, corporate entities interact with the intermediary, say a 'bank', whereas in the other, they directly approach the 'public' for finance. This distinction between a 'bank-based' and a 'market-based' system is not a watertight compartment; on the contrary, it has become blurred in recent years with the institutionalization of the sources of finance all over the world. The blurring of the distinction has emanated from the gradual spread of universal banking, spanning the entire range of financial services across commercial banking, insurance, and securities (investment as well as underwriting). This has been fortified by the emergence of institutional investors, in the capital market, including mutual funds, which, for example, have an asset base of as much as 70 per cent of GDP in the US.

There are also historical reasons for this emerging convergence. A number of countries, including the USA segregated banking and securities trading in their financial licensing laws as it was believed that direct commercial bank involvement in corporate securities would involve significant conflicts of interest. It was only recently that the US Financial Services Modernization Act of 1999 repealed the Glass–Steagall Act of 1933, which had prohibited commercial banks from underwriting, holding, or dealing in corporate securities, whether directly or through securities affiliates. A number of EMEs, such as Argentina (1991), Chile (1997–8), Indonesia (1995), and Malaysia (1991) have also recently liberalized restrictions governing banks' exposures to the capital markets.

Beyond the partition based on risk characteristics, it will be recognized that the need for diversification of the financial structure is also driven by the demand for funds of different tenors. Banks, for example, are a natural source of working capital because their resource base essentially emanates from the economy's transaction processes and the funds available with them are of a short-term nature. Bond markets are relatively more flexible because they can mediate both the short-term corporate funds as well as long-term household saving. However, in the absence of developed capital markets, there arises a need for specialized financial institutions—the so-called DFIs—which provide project finance.

The process of corporate financing is changing all over the world. There has been, for example, a sharp jump in market-based financing during the 1990s driven by a combination of financial liberalization and high growth. Private bond markets grew especially rapidly, jumping 500 per cent between 1980–5 and 1992–7 by one estimate (see Domowitz, Glen, and Madhavan, 2000, for details) outstripping bank credit offtake. Equity markets, especially in the G-4 markets and the East Asian tigers, also grew explosively—although much slower than that of the bond market. Corporate bond markets remain underdeveloped in most emerging markets because they are more difficult to develop than equity markets.

THE PRE-REFORM MODEL OF INDUSTRIAL FINANCE IN INDIA

How did India fare in the domain of industrial finance? The Indian economy, like most of the former colonial economies, adopted a path of planned development after Independence. This was, in a sense, dictated by the compulsions of contemporary political economy. While there was a wide consensus that economic growth could only spring from large-scale industrialization, in consonance with the contemporary big-push theories of economic development, it was thought that firms lacked the resources to finance such rapid growth. The strong preference for self-reliant growth in view of the mercantilist roots of colonialism, reinforced by faith in the nation-building capacity of the polity shaped by the successful freedom movement, led to a state-led development strategy during the 1950s. This preference was also reinforced by the perceived success of the state-led Russian model that was so visible in the immediate post-World War II period.

The industrial financing strategy adopted in the 1950s centred around the government as the primary entrepreneur in the economy. The state-led development initiatives had two distinct avenues, namely, (a) direct investment from the government budget (such as in case of irrigation projects, construction of dams, and railways), and (b) public enterprises (such as the steel plants—'the temples of modern India') often funded by budgetary provisions and government guaranteed bonds. This was reinforced by the channelling of public saving by an elaborate banking network to the 'socially productive' uses by an elaborate mechanism of directed credit programmes and concessional interest rates for 'priority sectors'.

As a result, the role of the financial system was restricted to the channelling of resources from the savers to the users in line with the 'socially productive' pattern of resource allocation, charted by the planning process. The emphasis, thus, lay in building a financial system with a widespread network, not only in terms of the geographical spread and socio-economic reach but also, in the functional sense, in terms of specialized forms of finance, through DFIs. The resultant financing strategy for industrialization, as it then emerged, rested on four building blocks:

1. Banks would provide short-term working capital, with appropriate allocations for the priority sector.
2. DFIs would provide medium- to longer-term funds for the corporate sector.
3. Since banks had a readymade access to cheap resources by way of banking transactions, the government sought to provide a cushion to DFIs by offering guarantees on bonds issued by them along with special access to concessional funds from the Reserve Bank.
4. Corporate entities could supplement these forms of funding by resource mobilization from the capital market, but this also needed government approval within the constraints of the credit allocation process.

A natural corollary of the planning process was then the conscious adoption of a model of the bank-based mode of financing as against a model of market-based financing, which was adopted in some emerging countries. Although the capital markets in India were among the oldest in Asia, the role of equity as a mode of financing was not considered as important because of the limited attraction that risk capital was perceived to have for projects with a long gestation lag.

There can be little doubt that the basic objective of developing an extensive financial network was, by and large, fulfilled by the early 1990s, especially following the spread of the branch bank network following the bank nationalizations of 1969 and 1980 (Table 3.2).

Table 3.2 Progress of Commercial Banking in India

Indicator	June 1969	June 1980	March 1990	March 2000	March 2002
1. Number of SCBs of which:	73	148	270	297	293
RRBs	–	73	196	196	196
Other SCBs	–	75	74	101	97
2. Number of bank offices	8262	32,419	59,752	67,868	68,195
3. Per capita deposits (Rs)	88	494	2098	8542	11,008
4. Per capita credit (Rs)	68	327	1275	4555	5927
5. Population per bank branch (thousand)	64	21	14	15	15

Source: *Statistical Tables Relating to Banks in India*, RBI.

The corporate financing strategy, as it evolved, was, however, inextricably linked to the fiscal position, because of the assumption that public investment would eventually generate surpluses for the social good. As fiscal deficits began to enlarge, the entire financial system began to be geared to funding the government's budgetary needs. Banks' SLR, originally a prudential requirement for solvency, was steadily raised to provide a captive market for public debt. Although interest rates were initially kept artificially low, even at the cost of financial repression, to contain the interest cost of public debt, the return on government securities was steadily raised to enhance their attractiveness to the market. As it got increasingly difficult to get voluntary subscriptions even at higher rates of return, the government resorted to a large-scale monetization of the fiscal deficit by the end-1980s. Concomitantly, the Reserve Bank had to raise reserve requirements in order to contain the inflationary impact of deficit financing. By the early 1990s, statutory pre-emptions of banks amounted to over 60 per cent of deposit mobilization. This process was accentuated by the government ownership of banks (Table 3.3).

Thus, the difficulty was that the Indian financial system, though extensive, was limited in its ability to allocate resources efficiently. A number of structural bottlenecks emerged in the process. First, a combination of an administered interest rate regime and directed credit controls prevented proper pricing of

Table 3.3 Ownership Pattern of Banks (in 2001)

Country	Per cent of total bank assets (government-owned)
India	80
South Korea	30
Thailand	31
Indonesia	44
Malaysia	0
UK	0
Germany	42
Canada	0
USA	0

Source: Levine (2001).

resources. Second, most financial intermediaries remained confined to markets relating to their area of operation because of balance sheet restrictions, leading to market segmentation. Finally, there was the problem of missing markets, especially at the shorter end, with caps even on the inter-bank rate. Hence, although the Indian banking system has grown tremendously, it has a long way to go. Even relative to other developing countries, the ratio of bank assets/GDP for India continues to be low (Figure 3.1).

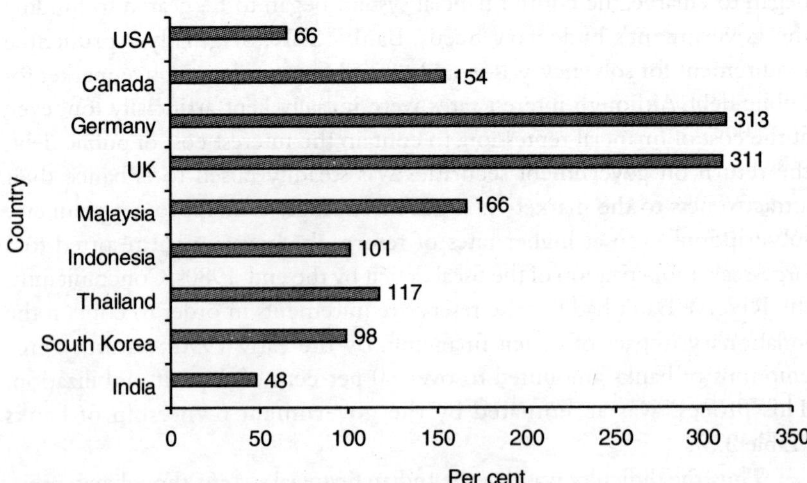

Figure 3.1 Total Bank Assets–GDP Ratio

Source: Barth, Caprio, and Levine (2001).

The role of banks as financial intermediaries can, therefore, be expected to grow significantly in the years to come. Surprisingly, the population serviced by a bank branch is also much higher in the Indian case than in many other countries (Figure 3.2).

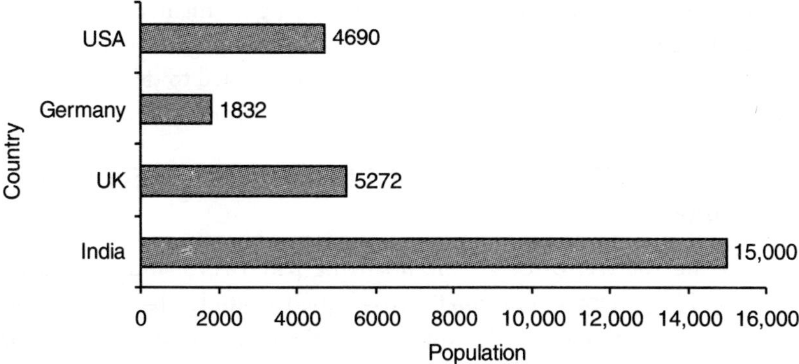

Figure 3.2 Population per Bank Branch

Source: Barth, Caprio, and Levine (2001).

It is against this backdrop that financial sector reforms were initiated in the early 1990s. There was clearly the need to reduce the role of government in the allocation of resources in the economy. A competitive environment was sought to be created in the financial sector to enhance the allocative efficiency of financial markets as a whole. Such financial sector reforms would then accelerate the overall economic growth process.

At the heart of financial reforms lay the need to contain the propensity of the government to pre-empt resources from financial institutions through *fiat*. The 1990s saw three fundamental changes in the relationship between the fisc and the financial system. First, the government securities market was transformed to a market-determined price discovery process by switching over to an auction mechanism for sale. This enabled the rest of the segments of the financial markets to price off this market. Second, the reduction in the statutory liquidity requirements to the minimum of 25 per cent of demand and time liabilities freed resources of the banking system for credit. However, PSBs presently continue to hold about 40 per cent SLR bonds voluntarily. Third, the phasing out of the process of automatic monetization of the fiscal deficit, rendered a sense of autonomy to the Reserve Bank and enabled it to gradually cut cash reserve requirement to the current level of 4.5 per cent.

The traditional model of industrial financing thus began to crumble by the mid-1990s. The dismantling of the administered structure of interest rates allowed the emergence of market-based interest rates so that resources could be allocated by market signals. Besides, the gradual withdrawal of restrictions on both the assets and the liabilities of the banks and the non-bank financial institutions enabled them to optimize their portfolios across instruments of varying risk and tenor according to their commercial judgement, consistent with the process of price discovery. Further, concessions, such as availability of government guarantees and central bank funding for financial institutions, were gradually phased out in the process of market integration. By the late 1990s, therefore, the Indian financial system was enabled to develop in such a way as to compete in the increasingly open economy.

SOURCES OF FINANCE FOR INDIAN INDUSTRIES DURING THE 1990s

It is now instructive to review the financing patterns for industry during the 1990s. The general impression that has gained ground is that bank finance for industry has gone down. A closer look at the major sources of industrial finance as a proportion of GDP (Table 3.4) brings out clearly the following stylized facts. First, banks have kept up their credit to industry. Not only has there been an increase in the proportion of conventional credit to GDP, in addition there has also been resource flow in the form of investments in non-SLR instruments—such as commercial paper, corporate bonds, and equity. Second, financing from FIs to industry has clearly fallen.[1] The decline has

Table 3.4 Major Sources of Industrial Finance

(percentage of GDP at current market prices)

Year	Banks		DFIs	Capital market	Total
	Credit	Non-SLR investments			
1970s	1.8	–	0.3	0.1	2.2
1980s	2.7	–	0.7	0.6	4.0
1990s	2.6	–	1.0	1.2	4.8
1992-3 to 1996–7	2.9	–	1.0	1.9	5.8
1997-8 to 2001–2	2.7	0.7[a]	0.6	0.2	4.2

Notes: [a] Non-substantial prior to mid-1990s.

1. Banks' support includes conventional credit in the form of loans and advances and bills rediscounted.
2. Capital market support to the industrial sector has been taken to be new capital issues by non-government public limited companies (that is ordinary shares, preference shares, and debentures) and their ordinary shares.

Source: *Handbook of Statistics on the Indian Economy 2002–03*, RBI.

been sharper in recent years because of the conversion of Industrial Credit and Investment Corporation of India (ICICI) into a bank as well as the problems besetting Industrial Finance Corporation of India (IFCI). The key change that took place in the late 1990s was the virtual collapse of the capital market as a source of industrial finance. Correspondingly, as might be expected, the demand for debt from the DFIs also fell, which was compensated to a certain extent by the participation of banks in subscribing to bond issues and other debt instruments of corporate entities through the private placement route. The exuberance of investment activity in the mid-1990s also led to the creation of over capacity in industry, including some uncompetitive capacity that led to erosion of profits which, in turn, perhaps explains the poor performance of the stock market during this latter period. With the recovery of corporate profits in 2002–3 and its continuation in 2003–4, the stock market has recorded high growth since May 2003. With the prevailing low interest rates, and a recovery of the stock market, we can now expect some increase in industrial investment demand.

Overall also, non-food credit has increased as a proportion of GDP in the past few decades reflecting both the demand for credit per se as well as an acceleration in the process of monetization with the spread of branch banking. This ratio continued to increase during the post-reform period as well though it had fallen somewhat in the early 1990s, even though the process of monetization is now more or less complete (Figure 3.3). This, in turn, suggests that there has been no credit constraint as far as industry is concerned during the late 1990s.

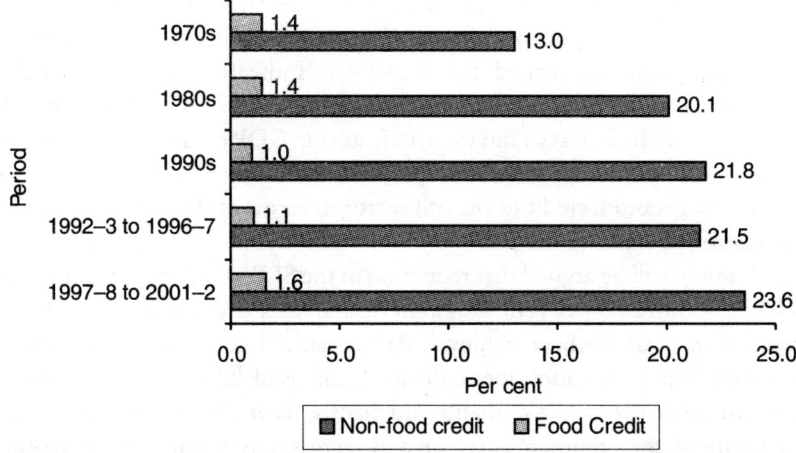

Figure 3.3 Food and Non-food Credit (as per cent of GDP at current market prices)

Source: RBI.

Thus there is reasonable evidence, at least in the aggregative sense, to suggest that Indian industry has not been starved of bank credit in recent years. A related question is the adequacy of finance across all sectors. Were there any specific sectors that did not get adequate finance? The picture is really no different when we look at the sectoral numbers (Table 3.5).[2]

Table 3.5 Sectoral Distribution of Non-food Gross Bank Credit

(per cent of relevant GDP)

Year	Agricultural credit/ agricultural GDP	Industrial credit/ manufacturing GDP	SSI[a] credit/ SSI GDP	Non-food gross bank credit/ GDP
1980s	10.0	65.6	38.9	19.9
1990s	9.2	68.4	43.8	20.6
1992–3 to 1996–7	8.9	65.9	42.4	20.1
1997–8 to 2001–2	10.0	71.9	45.3	21.6

Notes: [a] SSI—small-scale industries.

Source:

1. *Handbook of Statistics on the Indian Economy 2002–03*, RBI, for sectoral deployment of credit data.
2. *National Accounts Statistics*, CSO for manufacturing and agricultural GDP.
3. Author's calculations for SSI GDP.

The correct way to evaluate adequacy of the trend in sectoral credit is to look at it as a proportion of sectoral value added. Insofar as the sectoral credit trends are concerned, the above data indicate that the fall in the agricultural credit–agricultural GDP ratio during the 1990s has been arrested in recent years. In fact, as a ratio to manufacturing GDP, credit to the industrial sector has experienced a steady upward trend. Interestingly, contrary to popular impression, credit to the SSI sector in terms of the ratio to its GDP has exhibited a steady increase.

It might still be argued that reduction in the SLR stipulations from about 38.5 per cent to 25 per cent should have spurred a larger quantum of bank credit than what has been achieved. At the same time, while the reduction in statutory pre-emptions does enhance credit availability, the actual supply is contingent on credit demand and banks' own allocations across the government, the commercial sector, and increasingly, the rest of the world. With the increase in fiscal deficit of the government in the late 1990s, at a macro level, we could not expect an overall reduction in banks' subscription to SLR bonds. However, if there had been buoyant private sector credit demand we would have observed hardening of real interest rates, rather than the softening that has been observed in the last two to three years.

The more serious issues in the flow of resources to industry in the late 1990s thus centre around the problem of the gradual shrinkage of DFIs, as a sector, on the one hand and the lacklustre performance in the functioning of the capital market, on the other hand. There is also the issue of corporate profitability which might have affected the latter phenomenon.

Comparison of Banks and FIs

The process of financial sector reform has changed the operating environment in which the financial institutions, banks, and non-bank intermediaries operate. Until the early 1990s, the role of the financial system in India was primarily restricted to the function of channelling resources from the surplus to deficit sectors. Reforms in the financial sector created a deregulated environment and enabled relatively free play of market forces. It also altered the organizational structure, ownership pattern, and domain of operations of institutions and infused greater competition. In order to appreciate the consequential impact on the resource flow, it is useful to study the impact of financial sector reforms on each segment of financial intermediaries.

In the case of banks, there have been, in particular, three clear elements of change. First, banks now have greater operational flexibility and functional autonomy in terms of pricing and resource allocation. Second, the strengthening of prudential norms has resulted in the clean-up of balance sheets of banks and reinforced financial stability. Third, the banking sector is facing increased pressure of competition, from both within the banking system, with the emergence of new banks, and from other intermediaries, and to some extent, from the capital market.

There is very little doubt that the banking sector has recorded improvements in profitability, efficiency (in terms of intermediation costs), and asset quality in the 1990s. Within the commercial banking system, PSBs, however, continue to have higher interest rate spreads but at the same time earn lower rates of return, reflecting higher operating costs. Private sector banks, on the other hand, appear to have lower spreads as well as lower operating expenses comparable to the banking system in G-3 countries (Table 3.6). At the same time, asset quality is weaker so that loan loss provisions continue to be higher. This suggests that, whereas there is greater scope for enhancing the asset quality of banks in general, PSBs, in particular, need to reduce operating costs further. Although higher administrative expenses are often explained away by the large branch network, it should be borne in mind that banks in the G-3 countries actually have a lower ratio of population per branch ratio (see Figure 3.2).

Table 3.6 Banking Sector Performance

(per cent of assets)

Variable	India (1999)		G-3 (1999) countries
	Public sector banks	New private sector banks	
Spread	2.8	2.0	2.0
Other income	1.2	1.5	1.0
Operating cost	2.7	1.7	1.8
Loan losses	1.0	0.8	0.3
Net profits	0.4	1.0	0.8[a]

Note: [a] Refers to pre-tax profits.

Source: *Report on Currency and Finance, 2001–02*; *Report of Trend and Progress of Banking in India, 1999–2000*, RBI.

Financial Institutions

The operating environment of DFIs underwent a radical change in the 1990s. DFIs are facing new challenges both on the asset and the liability sides. Concessional sources of funds have dried up and financial institutions are raising resources including short-term funds at market-related rates. On the asset side, the distinction between banks and DFIs is getting blurred as both are offering long-term and short-term financing. Further, both banks and DFIs together face competition from market-based modes of financing.

The difficulties faced by the DFIs in the late 1990s are reflected in a gradual shrinkage of their balance sheets. Lending by the DFIs has fallen continuously over the last five to seven years. This has led to a growing body of opinion that DFIs are intrinsically uncompetitive, especially because of a legacy of high-cost long-term liabilities and poor asset quality. A closer look at the balance sheets suggests a mixed bag.

The most striking feature is that the profitability of DFIs as a group remains, by and large, comparable to that of banks (Figure 3.4). This is essentially because operating costs of DFIs are lower than that of banks, because these financial institutions do not have a wide branch network.

This advantage of low operating costs is, however, largely neutralized by the fact that their interest costs are higher than banks (Figure 3.5). While it is true that interest costs are likely to be always higher because DFIs raise longer-term funds, the shorter tenor of the banks liabilities allows them a far greater degree of manoeuvrability enabling them to cut interest expenses faster in a scenario of declining interest rates. Another issue is that while

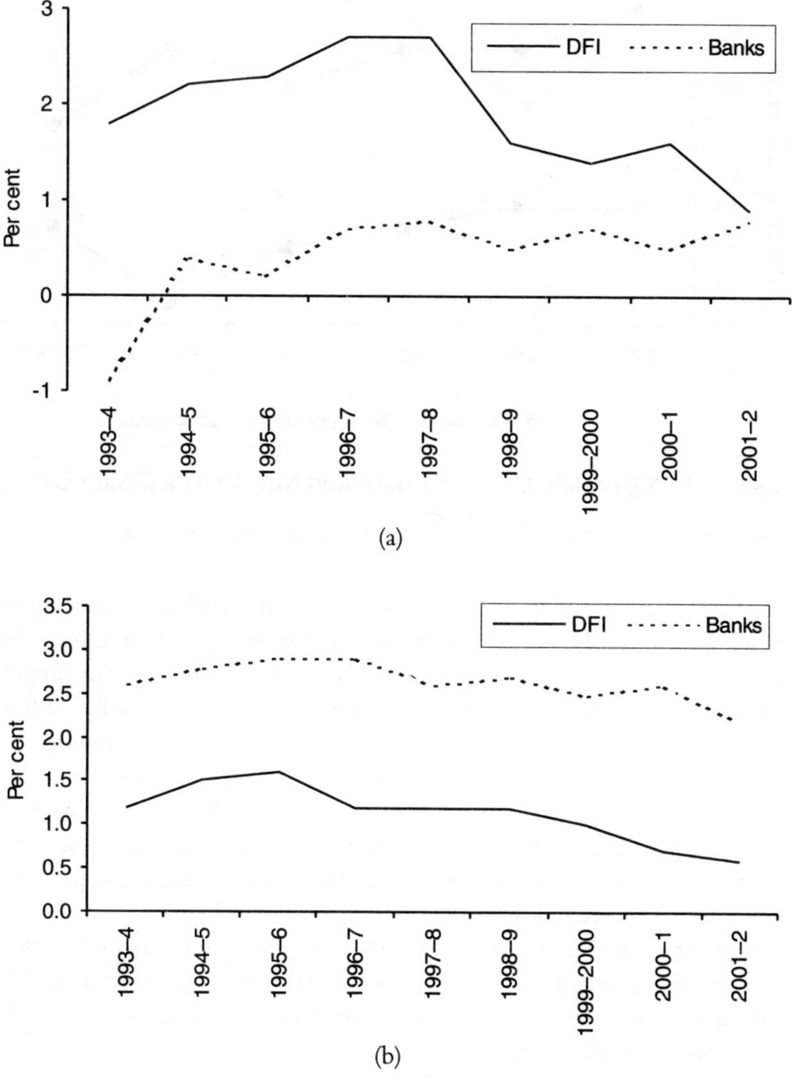

Figure 3.4 Banks vis-à-vis DFIs: (a) Net Profits and (b) Other Operating Expenses (per cent of total assets)

Source: *Report on Trend and Progress in Banking*, various issues, RBI.

interest income for DFIs is typically higher than that of banks because of the longer tenor of commitments, the spread between the two has been narrowing in recent years with the drying up of the demand for project finance as well as the emergence of alternate sources of longer-term funding.

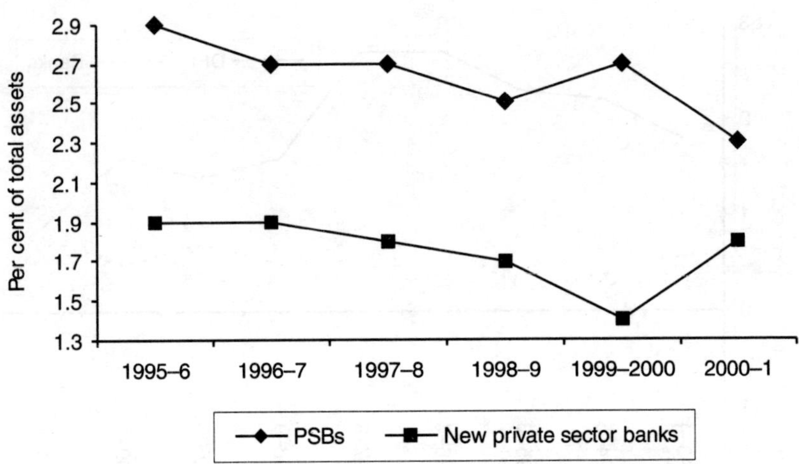

Figure 3.5 Operating Costs of Public and New Private Sector Banks

Source: *Report on Trend and Progress in Banking*, various issues, RBI.

Together with the rigidity in interest expenses, this has been squeezing the profitability of DFIs. An interesting fact is that the operating expenses of new private sector banks are comparable to that of the DFIs. This suggests that financial institutions are likely, sooner than later, to face a challenge from new private sector banks whose interest costs are much lower (Figure 3.6).

It is thus not entirely obvious, conventional wisdom notwithstanding, that DFIs cannot be competitive. There is no doubt that, with no access to current deposits, their average cost of funds will always be higher than that of banks. But this is compensated by lower operating costs because they typically do not need a large branch network. But as banks continue to cut down their own operating expenses, DFIs will also have to gradually reduce their operating costs further in order to maintain their commercial viability. This underscores the need for DFIs to pay greater attention to their NPAs and to address legacy issues.

Bank Financing of Long-Term Assets

The traditional model of corporate financing was based on a clear-cut partition of roles: banks were to fund working capital requirements while DFIs (and to the extent possible, the capital market) were to cater to longer-term financing needs of the economy. The downscaling of operations of DFIs, together with sluggishness in the capital markets in recent years, has created a gap at the longer end of the institutional financing spectrum in the Indian economy. This inevitably brings us to the possible role that banks could play in bridging this gap.

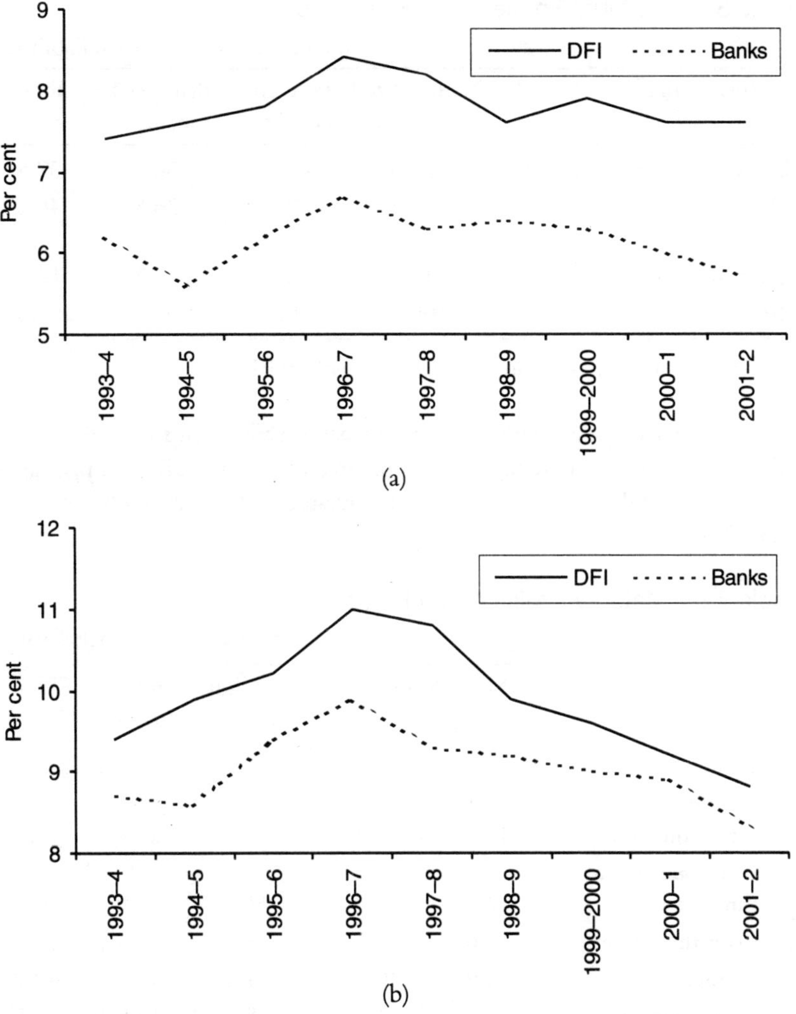

Figure 3.6 Banks vis-à-vis DFIs: (a) Interest Cost and (b) Interest Income (per cent of total assets)

Source: *Report on Trend and Progress in Banking*, various issues, RBI.

The tenure of funds provided by banks either as loans or investments depends critically on the overall asset–liability position. An inherent difficulty in this regard is that since deposit liabilities of banks often tend to be of relatively shorter maturity, long-term lending could induce the problem of asset–liability mismatches. The maturity structure of commercial bank deposits in 2002 shows that less than one fifth is of a tenor of more than three years and less than 7.0 per cent for private banks (Table 3.7).

Table 3.7 Maturity Profile of Bank Liabilities

(percentage share in total liabilities)

Maturity range	SBI	Nationalized banks	Foreign banks	Indian private banks	Total
Up to one year	19.3	35.5	61.9	56.5	37.8
Over one year to three years	59.4	47.5	17.6	36.8	46.1
Over three years	21.3	17.0	20.5	6.7	16.1
Total	100.0	100.0	100.0	100.0	100.0

Source: *Statistical Tables Relating to Banks in India*, RBI.

On the asset side, nearly 40 per cent has already been invested in assets of over three years maturity, mostly in investment instruments, primarily SLR bonds. Only about 10 per cent is invested in loans and advances (see Table 3.8).

Table 3.8 Maturity Profile of Bank Assets

(percentage share in total assets)

Maturity Range	SBI	Nationalised Banks	Foreign Banks	Indian Private Banks	Total
Loans and advances	44.1	53.5	58.4	52.3	51.1
Up to one year	19.0	21.9	38.3	25.9	23.1
Over one year to three years	14.5	17.9	11.9	19.0	16.8
Over three years	10.6	13.7	8.1	7.4	11.2
Investments	55.9	46.5	41.6	47.7	48.9
Up to one year	9.1	3.9	18.8	14.8	8.5
Over one year to three years	11.3	6.0	9.7	10.7	8.6
Over three years	35.5	36.6	13.1	22.3	31.7
Total	100.0	100.0	100.0	100.0	100.0

Source: *Statistical Tables Relating to Banks in India*, RBI.

In view of the large demand by the Central and state governments for funds for long-dated government paper, there is little flexibility left for extension of longer-term credit by banks to infrastructure, industry, agriculture, and other productive sectors. Any larger investment by banks in longer-term assets could result in asset–liability mismatches. This analysis of the relative roles of banks and financial institutions in term lending for financing growth suggests that there is a greater need to think about the future of DFIs. The structure of their relative costs suggests that if the legacy problems of DFIs are addressed they may not be intrinsically uncompetitive in their financing operations. They will have to improve their operating efficiency through the use of technology and other means in order to bring down operating costs further. Their comparative advantage in relevant skills for appraising projects will continue to give them an edge over commercial banks in their operations. They will also need to diversify their operations to take advantage of the new opportunities offered by the opening of the capital market and use of new investment techniques around instruments.

Banks also have some capacity to invest in longer-term assets, but this capacity will remain highly limited till the fiscal deficit remains as high as it is and government demand for investment in long-dated bonds remains high, even though they are, of course, tradable. Some enhancement of their capacity to invest in infrastructure, industry, and agriculture in longer gestation projects can be enhanced by allowing a limited recourse to longer-term bond issues.

CAPITAL MARKETS

The Indian capital market began to expand in the late 1980s (Table 3.9). This was abetted by wide-ranging reforms in the capital markets, in terms of reviving the process of price discovery, enhancing transparency, and improving trading and settlement practices. The reforms in the capital markets during the 1990s in terms of market microstructure and transactions have ensured that the Indian capital market in particular is now comparable to the capital markets in most developed markets. The early 1990s saw a greater willingness of the saver to place funds in capital market instruments on the

Table 3.9 Capital Market Indicators

(percentage of GDP)

Year	BSE[a] market capitalization	New equity issues
1980s	9.2	0.2
1990s	37.0	0.7
1992–3 to 1996–7	37.8	1.1
1997–8 to 2001–2	33.8	0.1
2002–3	23.1	0.01

Note: [a] BSE—Bombay Stock Exchange.

Source: *Handbook of Statistics on the Indian Economy 2002–03*, RBI.

supply side as well as an enthusiasm of corporate entities to take recourse to capital market instruments on the demand side. The size of the capital market is now comparable to other developing countries but there is still a long way to go. It is important to note that developed economies with bank-based systems, such as Germany and Japan, also have capital markets with substantial market capitalization in relation to GDP (Table 3.10).

Table 3.10 Capitalization of Stock Markets

(percentage of GDP)

Economy	1990	1999
Japan	98	105
Germany	22	68
UK	86	203
USA	53	182
Indonesia	7	45
Malaysia	110	184
Thailand	28	47
India	12	41

Source: *World Development Indicators*, 2001.

While there was a sharp increase in market capitalization as a percentage of GDP during the 1990s, the share of capital issues to GDP, a measure of resource mobilization by the capital markets, followed an inverted U-curve during the 1990s. The spurt in capital issues beyond 1.0 per cent of GDP during 1993–6 could not be sustained with the onset of the economic slowdown in the latter half of the 1990s. As a result, capital issues, especially equity issues, dwindled to the 1970s' levels (as a proportion of GDP) in the latter half of the 1990s. In fact, public capital issues by non-government public limited companies declined to 0.2 per cent of GDP during 1998–2002 from 1.9 per cent during 1992–7 and 0.6 per cent during the 1980s. Besides, public equity issues by non-government public limited companies declined to 0.1 per cent of GDP during 1998–2002 from 1.1 per cent during 1992–7 and 0.7 per cent during the 1980s.

The market for corporate debt is still in the process of development in the Indian economy, as is the case with most developing economies. The private placement market has emerged as an important source of resource mobilization in the Indian debt market. The first steps in development of the debt market have been taken through development of the government securities market. The issue of government bonds through auction and their active trading by banks have led to the emergence of a sovereign yield curve.

Steps have also been taken, though still in their infancy, to enable active trading of government securities in the stock exchanges. As this market grows and as steps are taken to regulate the private placement market, the corporate bond market will also develop. Creditworthy corporate borrowers will then be able to raise longer-term funds for financing their growth.

After the exuberance of the stock market in the mid-1990s and its decline thereafter, a large number of individual investors took flight to safety in bank deposits, safe retirement instruments, and insurance. It remains to be seen when and how fast such savers return to the capital market so that it performs its intermediary function efficiently.

PATTERN OF INDUSTRIAL FINANCE AMONG INDIAN CORPORATES

Having run through the supply side of the story, let me now turn to the demand side of industrial finance in India. An interesting shift in the pattern of financing of the Indian corporate sector needs to be highlighted in this context (Table 3.11). During the 1980s to mid-1990s, internal sources as a percentage of total sources of funds ranged between 30–35 per cent, while during recent years it has increased to more than 40 per cent; in fact for 2000–1, the proportion of internal sources touched nearly 60 per cent. Correspondingly, there has been a reduction in the reliance on external financing.

The question, however, remains as to whether this reflects the effect of substitution of internal sources for external sources or the scale effect of an external constraint. In terms of external funding, a number of interesting trends emerge. The share of equity increased in the 1990s. Besides, there was a shift to equity from debentures, especially during the mid-1990s when the equity issues commanded a large premium in the public issues markets. The share of capital market-based intermediaries has increased somewhat pulling down the debt-equity ratio. The overall share of borrowings, at about one third, remains, by and large, intact. There has been a greater reliance on internal resources during the downturn during the latter half of the 1990s. It is not clear at this stage whether this trend would change with an upturn in the capital market.

It is now appropriate to arrive at broad generalizations from the sources side of financing. First of all, bank credit has increased, but only marginally; the important aspect is that it has not gone down, contrary to the general belief. Second, banks continue to prefer investing in government securities despite the reduction in SLR requirements. Third, flows from DFIs have reduced, but they may not be uncompetitive intrinsically. While their interest costs are high, they have managed to curtail operating costs. Finally, the

Table 3.11 Pattern of Sources of Funds for Indian Corporates

(per cent of total sources of funds)

Item	1985–6 to 1990–1	1991–2 to 2000–1	1992–3 to 1996–7	1997–8 to 2000–1
Internal sources	34.1	35.7	31.3	43.1
External sources	65.9	64.3	68.7	56.9
of which				
(a) Equity capital	7.0	16.1	20.5	12.8
(b) Borrowings	36.2	32.0	33.2	28.3
Debentures	10.3	6.2	5.2	6.1
From Banks	12.7	10.0	10.7	9.4
From FIs	8.4	9.5	8.3	9.8
(c) Trade dues and other current liabilities	22.5	15.9	14.8	15.3
Total	100.0	100.0	100.0	100.0

Note: Data pertain to non-government, non-financial public Ltd companies.

Source: *Report on Currency and Finance, 1998–99*, RBI for data up to 1997–8, and articles on 'Finances of Public Limited Companies', *RBI Bulletins* (various issues) for subsequent years.

contraction in the capital market during the last five years has been dramatic. Overall, corporates have depended more on internal sources of financing during the second half of the 1990s.

SUPPLY OF FUNDS

Household financial savings are the main source of funds in the Indian financial system. Private savings performance, at about 25 per cent of GDP, has been reasonably impressive by international standards, perhaps with the exception of some of the East Asian countries. Reflecting the gradual willingness to invest in risk capital since the 1980s, the share of financial scrips amounted to almost 10 per cent of total household saving by the mid-1990s (Table 3.12). The late 1990s, however, witnessed a reversal of this process, with a flight to the safety of bank deposits and social security. The present indications are that we can expect this continuing shift to life insurance, pension funds, and so on, although there could be a return to the capital market if it does well for some time. As regards the other sources of saving, the fiscal deficit continues to act as a drag, leading to negative public sector dissavings, which pull down the overall savings of the country.

Table 3.12 Composition of Financial Savings Portfolio of Indian Households

(per cent of financial savings)

Item	1970s	1980s	1990s	1992–3 to 1996–7	1997–8 to 2001–2
1. Currency	18.8	16.1	11.9	12.5	10.0
2. Net bank deposits	32.7	22.8	27.0	25.9	31.4
3. Social security	41.0	47.8	44.2	39.4	54.2
(a) Life fund	12.1	10.3	11.8	11.0	14.4
(b) Provident fund and pension fund	26.3	23.8	21.9	20.5	23.9
(c) Net claims on government	2.6	13.7	10.5	7.9	15.9
4. Non-bank saving instruments	7.4	13.3	17.0	22.3	4.4
(a) Net non-banking deposits	1.1	3.7	5.6	9.9	1.9
(b) Shares and debentures	2.0	5.3	8.2	9.5	4.0
(c) Units of Unit Trust of India (UTI)	0.6	3.0	4.4	3.9	0.2
(d) Trade debt	3.7	1.3	−1.2	−1.0	−1.7
5. Total	100.0	100.0	100.0	100.0	100.0
Memo Item: Household Financial Saving (as % of GDP at current market prices)	4.6	6.8	10.0	10.2	10.4

Notes:

1. Net Bank Deposits = Bank Deposits – Bank Advances – Loans and Advances from Co-operative Non-Credit Societies.
2. Net Non-Banking Deposits = Non-Banking Deposits – Loans and Advances from Other Financial Institutions.
3. Net Claims on Government = Claims on Government – Loans and Advances from Government.
4. Saving in Trade Debt is 'Change in trade dues in respect of sundry creditors *minus* changes in loans and advances to sundry debtors', from the Company Finance Studies.

Source: *Handbook of Statistics on the Indian Economy*, 2002–03.

OPTIONS FOR LONGER-TERM FINANCE

Against the backdrop of the discussion on various aspects of financing patterns, sources of funds, maturity structure of assets and liabilities of banks and DFIs, it is apposite to discuss the options available for financing investment for growth. There are, of course, many sources of project finance available: banks, insurance companies, DFIs, pension funds, leasing companies, investment management companies, and individuals. It is perhaps useful to begin by exploring the options available within the existing institutional framework and then turn to other possible innovations.

Existing Institutional Framework

We have already observed that the maturity structure of the liabilities of banks is essentially short term in nature. On the asset side, they already hold large volumes of long-term government paper, which is in tradable form. The composition of assets suggests that banks are less averse to taking on interest rate risk than credit risk. Given the portfolio choice, it seems to make sense for banks to keep the maturity of their loans short. It is therefore necessary to change the perception of banks regarding credit risk. An added set of institutional sources of finance is emerging with the increasing magnitude of funds flowing to mutual funds, insurance, and pension. The size of the mutual fund industry in the Indian economy is still very small as compared with that of developed countries. Contractual savings are yet another source of project finance. There are two sets of completely opposing views on the investment of such savings. The first advocates higher return and hence advocates investment in the equity market, while the proponents of safety-first advocate investment in gilt-edged securities. Both sets of arguments are equally strong and the international experience does not provide a definitive guide one way or the other. At the same time, the increasing requirement of funds going to social securities augers well as a potential source of productive investment.

A second set of options centre around possible innovations within the existing institutional framework. Banks (and FIs) could play an innovative role in project finance by utilizing and improving on their appraisal expertise. This could be achieved through longer-term credit enhancements, take-out financing, special purpose vehicles and guarantees of corporate bonds. A typical long-term project faces the highest risk in initial years and cash flows usually stabilize after five to seven years. The basic idea is that banks and FIs can take initial risks through medium-term lending and as cash flows become secure, the loans could be securitized, and sold to those institutions that have a longer-term liability structure. Another option is the marketization of a mix of loans, such as, Jumbo Mortgages. This kind of securitization of all kinds of assets is especially appealing because it can encompass even loans to relatively SSIs. The basic philosophy is for banks and DFIs to take on the initial risks and thereafter package the risks into different baskets to match varying risk appetites in the market.

There is, of course, some long-term bank lending that is already being extended. A new competitor to project finance is emerging in the form of housing loans. Current indications are that the housing finance is likely to keep increasing, especially as the default rate is still relatively low. Clearly, banks seem to prefer interest rate risk to credit risk, and as long as the fiscal deficit is high, this option will always be available to them.

What does the future hold for project finance from the DFIs? In the Indian case, ICICI is already a bank, but presumably has the expertise to do project financing. IFCI is in great difficulty. Industrial Development Bank of India (IDBI) is in process of restructuring. A number of financial institutions are still in the business of long-term project financing: Infrastructure Development Finance Company (IDFC) for infrastructure and Small Industries Development Bank of India (SIDBI) for funding SSIs. A serious rethinking needs to be done about the future of these DFIs. DFIs, as has been observed earlier, are not intrinsically non-competitive. If their legacy problems can be sorted out, it is possible to evolve a future role for them. India is not yet at a stage where it can fund growth exclusively out of market-based approach.

There is very little alternative and it is too early to give up the bank/DFI-based financing for industrial investment at the present juncture because markets are not deep enough to securitize loans. There are other developments that are creating a more enabling environment for a long-term credit culture. There are several ways in which creditors' rights are being strengthened, which should go a long way in mitigating the risks of large-scale project financing. These include initiatives such as the setting up of Debt Recovery Tribunals (DRTs), the introduction of Corporate Debt Recovery (CDR) mechanisms, and the emergence of ARCs following the passage of the SARFAESI Act, 2002. It is hoped that all this would make securitization of assets easier. Besides, the institution of the CIB as a credit registry is also likely to reduce information asymmetries and cut down on transaction costs such as project appraisal.

Development of the Corporate Debt Market

A necessary condition for the process of asset securitization is the evolution of a deep and liquid corporate debt market. As I have already mentioned, the corporate debt market has not fully developed in the Indian context, though there is some activity in recent years, especially in the private placement segment.

Several pre-conditions for the evolution of a successful corporate debt market are now in place. These include a well-functioning market for government securities, well developed infrastructure for retail debt, a liquid money market, an efficient clearing and settlement system, a credible credit rating system, and a formal regulatory framework. At the same time, the lack of good quality issuers, institutional investors, and supporting infrastructure continue to constrain market development. There is also the need to enhance public disclosure, standardize products, put in place effective bankruptcy laws, and use technology to reduce transaction costs further (Mohan, 2003).

MARKET-BASED FINANCING

A final set of possibilities hinge around a shift in emphasis towards a market-based approach. Could the capital markets provide the long-term funds to industry by directly tapping the long-term savings potential in the economy? Indian households are typically risk averse and there has been a massive flight to the safety of bank deposits and contractual saving instruments. At the same time, the continuing increase in the saving rate of households suggests that there is no supply constraint in terms of financial resources available.

The challenge is really to harness these savings into risk capital. In a country like India, where a large number of retail investors enter the equity markets directly, there is great potential to develop institutional intermediaries to tap these funds. In contrast, the investor profile in most developed countries is relatively more institutional, with mutual funds and pension funds often accounting for a large proportion of the trade. This effectively means that investors in India bear far more risks than their counterparts in developed economies, who are able to spread their risk profile by, say, buying units of a large mutual fund, with the necessary technical expertise of investment management. The emerging pool of institutional investors in the equity markets, therefore, needs to tap the savings potential much more effectively. The UTI was able to successfully perform this assignment of transforming household saving into equity financing till guaranteed returns eroded its very sustainability.

The expansion of the mutual fund industry thus becomes a target candidate for higher resource mobilization from the capital markets. The size of the mutual fund industry in the Indian economy is still very small as compared with that of developed countries. Besides, mutual funds have been exiting the equity markets mainly because of better opportunities in the debt markets. Further, insurance companies and pension funds could be tapped with appropriate risk management. Investment funds—a category of non-banking financial companies in the Indian context—also provide an avenue for channelling funds into the stock markets, although the very logic of investment management carries an inherent bias for operations in the secondary market rather than the primary market. Venture capital funds with specialization in certain regions and certain sectors provide another possibility, although in the Indian case thus far, their portfolio is still not very large and often carries a preference for later-stage projects with a smaller gestation lag rather than projects at the absolute initial stages.

SUMMARY

It is now time to take stock of where we stand. While reviewing the trends in industrial finance during the last three decades, certain stylized facts stand out:

1. Bank credit to industry and agriculture has increased as a proportion of their respective sectoral GDP—but not as much as it might have compared with the size of the reduction in SLR.
2. Given the current maturity profile of their assets and liabilities and the existing fiscal deficit, banks' ability to lend in the medium and long term seems to be limited.
3. DFIs are not intrinsically uncompetitive but they need to clean up their legacy of bad debts, emphasize their strengths, and enhance their market orientation.
4. Adequate savings are available in the economy. The issue is to channel them for investment for growth.

The Indian financial system, thus, needs to look at new ways of doing business, in terms of knowledge-based banking and better management of information. It is necessary to tailor the new institutional funds to long-term investments. Besides, the next stage of industrial financing would depend on an accelerated development of the bond market facilitating the securitization of corporate lending.

In terms of the broad framework of industrial financing, it is clear that there is sufficient room for a greater role for market financing. At the same time, this does not mean that the Indian economy is ready for a shift to a market-based system of finance. The panacea to the present challenges in industrial financing hinges on the ability to design an appropriate mix of the bank- and the market-based systems of financing.

AFTERWORD

By 2004, both the major DFIs, which had played a substantial role in term-lending in the preceding three or four decades, had turned into banks. Other DFIs continue to be plagued by weaknesses. Thus, the responsibility of long-term project debt financing is now largely on banks, supported by domestic capital markets and external financing. While the various limitations on banks' ability to fund long-term assets—such as maturity mismatches on account of relatively short-term deposits and pre-emptions on account of SLR requirements—still remain, banks are increasingly able to fund long-term infrastructure projects. The share of credit to industry in overall bank credit has stabilized at around 38 per cent over 2004–7. More importantly, credit intensity of the industry—the ratio of outstanding credit to industry to industrial GDP—has exhibited a significant increase: from 57 per cent in March 2000 to 81 per cent by March 2007. It is much higher than that in other major countries such as Brazil, Germany, Indonesia, Malaysia, Thailand, UK and the US. The share of long-term credit to industry in the overall credit to industry has more than doubled from 19 per cent in March 2000 to 44 per cent by March 2007; over the same period, the share of credit to infrastructure sector in the total industrial credit has increased from 1.7 per cent to 7.4 per cent.

Resources raised from the domestic equity market recovered to 0.6 per cent of GDP during 2003–8 from 0.2 per cent during 1997–2003, but were still lower than that of 1.9 per cent during 1991–7.

There was a significant improvement in corporate profitability during 2003–8, reflecting a variety of factors such as robust sales growth, reduction in debt servicing costs, balance sheet restructuring and efficiency gains. Net profits of sampled corporates grew by an average of 43 per cent per annum during 2003–8, much higher than the annual average of 8 per cent during 1997–2003 and 21 per cent during 1991–7. Consequently, internal financing from retained profits emerged as the most significant source for corporate financing.

Finally, net flows from foreign sources—American Depository Receipts (ADRs), Global Depository Receipts (GDRs), FDI and external commercial borrowings taken together—rose from an average of 1.0 per cent of GDP during 1991–7 and 1.4 per cent during 1997–2003 to 3.3 per cent during 2003–8.

Thus, the overall flow of institutional finance to industry, from both domestic and foreign sources, has witnessed sustained increase in recent years. However, some of the potential markets for funds—such as the corporate bond market—are yet to see any significant progress. But there is a growing recognition that the corporate bond market needs to be developed on a priority basis to meet the long-term funding need of the industry.

Notes

[1] In order to obtain DFIs' support to the industrial sector, estimates of sanctions and disbursements of DFIs, being in gross terms (that is, without taking account of the repayments), may have been misleading. Instead, we have taken the investments

and loans and advances of the major DFIs. In particular, in order to arrive at an estimate of DFIs' support to industrial finance, we have added the following items, namely, investments and credit to industrial concerns by IDBI, equity investments, debentures, and loans and advances of IFCI; investments in bonds and equity and rupee and foreign currency loans of ICICI, credit by Industrial Investment Bank of India (IIBI) (since investments are negligible); loans and advances and investments (including government securities in absence of break-up) of Securities and Futures Commissions; and loans and advances to industrial concerns and commercial investments of SIDBI.

[2] The demand for credit, when seen as an essential input to the production process, has to be linked to the value added. While for aggregate non-food gross bank credit, GDP at current prices would be the appropriate normalization factor, for credit going to agriculture and industrial sectors, as well as, to the SSI sector, we have tried to capture their appropriate contribution in value added. For credit going to the agricultural and industrial sectors, we have taken GDP (at current factor cost) originating in 'agriculture and allied activities' and 'manufacturing', respectively. As far as 'GDP originating in the SSI sector' is concerned, there is no readymade estimate—therefore, we have taken the GDP originating in unregistered manufacturing and added to it the contribution of the SSI sector in organized manufacturing as revealed from the Annual Survey of Industries (Mohan, 2002).

References

Acharya, S. (2002), 'Macroeconomic Management in the Nineties,' *Economic and Political Weekly*, 37, pp. 1515–38.

Barth, J.R., G. Caprio Jr., and R. Levine (2001), *The Regulation and Supervision of Banks around the World: A New Database*, World Bank, Washington, DC.

Domowitz, L., J. Glen, and A. Madhavan (2000), *International Evidence on Aggregate Corporate Financing Decisions*, World Bank, Washington, DC.

Government of India (1991), *Report of the Committee on the Financial System*, RBI, Mumbai.

_____ (1998), *Report of the Committee on Banking Sector Reforms*, Government of India, New Delhi.

Levine, R. (1997), 'Financial Development and Economic Growth: Views and Agenda', *Journal of Economic Literature*, 35, pp. 688–726.

Mohan, R. (2002), 'Small Scale Industrial Policy: A Critical Evaluation,' in A. Krueger (ed.), *Economic Policy Reforms and the Indian Economy*, Oxford University Press, New Delhi.

_____ (2003), 'Developing the Corporate Debt Market in India,' presentation at the 3rd Invest India Debt Market Round Table, 6 May 2003, available at *http://www.rbi.org.in*.

RBI (2003a), *Report on Currency and Finance 2002-03*, RBI, Mumbai.

_____ , *Report on Trend and Progress of Banking in India*, RBI various issues, Mumbai.

Rajan, R. and L. Zingales (2003), *Saving Capitalism from the Capitalists*, Crown Business, New York.

4 Agricultural Credit in India

Status, Issues, and Future Agenda*

INTRODUCTION: HISTORICAL OVERVIEW OF AGRICULTURAL CREDIT IN INDIA

RISK IN INDIAN FARMING

Settled agriculture in India has had a long history because of the fertile plains of northern India irrigated by the Indus, the Ganga–Yamuna river systems, and the Brahmaputra in the east. Southern India has its own river systems and has, moreover, been characterized by its impressive history of sophisticated water management systems: perhaps among the most developed historically. As a consequence of this natural fertility and abundant availability of water, ironically, population density grew early in India, and along with that different degrees of poverty.

Despite the existence of these river systems, agriculture in India has always been heavily dependent on the monsoons and has hence been an inherently risky activity. At different times we have also had onerous rural tax systems under different empires, most recently under the British. Indigenous systems of credit had to develop as a consequence of seasonal needs and fluctuations in order to facilitate smoothing of consumption pattern of farmers over the year. With the intermittent failure of the monsoons and other customary vicissitudes of farming, rural indebtedness has been a serious and continuous characteristic of Indian agriculture. Because of the high risk inherent in traditional farming activity, the prevalence of high interest rates was the norm rather than an exception, and the concomitant exploitation and misery often resulted. Development of rural credit systems has, therefore, been found to be intrinsically very difficult and, as we will see, an issue of continuing official concern for over a century.

* Lecture delivered at the 17th National Conference of Agricultural Marketing, Indian Society of Agricultural Marketing, Hyderabad, on 5 February 2004. Reprinted from *Economic and Political Weekly*, Vol. 41, No. 11, 18 March 2006.

Early Attention to Agricultural Credit

These problems began to engage the attention of even the British colonial government as early as the 1870s: the practice of extending institutional credit to agriculture can be traced back to that period when farmers were provided with such credit by the government during drought years. Thinking to do with credit cooperation began in the latter part of the nineteenth century. Finally, the Cooperative Societies Act was passed in 1904 and cooperatives were seen as the premier institutions for disbursing agricultural credit. 'For some decades, that is, since long before the organization of the Reserve Bank, great faith has been placed in India in the potentialities of the cooperative organization to serve the credit needs of the country, especially of the rural sector' (RBI, 1970, p. 68). The early years of the twentieth century were characterized by continuous official attention to the provision of rural credit: a new Act was passed in 1912 giving legal recognition to credit societies and the like (a precursor of micro-finance); the Maclagan Committee on Cooperation in India issued a report in 1915 advocating the establishment of provincial cooperative banks, which got established in almost all provinces by 1930 thus giving rise to the three-tier cooperative credit structure; the Royal Commission on Agriculture further examined the programme of rural credit in 1926–7; Malcolm Darling submitted another report on co-operative credit to the Government of India in 1935, just before the founding of the RBI. This continuing concern reflected the intrinsic problems of extension of rural credit which, to some extent, find resonance even today. It was then reported that in many provinces credit overdues to these credit co-operative institutions constituted 60–70 per cent of the outstanding principal due.

It was in 1935 that the Reserve Bank was founded: the RBI Act is unusual among central banks to have specific provision for attention to agricultural credit. Section 54 of the Act enjoined the Reserve Bank to set up an Agriculture Credit Department which was to have an expert staff to advise the Central Government, state governments, state cooperative banks, and other banks, and to coordinate RBI functions for agricultural credit. Section 17 of the Act empowered it to provide agricultural credit through state cooperative banks or any other banks engaged in the business of agricultural credit.

Among the first activities of the Reserve Bank in agricultural credit were two studies: one in 1936 and the other in 1937. It was found that almost the entire finance required by agriculturalists was supplied by money lenders and that cooperatives and other agencies played a negligible part. During the period between 1935 and 1950, the Reserve Bank was very active in continuing the attempt to re-invigorate the cooperative credit movement through a variety of initiatives. Besides providing financial accommodation to the cooperative movement, the RBI played a central role in the task of building the cooperative credit structure, which gradually evolved into two separate arms, one for short-term credit and another for long-term credit—a structure that still exists today. The continuing intense concern with the provision of rural credit continued in the post-war years: more than half a dozen committees were appointed between 1945 and 1950. Despite all these efforts, even by 1951 the provision of credit through cooperatives remained meagre with only 3.3 per cent of the cultivators having access to credit from cooperatives and 0.9 per cent from commercial banks. Furthermore, the funds supplied by the money lenders were subject to high interest rates and other usurious practices and, accordingly, legislation on money lending was advocated to check such malpractices.

The foundation for building a broader credit infrastructure for rural credit was laid by the Report of the All-India Rural Credit Survey (RBI, 1954). The Committee of Direction that conducted this survey observed that agricultural credit fell short of the right quantity, was not of the right type, did not serve the right purpose, and often failed to go to the right people. The Committee also observed that the performance of cooperatives in the sphere of agricultural credit was deficient in more than one way, but at the same time, cooperatives had a vital role in channelling credit to the farmers and therefore summed up that, 'Co-operation has failed, but Co-operation must succeed'.

The Committee, apart from visualizing cooperatives as an exclusive agency for providing credit to agriculture, urged a well-defined role for commercial banks in delivering credit for agriculture in specialized areas, such as marketing, processing, storage, and warehousing. Towards this end, it recommended establishment of the State Bank of India and through it, extension of commercial banking facilities to rural and semi-urban areas. Thus, concern with the inadequate extension of agricultural credit had a significant role in the founding of both the RBI and transformation of the Imperial Bank of India into the State Bank of India.

THE PERIOD OF SUBSTANTIAL CHANGE: 1960s TO THE 1980s

The inadequacy of rural credit continued to engage the attention of the Reserve Bank and the government throughout the 1950s and 1960s. The Agricultural Refinance Corporation (AgRC) was set up by the Reserve Bank in 1963 to provide funds by way of refinance, but credit cooperatives still did not function too well.

Consequently, the All-India Rural Credit Review Committee (Chairman: B.Venkatappiah) was set up in July 1966 to, inter alia, review the supply of rural credit in the context of the Fourth Five Year Plan, in general, and the requirements of the intensive programmes of agricultural production in different parts of the country, in particular, as also to make recommendations for improving the flow of agricultural credit. After a comprehensive review, the Committee recommended that the commercial banks should play a complementary role, along with cooperatives, in extending rural credit. The social control and the subsequent nationalization of major commercial banks in 1969 (and in 1980) acted as a catalyst in providing momentum to the efforts of leveraging the commercial banking system for extending agricultural credit. The outreach of banks was enlarged considerably within a relatively short period of time. The concept of priority sector was introduced in 1969 to underscore the imperative of financing certain neglected sectors such as agriculture. The channelling of credit to the priority sectors was sought to be achieved through the stipulation that a certain proportion of the total net bank credit be deployed in these sectors by specific target dates.[1] Decentralized credit planning through the Lead Bank Scheme was also introduced, under which, each district was placed with one of the commercial banks (called the district Lead Bank) to spearhead the credit allocation for, inter alia, agricultural lending. In order to emphasize the developmental and promotional role assigned to the AgRC in addition to refinancing, the Corporation was renamed as the Agricultural Refinance and Development Corporation (ARDC) by an amendment to the Act in 1975.

It was also the case that the 1950s and 1960s had been characterized by a big industrial push with inadequate attention being given to agriculture. It was the 1965–7 drought that brought matters to a head and focused concentrated attention to agriculture. The Green Revolution then followed in the late 1960s and 1970s necessitating adequate availability of credit that could enable the purchase of inputs such as fertilizer, high yielding varieties of seeds, pump sets for irrigation, and the like.

Despite all these efforts, the flow of credit to the agricultural sector failed to exhibit any appreciable improvement due mainly to the fact that commercial banks were not tuned to the needs and requirements of the small and marginal farmers, while the cooperatives, on the other hand, lacked resources to meet the expected demand. The solution that was found involved the establishment of a separate banking structure, capable of combining the local feel and familiarity of rural problems characteristic of cooperatives and the professionalism and large resource base of commercial banks. Following the recommendations of the Narasimham Working Group (1975), RRBs were set up. Thus, by the end of 1977, there emerged three separate institutions for providing rural credit, which is often described as the 'multi-agency approach'.

Following the recommendations of the 'Committee to Review Arrangements for Institutional Credit for Agriculture and Rural Development', the NABARD was set up in 1982 for providing credit for promotion of, among others things, agriculture. NABARD took over the entire undertaking of the ARDC and the refinancing functions of the RBI in relation to state co-operatives and RRBs. NABARD is the apex institution which has been entrusted with a pivotal role in the sphere of policy planning and providing refinance facilities to RFIs to augment their resource base. Since its inception, the NABARD has played a central role in providing financial assistance, facilitating institutional development, and encouraging promotional efforts in the area of rural credit. NABARD also administers the Rural Infrastructure Development Fund (RIDF), which was set up in 1995–6; the corpus of RIDF is contributed by SCBs to the extent of their shortfall in agricultural lending under the priority sector targets. NABARD has been playing a catalytic role in micro-credit through the conduit of Self-Help Groups (SHGs).

THE PERIOD OF INTROSPECTION AND REFORMS: 1991 TO THE PRESENT

Notwithstanding the impressive geographical spread, functional reach and consequent decline in the influence of informal sources of credit, RFIs were characterized by several weaknesses, namely, decline in productivity and efficiency, erosion of repayment ethics, and profitability. On the eve of the 1991 reforms, the rural credit delivery system was again found to be in a poor shape (R.V. Gupta Committee, 1998).

The Report of the Committee on the Financial System (Government of India, 1991) and Report of the Committee on the Banking Sector Reforms (Government of India, 1998) provided the blue print for carrying out overall financial sector reforms during the1990s. Furthermore, weaknesses in the performance of RFIs since 1991 resulted in setting up of various committees/working groups/task forces to look into their operations such as: 'High-level Committee on Agricultural Credit through Commercial Banks' (Gupta, RBI, 1998), 'Task Force to Study the Functions of Cooperative Credit System and to Suggest Measures for its Strengthening' (Capoor, 1999), 'Expert Committee on Rural Credit' (Vyas, 2001), and 'Working Group to Suggest Amendments in the Regional Rural Banks Act, 1976' (Government of India, 2002). These committees/working groups/task forces made far-reaching recommendations having a bearing on agricultural credit. While the Capoor Task Force suggested adoption of a Model Co-operative Act, setting up of a Co-operative Rehabilitation and Development Fund at NABARD and Mutual Assistance Fund at the state level, the Vyas Committee (2001) recommended restoration of health of Primary Agricultural Credit

Societies (PACS) by scrapping the cadre system, selective delayering of cooperatives credit structure, and integration of short-term and long-term structures. The Madhava Rao Task Force (2002) had, in addition to suggesting diversification of the business of RRBs, recommended introduction of capital adequacy norms for RRBs in a phased manner, along with the RRB-specific amount of equity based on the risk-weighted assets ratio.

The financial sector reforms formed an integral part of the overall structural reforms initiated in 1991 and included various measures in the area of agricultural credit such as deregulation of interest rates of cooperatives and RRBs; deregulation of lending rates of commercial banks for loans above Rs 2 lakh; recapitalization of select RRBs; introduction of prudential accounting norms and provisioning requirements for all rural credit agencies; increased refinance support from RBI and capital contribution to NABARD; constitution of the RIDF in NABARD for infrastructure projects; introduction of KCC; and stipulation of interest rate not exceeding 9 per cent for crop loans up to Rs 50,000 extended by the PSBs.

Summary

Thus, concern with the inadequacy of agricultural credit has had more than a century of tortuous history. The agricultural credit system (Figure 4.1), as it has emerged, has been a product of both evolution and intervention and symbolizes the system's response to the stimuli from continuing dissatisfaction with credit delivery. The concern for food security and the need for building up buffer stocks, which guided the Green Revolution, created both enhanced and diversified type of credit requirements for agricultural production. In India, a 'supply-leading approach' to the institutional development for agriculture credit has been followed.

ASSESSMENT OF PROGRESS IN AGRICULTURAL CREDIT

Agricultural credit clearly started to grow after bank nationalization (Figure 4.2), and it has been growing continuously since then. With all the concerns and scepticism expressed, the difficult and continuous changes in institutional credit have indeed borne fruit. Over the years there has been a significant increase in the access of rural cultivators to institutional credit and, simultaneously, the role of informal agencies, including money lenders, as source of credit has declined. According to the AIDIS 1991–92, the relative shares of institutional agencies in the total cash debt of rural cultivators increased from 31.7 per cent in 1971 to 63.2 per cent in 1981 and further to 66.3 per cent in 1991.

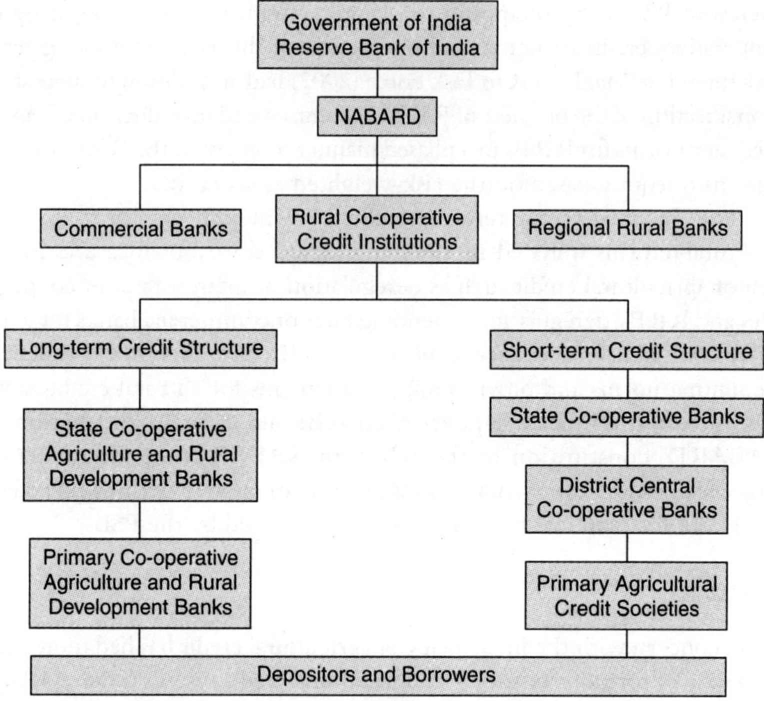

Figure 4.1 Structure of Agricultural Credit System in India

Source: RBI.

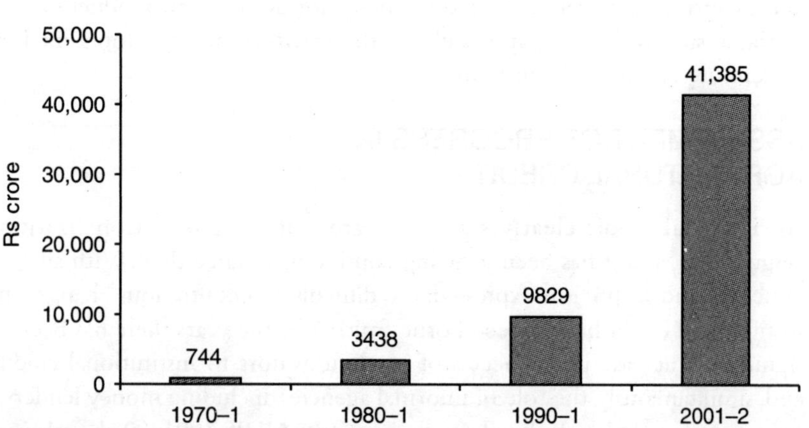

Figure 4.2 Total Direct Institutional Credit

Source: *Handbook of Statistics on Indian Economy, 2002–3*, RBI.

Nonetheless, recent years have again been characterized by a concern over the falling share of agricultural credit as a proportion of total credit. This is indeed true, but is this the correct metric to look at the progress of agricultural credit? What would be more relevant is to evaluate agricultural credit as a proportion of agricultural GDP, or short-term credit as a proportion of the value of inputs, or long-term credit as a proportion of private investment.

As might be expected, the share of agricultural GDP has been falling as a share of total GDP. Hence credit to agriculture may also be expected to fall as a proportion of total credit, assuming relative stability in the share of purchased inputs as a proportion of value added. What is interesting is that the share of agricultural credit as a proportion of agricultural GDP has been rising continuously since the 1950s, and even as a proportion of total GDP until the 1980s. There was indeed a fall in the mid-1990s, but has again risen now (Table 4.1). It is true, however, that agricultural credit has indeed fallen as a proportion of total credit.

Table 4.1 Ratio of Direct Agricultural Credit (Disbursements) to Agricultural GDP, Total GDP, and Total Credit

(per cent)

	Agricultural credit/ agricultural GDP	Agricultural credit/ total GDP	Agricultural credit/ CS
1950–1	0.5	0.3	–
1960–1	3.3	1.3	–
1970s	5.4	2.1	10.8
1980s	8.3	2.6	8.5
1990s	7.4	2.0	6.4
2001–2	8.7	2.0	5.5

Notes: 1. Agricultural credit: Direct credit for agricultural and allied activities extended by co-operatives, commercial banks, and RRBs.
2. Total GDP and agricultural GDP are at factor cost and at current prices.
3. CS–Other banks' credit to commercial sector (outstanding) proxy for total credit.

Source: *Report on Currency and Finance*, RBI; various issues, *Handbook of Statistics on Indian Economy, 2002–03*, RBI.

The existing agricultural credit system is geared to the needs of foodgrains production: with the share of foodgrains production falling as a proportion of total agricultural production, it is all the more creditable that agriculture credit has not fallen as a proportion of agricultural GDP. With the share of agriculture in GDP falling continuously, from 36 per cent in 1981 to 29 per cent in 1991 and 22 per cent in 2001, it is to be expected that the share of agricultural credit would also fall as a proportion of total credit, unless this trend is corrected by increasing commercialization of agriculture.

The age old problem of rural credit has been the excessive reliance of borrowers on money lenders and other informal sources that have entailed usurious interest rates and exploitation. It is quite remarkable how long it has taken to really substitute institutional credit for informal money lending channels and how tortuous the process of change has been: change of any significance took over fifty years from the beginning of serious attention in the 1930s to the 1980s (see Table 4.2). It was the nationalization of banks in 1969 and subsequent spread of rural bank branches that has really made a difference in reducing, finally, the share of money lenders in agricultural credit.

Table 4.2 Relative Share of Borrowing of Cultivator (Households from Different Sources)

(per cent)

Sources of credit	1951	1961	1971	1981	1991
Non-institutional	92.7	81.3	68.3	36.8	30.6
of which					
Money lenders	69.7	49.2	36.1	16.1	17.5
Institutional	7.3	18.7	31.7	63.2	66.3
of which					
Cooperative societies/banks	3.3	2.6	22.0	29.8	35.2
Commercial banks	0.9	0.6	2.4	28.8	35.2
Unspecified	–	–	–	–	3.1
Total	100.0	100.0	100.0	100.0	100.0

Source: AIDIS, *RBI Bulletin*, February 2000.

As documented in the last section, it has taken drastic action ranging from the formation of co-operatives to bank nationalization, setting up of RRBs, and the like. The Indian record of extension of rural credit is quite a story of institutional innovation.

The remarkable feature of agricultural credit extension in India is the widespread network of RFIs. Following the first phase of nationalization of commercial banks in 1969, large scale branch expansion was undertaken with a view to creating a strong institutional base in rural areas. At the time of nationalization in June 1969, the total number of rural offices of SCBs was 1833, which then increased significantly to 32,406 by March 2003. The number of co-operative institutions catering to agriculture went up from 95,871 at end-June 1980 to over 1,10,000 at present. The share of the rural branches of SCBs (including RRBs) in total increased sharply from 22 per cent in June 1969 to 47 per cent by March 2003. The main story in the expansion of rural credit in the 1980s and 1990s has been the ascendancy of commercial banks, along with RRBs, with a corresponding fall in the share of cooperatives (see Table 4.3). This is reflected in the increasing concern in recent years over the effectiveness, governance, and financial health of rural cooperative banks. Just under half of rural credit continues to be extended by them and hence it is essential that they be revitalized and put on a sound business footing.

Table 4.3 Decadal Average Share of Institutions in Direct Agricultural Credit (Disbursements)

(per cent)

Period	Co-operatives	RRBs	Commercial banks
1970s	79.5	2.3	21.0
1980s	55.9	5.3	38.9
1990s	51.5	6.2	42.3
2001–2	44.0	11.0	45.0

Note: Direct agricultural credit (disbursements) from 1975–6 for RRBs and 1971–2 for commercial banks.

Source: *Handbook of Statistics on Indian Economy, 2002–03*, RBI.

There has been increasing expression of concern on the extension of agricultural credit in the 1990s. There has actually been continuous growth in the number of accounts in all categories of farm size in the case of commercial banks (Figure 4.3).

It is probably the case that the introduction of KCCs has also aided this process in the recent years. But it is equally true that the share of small farms in total credit appears to be falling to a certain extent (Figure 4.4).

This trend needs to be analysed carefully and is a good topic for further research. Are larger farmers becoming more productive and commercial with higher intensity of bought-out inputs, thus requiring higher levels of credit? Or are small farmers becoming unviable, making it difficult for banks to finance them? Or, are banks becoming more risk averse and hence reluctant to lend?

There is some evidence to the contrary. Available data suggest that agricultural credit has been rising in recent years as a share of both the value of inputs or the value of output (see Table 4.4). Moreover, long-term credit

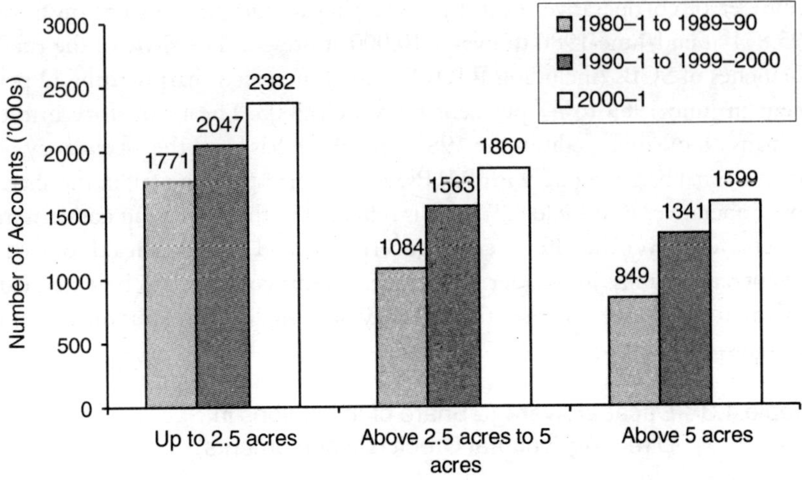

Figure 4.3 Average Number of Accounts (size-wise)

Source: *Handbook of Statistics on Indian Economy, 2002–03*, RBI.

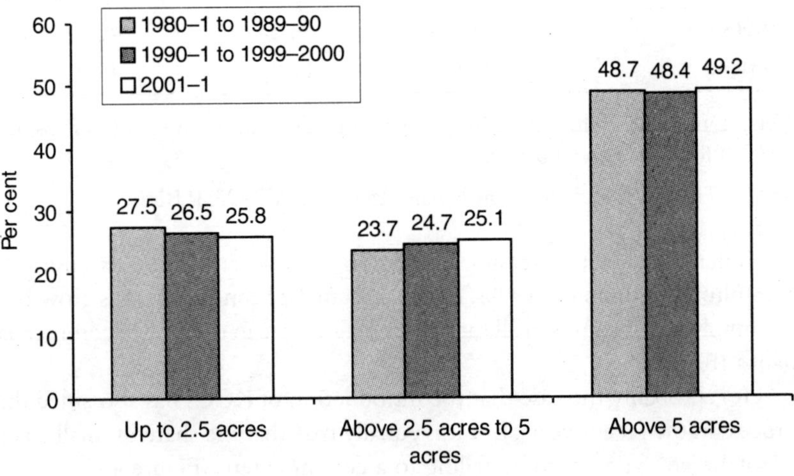

Figure 4.4 Average Share of Loan Outstanding

Source: *Handbook of Statistics on Indian Economy, 2002–03*, RBI.

as a share of private investment has also been rising in the 1990s (see Table 4.5). Thus, it is probably fair to say that the agricultural credit effort has not really been slackening in the 1990s. It is also possible that with credit intensity going up in this fashion it could, ironically, also lead to greater risk on the part of borrowers because of greater indebtedness.

Table 4.4 Gross Value of Outputs, Value of Inputs, and Short-term Credit

(Rs crore at 1993–4 prices)

Year	Gross value of outputs	Value of inputs	Short-term credit	Short-term credit as percentage to	
				Value of inputs	Value of outputs
1993–4	2,04,874	27,413	9752	35.6	4.8
1996–7	2,32,833	30,735	13,330	43.4	5.7
1998–9	2,45,413	34,566	14,642	42.4	6.0

Source: Pant Joshi (2003).

Table 4.5 Private Capital Formation and Share of Long-term Credit

(Rs crore)

Year	Private sector capital formation	Investment credit	Proportion (%)
1980–1	2843	1335	47.0
1990–1	8402	4208	50.1
1998–9	19,311	13,264	68.7

Source: Pant Joshi (2003).

Regional Distribution

Among the striking features of the agricultural credit scene in India are the wide regional disparities in the disbursement of agricultural credit by SCBs (excluding RRBs). The correct way to evaluate the performance of agricultural credit is to look at the ratio of agricultural credit to state agricultural value added. It is difficult to obtain these data. So, as a second best, we can look at agricultural credit as a proportion of NSDP. The southern states stand out with a substantially higher share of agricultural credit (see Tables 4.6 and 4.7), followed by the northern and central regions. Whereas the ratio for the southern region increased during the latter part of the 1990s, it remained stationary for the northern, central, and north-eastern regions. It is also notable that the southern states have a much more active cooperative movement (not covered in the data reported here), and hence their share of agricultural credit is likely to be even higher. The low share of the western region is surprising, but could be because of the very active role of co-operatives in this region. The eastern and north-eastern regions clearly get a very low share.

Table 4.6 Region-wise Ratio of Agricultural Credit to Net State Domestic Product (NSDP)

(per cent)

Region	1991–5 (average)	1996–2001 (average)
Northern	0.7	1.0
North-eastern	0.2	0.2
Eastern	0.5	0.5
Central	0.7	1.0
Western	0.7	0.7
Southern	1.6	2.0
All-India	0.9	1.0

Notes: 1. Agricultural credit relates to direct finance to agriculture and allied activities by all SCBs (disbursements—short-term and long-term).
2. NSDP is at current prices.

Source: *Economic Survey*, various issues; RBI.

Table 4.7 Region-wise Share of Agriculture and Allied Sector Credit (Short-term and Long-term) Disbursements

(per cent)

Region	1990–1	1995–6	2001–2
Northern	12.9	11.6	19.9
North-eastern	0.4	0.4	0.5
Eastern	8.3	6.4	7.4
Central	16.9	16.4	14.1
Western	13.6	17.1	14.4
Southern	47.9	48.0	43.8
All-India	100.0	100.0	100.0

Note: Agricultural credit relates to direct finance to agricultural and allied activities of all SCBs (disbursements—short-term and long-term).

Source: RBI.

Some information is also available on a per capita basis and, as may be expected, the southern region really stands out in terms of exposure to agricultural credit. The per capita extension of agricultural credit in the eastern and north-eastern regions is extremely low (see Table 4.8). Since these data pertain to commercial banks, the puzzle before us is why should such stark differences exist between regions? Given that Punjab, Haryana, and western UP are the centres of the Green Revolution, one would have expected a higher intensity of agricultural credit in the northern region and why do PSBs, with similar management and staff, behave so differently between regions? If it is possible for banks to do direct lending for agriculture in the southern states, why not in the other regions? And why should the differences be so large? Incidentally, it is notable that the rural stress that has emerged in recent years after repeated droughts has been concentrated in the southern region. Ironically, it is possible that this may have occurred as a consequence of the relative success of the agricultural credit effort in this region. All these issues need much greater research so that our continuing search for viable agricultural credit extension is informed by appropriate knowledge.

Table 4.8 Region-wise Trends in Agricultural and Allied Sector Credit Per Capita

(Rupees)

Region	1991–5	1996–2001
Northern	60	153
North-eastern	9	17
Eastern	21	42
Central	36	86
Western	67	134
Southern	157	280
All-India	67	128

Note: Ratios obtained by dividing the average direct finance to agricultural and allied activities of all SCBs (disbursements—short term and long-term) during the period 1991–5 and 1996–2001 by the total region-wise population in 1991 and 2001, respectively.

Source: *Economic Survey*, various issues; RBI.

Non-performing Assets (NPAs)

I started with the core issue of risk in agriculture and how that is a key determinant of all the problems encountered in agricultural lending. I would, therefore, briefly like to examine the record of NPAs in agriculture for commercial banks. Is the hesitation of banks to lend for agriculture really caused by the experience of a much higher level of NPAs? It is found that the proportions of NPAs are indeed higher for agriculture than they are for the non-priority sector. However, they are not as high as those for SSIs and for other priority sectors. In fact, for private sector banks, agricultural NPAs are as low as 5 per cent of total outstanding advances to agriculture and are lower than for the non-priority sector (see Table 4.9). In fact, it is likely that if public sector enterprises are excluded from the data for the non-priority sector, the performance of NPAs in agriculture may not be much higher than for lending to the non-priority sector private sector credit exposure as a whole. These data do suggest that agricultural lending may be more risky than non-priority sectors, but the difference is probably not large enough to warrant excessive caution in bank lending for agricultural purposes.

Table 4.9 Sector-wise Average Non-performing Assets of Banks (2001–3)

(Rs Crore)

	Agriculture	Small scale	Others	Total priority sector	Non-priority sector
Public Sector Banks					
Average NPAs	7635	10,362	6748	24,745	28,764
Average NPAs as a per cent of average outstanding advances	12.0	20.6	12.2	14.2	9.4
Private Sector Banks					
Average NPAs	433	1249	593	2275	9271
Average NPAs as a per cent of average outstanding advances	5.1	15.9	5.3	8.1	10.2

Source: *Report on Trend and Progress of Banking in India*, various issues, RBI.

Summary

What have we learnt from this brief summary of the record of agricultural credit? First, after about seventy years of constant efforts, institutional credit is indeed reaching a substantial proportion of farmers. Second, with the share of agricultural GDP falling in total GDP, it is to be expected that the share of agricultural credit will go down as a proportion of total credit. But we do need to ensure that it does not fall as a share of agricultural GDP, and that it in fact intensifies. Third, what is needed is a better analysis by banks on where the risks are in the extension of agricultural credit, and to then find market-oriented solutions for mitigating such risks. Where the mitigation of such risk involves positive externalities, and the promotion of public good, methods of appropriate government intervention would need to be identified and considered. Fourth, there is an urgent need for the adoption of the best modern techniques for risk management in agriculture, including a clearer distribution between risky and less risky borrowers. Fifth, banks need to adopt a more specialized approach as between different agricultural sectors and regions in order to achieve a better understanding of agricultural credit needs and risks on a disaggregated basis: which sectors and regions are more credit worthy and which less so? Which agricultural activities and regions are getting more credit and why? Business as usual and a blanket approach will no longer do. Sixth, there is an increasing need for allied activities and term lending, and hence a change in our traditional view of what constitutes agriculture and how it should be promoted.

It is to these issues that I now turn.

THE CHANGING FACE OF AGRICULTURE

Changes in the Demand for Food

The defining characteristic of the 1980s and 1990s has been the overall acceleration in economic growth of the country (see Table 4.10). Whereas per capita annual income growth was only about 1.2 per cent for about thirty years until 1980 or so, growth has been accelerating in the 1980s and 1990s. With the perceptible fall in population growth in the 1990s a similar level of overall GDP growth still implies higher per capita income growth. The consequence is that Indian annual per capita income is now about US$ 500 which is pushing India into the group of middle income countries.

Table 4.10 Growth of the Indian Economy

(annual growth rate in per cent per year)

Year	Gross National Product (GNP)	Per capita
1950–80	3.5	1.2
1980–90	5.7	3.4
1990–2000	5.8	3.6

Source: *National Accounts Statistics*, Central Statistical Organisation.

When annual per capita growth is in the region of 1.2 per cent, it is barely palpable, even cumulatively over ten years. When, however, per capita income growth ascends to around 3.5 per cent per year, it starts becoming palpable on a cumulative basis and leads to perceptible shifts in the demand pattern. Although there is some dispute on the measurement of poverty, the official estimates of poverty and of most academic analysts suggest that there has been substantial reduction in absolute poverty levels between the 1970s and late 1990s (see Figure 4.5). With measured poverty having fallen to around 26 per cent, from the late 1970s levels of around 50 per cent, the pattern of demand for food has been changing correspondingly.

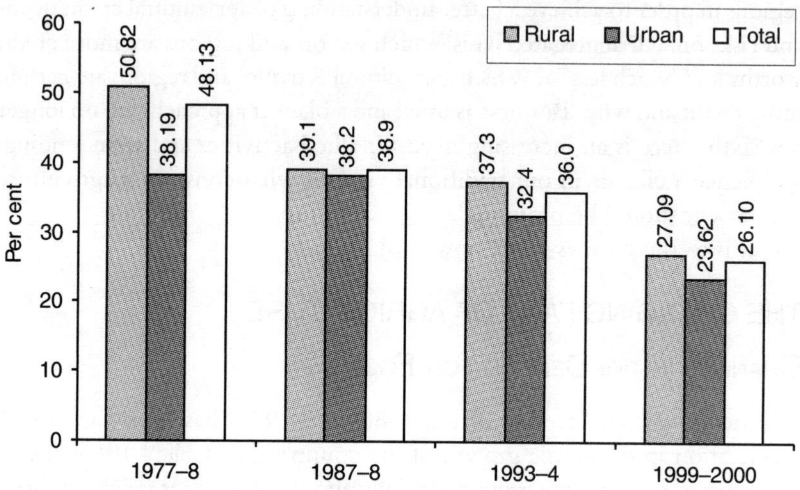

Figure 4.5 Percentage of Persons below Poverty Line (1977–8 to 1999–2000)

Source: *Sixth Five Year Plan*, Planning Commission and *Agricultural Statistics at a Glance*, various issues.

The key observation to be made is that there has been a steep fall in the share of cereals in total household food expenditure over the last thirty years: from just under 60 per cent in the late 1960s to less than 40 per cent in the late 1990s in rural areas; and from over 35 per cent in the late 1960s to 25 per cent in the late 1990s in urban areas (Table 4.11).

Table 4.11 Share of Cereals and Non-cereal Items in Total Monthly Per Capita Expenditure on Food: Rural and Urban Areas

(per cent)

		1969–70	1987–8	1993–4	1999–2000
Rural	Cereals	56.0	41.0	38.3	37.3
	Non-cereals	44.0	59.0	61.7	62.7
Urban	Cereals	36.6	26.5	25.7	25.7
	Non-cereals	63.4	73.5	74.3	74.3

Source: Various NSS Rounds on Household Consumption Expenditure.

Moreover, there has been similar change in the household expenditure on food as a proportion of total expenditure in both rural and urban areas. In rural areas, the expenditure on non-food items has shot up from 26 per cent of the total in 1969–70 to 41 per cent in 1999–2000. In urban areas, this proportion has gone up from about 34 per cent to 52 per cent over the same period (see Table 4.12).

Table 4.12 Share of Food and Non-food Items in Total Monthly Per Capita Expenditure: Rural and Urban Areas

(per cent)

		1969–70	1987–8	1993–4	1999–2000
Rural	Food	73.7	63.8	63.2	59.4
	Non-food	26.3	36.2	36.8	40.6
Urban	Food	65.7	55.9	54.7	48.1
	Non-food	34.3	44.1	45.3	51.9

Source: Various NSS Rounds on Household Consumption Expenditure.

Thus household expenditure on cereals has been shrinking as a proportion of total expenditure in the last thirty to thirty-five years, and this trend may be expected to continue in the years to come. It is quite clear that with progressive and continuous increases in income and poverty reduction, the Indian diet is gradually becoming more diversified. The composition of products in the supply of food will also have to reflect this with the passage of time. With acceleration in economic growth, this change will probably take place faster.

From a policy perspective, the key lesson from this change in demand pattern is that Indian agricultural policy will need to shift its almost exclusive attention from the production of foodgrains to the promotion of all the other food products. The quest for higher agricultural growth, and large accelerated economic growth in rural areas, therefore, requires a shift of policy attention to a much more diversified approach involving growth of production of products such as meat, fish, poultry, vegetables, fruits, and the like.

Changes in the Supply Pattern of Food

India is already a very large producer of fruits and vegetables. It is ranked among the top five producers in a range of items such as bananas, mangoes, papayas, and pineapples, among fruits; and brinjal, cabbage, cauliflower, peas, onions, and potatoes, among vegetables. India is perhaps the second largest producer of both fruits and vegetables (see Table 4.13).

Table 4.13 India's Position in World Production of Fruits and Vegetables

Crop	Rank	Crop	Rank
Apple	10	Brinjal	2
Banana	1	Cabbage	2
Mango	1	Cauliflower	1
Papaya	2	Peas	1
Pineapple	4	Onion	2
Grapes	10	Potato	3
Total fruits	2	Total vegetables	2
Coconut	3	Cashew	1

Source: Indian Horticulture Database–2001.

As incomes increase and diet diversification takes place, the demand for fruits and vegetables will grow correspondingly, and hence we can expect huge changes to take place in the supply response to such emerging demand. The production growth in these items is likely to accelerate significantly if appropriate conditions are created for such an expansion. Correspondingly, such expansion will give rise to huge possibilities for food processing. Although India is indeed a very large producer of fruits and vegetables, our productivity levels continue to be very low: Indian yields are significantly below the world average in vegetables (Table 4.14).

Table 4.14 Yields in Vegetables: India and the World

(Quintals per hectare)

	1990	1995	2000	2002	2003
World	149	155	166	169	168
China	177	188	189	196	192
India	102	102	131	125	129

Note: Vegetables include melons.

Source: FAO Stat 2004.

One successful example of policy attention in the non-foodgrains area is that of milk. Ever since the creation of the National Dairy Development Board (NDDB), the production of milk has increased tremendously, as has its distribution over most parts of the country. The production of milk increased from around 56 million tonnes in 1991–2 to about 80 million tonnes by 2000–1. This development took place only as a result of focused attention to technology development, extension, provision of input supply, procurement, distribution, and marketing, along with corresponding appropriate institutional development. The success achieved in both the acceleration of growth in foodgrains production since the early 1970s and milk production later owed much to specific policy analysis and subsequent policy action accompanied with institutional development—including that of the provision of credit. The key innovation made by the NDDB was to find a way of expanding production by small producers located over different regions, while concentrating technology investment centrally and then extending it to the producers.

Just as research and development (R&D) activities and marketing were very important in the production and adaptation of high yielding seed varieties for wheat and rice, and expanding milk production, productivity increases in other areas such as horticulture will also need similar intensity of investment in appropriate R&D, and special marketing efforts increasingly involving public/private partnership.

ELEMENTS OF A NEW APPROACH

The changing demand pattern for food involves a reordering of priorities in organizing appropriate matching supply responses. Besides promoting diversification, there is also a need for value addition in agricultural production for increasing rural employment and incomes. Interestingly, very significant changes are taking place in the agricultural sector in this regard. There are incipient signs of a much closer connection between primary producers, trade intermediaries, food processing entities, and the eventual marketing of value-added products. With the share of unprocessed foods falling, the real growth area in the agricultural sector is in value-added food products such as meat, poultry, fish, vegetables, fruits, and the like. There is an accelerating move of consumers to basic processed foods such as atta, packaged milk, fresh poultry, soft drinks, processed meat and poultry, and the like (Mohan, 2002).

Supporting policy changes and investments are required to facilitate agricultural diversification and value-addition. The task of the policymakers in designing an appropriate package of measures becomes more challenging considering the fact that the new growth areas of agriculture are characterized by a high degree of heterogeneity, unlike in the case of wheat, rice, and milk. There is a multiplicity of varieties that can be produced in each of these product groups, production is often regionally concentrated, the production and marketing conditions differ significantly, and the input requirements are equally heterogeneous. Hence, policies and programmes that are to be designed to support higher productivity and production in these areas need to be much more regionally disaggregated and knowledge intensive.

In the new growth areas of agriculture, the importance of post-harvest activities such as storage, transportation, processing, and marketing of non-cereal products increases, which leads to greater links between agricultural diversification and rural industrialization. The success of this strategy would, however, depend crucially on developing adequate i frastructural and other support systems.

The monopoly of government-regulated wholesale markets has prevented development of a competitive marketing system in the country, providing no help to farmers in direct marketing, organized retailing, developing smooth raw material supply systems for agro-processing industries, and the adoption of innovative marketing system and technologies. An efficient agricultural marketing system is essential for development of the agricultural sector as it provides outlets and incentives for increased production and the marketing system contributes greatly to the commercialization of subsistence farmers. Worldwide, governments have recognized the importance of liberalized agricultural markets. If the agricultural markets are to be developed in private and cooperative sectors and are to be provided a competitive environment vis-à-vis regulated markets, the existing framework of State Agricultural Produce Marketing Committee (APMC) Acts will have to undergo a change. In this context, the Model Agricultural Produce Marketing (Development & Regulation) Act, 2003 circulated in September 2003 acquires significance. Ten states have initiated legal or administrative action for direct marketing and 'contract farming' arrangements in line with the Model Act. Other states need to follow suit.

As mere policy reforms in these areas would be inadequate, corresponding investment in rural infrastructure is required for closer connection between the farmer and the market. The government has already launched an ambitious rural roads programme, namely the Prime Minister's Gram Sadak Yojana. As village connectivity is actually achieved through the construction of rural roads, it will become possible to make other investments that are required for farm to market transfer of agricultural products. The experience of states such as Tamil Nadu, Punjab, Haryana, Kerala, and Goa, where rural connectivity through roads was achieved much earlier, suggests that such a programme is more successful when conducted in a decentralized framework.

Heavy investments need to be made in establishing cold chains across the country such as cold storage, transport facilities, and the like. The kind of storage and transportation facilities required will differ from product to product and from region to region. It would be best accomplished in a decentralized private sector framework with appropriate policies and supportive financing facilities.

The banking system in India is, at present, geared more to financing the traditional crops such as cereals. However, it needs to reorient itself to meet the changing requirements of commercializing agriculture. Credit requirements would go up due to purchased-input-intensive and heterogeneous production cycles of the new areas of agriculture. This would also call for designing innovative schemes and products which recognize the differing nature of agri-business and supply chains for different products. Newer forms of credit assessment and risk management systems may also have to be put in place, besides upgrading skills and changes in attitudes and mind-sets. The rural credit system has been bypassed by the revolution in IT. The banking system may also have to address the problem of 'financial dualism', characterized by faster modernization of urban financial markets compared with their rural counterparts and the 'digital divide' which separates those using modern computers and communication technologies from those who do not. Financial dualism could result in large farmers, agri-business and rural industries obtaining financial services from modern urban financial institutions, while small and marginal farmers and landless labourers may have to depend on micro finance and personal savings. IT has to be used to facilitate transformation in various processes of rural credit. In this regard, it is suggested that each bank should form a special task force to look into the entire gamut of credit in the context of the agricultural transformation. The best results could be obtained if these task forces are staffed with enthusiastic young bankers with penchant for innovation.

Experience shows that the Green Revolution was largely aided by domestic and international research and extension efforts. While traditionally this has been concentrated exclusively in the government, in these new areas of agriculture, measures need to be taken to encourage the private sector to invest in R&D and extension activities.

Several South-East and East Asian countries, which adopted agricultural diversification and rural industrialization as a strategy for rural development, have witnessed a move away from cereals to non-cereal production. This was spurred by the structural changes, which accompanied the long-term contraction of agriculture in the economy, the decline in the real prices of cereals following the success of Green Revolution, as also the changes in the consumption pattern due to rising incomes and urbanization. Agricultural diversification has been seen as a desirable response to these demand and supply changes and was explicitly incorporated into many countries' agricultural policies and rural development strategies (Goletti, 1999). Thus, fundamental changes in the diets of the population in developing countries in Asia has been a major factor in the evolution of cereal supply and demand and agricultural diversification (Rosegrant and Hazell, 2000). Agro-based rural industries were recognized as providing not only high value products and income to the rural population but also employment to large rural non-farm population which could not be absorbed by the rapidly expanding industrial and services sector. This strategy was followed in several countries like Taiwan and Malaysia in the 1960s and Thailand, the Philippines, and Indonesia in the 1970s and 1980s.

The rapid transformation that has been observed in these areas in South-East Asian countries in the last twenty years provides pointers to what can be expected in the years to come. One key area of change that has occurred is in the modernization of retail grocery structures. Most cultures in a transitional phase attach great importance to personalized shopping for daily needs. The small corner stores are well distributed across towns and cities. The situation in East Asia was similar until the 1980s. However, tremendous change has taken place in retail grocery structures in these countries over the last fifteen years. In Taiwan, for example, whereas only about 2 per cent of groceries were sold in modern retail formats such as super markets in the mid-1980s, this proportion has now shot up to more than 65 per cent. A similar change has taken place from 0 to 50 per cent over the same period in Thailand. Even in Indonesia, about 25 per cent of groceries are now bought in modern supermarkets. Modern retailing firms are much more efficient than traditional firms. Their costs can be as much as 20 per cent lower than in traditional firms. Contrary to popular perception, they actually generate greater employment. The economies of scale provide for greater variety in product stocks; they provide a demand pull factor from consumers to producers; and they help in reducing the difference between the retail and farm gate prices. Overall, they help in accelerating growth in the whole food chain thereby leading to higher agricultural growth and, more importantly, higher employment growth in the whole food chain from the farm, food processing, logistics, and retailing.

To sum up, the income and consumption changes, described above, have ushered in a new demand structure for rural products that has gone largely unnoticed. Traditional approaches to agriculture, which focussed on foodgrain production, will only bring agricultural stagnation and employment distress in rural areas. The need of the hour is to promote agricultural diversification, encourage production of other food products, invest actively in rural infrastructure, and enable greater food processing and value addition to agricultural production, which would create new avenues for rural employment and income.

SUMMARY

Agricultural credit has played a vital role in supporting agricultural production in India. The Green Revolution characterized by a greater use of inputs such as fertilizers, seeds, and other inputs increased credit requirements which were provided by the agricultural financial institutions. Though the outreach and the amount of agricultural credit have increased over the years, several weaknesses have crept in which have affected the viability and sustainability of these institutions. Furthermore, an antiquated legal framework and outdated tenancy laws have hampered the flow of credit and the development of strong and efficient agricultural credit institutions.

A review of performance of agricultural credit in India reveals that though the overall flow of institutional credit has increased over the years, there are several gaps in the system such as inadequate provision of credit to small and marginal farmers, paucity of medium- and long-term lending, limited deposit mobilization, and heavy dependence on borrowed funds by major agricultural credit purveyors. These have major implications for agricultural development as also the well being of the farming community. Efforts are therefore required to address and rectify these issues.

Following the changes in the consumption and the dietary patterns from cereals to non-cereal products, a silent transformation is taking place in the rural areas calling for diversification in agricultural production and value-addition processes in order to protect employment and incomes of the rural population. In the changed scenario, strong and viable agricultural financial institutions are needed to cater to the requirements of finance for building the necessary institutional and marketing infrastructure.

What is needed in agriculture now is a new mission mode akin to what was done in the 1970s with the Green Revolution. The difference is that then we concentrated countrywide on two relatively homogeneous products so that the countrywide strategy could also be similarly homogeneous. The approach was a package approach, which attempted to bring together technology inputs (focused investment in new agricultural universities, regionally distributed, with complementary organization of agricultural extension services) along with provision of infrastructure inputs like power at subsidized costs, arrangements for the supply of bought out inputs like seeds, fertilizers, tractors, and most importantly, corresponding arrangements for credit provision through the then recently nationalized banking system. This model has clearly delivered results in the sense that India has become self sufficient in food and we have effectively brought food security. However, the model has not changed much since then and various ills have resulted: the persistence of high fertilizer subsidies, power subsidies, and minimum support prices that may now act as a disincentive for crop diversification. We, therefore, need a major review of agriculture policy to meet the changing needs of both producers and consumers.

The difference now is that we need initiatives in a disaggregated manner in many different segments of agriculture and agro industry: horticulture, aquaculture, pisciculture, dairying, sericulture, poultry, vegetables, meat, food processing, other agro-processing, and the like.

So what we need to do is to initiate a nationwide major mission programme for different activities, regionally disaggregated, in a similar package mode. The packages will have to be different for each activity and location. To begin with, expert teams will have to be formed for each agro-climate zone focusing on the relevant activities there. These teams can then design the package that needs to be put together in each place. The basic ingredients of each package can be similar: provision of technology inputs, infrastructure, extension services, arrangements for the supply of inputs, and the corresponding credit model. A key difference in approach would have to be the much greater involvement of region specific market participants, and of private sector suppliers in all these activities, and credit suppliers ranging from PSBs, cooperative banks, the new private sector banks and micro-credit suppliers, specially SHGs.

AFTERWORD

Reflecting the concerted policy initiatives to improve the flow of credit to agriculture, there has been a significant expansion in credit to agriculture since the turn of this decade. Average annual growth in agricultural credit extended by the SCBs, which had decelerated from 18 per cent per annum during the 1980s to 11 per cent during the 1990s, jumped to 26 per cent during 2000–7. The share of agricultural credit in total credit of SCBs increased from 9.9 per cent in March 2000 to 11.8 per cent by March 2007. The ratio of agricultural credit to agricultural GDP jumped from 10 per cent to 29 per cent in the same period.

Efforts are also on to revitalize both short-term and long-term rural cooperative institutions, and the RRBs too are being strengthened.

In the context of significant jump in bank credit to agriculture since 2000, the results of the latest AIDIS appear to be somewhat puzzling. According to the survey results, the share of institutional lenders (such as banks) in total debt of cultivator households reversed its increasing trend in 2002, while that of non-institutional sources (such as moneylenders) rose. These data need to be analysed more closely to arrive at a more informed judgement (see *Report on Currency and Finance*, 2006–08, RBI). First, the AIDIS data pertain to 2002 and therefore, do not capture the significant jump in bank credit to agricultural and rural sectors that has occurred since then. Second, the overall indebtedness reported to the banking sector by the AIDIS survey is found to be significantly lower than that reported by banks themselves. Finally, some other survey results suggest that a large portion of loans taken by the indebted households is for meeting financial emergency, medical emergency, and social obligations. Such expenditures cannot be financed easily by banks and other institutional agencies and may lead to higher reliance on non-institutional source. It is thus debatable whether increased reliance on non-institutional sources of finance is a failure of the formal financial system or a reflection of the weaknesses of the prevailing social security systems in the country. Whereas there may be a case for more thorough analysis of the various data sources, there is still a large scope for more financial inclusion. The recent policy initiatives for more financial inclusion would need to be continued and intensified.

Note

[1] At present, SCBs (excluding RRBs) are expected to ensure that the priority sector advances constitute 40 per cent of their net bank credit and that within the overall lending target of 40 per cent, 18 per cent of net bank credit goes to agricultural sector. To ensure that the focus of banks on direct category of agricultural advances does not get diluted, lendings under indirect category should not exceed one-fourth of the agricultural sub-target of 18 per cent, that is, 4.5 per cent of net bank credit.

References

All-India Rural Credit Review Committee (Chairman: B. Venkatappiah).

Capoor, J. (1999), 'Structural Reforms in Agricultural and Rural Development Banks', *Reserve Bank of India Bulletin*, 53 (10), October, pp. 1185–90.

Government of India, *Economic Survey*, various issues, Ministry of Finance, New Delhi.

——— (1991), *Report of the Committee on the Financial System*, Ministry of Finance, New Delhi.

——— (1998), *Report of the Committee on the Banking Sector Reforms*, Ministry of Finance, New Delhi.

——— (2002), *Report of the Working Group to Suggest Amendments in the Regional Rural Banks Act, 1976*, Ministry of Finance, New Delhi.

Goletti, F. (1999), *Agricultural Diversification and Rural Industrialisation as a Strategy for Rural Income Growth and Poverty Reduction in Indochina and Myanmar*, IFPRI, Washington, DC, June.

Mohan, R. (2002), *A Decade After 1991: New Challenges Facing the Indian Economy*, 28th Frank Moraes Lecture delivered at Chennai on 26 July, organized by United Writers Association and the Frank Moraes Foundation, *RBI Bulletin*, November.

NABARD, *Annual Report*, various issues.

——— (1999), *Report of the Task Force on Supportive Policy and Regulatory Framework for Microfinance*, October.

——— (2001), *Report of the Expert Committee on Rural Credit*.

Pant Joshi, D. (2003), 'Indian Agriculture Perspectives', *Prajnan*, 32 (1), pp. 7–36.

Reserve Bank of India (1954), *Report of the All-India Rural Credit Survey Committee*, 1951–52.

——— (1970), *Reserve Bank of History* (Volume I).

——— *Annual Report*, various issues, Mumbai.

Reserve Bank of India (1984), *Functions and Working.*

_____ (1985), *Report of the Committee to Review the Working of Monetary System in India.*

_____ *Handbook of Statistics on the Indian Economy*, various issues, Mumbai.

_____ *Reserve Bank of India Bulletins*, various issues, Mumbai.

_____ *Report on Currency and Finance,* various issues, Mumbai.

_____ *Report on Trend and Progress of Banking in India*, various issues, Mumbai.

_____ (1998), *Report of the High Level Committee on Agricultural Credit through Commercial Banks.*

_____ (1999), *Report of the Task Force on Revival/Restructuring for Co-operating Banks*, Mumbai.

_____ (2000), *All-India Rural Debt and Investment Surveys, Reserve Bank of India Bulletin*, February.

_____ (2004), *Report of the Advisory Committee on Flow of Credit to Agriculture and Related Activities from Banking System*, June.

Report of the Committee on Co-operation in India (1915), Maclagan Committee.

Rosegrant, M.W. and B.R.P. Hazell (2000), *Transforming the Rural Asian Economy: The Unfinished Revolution*, Oxford University Press, Hong Kong.

5 Ownership and Governance in Private Sector Banks in India*

On 2 July 2004, the RBI issued draft guidelines on ownership and governance in private sector banks in India. These guidelines were placed in the public domain for wider debate and feedback. The RBI is to put out a second draft and then finalize the policy taking into account the feedback received. The intention is to continue strengthening the Indian banking system and keep moving towards international best practice through a consultative process.

If the importance of the issue of ownership and governance in banks is to be gauged by the number of responses received to any public document issued by the RBI, then I would say that it is overwhelmingly important!

We had said in the guidelines that banks are special. Several responses have been received asking us what we mean by 'special'. Banks are financial intermediaries critical for mobilizing public savings and for deploying them to provide safety and return to the savers. They thus have fiduciary responsibility. The deployment of funds mobilized through deposits involves banks in financing economic activity and providing the lifeline for the payments system. The banking system is something that is central to a nation's economy irrespective of the fact whether the banks are owned locally or are foreign-owned.

The owners or shareholders of the banks have only a minor stake, and considering the leveraging capacity of banks (more than ten to one), it puts them in control of very large volume of public funds of which their own stake is miniscule. In a sense, therefore, they act as trustees and as such must be fit and proper for the deployment of funds entrusted to them. The sustained stable and continuing operations depend on the public confidence in individual banks and the banking system. The speed with which a bank under a run can collapse is incomparable with any other organization. For a

* Address by the author at Conference on Ownership and Governance in Private Sector Banking organized by Confederation of Indian Industries at Mumbai on 9 September 2004.

developing economy like ours there is also much less tolerance for downside risk among depositors many of whom place their life savings in the banks. Hence from a moral, social, political, and human angle, there is a more onerous responsibility on the regulator. Millions of depositors of the banks whose funds are entrusted with the bank are not in control of their management.

Thus, concentrated shareholding in banks controlling huge public funds does pose issues related to the risk of concentration of ownership because of the moral hazard problem and linkages of owners with businesses. Hence diversification of ownership is desirable as also ensuring fit and proper status of such owners and directors. At the same time with diversified ownership, there is, perhaps, even greater concern over corporate governance and professional management. In view of this, apart from ensuring fit and proper considerations, in order to safeguard depositors interest and ensure systemic stability, the regulatory and supervisory framework has to ensure that banks have adequate capital to cushion risks that are inevitable in their operations, follow prudent and transparent accounting practices, and are managed in accordance with the best practices for risk management. Seen from this standpoint, great responsibility is imposed on the regulator.

The issue that has been raised is: why now? What is new that these concerns are being raised now? After nationalization of major banks in 1969 and in 1980, in a sense, being government-owned, the issue did not arise till recently. As part of financial sector reform and keeping in view the growth needs of the economy it is expected that the significance and share of the private sector banks will increase as also public shareholding in the PSBs within the current policy framework. The banks are expected to grow with the economy. There is also opening up of the economy and increasing integration with the global economy. As this happens, the regulator has to ensure that the banking system is strong, healthy, and resilient to withstand shocks. We also want to ensure that transparency improves and want to move to international best practices in regulation, supervision, risk management while at the same time calibrating the suitability to the domestic conditions and needs at the current stage of development.

KEY FEATURES OF THE GUIDELINES

To begin with, let me enumerate the salient features of the guidelines.

1. All shareholding of 5 per cent and above representing important shareholding will have to meet the 'fit and proper' tests of competence, reputation, track record, integrity, satisfactory outcome of financial vetting, source of funds, and so on. Where the applicant is a body corporate, fit and proper would include good corporate

governance, financial strength, and integrity in addition to the assessment of individuals and other entities associated with the body corporate as enumerated above.

2. In the interest of diversified ownership of banks, the objective will be to ensure that no single entity or group of related entities have shareholding or control, directly or indirectly, in any bank in excess of 10 per cent of the paid up capital of the private sector bank. Any higher level of acquisition will be with the prior approval of the RBI and in accordance with the guidelines of 3 February 2004. These guidelines state that where acquisition or investment takes the shareholding of the applicant to a level of 10 per cent or more and up to 30 per cent, the RBI will also take into account other factors including but not limited to the following: (a) source and stability of the funds for the acquisition and the ability to access financial markets as a source of continuing financial support for the bank; (b) the business record and experience of the applicant including any experience of acquisition of companies; (c) the extent to which the corporate structure of the applicant will be in consonance with effective supervision and regulation of the bank; and (d) in case the applicant is a financial entity, whether the applicant is a widely held entity, publicly listed, and a well-established regulated financial entity in good standing in the financial community. In addition as indicated in the July draft, where the investing entity is a corporate entity, it will be seen whether there is diversified shareholding of the investing entity. For acquisition or investment exceeding the level of 30 per cent, the criteria will also take into account but will not be limited to whether (a) the acquisition is in public interest; (b) the desirability of diversified ownership of banks; (c) the soundness and feasibility of the plans of the applicant for the future conduct and development of the business of the bank; and (d) shareholder agreements and their impact on control and management of the bank.
3. The main difference between the February guidelines and the July draft is that the latter requires prior approval for shareholding above 10 per cent and is also applicable for existing shareholding above such level. The criteria laid down in the guidelines will be applicable equally for higher level of acquisitions as also for a time-bound plan for continuance or reduction in cases where the limits exceed those indicated.
4. A minimum of Rs 300 crore of net worth is perceived as being desirable on grounds of optimal operations and systemic stability. Banks with net worth lower than Rs 300 crore will be encouraged

to increase it to this level through organic or inorganic growth within a reasonable period.

5. In case of new licenses, the promoter's shareholding will normally be expected to be brought down to 10 per cent in a period of three years even if it is higher to begin with.
6. Large industrial houses as per existing policy will be permitted strategic investment in banks up to 10 per cent, subject to fulfilling the other criteria.
7. While guidelines have already been issued to banks and FIs in India to minimize cross-holding to 5 per cent, symmetrically, the draft guidelines require foreign banks operating in India to restrict their acquisition (either directly or through any entity in the group) of shareholding in Indian banks to 5 per cent.
8. The maximum limits for portfolio investment through stock exchanges by individual non-resident Indians (NRIs) and Foreign Institutional Investors (FIIs) at 5 per cent and 10 per cent, respectively, and aggregate limits at 10 per cent (can be raised to 24 per cent through special resolution of general body) and 24 per cent (can be raised to 49 per cent through special resolution of general body), respectively, currently permissible, as reiterated in the Government of India press note of 5 March 2004, have been retained in the draft guidelines. These will be subject to the government's policy in this regard. All cases of acquisition or holding of 5 per cent and above, in case of FIIs, will require acknowledgment by RBI as per 3 February 2004 guidelines. Where the investing entity is a 'sub account', full details of the investor/s and other particulars required for due diligence will be called for.
9. While most of the elements of the draft guidelines in case of directors have been implemented already, the provision relating to the desirable practice of having not more than one member of family as close relative or associate on the Board of a bank is yet to be introduced.
10. All transition arrangements for compliance with the guidelines for existing holdings will be subject to submission of time-bound action plans by the concerned banks. The intention as already indicated will be to move towards the desired objectives in as non-disruptive a manner as possible.
11. Continuing compliance of 'fit and proper' criteria for shareholders and directors will have to be ensured by the bank on an ongoing basis subject to independent verification by RBI where felt necessary.

How did we come to devise these guidelines? For this, apart from an internal review, we scanned international practice.

INTERNATIONAL APPROACHES

Internationally, the regulatory/supervisory approach has been evolving into cohesive and inclusive regulatory paradigm involving three different monitoring perspectives on the overall functioning of banks:

1. an enabling and proactive regulatory and supervisory oversight;
2. internal control through a vibrant and professional Board and;
3. market discipline.

All three in isolation have their limitations and are effective differentially based on the overall systemic contexts such as the level of maturity of the economy, and hence the markets; the efficacy of the legal system and the resolution mechanisms in place; the prevalent business culture, etc. Market discipline may not be very effective till transparent disclosure requirements are put in place. Even then the ability of the market to discipline the constituents would depend on its own structural strength as well as the economic setting in which it operates. Therefore a significant level of reliance has to be placed on internal control effected through Board oversight.

An important factor, in this context, that defines the business culture is what has come to be termed as 'corporate governance'. It is a nebulous concept whose essential elements were part of the business ethos in all societies but which has in recent times come under sharp focus and acquired a heightened significance partly due to the process of globalization and the increasingly overarching role of business on the society at large.

From a banking industry perspective, corporate governance involves the manner in which the business and affairs of individual institutions are governed by their boards of directors and senior management, affecting how banks:[1]

1. set corporate objectives (including generating economic returns to owners);
2. run the day-to-day operations of the business;
3. consider the interests of recognized stakeholders;
4. align corporate activities and behaviours with the expectation that banks will operate in a safe and sound manner, and in compliance with applicable laws and regulations; and
5. protect the interests of depositors.

The two major concerns that arise in context of corporate governance in banks and need to be addressed are (a) the concentration of ownership and (b) the type of people who control the bank. Diversified ownership becomes a necessary postulate as it provides balancing stakes which may not be possible otherwise, even in the case of voting right limits. A related concern is the 'quality' of control over the functioning of banks manifest in the credentials of the various stakeholders.

A survey of the regulatory regimes in major countries brings out that most of the regimes address these two concerns through a set of restrictions on the ownership of bank stock on the following parameters:

1. quantum of ownership by single person/associated persons;
2. ownership restrictions for domestic entities based on nature of entity;
3. non-bank financial firms;
4. non-financial entities;
5. other banks; and
6. ownership restrictions for foreign entities.

Major inferences that can be drawn from the international practices are discussed in the following paragraphs.

In most of the countries, ownership concentration is regulated through a layered threshold structure as per which any person wishing to acquire/increase shareholding in a bank beyond those thresholds would be required to seek regulatory approval. The qualifying threshold level in most countries is 10 per cent. Most of the countries though do not have an explicit cap on the maximum shareholding by a single person/entity. The above structure applies to direct as well as indirect control by a person singly or jointly through a group of associates or related parties.

The regulators give approvals on a case to case basis, subject to a number of considerations including the overall sectoral impact of the transaction and the satisfaction of 'fit and proper' principles by the person(s) acquiring the stake.

Acquirers of shares beyond thresholds need to provide comprehensive information to the authorities for their approval including the intent of purchase, terms and conditions, if any, manner of acquisition, source of funds, etc.

In terms of the nature of the entity, non-banking financial firms and non-financial firms are permitted to acquire shares in banks subject to the overall ceilings in respect of single entity in most countries albeit with regulatory approval in most cases. The non-discriminative treatment of the two classes of entities is reflected in dovetailing of the restrictive clauses, wherever applicable, with the norms on ownership by single entity.

Cross-holding amongst banks, that is, acquiring shares in a bank by another bank, directly or indirectly, is subject to regulatory approval in most of the regimes and the thresholds, in some cases, are lower than those for non-bank entities.

BACKGROUND FOR THE DRAFT GUIDELINES

Having dealt with the international approaches, I would like to highlight some facts and developments which should serve as background information for this chapter.

1. Unlike in many other countries, the various laws relating to banking in India [Banking Regulation Act 1949, Banking Companies (Acquisition and Transfer of Undertakings) Act, 1970 and 1980; the State Bank of India Act 1955, the State Bank of India (Subsidiary Banks) Act, 1959] do not provide for prior approval of the regulator for acquisition of significant ownership in banks—either in the public sector or in the private sector. There is, therefore, a need for an articulation of policy in public interest and depositor's interest.
2. On 3 February 2004, the Reserve Bank came out with the guidelines for acknowledgment for acquisition and transfer of shares in private sector banks. These guidelines took into account the emerging trends in banking and international practices. For the first time, it was spelt out that the term 'holding' will refer to both direct and indirect, beneficial or otherwise and will be computed with reference to the holding of the applicant, relatives, and associates.
3. On 5 March 2004, press note 4 was issued by the Government of India covering foreign investment in banking. The operational guidelines are yet to be issued. Hence the draft guidelines do not cover the policy in regard to investment by foreign banks or form of presence of foreign banks for which there will be separate guidelines. Before issuing these, it is felt necessary to streamline the national policy for ownership, domestic and foreign, and governance.
4. On 25 June 2004, 'fit and proper' criteria for directors of private sector banks were spelt out by the RBI based on qualification, expertise, track record, and integrity of persons to be appointed as directors of banks. The process of due diligence is to be undertaken by the bank at the time of appointment and renewal.
5. On 6 July 2004, banks/FIs were advised that they should not acquire any fresh stake in a bank's equity shares, if by such acquisition, the investing bank's/FI's holding exceeds 5 per cent of the investee bank's equity capital.

WHY ARE THE GUIDELINES BEING MADE APPLICABLE FOR EXISTING BANKS?

The banking sector is already quite large and widespread. There are several banks of varying sizes, composition of shareholding, and directors. The issues of size and governance are extremely important from the financial stability point of view. This draft policy is in consonance of treating banks as special and is setting upfront a road map in a transparent manner for the existing investors to align their policies and potential investors to make informed decisions. The intention of the policy is to ensure adequate capital and consolidation in the banking industry with the regulator being aware of the intention of existing and potential shareholders. Since one of the fundamental presumption in the policy is that any shareholding above 10 per cent would have to satisfy the regulator of the fit and proper status and sound governance principles on a continuing basis, it is necessary that the same principles are applicable to existing owners but done so in a non-disruptive and consultative fashion. In regard to banks permitted recently or rehabilitated recently on the basis of specific approvals, the commitments made as part of the approval process would undoubtedly be taken into account as also continuing compliance with 'fit and proper' and sound governance. The same criteria as applicable for higher level of ownership as articulated in the 3 February 2004 would form the basis for dealing with the cases under transition as well.

This discussion chapter is an illustration to the consultative process that has been increasingly adopted in the policymaking by the Reserve Bank. As far as banking business is concerned, we appreciate the role of promoters in general and strategic investors in particular, although the distinction between them is often blurred in practice. The comments on the first draft of these guidelines on ownership and governance will definitely enable us to fine-tune the policy for the better.

Note

[1] Basel Committee on Banking Supervision, *Enhancing Corporate Governance in Banking Organisations*, 1999.

6 Reforms, Productivity, and Efficiency in Banking*

Issues of productivity and efficiency have been at the centre stage of discussions in recent years. Nowhere is this truer than the financial sector, which is perceived to be the 'brain' of the economy (Stiglitz, 1998). Even within the financial sector, given the dominance of bank-based financial systems in most emerging markets including ours and the systemic importance of banks in the financial system, the banking sector continues to be the centre of attention for academia and policymakers alike. Not surprisingly therefore, performance of the banking sector has repercussions across the length and breadth of the economy. As a central banker, the obvious topic for me to discuss in this chapter relates to productivity and efficiency in Indian banking.

The objective of reforms in general is to accelerate the growth momentum of the economy, defined in terms of per capita income. Typically, improvements in the growth rate can be effected through three, not necessarily mutually exclusive, channels: improving productivity of capital, through investments in human capital and raising total factor productivity (TFP).

The quality of functioning of the financial sector can be expected to affect the functioning and productivity of all sectors of the economy. Efficient financial intermediation should help in improving economy-wide resource allocation, thereby promoting productivity growth all round. Thus discussion on economic efficiency and productivity should involve analysis of developments in the financial sector. Improvements in the financing of physical and human capital, both in terms of increasing magnitudes and in terms of allocative efficiency, should raise efficiency and productivity across the economy. This approach justifies the choice of my topic in this chapter.

* Address delivered at the 21st Annual General Meeting and Conference of the Pakistan Society of Development Economists at Islamabad in December 2005. Reprinted from *Pakistan Development Review*, Vol. 44, No. 4, Part I (2005).

Financial intermediation is essential to the promotion of both extensive and intensive growth. The efficient intermediation of funds from savers to users enables the application of available resources to their most productive uses. The more efficient a financial system is in such resource generation and in its allocation, the greater is its contribution to productivity and economic growth. As resource allocation improves and real returns increase, savings would presumably respond and higher resource generation should result. Thus, development of the financial system is essential to the generation of higher productivity and economic growth.

This chapter is structured along the following lines. First, I will explore in brief the impact of banking sector productivity on the rest of the economy. This is relevant in view of the fact that any discussion on productivity and efficiency issues in banking would need to be judged in conjunction with the level of financial development and other country-specific features. This will be followed by a brief review of banking sector reforms in India. The subsequent section will examine, in some detail, the trends in productivity and efficiency in Indian banking. The concluding remarks will be in the nature of the way ahead on areas germane to this sector at the present juncture.

HOW DOES PRODUCTIVITY IN BANKING INFLUENCE THE REST OF THE ECONOMY?

Economic history provides support for the fact that financial development makes a fundamental contribution to growth. Financial development helped in the promotion of industrialization in developed countries by facilitating the mobilization of capital for large investments. Well-functioning banks or other financial intermediaries such as venture capital funds also spur technological innovation by identifying and funding entrepreneurs who are perceived to have the best chances of developing new products successfully and for implementing innovative production processes.

Recent research has provided robust evidence supporting the view that financial development contributes to economic growth.

1. At the cross-country level, various measures of financial development (including measures of financial sector assets, domestic credit to private sectors, and stock market capitalization) are found to be positively related to economic growth.
2. Other studies establish a positive relationship between financial development and growth at the industry level (Rajan and Zingales, 1998).
3. Similarly, at the firm level, firms in countries with deeper financial development are able to obtain more external funds and thereby are enabled to grow faster (Demirgúc-Kunt and Maksimovic, 1998).

A basic indicator of financial development is the contribution of finance-related activities to GDP. The share of real GDP originating from finance-related activities in India tripled from just around 2 per cent during the 1970s to around 6 per cent during the 1990s and further to 7 per cent during the first half of this decade. Within the services sector, the share of finance rose from less than 5 per cent to more than 12 per cent over the same period (Table 6.1).

Table 6.1 Share of Real GDP Originating in Banking and Insurance

(per cent)

Period	Share of banking and insurance in GDP	Share of banking and insurance in services
1970–1 to 1974–5	1.8	4.6
1975–6 to 1979–80	2.2	5.4
1980–1 to 1984–5	2.5	5.9
1985–6 to 1992–3	3.9	8.5
1993–4 to 1998–9	5.8	11.8
1999–2000 to 2003–4	6.7	12.3

Source: Computed from *National Accounts Statistics*, Central Statistical Organisation.

The broad-based indicators of financial development, as culled from the flow-of-funds accounts, are also testimony to gradual widening and deepening of the economy. Most of the commonly tracked ratios exhibited an upward trend during the 1970s and 1980s, while moderate fluctuations in these ratios were observed during the 1990s (Table 6.2). What is of interest is that the finance ratio (FR), a proxy for financial deepening, witnessed remarkable improvement over this period.

When we move away from these broad-based indicators to more specific liquidity- and credit-based indicators, a similar picture emerges. Illustratively, the ratio of aggregate deposits to GDP exceeded 65 per cent during the first half of the current decade; M3/GDP has averaged around 50 per cent over the same period. At a slightly more disaggregated level, while bank credit to government has witnessed some tapering off in the second half of the 1990s, credit to the commercial sector averaged over 30 per cent of GDP during the first half of the current decade (Table 6.3). These observations are particularly relevant from the standpoint of the role of banks in the intermediation process. Juxtaposed with the financial sector reforms, this suggests that the enhanced freedom of banks since the liberalization process has provided them with the flexibility in resource mobilization and

Table 6.2 Flow of Funds-based Indicators of Financial Development

Period	FR	FIR	NIR	IR
1970–1 to 1974–5	0.2	1.4	0.8	0.8
1975–6 to 1979–80	0.3	1.8	1.0	0.7
1980–1 to 1984–5	0.3	2.4	1.4	0.7
1985–6 to 1989–90	0.4	2.4	1.4	0.7
1991–2	0.5	2.9	1.6	0.8
1994–5	0.5	2.4	1.2	0.9
1995–6	0.5	2.3	1.3	0.7

Notes: FR = Finance ratio =Total issues/national income (net national product at current prices); FIR = Financial inter-relations ratio =Total issues/net domestic capital formation; NIR = New issue ratio = Primary issues/net domestic capital formation; IR = Inter-relations ratio = Secondary issues (i.e., issues by banks and other financial institutions)/primary issues.[1]

Source: RBI.

deployment, which has manifested itself in the uptrend in these ratios. Thus financial deepening has been taking place continuously in India and is still in progress.

Studies by the Reserve Bank (RBI, 2000) on the association between finance and growth for an extended time span from 1971–2 to 1999–2000 find that the causality between finance (proxied by real M3 growth) and growth (proxied by real GDP growth) is bi-directional. However, in the

Table 6.3 Liquidity- and Credit-based Indicators of Financial Development

(per cent of GDP at current market prices)

Period	Aggregate deposits	M3	Bank credit to the government	Bank credit to commercial sector
1970–1 to 1974–5	16.4	25.9	13.3	15.6
1975–6 to 1979–80	24.1	33.0	14.0	21.8
1980–1 to 1984–5	30.0	39.1	18.7	26.9
1985–6 to 1989–90	36.1	45.4	22.9	30.3
1990–1 to 1994–5	39.6	49.3	23.6	29.0
1995–6 to 1999–2000	43.8	53.8	21.9	28.6
2000–1 to 2004–5	54.7	65.3	24.9	33.5

Source: RBI.

absence of any structural model underlying such relationships, these 'causality' estimates can only be interpreted in terms of the predictive content of each of the variables. Subsequent research on the inter-linkage between finance and growth in India has veered around to the view that the Indian growth process has essentially been 'finance-led': expansion in the financial sector played an enabling role in promoting capital accumulation, which, in turn, engendered higher growth (Bell and Rousseau, 2001). Typically, however, studies of this genre tend to be susceptible to the time period and choice of variables, so that a different period with another set of variables could possibly lead to different conclusions. What is, however, accepted is that finance did play a role in influencing the growth process in India, although such observations related to financial deepening have little to say about efficiency and productivity growth.

The aforesaid observations do not take into account the changing dynamics of the financial system. The traditional classification of the financial system as bank- or market-based often tends to be static; in contrast, financial systems evolve and develop over time in response to changes in the institutional environment, legal set up, and other country-specific features. This has been the case in India as well. Many of you would be aware that cross-country classifications of financial system have typically classified India as a 'bank-based' system. This is not surprising, since banks have traditionally been the dominant financial intermediaries. However, the relative share of banks in total financial sector assets, which was nearly three-fourths in the early 1980s, came down gradually over a period of time and has hovered around the two-thirds mark since the 1990s (Ray and Sengupta, 2004).

More importantly however, following the rapid growth of stock markets since the 1990s, the role of 'market-based' finance has been on the rise. The most commonly employed measure of financial system orientation—the ratio of market capitalization to bank assets—supports this observation (Table 6.4). This suggests that not only have financial institutions gained in terms of financial assets, but there is also considerable potential for market financing to develop. However, the magnitude of market capitalization is obviously dependent on the vagaries of the stock market: it is not expected to exhibit a consistent increase as a ratio of GDP, whereas the growth in bank assets/GDP ratio is much more regular.

Whereas financial deepening is easier to measure, analysing productivity and efficiency changes in banking is more complex and needs to be viewed in relation to the changing contours of the banking industry in India.

Table 6.4 Financial System Orientation

(per cent of GDP at current market prices)

As at end	Assets of SCBs	Market capitalization at BSE	Financial system orientation
(1)	(2)	(3)	(4)=(3)/(2)×100
December 1970	17.9	3.8	21.3
December 1975	21.0	2.6	11.0
December 1980	40.0	3.8	9.3
December 1985	46.8	7.4	15.2
March 1991	56.3	16.0	28.4
March 1995	51.6	43.1	83.5
March 2000	59.1	46.8	79.3
March 2003	69.0	23.2	33.7
March 2004	71.6	43.5	60.8
March 2005	75.9	54.7	72.1

Note: BSE: Bombay Stock Exchange, Mumbai

Source: Computed from *Handbook of Statistics on the Indian Economy*, RBI.

CONTOURS OF INDIAN BANKING SECTOR REFORMS[2]

The transformation of the banking sector in India needs to be viewed in light of the overall economic reforms process along with the rapid changes that have been taking place in the global environment within which banks operate. The global forces of change include technological innovation, the deregulation of financial services internationally, our own increasing exposure to international competition, and, equally important, changes in corporate behaviour such as growing disintermediation and increasing emphasis on shareholder value. Recent banking crises in Asia, Latin America, and elsewhere have accentuated these pressures.

India embarked on a strategy of economic reforms in the wake of a serious BoP crisis in 1991; a central plank of the reforms was reform in the financial sector and, with banks being the mainstay of financial intermediation, the banking sector. The objective of the banking sector reforms was to promote a diversified, efficient, and competitive financial system with the ultimate objective of improving the allocative efficiency of resources through operational flexibility, improved financial viability, and institutional strengthening. A summary profile of the banking industry over the last fifteen years is presented in Table 6.5.

Table 6.5 Summary Profile of the Banking Industry: 1990–1 to 2004–5

Year/bank group	1990–1			1995–6			2004–5		
	PSB	Private	Foreign	PSB	Private	Foreign	PSB	Private	Foreign
1. No. of banks	28	25	23	27	35(8)	29	28	29(9)	31
(a) Listed	–	–	–	2	9(3)	–	20	18(7)	–
(b) Non-listed	–	–	–	25	26(5)	–	8	11(2)	–
2. Share (in per cent) of									
(a) Assets	91.4	3.7	4.9	84.5	6.5(1.5)	7.9	75.3	18.2(12.5)	6.5
(b) Deposits	92.0	4.0	4.0	85.4	6.6(1.3)	6.7	78.0	17.3(10.9)	4.7
(c) Credit	93.0	4.0	3.0	82.4	6.8(1.9)	8.9	73.2	20.0(13.9)	6.8
(d) Income	89.4	3.3	7.3	82.5	8.2	9.4	76.4	16.9	6.7
(e) Expenses	90.0	3.3	6.8	84.1	7.5	8.4	76.7	16.9	6.4
(f) Profit	68.5	4.1	27.4	-33.3	55.6	77.8	74.2	16.4	9.4
3. Memo									
Bank asset/GDP (per cent)	–	56.3	–	–	50.4	–	–	80.4	–

Note: PSB: public sector banks; listed: banks listed on recognized stock exchanges. Figures in brackets under private pertain to de novo private banks.

Source: RBI.

The financial system in India by the late 1980s was characterized by dominant government ownership of banks and financial institutions, widespread use of administered and variegated interest rates, and financial repression through forced financing of government fiscal deficits by banks and through monetization. Thus, although a great degree of financial deepening had indeed taken place and financial savings had increased continuously, financial markets were not really functioning, and there was little price discovery in terms of the cost of money, that is, interest rates. The efficiency- and productivity-enhancing function of the financial system was severely handicapped. Hence, a widespread financial sector reform effort has been underway since 1991.

Let me briefly sum up the major areas of banking sector reforms:[3]

1. Financial repression through statutory pre-emptions has been reduced, while stepping up prudential regulations at the same time.
2. Interest rates have been progressively deregulated on both the deposit and lending sides (Box 6.1).

Restoration of the health of the banking system has involved:

1. Restoration of PSBs' net worth achieved through recapitalization where needed (total cost less than one per cent of GDP).
2. Competition increased through entry of new private sector banks and foreign banks.
3. Higher levels and standards of disclosure achieved to enhance market transparency.
4. Bank regulation and supervision strengthened towards international best practice.
5. Micro prudential measures instituted.
6. Supervision process streamlined with combination of on-site and off-site surveillance along with external auditing.
7. Risk based supervision introduced.
8. Process of structured and discretionary intervention introduced for problem banks through a prompt corrective action (PCA) mechanism.
9. Ownership of PSBs has been broadened through disinvestment up to 49 per cent, and banks have been listed (Table 6.6).
10. Mechanism for greater regulatory coordination instituted for regulation and supervision of financial conglomerates.
11. Measures taken to strengthen creditor rights (still in process).

Box 6.1: Interest Rate Deregulation

Deposit Rate Deregulation

1. April 1992: (a) Interest rates freed between forty-six days and three years and over, but ceiling prescribed, (b) October 1995: Ceiling removed for deposits over two years.
2. July 1996: Ceiling removed for deposits over one year.
3. October 1997: Interest rates on term deposits completely deregulated.
4. 2004: Minimum maturity for term deposits reduced to seven days.

Lending Rate Deregulation

1. 1992–3: Six categories of lending rates
   (a) Five slabs for below Rs 2 lakh
   (b) Minimum lending rate above Rs 2 lakh.
2. October 1994: Lending rate freed for loans above Rs 2 lakh and minimum rate abolished.
3. October 1996: Banks to specify maximum spread over PLR.
4. 1997–8: Separate PLRs permitted for cash credit/demand loans and term loans above three years. Floating rate permitted.
5. 1998–9: PLR made ceiling for loans upto Rs 2 lakh.
6. 1999–2000: Tenor linked PLR introduced.
7. 2001–2: PLR made benchmark rate; sub-PLR permitted for loans above Rs 2 lakh.
8. 2002–3: Bank-wise PLRs made transparent on RBI website.
9. 2003–4: Computation of benchmark PLR rationalized; tenor linked PLRs abolished.

Source: RBI.

Table 6.6 Private Shareholding in Public Sector Banks (as on 31 March 2005)

Shareholding (in per cent)	Number of banks[a]
Up to 10	4
More than 10 and up to 20	–
More than 20 and up to 30	5
More than 30 and up to 40	6
More than 40 and up to 49	6

Note: [a] Comprising 19 nationalized banks, State Bank of India, and IDBI Ltd.

Source: *Report on Trend and Progress of Banking in India, 2004–5*, RBI.

As the banking system has been liberalized and has become increasingly market-oriented and financial markets have developed concurrently, the conduct of monetary policy has also been tailored to take into account the realities of the changing environment (switch from direct to indirect instruments).

This macro approach to financial monitoring has enabled policymakers to fine-tune their regulatory stance in consonance with the changing market and institutional dynamics so as to balance growth and stability concerns. For instance, despite the gradual tightening of prudential norms, the ratio of non-performing loans (NPLs) to total loans, which was at a high of 15.7 per cent for SCBs at end-March 1997, has declined by more than two-thirds to 5.2 per cent at end-March 2005 (Table 6.7). Net NPLs also witnessed a significant decline, driven by the improvements in loan loss provisioning and improved recovery management, which comprises over half of the total provisions and contingencies. Capital adequacy of the banking sector also recorded a marked improvement and reached 12.8 per cent at end-March 2005, well above the stipulated level of 9 per cent. Banks have also been

Table 6.7 Non-performing Loans of Different Bank Groups: 1994–2005

(per cent to total advances)

Year (end-March)	PSB	Old private banks	New private banks	Foreign banks	Memo: NPL/ total loans (per cent)—2004
1994	24.8	–	–	–	China: 15.6
1995	19.5	–	–	–	Indonesia: 13.4
1996	18.0	–	–	–	Korea: 1.7
1997	17.8	10.7	2.6	4.3	Malaysia: 11.6[a]
1998	16.0	10.9	3.5	6.4	Argentina: 17.5[a]
1999	15.9	13.1	6.2	7.6	Brazil: 3.9
2000	14.0	10.8	4.1	7.0	US: 0.8
2001	12.4	10.9	5.1	6.8	UK: 2.2
2002	11.1	11.0	8.9	5.4	Japan: 2.9
2003	9.4	8.9	6.7	5.3	
2004	7.8	7.6	5.0	4.6	
2005	5.5	6.0	3.6	2.8	Global range: [0.3 to 30.0]

Note: [a] relates to 2005.

Source: Computed from *Statistical Tables Relating to Banks in India*, RBI, various years.

sensitized to develop robust risk management systems for credit and operational risks and focus on their asset–liability maturity profile to withstand adverse movements in market risk parameters such as interest rates and take corrective measures.

Another heartening development in banks' balance sheets, driven by the twin forces of international accounting irregularities and regulatory initiatives, has been the increasing focus on corporate governance. As part of their Annual Report, banks presently disclose, under the head 'Report on Corporate Governance', details of their boards of directors, number of board meetings attended by members, details of the various sub-committees of the boards, and, provided the banks are listed, information on their stock price movements. This is complemented with the banks' philosophy on corporate governance and the enabling mechanisms undertaken by the banks to achieve their philosophy. As you would be aware, such listing is an important component of the process of 'market discipline', which complements the regulatory initiatives undertaken by the authorities. To take the governance process in banks a step further, we had some time back issued guidelines laying down transparent criteria for determining the 'fit and proper' status of owners and directors in private banks. Given our focus on a consultative approach to policy formulation, the document was posted on the RBI website for encouraging a debate on this issue. On the basis of the feedback received, the draft is being reviewed before final guidelines can be issued to banks.

The whole policy reform process has been designed to make the banking system more market oriented to enable efficient price discovery and to induce greater internal efficiency in the resource allocation process. Thus, whereas the efforts in the 1960s, 1970s, and 1980s were essentially devoted to financial deepening, the focus of reforms in the past decade and a half has been engendering greater efficiency and productivity in the banking system in particular, and in the financial sector as a whole. How well have we succeeded?

EFFICIENCY AND PRODUCTIVITY ANALYSIS IN BANKING

In recent times, a significant body of literature has evolved which explores the performance of financial institutions in the wake of financial liberalization. These studies are essentially microeconomic in nature and seek to analyse the efficiency and productivity of banking systems. Such analysis is of relevance from the policy standpoint, because as the finance-growth literature suggests, if banks become better-functioning entities, this is expected to be reflected in safety and soundness of the financial system and, ultimately, would lead to increases in the rate of economic growth. More importantly, such analysis is useful in enabling policymakers to identify the success or failure of policy initiatives or, alternatively, highlight different strategies undertaken by banking firms which contribute to their successes.

A priori, deregulation is expected to unleash competitive forces. Such competition would, in turn, enable banks to alter their input and output mix, which when combined with technological developments facilitates increase in output that raises overall bank productivity and efficiency. Second, liberal entry of de novo private and foreign banks as a part of the deregulation process is expected to raise bank efficiency, productivity, and technology levels, because de novo private/foreign banks are associated with superior management practices and technology, which can be fruitfully imbibed by those which are not. A third strand of thinking, borrowing from the public choice framework, contends that different ownership structures may engender different efficiency levels. The theoretical argument is straightforward: lack of capital market discipline weakens owners' control over management, enabling the latter to pursue their own interests, and provides fewer incentives for them to be efficient. Finally, as banking in the current world is technology driven and technological progress itself is scale augmenting, the relationship between bank size and efficiency becomes important. Sceptics, on the contrary, argue that deregulation is, in general, accompanied by an increase in banks' operational cost and could induce financial fragility due to over-expansion of banking activity. Thus, productivity gains after deregulation could be temporary and not sustainable in the long run. As a result, evidence in support of a unidirectional relationship between deregulation and efficiency/productivity is not conclusive.

Besides various methods of estimation, the efficiency and productivity studies in banking are constrained by the absence of precise definitions of inputs and outputs of banks. As a result, several approaches exist and the appropriateness of each approach varies according to the circumstances (Box 6.2).

Competition and Profitability of Indian Banks

Beginning from 1992, Indian banks were gradually exposed to the rigours of domestic and international competition. Newly opened banks from the private sector and entry and expansion of several foreign banks resulted in greater competition in both deposit and credit markets. Consequent to these developments, there has been a consistent decline in the share of public sector banks in total assets of commercial banks. The evidence of competitive pressure is well supported from the declining trend of Herfindahl's concentration index (Table 6.8).[5] Notwithstanding such transformation, the PSBs still remain the mainstay, accounting for nearly three-fourths of assets

Box 6.2: Inputs and Outputs of Commercial Banks

Banks are typically multi-input and multi-output firms. As a result, defining what constitutes 'input' and 'output' is fraught with difficulties, since many of the financial services are jointly produced and prices are typically assigned to a bundle of financial services. Additionally, banks may not be homogeneous with respect to the types of outputs actually produced. In view of these complexities, four approaches have come to dominate the literature on banking output: the production approach, the intermediation approach, the operating (income-based) approach, and more recently, the modern approach.

Under the *production approach*, banks are primarily viewed as providers of services to customers. The input set under this approach includes physical variables (for example, labour, material, space, or information systems) and the outputs represent the services provided to customers and are best measured by the number of deposit and loan accounts.

Under the *intermediation approach*, financial institutions are viewed as intermediating funds between savers and investors. Banks produce intermediation services through the collection of deposits and other liabilities and their application in interest-earning assets, such as loans, securities, and other investments. This approach includes both operating and interest expenses as inputs, whereas loans and other major assets count as outputs. In principle, there are three variant of intermediation approach, namely, the *asset approach*, the *user cost* approach, and *value-added approach*. The *asset approach* is a reduced form modelling of the banking activity, focusing exclusively on the role of banks as financial intermediaries between depositors and final uses of bank assets. Deposits and other liabilities, together with real resources (labour and physical capital) are defined as inputs, whereas the output set includes earning assets such as loans and investments. The *user cost approach* determines whether a financial product is an input or an output on the basis of its net contribution to bank revenue. If the financial returns on an asset exceed the opportunity cost of the funds or alternately, if the financial costs of a liability are less than the opportunity cost, they are considered as outputs; otherwise, they are considered as inputs. The *value-added approach* identifies major categories of produced deposits and loans as outputs because they form a significant proportion of value added.

The *operating approach* (or *income-based approach)* views banks as business units with the final objective of generating revenue from the total cost incurred for running the business. Accordingly, it defines banks' output as the total revenue (interest and non-interest) and inputs as the total expenses (interest and operating expenses).

Finally, the *modern approach* seeks to integrate some measure for risk, agency costs, and quality of bank services. In this approach, the individual components of CAMEL[4] are derived from the financial tables of the banks and are used as variables in the performance analysis.

Source: Adapted from Berger and Humphrey (1992) and Frexias and Rochet (1997).

and income. It is also important to note that PSBs have responded to the new challenges of competition, as reflected in the increase in the share of these banks in the overall profit of the banking sector. From the position of net loss in the mid-1990s, in recent years the share of PSBs in the profit of the commercial banking system has become broadly commensurate with their share in assets, indicating a broad convergence of profitability across various bank groups. This suggests that, with operational flexibility, PSBs are competing relatively effectively with private sector and foreign banks. The 'market discipline' imposed by the listing of most PSBs has also probably contributed to this improved performance. PSB managements are now probably more attuned to the market consequences of their activities (Mohan, 2005).

Table 6.8 Herfindahl's Index of Concentration on Deposits and Credit of SCBs: 1992–2004

Year (end-March)	Deposit	Credit
1992	8.1	10.4
1993	7.6	10.1
1994	7.4	8.6
1995	7.0	7.9
1996	6.9	7.8
1997	6.7	7.3
1998	6.6	7.4
1999	7.1	7.2
2000	6.9	6.9
2001	7.3	6.7
2002	7.1	6.0
2003	6.9	6.0
2004	6.3	5.8

Source: Author's calculations.

Since the late 1990s, in line with the benign interest rate regime, both interest income and interest expenditure of banks as proportions of total assets have declined. However, interest expenditure declined faster than interest income, resulting in an increase in net interest income. Moreover, non-interest income, which emanates mostly from fee-based activities, has been increasing consistently in the post-reform period. For example, non-interest income as a proportion of total assets of the banking sector increased from 1.2 per cent in 1993 to more than 2 per cent in 2004 (Table 6.9). In this context, it is also appropriate to mention that Indian banks, in particular the PSBs, are yet to catch up fully with their foreign counterparts.

Table 6.9 Non-interest Income of SCBs: 1992–2004

(percentage to total assets)

Year (end-March)	Public sector banks	Indian private banks	Foreign banks	All SCBs
1992	1.22	1.03	3.40	1.38
1993	1.19	1.13	0.99	1.17
1994	1.26	1.34	2.22	1.34
1995	1.26	1.43	2.46	1.36
1996	1.39	1.68	2.35	1.49
1997	1.32	1.64	2.54	1.45
1998	1.33	1.94	2.96	1.52
1999	1.22	1.36	2.46	1.33
2000	1.28	1.67	2.60	1.43
2001	1.22	1.28	2.47	1.32
2002	1.43	1.59	2.91	1.57
2003	1.66	2.45	2.64	1.86
2004	1.91	2.08	2.98	2.01

Source: Computed from *Statistical Tables Relating to Banks in India*, RBI, various years.

EFFICIENCY OF INDIAN BANKS

Improvements in efficiency of the banking system are expected to be reflected, inter alia, in a reduction in operating expenditure, interest spread and cost of intermediation in general. Several indicators have been employed in the literature to compare banking production costs across time. Illustratively, intermediation cost, defined as the ratio of operating expense to total assets, witnessed a gradual reduction in the post reform period across various bank groups barring foreign banks (Table 6.10). This decline in intermediation cost needs to be weighed against the large expenditures incurred in upgradation of IT and institution of 'core banking' solutions. Admittedly, intermediation costs of banks in India still tend to be higher than those in developed banking markets.

At a more disaggregated level, it is evident that[6] Indian banks have improved their efficiency in the post-reform period as evidenced from the declining trend in per unit cost of output, irrespective of the choice of outputs

Table 6.10 Intermediation Cost* of SCBs: 1992–2004

(percentage to total assets)

Year (end-March)	Public sector banks	Indian private banks	Foreign banks	All SCBs
1992	2.60	2.97	2.26	2.59
1993	2.64	2.71	2.70	2.65
1994	2.65	2.49	2.65	2.64
1995	2.83	2.35	2.73	2.79
1996	2.99	2.47	2.78	2.94
1997	2.88	2.36	3.04	2.85
1998	2.66	2.14	2.99	2.63
1999	2.65	2.04	3.40	2.65
2000	2.52	1.85	3.12	2.48
2001	2.72	1.87	3.05	2.64
2002	2.29	1.45	3.03	2.19
2003	2.25	1.99	2.79	2.24
2004	2.20	2.01	2.76	2.20

Note: * Intermediation cost = operating expenses.

Source: Computed from *Statistical Tables Relating to Banks in India*, RBI, various years.

(Table 6.11). The operating cost per unit of earning assets declined from 2.1 per cent in 1992 to 1.8 per cent in 2004; similarly, operating cost per unit of total volume of business declined from 3.4 per cent to 2.6 per cent during the same period. Among the components of operating expenses, employee cost per unit of output witnessed a noticeable decline in the post-reform period. This decline is discernible across all bank groups, and especially for PSBs in the post-2001 period consequent to the voluntary retirement scheme across several nationalized banks. On the other hand, the change in physical capital cost per unit of output has been marginal, reflecting the fact that Indian banks maintained a steady flow of investments towards physical capital formation, especially on automation and IT.

From the efficiency standpoint, the intermediation cost needs to be viewed in conjunction with non-interest income. Till 2001, the burden (the excess of non-interest expenditure over non-interest income as a percentage to total assets) of commercial banks hovered around 1 per cent to 1.5 per cent (Table 6.12). This gap between intermediation cost and income from fee-based activities has narrowed considerably in recent years. For example, the burden of Indian commercial banks declined from 1.2 per cent in 1992 to

Table 6.11 Operating Expense and its Components of SCBs: 1992–2004

(per cent)

Year (end-March)	Operating expense/earning assets[a]	Labour cost/ earning assets[a]	Non-labour cost/earning assets[a]	Operating expense/total business[b]	Labour cost/ total business[b]	Non-labour cost/total business[b]
1992	2.08	1.40	0.68	3.42	2.30	1.12
1993	2.14	1.43	0.72	3.51	2.34	1.17
1994	2.22	1.44	0.78	3.56	2.31	1.25
1995	2.32	1.54	0.78	3.74	2.48	1.26
1996	2.48	1.73	0.75	4.01	2.80	1.22
1997	2.36	1.60	0.76	3.84	2.60	1.24
1998	2.16	1.46	0.70	3.51	2.37	1.14
1999	2.21	1.47	0.74	3.55	2.35	1.20
2000	2.05	1.37	0.68	3.22	2.15	1.06
2001	2.16	1.47	0.69	3.36	2.28	1.07
2002	1.82	1.18	0.64	2.73	1.77	0.96
2003	1.81	1.13	0.69	2.65	1.65	1.00
2004	1.78	1.08	0.71	2.61	1.58	1.03

Notes: [a] Earning assets = credit + investment; [b] Total business = deposit +credit.

Source: Computed from *Statistical Tables Relating to Banks in India*, RBI, various years.

0.2 per cent in 2004. Moreover, there has been a lowering of the burden across bank groups in recent years. The improvement in respect of Indian private banks has been remarkable; their non-interest income in recent years has surpassed their intermediation cost and has resulted in a negative burden.

Table 6.12 Burden of SCBs: 1992–2004

(percentage to total assets)

Year (end-March)	Public sector banks	Indian private banks	Foreign banks	All SCBs
1992	1.37	1.94	–1.14	1.21
1993	1.45	1.57	1.70	1.48
1994	1.39	1.16	0.42	1.30
1995	1.57	0.92	0.27	1.43
1996	1.60	0.78	0.43	1.44
1997	1.56	0.72	0.50	1.40
1998	1.33	0.19	0.03	1.11
1999	1.44	0.69	0.94	1.32
2000	1.24	0.18	0.53	1.05
2001	1.51	0.59	0.59	1.32
2002	0.86	–0.14	0.12	0.63
2003	0.59	–0.46	0.15	0.38
2004	0.29	–0.07	–0.22	0.19

Note: Burden = non-interest expense *less* non-interest income. It reflects the extent to which non-interest expenses are recovered through non-interest income.

Source: Computed from *Statistical Tables Relating to Banks in India*, RBI, various years.

The cost–income ratio (defined as the ratio of operating expenses to total income less interest expense) of Indian banks showed a declining trend during the post-reform period. For example, Indian banks paid roughly 45 per cent of their net income towards managing labour and physical capital in 2004 as against nearly 72 per cent in 1993 (Table 6.13). In other words, Indian banks recorded a net cost saving of nearly 27 per cent of their net income during the post-reform period. According to the data reported in *The Banker 2004*, the cost–income ratio of world's largest banks varied markedly from a low of 48 per cent to a high of 116 per cent and the ratio around 60 per cent is an indicative benchmark (RBI, 2005). In that respect, the cost–income ratio of Indian banks is now comparable internationally. Among various ownership patterns, PSBs have tended to have relatively higher cost–income ratio as against private banks and foreign banks.

Table 6.13 Cost–Income Ratio of SCBs: 1992–2004

(per cent)

Year (end-March)	Public sector banks	Indian private banks	Foreign banks	All SCBs
1992	58.4	58.9	30.9	55.3
1993	73.7	66.8	59.2	71.9
1994	73.1	57.3	41.2	68.1
1995	67.6	52.2	40.6	63.5
1996	66.7	51.5	45.6	63.3
1997	64.3	51.3	45.6	61.0
1998	62.7	48.5	43.1	58.9
1999	65.9	58.9	56.9	64.3
2000	63.2	48.6	48.5	59.9
2001	67.0	51.8	50.0	63.4
2002	54.9	45.6	49.1	53.1
2003	47.8	45.1	46.5	47.2
2004	45.1	46.6	42.8	45.1

Note: Cost–income ratio = ratio of operating expenses to total income *less* interest expense. It measures the extent to which non-interest expense devours net total income.

Source: Computed from *Statistical Tables relating to Banks in India*, RBI, various years.

This explanation needs to be viewed in conjunction with the differential ownership profile of banks. Early studies (Sarkar, Sarkar, and Bhaumik, 1998) found somewhat weak evidence to suggest that ownership was an important determinant of performance. More recent studies exhibit mixed evidence: while certain studies (Keova, 2003) suggest ownership to have some effect on bank performance, others (for example, Bhaumik and Dimova, 2004) veer around the view that competition induced PSBs to eliminate the performance gap that existed between them and both domestic and foreign and private sector banks. More recent research reported differences in the efficiency of Indian commercial banks with different ownership status, level of non-performing loans, size, and asset quality (Das and Ghosh, 2006). More importantly, their study uncovered evidence that PSBs recorded higher efficiency gains in the post-reform period. Clearly, the evidence here is not conclusive, because comparisons are beset with several difficulties. Given the size and variety of PSBs, it is possible to find banks that could equal the good private sector banks as well as bad ones. In addition, PSBs have to reckon with 'legacy' problems, such as many of the NPAs that they have been saddled with. Some PSBs operate in relatively backward areas with limited discretion to pull out from such areas. The question still remains: whether there is a better payoff in enabling PSBs to improve their performance while promoting private sector banks, as compared with an alternative policy that provides for transfer of ownership and control from the public to the private sector. Will greater scope for mergers and acquisitions within and between public and private sector add to greater efficiency?

Another important indicator of efficiency of banks is net interest margin (NIM), defined as the excess of interest income over interest expense, scaled by total bank assets. Broadly speaking, this ratio reflects the allocative efficiency of financial intermediation, a lower ratio being indicative of higher efficiency. It is quite reasonable to believe that the decline in deposit rates ushered by the deregulation process will be manifested in the lending behaviour of banks. In practice, however, lending rates have tended to be sticky downwards and seem to operate with a time lag. Historically the NIM of Indian banks is rather high. Around the onset of the reform process in 1992, the NIM of Indian banks was about 3.3 per cent (Table 6.14). Thereafter, it recorded a relatively modest decline to around 3 per cent in recent years. And traditionally, it is

Table 6.14 Spread of SCBs: 1992–2004

(percentage to total assets)

Year (end-March)	Public sector banks	Indian private banks	Foreign banks	All SCBs
1992	3.22	4.01	3.90	3.30
1993	2.39	2.92	3.57	2.51
1994	2.36	3.01	4.20	2.54
1995	2.92	3.07	4.27	3.03
1996	3.10	3.10	3.76	3.15
1997	3.16	2.95	4.13	3.22
1998	2.91	2.46	3.97	2.95
1999	2.81	2.11	3.51	2.79
2000	2.70	2.13	3.85	2.72
2001	2.84	2.33	3.64	2.84
2002	2.73	1.58	3.25	2.57
2003	2.52	1.96	3.36	2.48
2004	2.97	2.24	3.47	2.87

Note: Spread = interest earned – interest paid.

Source: *Report on Trend and Progress of Banking in India*, RBI, various years.

the foreign banks, which by virtue of their ability to mobilize low-cost deposits, have the highest NIMs, whereas those for private banks have been the lowest in recent years. These comparisons are not watertight: typically, small and medium banks had high NIM until 1997.[7] Thereafter, NIM for big banks recorded a rise. Contextually, it may be mentioned that banks in most developed countries and several emerging economies have NIM (as a percentage to total assets) of around 2 per cent. This provides some indication that competition in banking still has some way to go in India.

PRODUCTIVITY

Studies on productivity in Indian banking have only begun to emanate of late. A recent study found that TFP growth has improved marginally in the post-deregulation period, but there was little evidence of narrowing of productivity differentials across ownership categories following deregulation (Kumbhakar and Sarkar, 2003). Among various productivity indicators, labour productivity indicators like business per employee and profit per employee are most commonly used. In addition, business per branch is also used to judge branch-level productivity. The business per employee of Indian banks increased over three-fold in real terms from Rs 5.4 million in 1992 to Rs 16.3 million in 2004, exhibiting an annual compound growth rate of nearly 9 per cent (Table 6.15). At the same time, the profit per employee increased more than five-fold: from Rs 20,000 to Rs 150,000 over the same period, implying a compound growth of around 17 per cent. Branch productivity also recorded concomitant improvements. Overall, the balance of evidence suggests distinctive productivity improvements in the banking sector over the reform period. The extant literature suggests that such improvements could be driven by two factors: technological improvement, which expands the range of production possibilities, and a catching up effect, as peer pressure amongst banks compels them to raise productivity levels. In the context of gradual deregulation of financial sector, several factors could have been at work: a significant shift of the best-practice frontier, driven by a combination of technological advances, financial innovation, and different strategies pursued by banks suited to their business philosophy and risk-return profile, changing composition of banks' input–output, and reduction in total cost due to improvements in overall efficiency. While it is difficult to pinpoint the relative mix of these factors in raising productivity, the bottomline is clear: Indian banks witnessed significant productivity improvements, post-reforms.

In a wider framework, cross-country studies of deregulation and productivity growth of banks report divergent views. Typically, cross-country comparisons are often fraught with difficulties, not only because of the different regulatory and economic regimes encountered by financial entities,

Table 6.15 Select Productivity Indicators of SCBs

(Rs million at 1993–4 prices)

Year	Business per employee	Profit per employee	Business per branch
1992	5.4	0.02	109.9
1993	5.4	-0.05	110.4
1994	5.4	-0.04	109.2
1995	5.6	0.02	113.0
1996	6.0	0.01	119.6
1997	6.6	0.04	129.0
1998	7.5	0.05	144.9
1999	8.4	0.03	158.7
2000	9.7	0.05	179.4
2001	11.5	0.05	196.2
2002	13.7	0.09	214.9
2003	15.0	0.12	234.8
2004	16.3	0.15	254.5

Source: *Statistical Tables Relating to Banks in India*, RBI.

but also owing to the differential quality of services associated with deposits and loans in different countries. Maudos and Pastor (2001) analysed the cost and profit efficiency across fourteen European Union (EU) economies, as well as Japan and the US. The results uncovered the evidence that, since the start of the 1990s increasing competition has led to gains in profit efficiency in the US and Europe but not so in the Japanese banking system. Their results also show that the variance in profitability between countries would be considerably reduced if inefficiencies were eliminated, efficiency gains thus being a very important source of improvement in profitability. A recent study in the Asian context analysed various efficiency measures of South-East Asian (Indonesia, Korea, Malaysia, Philippines, and Thailand) banks in the context of corporate governance (Williams and Nguyen, 2005). Although the motivation of the study was different, their empirical results found economic justification for the policy of bank privatization.

Let me encapsulate this section by making some general comments on the efficiency and productivity growth of Indian banks vis-à-vis leading Asian nations such as China and Korea. As far as real growth (adjusted for price movement and exchange rate fluctuations) in banking business is concerned, Indian banks are favourably placed. In recent years, the real growth of deposits and of loans of Indian banks were noticeably higher than those of other

Asian countries such as China and Korea. At the same time, profitability of Indian banks, as determined by the return on assets, is also much higher (Tables 6.16–6.19). The intermediation cost of Indian banks seems to be relatively higher than that of Korea and China. Nonetheless, higher operating cost in India is well compensated by the higher non-interest income, as

Table 6.16 Spread (Net Interest Margin) of Banks of Major Asian Countries

(percentage to total assets)

Year	China	Indonesia	Korea	Malaysia	Philippines	Thailand	India
1996	1.86	2.92	1.70	2.91	4.07	2.57	3.07
1997	2.27	2.76	1.80	2.94	4.21	3.00	2.83
1998	2.16	-9.38	1.69	3.32	4.52	0.74	2.66
1999	1.83	-3.11	2.03	2.67	3.16	0.69	2.56
2000	1.76	2.21	2.06	3.02	2.54	1.43	2.74
2001	1.78	3.16	2.12	2.83	2.60	1.69	2.54
2002	1.78	3.61	2.33	2.70	2.29	1.84	2.74
2003	1.87	4.22	2.50	2.61	2.30	1.99	2.84

Note: The figures reported in this table for India are not strictly comparable with earlier tables because of different data sources.

Source: *BankScope*.

Table 6.17 Intermediation Cost (Operating Expense) of Banks of Major Asian Countries

(percentage to total assets)

Year	China	Indonesia	Korea	Malaysia	Philippines	Thailand	India
1996	1.23	2.39	2.24	1.42	3.52	1.50	2.77
1997	1.24	4.50	2.55	1.49	3.28	2.05	2.60
1998	1.40	4.04	2.53	1.68	3.67	2.54	2.58
1999	1.18	2.83	1.53	1.50	3.38	2.20	2.41
2000	1.12	2.72	1.46	1.70	3.32	1.98	2.57
2001	1.10	2.36	1.42	1.80	3.30	2.01	2.21
2002	1.05	2.73	1.39	1.73	3.16	1.78	2.22
2003	1.01	2.94	1.38	1.61	3.00	1.71	2.19

Note: The figures reported in this table for India are not strictly comparable with earlier tables because of different data sources.

Source: *BankScope*.

compared to other Asian countries. Finally, the labour productivity of the top four banks in India (which includes one de novo private bank) and the four state-owned Chinese banks indicates that except the private bank, the top three PSBs in India recorded much lower employee productivity. However, in the absence of data on employment for banks in other countries, it is difficult to ascertain the degree of labour productivity differentials across countries.

Table 6.18 Non-interest Income of Banks of Major Asian Countries

(percentage to total assets)

Year	China	Indonesia	Korea	Malaysia	Philippines	Thailand	India
1996	0.26	0.99	1.06	0.98	2.12	0.68	1.44
1997	0.24	2.97	0.93	1.10	1.73	1.00	1.49
1998	0.13	1.31	0.20	1.16	1.96	1.03	1.38
1999	0.17	1.96	0.99	1.00	1.95	0.97	1.47
2000	0.22	1.51	0.74	1.01	1.59	0.62	1.33
2001	0.22	1.08	1.28	1.15	1.73	0.73	1.49
2002	0.25	1.30	0.91	1.11	2.11	0.93	1.83
2003	0.25	1.46	0.80	0.94	2.16	0.95	1.97

Note: The figures reported in this table for India are not strictly comparable with earlier tables because of different data sources.

Source: *BankScope*.

Table 6.19 Net Profit of Banks of Major Asian Countries

(percentage to total assets)

Year	China	Indonesia	Korea	Malaysia	Philippines	Thailand	India
1996	0.29	1.01	0.17	1.40	2.06	–0.56	0.71
1997	0.30	–0.39	–0.84	1.03	1.63	–1.17	0.90
1998	0.20	–46.92	–3.10	0.04	0.85	–5.57	0.54
1999	0.17	–9.20	–1.40	0.96	0.10	–5.88	0.70
2000	0.21	0.46	–0.37	1.29	–0.03	–0.15	0.48
2001	0.20	0.87	0.76	0.68	0.48	1.46	0.69
2002	0.20	1.30	0.60	1.03	0.60	0.21	0.97
2003	0.12	1.61	0.15	1.08	1.08	0.63	1.14

Note: The figures reported in this table for India are not strictly comparable with earlier tables because of different data sources.

Source: *BankScope*.

A clear message emanating from these findings is the role of technology in driving productivity and efficiency improvements. In today's world of banking, technology is considered as the basic tool of the 'process engineers' of the organization. It is crucial for the design, control, and execution of service delivery in banks. Therefore, a key driver of efficiency and productivity in the banking industry today is the effective use of technology. This is a crucial prerequisite for capitalizing on future opportunities for the banking sector. In effect, it has become the key to servicing all customer segments—offering convenience to retail customer, corporates, and government clients. The increasing sophistication, flexibility, and complexity of products and servicing offerings makes the effective use of technology critical for managing the risks associated with banking business. However, the 'technological penetration' in India has been quite modest. According to data reported in the *World Development Indicators* database, as of 2002, the number of computers per 1000 persons was about seven in India compared to anywhere between 70–500 in most emerging markets and even higher in most developed economies.[8] Wide disparities exist within the banking sector as far as technological capabilities are concerned: the percentage of 'computer literate' employees as percentage of total staff in 2000 was around 20 per cent in PSBs compared with 100 per cent in new private and around 90 per cent in foreign banks (RBI, 2002). Data reported by the RBI suggests that nearly 71 per cent of branches of PSBs are fully computerized. However, computerization needs to go beyond the mere 'arithmeticals', to borrow a term from the Report of the Committee on Banking Sector Reforms (Government of India, 1998), and instead, needs to be leveraged optimally to achieve and maintain high service and efficiency standards. In fact, recent research on the role of technology in driving productivity improvements in banking demonstrates that computer employees and IT capital exhibit higher productivities than their respective non-computer employees and non-IT capital, respectively (Huang, 2005). The challenge, therefore, remains three-fold: acquiring the 'right' technology, deploying it optimally, and remaining cost-effective whilst delivering sustainable returns to shareholders. In effect, 'managing' technology so as to reap the maximum benefits remains a key challenge for the Indian banks.

WAY AHEAD

How do we see the future? In this context, I would like to share with you some of the issues that need to be kept in view while discussing productivity and efficiency in banks. Needless to state, these issues remain relevant, in varying degrees, in economies that share similar features in the banking sector, as ours.

First, SMEs constitute an important segment of the industrial and services sectors in India in view of their significant contributions to employment generation as also exports. With the emergence of new activities in the rural segment such as agri-clinics, contract farming, and rural housing with forward and backward linkages to SMEs, lending to SMEs has become a viable revenue proposition for banks. The Reserve Bank has also initiated several measures to streamline the flow of credit and address structural bottlenecks in credit delivery to this segment. Salient among these include fixing of self-set targets for financing, rationalization of cost of loans, expanding the outreach of formal credit, and formulation of comprehensive and more liberal policies for credit extension. PSBs have also been advised to constitute specialized SME branches in identified clusters/centres with preponderance of SMEs. A noteworthy development in this context has been the passage of the Credit Information Companies (Regulation) Act, 2005 in the Parliament. The Act is expected to encourage setting up of credit information companies and thereby, improve exchange of information on credit histories of borrowers. Coupled with appropriate risk assessment models and mechanisms, this is expected to lower transactions costs of banks. The overall effect of this process is likely to be reflected in a lowering of the risk premium embedded in interest rates charged to SMEs with positive spillovers for bank lending to the SME sector.

Although liberalization of financial services and competition has improved customer services, experience shows that customers' interests are not always accorded priority. More importantly, concerns have been raised with regard to banking practices that tend to exclude vast segments of the population. In this context, the Reserve Bank has announced its intention to implement policies to incentivize banks to provide extensive services responsive to the needs of the under-privileged. As part of the process, the Reserve Bank has recently advised all banks to make available a basic banking 'no frills' account either with 'nil' or very low minimum balances as well as charges that would make such accounts accessible to vast sections of population. The nature and number of transactions in such accounts could be restricted, but made known to the customer in advance in a transparent manner. Banks have been urged to give wide publicity to this facility so as to ensure greater financial inclusion.

The growth performance of the Indian economy during the last few years indicates a possible ratcheting up of the trend rate of growth from around 6 per cent to around 8 per cent per year. Yet, there is a need to undertake significant efforts to achieve higher rates of growth in a sustained manner. The current levels of investment might not be adequate to achieve such growth rates, even after accounting for reductions in the existing incremental capital–output ratios. Looking beyond the aspect of fiscal consolidation, action on several fronts needs to be pursued vigorously to step up growth rates. First is the issue of investment in agriculture and allied activities, a sector that produces 21 per cent of GDP, but supports nearly 60 per cent of the population. There is often substantial loss of output owing to inadequate storage and transport facilities and paucity of adequate food processing capacities. This necessitates greater public and private investment on these post-harvest facilities to not only increase value addition, but also to improve the agriculture-industry linkage. The second issue of import is the simplification of procedures. Cumbersome procedural formalities introduce delays and results in significant output losses. Added to these, the de-reservation of items from exclusive production under SSI units is likely to permit the sector reap economies of scale and scope and enhance competitiveness. The third is the issue of finances. The incipient investment boom in infrastructure, industry, and services will yield best results only if enormous resource flows are successfully intermediated at a low cost. This will depend on the ability of the financial sector to process information properly and to intermediate the extant savings into optimal investment by specific firms and sectors. The fourth aspect of stepping up investment is to address the deficiencies in infrastructure. The decline in public spending on infrastructure has not been adequately compensated by the private sector, possibly owing to difficulties in the regulatory environment. Therefore, nurturing an appropriate policy framework, with a conducive environment for public–private participation, remains the key to accelerating investment in infrastructure. The final aspect is the need to complement domestic investment with higher foreign investment, primarily in the form of foreign direct investment (FDI). Such investment is likely to trigger technology spillovers, assist human capital formation, and more generally, improve the efficiency of resource use.

Over the reform period, more and more banks have begun to get listed on the stock exchange, which, in its wake, has led to greater market discipline and concomitantly, and to an improvement in their governance aspects as well. This has led to a broadbasing of the ownership of PSBs. Such diversification of ownership has also led to a qualitative difference in their functioning, since there is induction of private shareholding as well as attendant issues of shareholder's value, as reflected by the market capitalization, board representation and interests of minority shareholders (Reddy, 2002). The issue of mixed ownership as an institutional structure where the government has controlling interest is a salient feature of bank governance in India. Such aspects of corporate governance in PSBs are important, not only because PSBs dominate the banking industry but also because it is likely that they would continue to remain in banking business. To the extent there is public ownership of PSBs, the multiple objectives of the government as owner and the complex principal–agent relationships need to be taken on board. Given the increased technical complexity of most business activities including banking and the rapid pace of change in financial markets and practices, PSBs would need to devise imaginative ways of responding to the evolving challenges within the context of mixed ownership. All in all, this is an exciting phase for PSBs to grow and prosper, and it is up to these banks to respond to the challenges.

Let me conclude: the chapter has traversed a modest terrain, focusing on the efficiency and productivity changes in Indian banking. The patterns of efficiency and technological change witnessed in Indian banking can be viewed as consistent with expectations in an industry undergoing rapid change in response to the forces of deregulation. In reaction to evolving market prospects, a few pioneering banks might adjust quickly to seize the emerging opportunities, while others respond cautiously. As deregulation gathers momentum, commercial banks would need to devise imaginative ways of augmenting their incomes and more importantly their fee-incomes so as to raise efficiency and productivity levels.

Notes

[1] Secondary issues refer to issues by financial intermediaries (that is, banks and other financial institutions). Therefore, secondary issues = sources of funds of banking sector + sources of funds of other financial sector. Primary issues refer to issues by all sectors other than financial intermediaries. FR captures the relationship between financial development and overall economic growth. The relationship between financial development and the growth of physical investment is captured by the financial inter-relations ratio (FIR). The NIR reflects the proportion of primary claims issued by non-financial institutions. IR captures the relative importance of financial institutions in financial transactions (Rangarajan and Jadhav, 1992).

[2] I have discussed the details of financial sector reforms in India elsewhere; see Mohan (2005).

[3] A detailed discussion on this aspect is contained in Bhide, Prasad, and Ghosh (2001).

[4] CAMEL is the acronym for capital adequacy, asset quality, management, earnings, and liquidity.

[5] Defined as the sum of squares of the market shares of individual banks. Decreases in the index generally indicate a loss of pricing power and an increase in competition.

[6] Total operating cost can be broken down into labour cost and cost of physical capital. To create per unit cost measure, we deflate the operating cost and its two components by either (a) the total earning assets (deposits plus investments), which is justified by the asset approach in measuring banking outputs, or (b) the aggregate of advances and deposits, which can be justified by the value-added approach in measuring banking outputs.

[7] Definitions of small, medium, and big banks are as follows: small banks are those with assets upto Rs 50 billion; medium banks are those with assets exceeding

Rs 50 billion and upto Rs 100 billion; big banks are those with assets exceeding Rs 100 billion and upto Rs 200 billion; and large banks are those with assets exceeding Rs 200 billion.

[8] The reported figure for Pakistan was 4.21 in 2001.

References

Bell, C. and P. Rousseau (2001), 'Post-Independence India: A Case of Finance-led Industrialization?', *Journal of Development Economics*, 65, pp. 153–75.

Berger, A.N. and D.B. Humphrey (1992), 'Measurement and Efficiency Issues in Commercial Banking,' in Z. Griliches (ed.), *Output Measurement in the Services Sector*, University of Chicago Press, Chicago, pp. 245–79.

Bhaumik, S.K. and R. Dimova (2004), 'How Important is Ownership in a Market with Level-Playing Field? The Indian Banking Sector Revisited', *Journal of Comparative Economics*, 32, pp. 165–80.

Bhide, M.G., A. Prasad, and S. Ghosh (2001), *Emerging Challenges in Indian Banking*, Working Paper No.103, Centre for Research in Economic Development and Policy Reform, Stanford University.

Das, Abhiman and Saibal Ghosh (2006), 'Financial Deregulation and Efficiency: An Empirical Analysis of Indian Banks during the Post Reform Period', *Review of Financial Economics*, 15, pp. 193–221.

Demirgúc-Kunt, A. and V. Maksimovic (1998), 'Law, Finance and Firm Growth', *Journal of Finance*, 53, pp. 2107–37.

Frexias, X. and J.C. Rochet (1997), *Microeconomics of Banking*, MIT Press, Cambridge, MA.

Government of India (1998), *Report of the Committee on Banking Sector Reforms*, New Delhi.

Huang, T.-H. (2005), 'A Study on the Productivities of IT Capital and Computer Labor: Firm-level Evidence from Taiwan's Banking Industry', *Journal of Productivity Analysis*, 24, pp. 241–57.

Koeva, P. (2003), 'The Performance of Indian Banks During Financial Liberalization', IMF Working Paper No.150, Washington, DC.

Kumbhakar, S. and S. Sarkar (2003), 'Deregulation, Ownership and Efficiency Change in Indian Banking: Evidence from India', *Journal of Money, Credit and Banking*, 35, pp. 403–14.

Maudos, J. and J.M. Pastor (2001), 'Cost and profit efficiency in banking: An international comparison of Europe, Japan and USA', *Applied Economics Letters*, 8, pp. 383–7.

Mohan, R. (2005), 'Financial Sector Reforms: Policies and Performance Analysis', *Economic and Political Weekly*, Special Issue on Money, Banking and Finance (March), 40, pp. 1106–21.

Rajan, R.G. and L. Zingales (1998), 'Financial Dependence and Growth', *American Economic Review*, 88, pp. 559–86.

Rangarajan, C. and N. Jadhav (1992), 'Issues in Financial Sector Reforms', in B. Jalan (ed.), *The Indian Economy*, Penguin Books India, Delhi.

Ray, P. and I. Sengupta (2004), 'Systemic Restructuring of Banks: The Indian Experience', *Journal of the Indian Bankers Association*, 74(4), pp. 4–19.

Reddy, Y.V. (2002), 'Public Sector Banks and the Governance Challenge: Indian Experience', lecture Delivered at the World Bank, IMF and Brookings Institutions Conference, April.

RBI (2000), *Report on Currency and Finance 1999-2000*, RBI, Mumbai.

_____ (2002), 'Expenditure Pattern and IT Initiatives of Banks', *RBI Bulletin*, December.

_____ (2005), *Report on Trend and Progress of Banking in India 2004-2005*, RBI, Mumbai.

Sarkar, J., S. Sarkar, and S.K. Bhaumik (1998), 'Does Ownership Always Matter? Evidence from the Indian Banking Industry', *Journal of Comparative Economics*, 26, pp. 262–81.

Stiglitz, J.E. (1998), 'More Instruments and Broader Goals: Moving Towards the Post-Washington Consensus', *WIDER Annual Lecture*, Helsinki.

Williams, J. and N. Nguyen (2005), 'Financial Liberalization, Crisis, and Restructuring: A Comparative Study of Bank Performance and Bank Governance in South East Asia', *Journal of Banking and Finance*, 29, pp. 2119–54.

7 Financial Sector Reforms and Monetary Policy*

Since the initiation of reforms in the early 1990s, the Indian economy has achieved high growth in an environment of macroeconomic and financial stability. The period has been marked by broad-based economic reforms that have touched every segment of the economy. These reforms were designed essentially to promote greater efficiency in the economy through promotion of greater competition. The story of Indian reforms is by now well documented (for example, Ahluwalia, 2002); nevertheless, what is less appreciated is that India achieved this acceleration in growth while maintaining price and financial stability. As a result of the growing openness, India was not insulated from exogenous shocks since the second half of the 1990s. These shocks, global as well as domestic, included a series of financial crises in Asia, Brazil, and Russia; 9/11 terrorist attacks in the United States; border tensions; sanctions imposed in the aftermath of nuclear tests; political uncertainties; changes in the government; and the current oil shock. Nonetheless, stability could be maintained in financial markets. Indeed, inflation has been contained since the mid-1990s to an average of around 5 per cent, distinctly lower than that of around 8 per cent per annum over the previous four decades. Simultaneously, the health of the financial sector has recorded very significant improvement.

India's path of reforms has been different from most other EMEs: it has been a measured, gradual, cautious, and steady process, devoid of many flourishes that could be observed in other countries. I shall argue in this chapter that reforms in the financial sector and monetary policy framework have been a key component of the overall reforms that provided the foundation of an increased price and financial stability. Reforms in these

* Paper presented by the author at the Conference on Economic Policy in Asia at Stanford, organized by Stanford Center for International Development and Stanford Institute for Economic Policy Research, on 2 June 2006.

sectors have been well sequenced, taking into account the state of the markets in the various segments.

The main objective of the financial sector reforms in India initiated in the early 1990s was to create an efficient, competitive, and stable financial sector that could then contribute in greater measure to stimulate growth. Concomitantly, the monetary policy framework made a phased shift from direct instruments of monetary management to an increasing reliance on indirect instruments. However, as appropriate monetary transmission cannot take place without efficient price discovery of interest rates and exchange rates in the overall functioning of financial markets, the corresponding development of the money market, government securities market, and the foreign exchange market became necessary. Reforms in the various segments, therefore, had to be coordinated. In this process, growing integration of the Indian economy with the rest of the world also had to be recognized and provided for.

Against this backdrop, the coverage of this chapter is three-fold. First, I will give a synoptic account of the reforms in financial sector and monetary policy. Second, this is followed by an assessment of these reforms in terms of outcomes and the health of the financial sector. Finally, lessons emerging from the Indian experience for issues of topical relevance for monetary authorities are considered in the final section.

FINANCIAL SECTOR AND MONETARY POLICY: OBJECTIVES AND REFORMS

Till the early 1990s the Indian financial sector could be described as a classic example of 'financial repression' *à la* McKinnon and Shaw. Monetary policy was subservient to the fisc. The financial system was characterized by extensive regulations such as administered interest rates, directed credit programmes, weak banking structure, lack of proper accounting and risk management systems, and lack of transparency in operations of major financial market participants (Mohan, 2004b). Such a system hindered efficient allocation of resources. Financial sector reforms initiated in the early 1990s have attempted to overcome these weaknesses in order to enhance efficiency of resource allocation in the economy.

Simultaneously, the Reserve Bank took a keen interest in the development of financial markets, especially the money, government securities, and forex markets in view of their critical role in the transmission mechanism of monetary policy. As for other central banks, the money market is the focal point for intervention by the Reserve Bank to equilibrate short-term liquidity flows on account of its linkages with the foreign exchange market. Similarly, the government securities market is important for the entire debt market as it serves as a benchmark for pricing other debt market instruments, thereby aiding the monetary transmission process across the yield curve. The Reserve Bank had, in fact, been making efforts since 1986 to develop institutions and infrastructure for these markets to facilitate price discovery. These efforts by the Reserve Bank to develop efficient, stable, and healthy financial markets accelerated after 1991. There has been close coordination between the Central Government and the Reserve Bank, as also between different regulators, which helped in orderly and smooth development of the financial markets in India.

What have been the major contours of the financial sector reforms in India? For the sake of completeness, it is useful to have a quick run-down of these:

1. removal of the erstwhile existing financial repression;
2. creation of an efficient, productive, and profitable financial sector;
3. enabling the process of price discovery by the market determination of interest rates that improves allocative efficiency of resources;
4. providing operational and functional autonomy to institutions;
5. preparing the financial system for increasing international competition;
6. opening the external sector in a calibrated manner; and
7. promoting financial stability in the wake of domestic and external shocks.

The financial sector reforms since the early 1990s could be analytically classified into two phases.[1] The first phase—or the first generation of reforms—was aimed at creating an efficient, productive, and profitable financial sector which would function in an environment of operational flexibility and functional autonomy. In the second phase, or the second generation reforms, which started in the mid-1990s, the emphasis of reforms has been on strengthening the financial system and introducing structural improvements. Against this brief overview of the philosophy of financial sector reforms, let me briefly touch upon reforms in various sectors and segments of the financial sector.

Banking Sector

The main objective of banking sector reforms was to promote a diversified, efficient, and competitive financial system with the ultimate goal of improving the allocative efficiency of resources through operational flexibility, improved financial viability, and institutional strengthening. The reforms have focused on removing financial repression through reductions in statutory pre-emptions, while stepping up prudential regulations at the same time.

Furthermore, interest rates on both deposits and lending of banks have been progressively deregulated (Box 7.1).

Box 7.1: Reforms in the Banking Sector

A. Competition-enhancing Measures

1. Granting of operational autonomy to PSBs, reduction of public ownership in PSBs by allowing them to raise capital from equity market up to 49 per cent of paid-up capital.
2. Transparent norms for entry of Indian private sector, foreign and joint-venture banks and insurance companies, permission for foreign investment in the financial sector in the form of FDI as well as portfolio investment, permission to banks to diversify product portfolio, and business activities.
3. Roadmap for presence of foreign banks and guidelines for mergers and amalgamation of private sector banks and banks and NBFCs.
4. Guidelines on ownership and governance in private sector banks.

B. Measures Enhancing Role of Market Forces

1. Sharp reduction in pre-emption through reserve requirement, market-determined pricing for government securities, disbanding of administered interest rates with a few exceptions, and enhanced transparency and disclosure norms to facilitate market discipline.
2. Introduction of pure inter-bank call money market, auction-based repos–reverse repos for short-term liquidity management, facilitation of improved payments, and settlement mechanism.
3. Significant advancement in dematerialization and markets for securitized assets are being developed.

C. Prudential Measures

1. Introduction and phased implementation of international best practices and norms on risk-weighted capital adequacy requirement, accounting, income recognition, provisioning, and exposure.
2. Measures to strengthen risk management through recognition of different components of risk, assignment of risk-weights to various asset classes, norms on connected lending, risk concentration, application of marked-to-market principle for investment portfolio, and limits on deployment of fund in sensitive activities.
3. 'Know Your Customer' and 'Anti-Money Laundering' guidelines, roadmap for Basel II, introduction of capital charge for market risk, higher graded provisioning for NPAs, guidelines for ownership and governance, securitization and debt restructuring mechanisms norms, etc.

Contd

Box 7.1 Contd

D. Institutional and Legal Measures

1. Setting up of Lok Adalats (people's courts), debt recovery tribunals, ARCs, settlement advisory committees, corporate debt restructuring mechanism, etc., for quicker recovery/restructuring.
2. Promulgation of Securitization and SARFAESI Act, 2002 and its subsequent amendment to ensure creditor rights.
3. Setting up of Credit Information Bureau of India Limited for information sharing on defaulters as also other borrowers.
4. Setting up of Clearing Corporation of India Ltd (CCIL) to act as central counterparty for facilitating payments and settlement system relating to fixed income securities and money market instruments.

E. Supervisory Measures

1. Establishment of the Board for Financial Supervision as the apex supervisory authority for commercial banks, financial institutions, and NBFCs.
2. Introduction of Capital Adequacy, Asset Quality, Management, Earnings, Liquidity, and Systems (CAMELS) supervisory rating system, move towards risk-based supervision (RBS), consolidated supervision of financial conglomerates, strengthening of off-site surveillance through control returns.
3. Recasting of the role of statutory auditors, increased internal control through strengthening of internal audit.
4. Strengthening corporate governance, enhanced due diligence on important shareholders, fit and proper tests for directors.

F. Technology Related Measures

1. Setting up of INFINET as the communication backbone for the financial sector, introduction of negotiated dealing system (NDS) for screen-based trading in government securities and Real-Time Gross Settlement (RTGS) system.

As the Indian banking system had become predominantly government-owned by the early 1990s, banking sector reforms essentially took a two-pronged approach. First, the level of competition was gradually increased within the banking system while simultaneously introducing international best practices in prudential regulation and supervision tailored to Indian requirements. In particular, special emphasis was placed on building up the risk management capabilities of Indian banks while measures were initiated to ensure flexibility, operational autonomy, and competition in the banking sector. Second, active steps were taken to improve the institutional arrangements including the legal framework and technological system. The supervisory system was revamped in view of the crucial role of supervision in the creation of an efficient banking system.

Measures to improve the health of the banking system have included (a) restoration of PSBs' net worth through recapitalization where needed; (b) streamlining of the supervision process with combination of on-site and off-site surveillance along with external auditing; (c) introduction of risk based supervision; (d) introduction of the process of structured and discretionary intervention for problem banks through a PCA mechanism; (e) institutionalization of a mechanism facilitating greater coordination for regulation and supervision of financial conglomerates; (f) strengthening creditor rights (still in process); and (g) increased emphasis on corporate governance.

Consistent with the policy approach to benchmark the banking system to the best international standards with emphasis on gradual harmonisation, all commercial banks in India are expected to start implementing BASEL II with effect from 31 March 2007—though a marginal stretching beyond this date should not be ruled out in view of the latest indications on the state of preparedness (Reddy, 2006a). Recognizing the differences in degrees of sophistication and development of the banking system, it has been decided that the banks will initially adopt the Standardized Approach for credit risk and the Basic Indicator Approach for operational risk. After adequate skills are developed, both by the banks and also by the supervisors, some of the banks may be allowed to migrate to the Internal Rating-based Approach. Although implementation of BASEL II will require more capital for banks in India, the cushion available in the system—at present, the Capital to Risk-weighted Assets Ratio (CRAR) is over 12 per cent—provides some comfort. In order to provide banks greater flexibility and avenues for meeting the capital requirements, the Reserve Bank has issued policy guidelines enabling issuance of several instruments by the banks, namely, innovative perpetual debt instruments, perpetual non-cumulative preference shares, redeemable cumulative preference shares, and hybrid debt instruments.

Reforms in the Monetary Policy Framework

The basic emphasis of monetary policy since the initiation of reforms has been to reduce market segmentation in the financial sector through increased interlinkages between various segments of the financial market including money, government security, and forex market. The key policy development that has enabled a more independent monetary policy environment as well as the development of government securities market was the discontinuation of automatic monetization of the government's fiscal deficit since April 1997 through an agreement between the government and the RBI in September 1994. In order to meet the challenges thrown by financial liberalization and the growing complexities of monetary management, the Reserve Bank switched from a monetary targeting framework to a multiple indicator approach from 1998–9. Short-term interest rates have emerged as the key indicators of the monetary policy stance. A significant shift is the move towards market-based instruments away from direct instruments of monetary management. In line with international trends, the Reserve Bank has put in place a liquidity management framework in which market liquidity is managed through a mix of open market (including repo) operations (OMOs), changes in reserve requirements and standing facilities, reinforced by changes in the policy rates, including the Bank Rate and the short-term (overnight) policy rate. In order to carry out these market operations effectively, the Reserve Bank has initiated several measures to strengthen the health of its balance sheet (RBI, 2004).

Over the past few years, the process of monetary policy formulation has become relatively more articulate, consultative, and participative with external orientation, while the internal work processes have also been re-engineered. A recent notable step in this direction is the constitution of a Technical Advisory Committee on Monetary Policy comprising external experts to advise the Reserve Bank on the stance of monetary policy (Box 7.2).

Box 7.2: Reforms in the Monetary Policy Framework

Objectives

1. Twin objectives of 'maintaining price stability' and 'ensuring availability of adequate credit to productive sectors of the economy to support growth' continue to govern the stance of monetary policy, though the relative emphasis on these objectives has varied depending on the importance of maintaining an appropriate balance.
2. Reflecting the increasing development of financial market and greater liberalization, use of broad money as an intermediate target has been de-emphasized and a multiple-indicator approach has been adopted.
3. Emphasis has been put on development of multiple instruments to transmit liquidity and interest rate signals in the short-term in a flexible and bi-directional manner.
4. Increase of the interlinkage between various segments of the financial market including money, government security, and forex markets.

Instruments

1. Move from direct instruments (such as administered interest rates, reserve requirements, selective credit control) to indirect instruments (such as OMOs, purchase and repurchase of government securities) for the conduct of monetary policy.

Contd

Box 7.2 Contd

2. Introduction of LAF, which operates through repo and reverse repo auctions and effectively provides a corridor for short-term interest rate. LAF has emerged as the tool for both liquidity management and also as a signalling device for interest rate in the overnight market.
3. Use of open market operations to deal with overall market liquidity situation especially those emanating from capital flows.
4. Introduction of MSS as an additional instrument to deal with enduring capital inflows without affecting short-term liquidity management role of LAF.

Developmental Measures

1. Discontinuation of automatic monetisation through an agreement between the government and the Reserve Bank. Rationalization of Treasury Bill market. Introduction of delivery versus payment (DVP) system and deepening of inter-bank repo market.
2. Introduction of Primary Dealers (PDs) in the government securities market to play the role of market maker.
3. Amendment of Securities Contracts Regulation Act (SCRA) to create the regulatory framework.
4. Deepening of government securities market by making the interest rates on such securities market-related. Introduction of auction of the government securities. Development of a risk-free credible yield curve in the government securities market as a benchmark for related markets.
5. Development of pure inter-bank call money market. Non-bank participants to participate in other money market instruments.
6. Introduction of automated screen-based trading in government securities through NDS. Setting up of risk-free payments and system in government securities through CCIL. Phased introduction of the RTGS system.
7. Deepening of forex market and increased autonomy of Authorized Dealers.

Institutional Measures

1. Setting up of Technical Advisory Committee on Monetary Policy with outside experts to review macroeconomic and monetary developments and advise the Reserve Bank on the stance of monetary policy.
2. Creation of a separate Financial Market Department within the RBI.

Following the reforms, the financial markets have now grown in size, depth, and activity paving the way for flexible use of indirect instruments by the Reserve Bank to pursue its objectives. It is recognized that stability in financial markets is critical for efficient price discovery. Excessive volatility in exchange rates and interest rates masks the underlying value of these variables and gives rise to confusing signals. Since both the exchange rate and interest rate are the key prices reflecting the cost of money, it is particularly important for the efficient functioning of the economy that they be market determined and be easily observed. The Reserve Bank has, therefore, put in place a liquidity management framework in the form of a LAF for the facilitation of forex and money market transactions that result in price discovery sans excessive volatility. The LAF coupled with OMOs and the Market Stabilization Scheme has provided the Reserve Bank greater flexibility to manage market liquidity in consonance with its policy stance. The introduction of LAF had several advantages (Mohan, 2006b).

1. First and foremost, it helped the transition from direct instruments of monetary control to indirect and, in the process, certain dead weight loss for the system was saved.
2. Second, it has provided monetary authorities with greater flexibility in determining both the quantum of adjustment as well as the rates by responding to the needs of the system on a daily basis.
3. Third, it enabled the Reserve Bank to modulate the supply of funds on a daily basis to meet day-to-day liquidity mismatches.
4. Fourth, it enabled the Reserve Bank to affect demand for funds through policy rate changes.
5. Fifth and most important, it helped stabilize short-term money market rates.

LAF has now emerged as the principal operating instrument of monetary policy. Although there is no formal targeting of a point overnight interest rate, the LAF is designed to nudge overnight interest rates within a specified corridor, the difference between the fixed repo and reverse repo rates currently being 100 basis points. The evidence suggests that this effort has been largely successful with the overnight interest rate moving out of this corridor for only a few brief periods. The LAF has enabled the Reserve Bank to de-emphasize targeting of bank reserves and focus increasingly on interest rates. This has helped in reducing the CRR without loss of monetary control.

Given the growing role played by expectations, the stance of monetary policy and its rationale are communicated to the public in a variety of ways. The enactment of the Fiscal Responsibility and Budget Management (FRBM) Act, 2003 has strengthened the institutional mechanism further: from April 2006 onwards, the Reserve Bank is no longer permitted to subscribe to government securities in the primary market. The development of the monetary policy framework has also involved a great deal of institutional initiatives to enable efficient functioning of the money market: development of appropriate trading, payments, and settlement systems along with technological infrastructure.

Financial Markets

The success of a framework that relies on indirect instruments of monetary management, such as interest rates, is contingent upon the extent and speed with which changes in the central bank's policy rate are transmitted to the spectrum of market interest rates and exchange rate in the economy and onward to the real sector. Given the critical role played by financial markets in this transmission mechanism, the Reserve Bank has taken a number of initiatives to develop a pure inter-bank money market. A noteworthy and desirable development has been the substantial migration of money market activity from the uncollateralized call money segment to the collateralized market repo and collateralized borrowing and lending obligations (CBLO) markets. The shift of activity from uncollateralized to collateralized segments of the market has largely resulted from measures relating to limiting the call market transactions to banks and PDs only. This policy-induced shift is in the interest of financial stability and is yielding results.

Concomitantly, efforts have been made to broaden and deepen the government securities market and foreign exchange market so as to enable the process of efficient price discovery in respect of interest rates and the exchange rate (Boxes 7.3 and 7.4).

Box 7.3: Reforms in the Government Securities Market

Institutional Measures

1. Administered interest rates on government securities were replaced by an auction system for price discovery.
2. Automatic monetisation of fiscal deficit through the issue of ad hoc Treasury Bills was phased out.
3. PDs were introduced as market makers in the government securities market.
4. For ensuring transparency in the trading of government securities, DVP settlement system was introduced.
5. Repurchase agreement (repo) was introduced as a tool of short-term liquidity adjustment. Subsequently, the LAF was introduced.
6. LAF operates through repo and reverse repo auctions and provide a corridor for short-term interest rate. LAF has emerged as the tool for both liquidity management and also signalling device for interest rates in the overnight market. The Second LAF (SLAF) was introduced in November 2005.
7. MSS has been introduced, which has expanded the instruments available to the Reserve Bank for managing the enduring surplus liquidity in the system.
8. Effective 1 April 2006, RBI has withdrawn from participating in primary market auctions of the government paper.

Contd

Box 7.3 Contd

9. Banks have been permitted to undertake PD business while PDs are being allowed to diversify their business.
10. Short sales in the government securities is being permitted in a calibrated manner while guidelines for 'when issued' market have been issued recently.

Increase in Instruments in the Government Securities Market

1. 91-day Treasury Bill was introduced for managing liquidity and benchmarking. Zero coupon bonds, floating rate bonds, capital indexed bonds were issued and exchange traded interest rate futures were introduced. Over-the-Counter (OTC) interest rate derivatives like interest rate swaps (IRS)/forward rate agreements (FRAs) were introduced.
2. Short sales in Government securities permitted, subject to certain conditions.
3. Repo status has been granted to the state government securities in order to improve secondary market liquidity.

Enabling Measures

1. FIIs were allowed to invest in the government securities subject to certain limits.
2. Introduction of automated screen-based trading in government securities through NDS.
3. Setting up of risk-free payments and settlement system in government securities through CCIL.
4. Introduction of trading in government securities on stock exchanges for promoting retailing in such securities, permitting non-banks to participate in repo market.

It is pertinent to note that the phased approach to development of financial markets has enabled RBI's withdrawal from the primary market since 1 April 2006. This step completes the transition to a fully market-based system in the government securities market. Looking ahead, as per the recommendations of the Twelfth Finance Commission, the Central Government would cease to raise resources on behalf of state governments, who, henceforth, have to access the market directly. Thus, state governments' capability in raising resources will be market-determined and based on their own financial health. In order to ensure a smooth transition to the new regime, restructuring of current institutional processes has already been initiated (Mohan, 2006c). These steps are helping to achieve the desired integration in the conduct of monetary operations.

As regards the foreign exchange market, reforms focused on market development with in-built prudential safeguards so that the market would not be destabilized in the process (Reddy, 2002). The move towards a market-based exchange rate regime in 1993 and the subsequent adoption of current account convertibility were the key measures in reforming the Indian foreign exchange market. Banks are increasingly being given greater autonomy to undertake foreign exchange operations. In order to deepen the foreign exchange market, a large number of products have been introduced and entry of new players has been allowed in the market (Box 7.4).

Summing up, reforms were designed to enable the process of efficient price discovery and induce greater internal efficiency in resource allocation within the banking system. While the policy measures in the pre-1990s period were essentially devoted to financial deepening, the focus of reforms in the last decade and a half has been engendering greater efficiency and productivity in the banking system. Reforms in the monetary policy framework were aimed at providing operational flexibility to the Reserve Bank in its conduct of monetary policy by relaxing the constraint imposed by passive monetization of the fisc.

FINANCIAL SECTOR AND MONETARY POLICY REFORMS: AN ASSESSMENT

BANKING SECTOR

An assessment of the banking sector shows that banks have experienced strong balance sheet growth in the post-reform period in an environment of operational flexibility. Improvement in the financial health of banks, reflected in significant improvement in capital adequacy and improved asset quality, is distinctly visible. It is noteworthy that this progress has been achieved despite the adoption of international best practices in prudential norms. Competitiveness and productivity gains have also been enabled by proactive technological deepening and flexible human resource management. These significant gains have been achieved even while renewing our goals of social banking, namely, maintaining the wide reach of the banking system and directing credit towards important but disadvantaged sectors of society. A brief discussion on the performance of the banking sector under the reform process is given in the following sub-sections.

Spread of Banking

The banking system's wide reach, judged in terms of expansion of branches and the growth of credit and deposits indicates continued financial deepening (Table 7.1). The population per bank branch has not changed much since the 1980s, and has remained at around 16,000.

Box 7.4: Reforms in the Foreign Exchange Market

Exchange Rate Regime

1. Evolution of exchange rate regime from a single-currency fixed-exchange rate system to fixing the value of rupee against a basket of currencies and further to market-determined floating exchange rate regime.
2. Adoption of convertibility of rupee for current account transactions with acceptance of Article VIII of the Articles of Agreement of the International Monetary Fund (IMF). De facto full capital account convertibility for non residents and calibrated liberalization of transactions undertaken for capital account purposes in the case of residents.

Institutional Framework

1. Replacement of the earlier Foreign Exchange Regulation Act (FERA), 1973 by the market-friendly Foreign Exchange Management Act, 1999. Delegation of considerable powers by RBI to authorized dealers to release foreign exchange for a variety of purposes.

Increase in Instruments in the Foreign Exchange Market

1. Development of rupee-foreign currency swap market.
2. Introduction of additional hedging instruments, such as, foreign currency-rupee options. Authorized dealers permitted to use innovative products like cross-currency options, IRS and currency swaps, caps/collars, and FRAs in the international forex market.

Liberalization Measures

1. Authorized dealers permitted to initiate trading positions, borrow, and invest in overseas market subject to certain specifications and ratification by respective Banks' Boards. Banks are also permitted to fix interest rates on non-resident deposits, subject to certain specifications, use derivative products for asset-liability management, and fix overnight open position limits and gap limits in the foreign exchange market, subject to ratification by the RBI.
2. Permission to various participants in the foreign exchange market, including exporters, Indians investing abroad, FIIs, to avail forward cover and enter into swap transactions without any limit subject to genuine underlying exposure.
3. FIIs and NRIs permitted to trade in exchange-traded derivative contracts subject to certain conditions.
4. Foreign exchange earners permitted to maintain foreign currency accounts. Residents are permitted to open such accounts within the general limit of US$ 25,000 per year.

Table 7.1 Progress of Commercial Banking in India

Item	1969	1980	1991	1995	2000	2005
1. No. of commercial banks	73	154	272	284	298	288
2. No. of bank offices of which	8262	34,594	60,570	64,234	67,868	68,339
Rural and semi-urban bank offices	5172	23,227	46,550	46,602	47,693	47,491
3. Population per office (thousands)	64	16	14	15	15	16
4. Per capita deposit (Rs)	88	738	2368	4242	8542	16,699
5. Per capita credit (Rs)	68	457	1434	2320	4555	10,135
6. Priority sector advances (per cent)	15	37	39	34	35	40
7. Deposits (per cent of national income)	16	36	48	48	54	65

Source: RBI.

In the post-reform period, banks have consistently maintained high rates of growth in their assets and liabilities. On the liability side, deposits continue to account for about 80 per cent of the total liabilities. On the asset side, the shares of loans and advances on the one hand and investments on the other hand have seen marked cycles, reflecting banks' portfolio preferences as well as growth cycles in the economy. The share of loans and advances declined in the second half of 1990s responding to slowdown in investment demand as well as tightening of prudential norms. With investment demand again picking up in the past three to four years, banks' credit portfolio has witnessed sharp growth. Banks' investment in gilts have accordingly seen a significant decline in the past one year, although it still remains above the minimum statutory requirement. Thus, while in the 1990s, greater investments and aversion to credit risk exposure may have deterred banks from undertaking their 'core function' of financial intermediation, namely, accepting deposits and extending credit, they seem to have struck a greater balance in recent years between investments and loans and advances. The improved atmosphere for recovery created in the recent years seems to have induced banks to put greater efforts in extending loans.

Capital Position and Asset Quality

Since the beginning of reforms, a set of micro-prudential measures have been stipulated aimed at imparting strength to the banking system as well as ensuring safety. With regard to prudential requirements, income recognition and asset classification (IRAC) norms have been strengthened to approach international best practice. Initially, while it was deemed to attain a CRAR of 8 per cent in a phased manner, it was subsequently raised to 9 per cent with effect from 1999–2000.

The overall capital position of commercial banks has witnessed a marked improvement during the reform period (Table 7.2). Illustratively, as at end-March 2005, eighty-six out of the eighty-eight commercial banks operating in India maintained CRAR at or above 9 per cent. The corresponding figure for 1995–6 was fifty-four out of ninety-two banks. Improved capitalization of PSBs was initially brought through substantial infusion of funds by government to recapitalize these banks. Subsequently, in order to mitigate the budgetary impact and to introduce market discipline, PSBs were allowed to raise funds from the market through equity issuance subject to the maintenance of 51 per cent public ownership. Ownership in PSBs is now well diversified. As at end-March 2005, the holding by the general public in six banks ranged between 40 per cent and 49 per cent and in twelve banks between 30 per cent and 49 per cent. It was only in four banks that the government holding was more than 90 per cent.

Despite tightening norms, there has been considerable improvement in the asset quality of banks. India transited to a 90-day NPL recognition norm (from 180-day norm) in 2004. Nonetheless, NPLs, as ratios of both total advances and assets, have declined substantially and consistently since the mid-1990s (Table 7.3). Improvement in the credit appraisal process, upturn of the business cycle, new initiatives for resolution of NPLs (including promulgation of the SARFAESI Act), and greater provisioning and write-off of NPLs enabled by greater profitability, have kept incremental NPLs low.

Table 7.2 Distribution of Commercial Banks according to Risk-weighted Capital Adequacy

(number of banks)

Year	Below 4 per cent	Between 4–9 per cent[a]	Between 9–10 per cent[b]	Above 10 per cent	Total
1995–6	8	9	33	42	92
2000–1	3	2	11	84	100
2004–5	1	1	8	78	88

Notes: [a] Relates to 4–8 per cent before 1999–2000; [b] Relates to 8–10 per cent before 1999–2000.

Source: RBI.

Table 7.3 Non-performing Loans (NPLs) of SCBs

(per cent)

Period	Gross NPL/ advances	Gross NPL/ assets	Net NPL/ advances	Net NPL/ assets
1996–7	15.7	7.0	8.1	3.3
1997–8	14.4	6.4	7.3	3.0
1998–9	14.7	6.2	7.6	2.9
1999–2000	12.7	5.5	6.8	2.7
2000–1	11.4	4.9	6.2	2.5
2001–2	10.4	4.6	5.5	2.3
2002–3	8.8	4.0	4.4	1.9
2003–4	7.2	3.3	2.9	1.2
2004–5	5.2	2.6	2.0	0.9

Source: RBI.

Competition and Efficiency

In consonance with the objective of enhancing efficiency and productivity of banks through greater competition—from new private sector banks and entry and expansion of several foreign banks—there has been a consistent decline in the share of PSBs in total assets of commercial banks. Notwithstanding such transformation, the PSBs still account for nearly three-fourths of assets and income. PSBs have also responded to the new challenges of competition, as reflected in their increased share in the overall profit of the banking sector. This suggests that, with operational flexibility, PSBs are competing relatively effectively with private sector and foreign banks. PSB managements are now probably more attuned to the market consequences of their activities (Mohan, 2006a). Shares of Indian private sector banks, especially new private sector banks established in the 1990s, in the total income and assets of the banking system have improved considerably since the mid-1990s (Table 7.4). The reduction in the asset share of foreign banks, however, is partially due to their increased focus on off-balance sheet non-fund-based business.

Efficiency gains are also reflected in containment of the operating expenditure as a proportion of total assets (Table 7.5). This has been achieved in spite of large expenditures incurred by Indian banks in installation and upgradation of IT and, in the case of PSBs, large expenditures under voluntary premature retirement of nearly 12 per cent of their total staff strength.

Table 7.4 Bank Group-wise Shares: Select Indicators

(per cent)

Items	1995–6	2000–1	2004–5
	Public Sector Banks		
Income	82.5	78.4	75.6
Expenditure	84.2	78.9	75.8
Total assets	84.4	79.5	74.4
Net profit	–39.1	67.4	73.3
Gross profit	74.3	69.9	75.9
	New Private Sector Banks		
Income	1.5	5.7	11.8
Expenditure	1.3	5.5	11.4
Total assets	1.5	6.1	12.9
Net profit	17.8	10.0	15.0
Gross profit	2.5	6.9	10.7
	Foreign Banks		
Income	9.4	9.1	7.0
Expenditure	8.3	8.8	6.6
Total assets	7.9	7.9	6.8
Net profit	79.8	14.8	9.7
Gross profit	15.6	15.7	9.0

Source: RBI.

Improvements in efficiency of the banking system are also reflected, inter alia, in costs of intermediation, which, defined as the ratio of operating expense to total assets, witnessed a gradual reduction in the post-reform period across various bank groups barring foreign banks (Table 7.6). However, intermediation costs of banks in India still tend to be higher than those in developed countries. Similarly, the cost–income ratio (defined as the ratio of operating expenses to total income less interest expense) of Indian banks has shown a declining trend during the post reform period. For example, Indian banks paid roughly 45 per cent of their net income towards managing labour and physical capital in 2004 as against nearly 72 per cent in 1993 (Mohan, 2006a). Indian banks thus recorded a net cost saving of nearly 27 per cent of their net income during the post-reform period.

Table 7.5 Earnings and Expenses of SCBs

(Rs billion)

Year	Total assets	Total earnings	Interest earnings	Total expenses	Interest expenses	Establishment expenses	Net Interest earning
1969	68	4	4	4	2	1	2
		(6.2)	(5.3)	(5.5)	(2.8)	(2.1)	(2.5)
1980	582	42	38	42	27	10	10
		(7.3)	(6.4)	(7.2)	(4.7)	(1.7)	(1.8)
1991	3275	304	275	297	190	76	86
		(9.3)	(8.4)	(9.1)	(5.8)	(2.3)	(2.6)
2000	11055	1149	992	1077	690	276	301
		(10.4)	(9.0)	(9.7)	(6.2)	(2.5)	(2.7)
2005	22,746	1867	1531	1660	866	491	665
		(8.2)	(6.7)	(7.3)	(3.8)	(2.2)	(2.9)

Note: Figures in brackets are ratios to total assets.

Source: RBI.

Productivity

What is most encouraging is the very significant improvement in the productivity of the Indian banking system, in terms of various productivity indicators. The business per employee of Indian banks increased over three-fold in real terms from Rs 5.4 million in 1992 to Rs 17.3 million in 2005, exhibiting an annual compound growth rate of more than 9 per cent (Table 7.7). The profit per employee increased from Rs 20,000 to Rs 130,000 over the same period, implying a compound growth of around 15.5 per cent. Branch productivity also recorded concomitant improvements. These improvements could be driven by two factors: technological improvement, which expands the range of production possibilities, and a catching up effect, as peer pressure amongst banks compels them to raise productivity levels. Here, the role of new business practices, new approaches, and expansion of the business that was introduced by the new private banks has been of the utmost importance.

Monetary Policy

What has been the impact of the monetary policy? From the innumerable dimensions of impact of monetary policy, let me focus on some select elements.

Table 7.6 Intermediation Cost of SCBs: 1996–2005

(percentage to total assets)

Year (end-March)	Public sector banks	New private banks	Foreign banks	All SCBs
1996	2.99	1.82	2.78	2.94
1997	2.88	1.94	3.04	2.85
1998	2.66	1.76	2.99	2.63
1999	2.65	1.74	3.40	2.65
2000	2.52	1.42	3.12	2.48
2001	2.72	1.75	3.05	2.64
2002	2.29	1.12	3.03	2.19
2003	2.25	1.95	2.79	2.24
2004	2.20	2.02	2.76	2.20
2005	2.03	2.06	2.85	2.09

Note: Intermediation cost = operating expenses.

Source: Computed from *Statistical Tables Relating to Banks in India*, RBI, various years.

Table 7.7 Select Productivity Indicators of SCBs

(Rs million at 1993–4 prices)

Year	Business per employee	Profit per employee	Business per branch
1992	5.4	0.02	109.9
1996	6.0	0.01	119.6
2000	9.7	0.05	179.4
2005	17.3	0.13	267.0

Source: *Statistical Tables Relating to Banks in India*, RBI.

Inflation

Turning to an assessment of monetary policy, it would be reasonable to assert that monetary policy has been largely successful in meeting its key objectives in the post-reforms period. Just as the late 1990s witnessed a fall in inflation worldwide, so too has India. Inflation has averaged close to 5 per cent per annum in the decade gone by, notably lower than that of 8 per cent in the previous four decades (Figure 7.1). Structural reforms since the early 1990s coupled with improved monetary-fiscal interface and reforms in the government securities market enabled better monetary management from the second half of the 1990s onwards. More importantly, the regime of low and stable inflation has, in turn, stabilized inflation expectations and inflation tolerance in the economy has come down. It is encouraging to note that despite record high international crude oil prices, inflation remains low and inflation expectations also remain stable. Since inflation expectations are a key determinant of the actual inflation outcome, and given the lags in monetary transmission, we have been taking pre-emptive measures to keep inflation expectations stable.[2] As discussed further below, a number of instruments, both existing as well as new, were employed to modulate liquidity conditions to achieve the desired objectives. A number of other factors such as increased competition, productivity gains, and strong corporate balance sheets have also contributed to this low and stable inflation environment, but it appears that calibrated monetary measures had a substantial role to play as well.

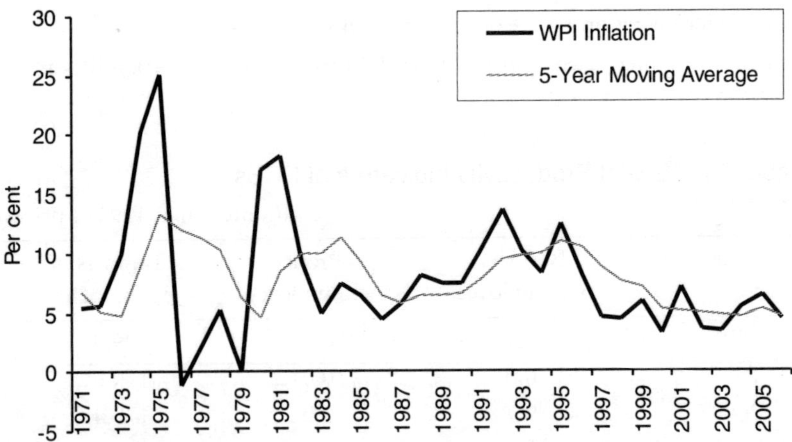

Figure 7.1 Wholesale Price Inflation in India

Source: RBI.

Challenges Posed by Large Capital Inflows

It is pertinent to note that inflation could be contained since the mid-1990s, despite challenges posed by large capital flows. Following the reforms in the external sector, foreign investment flows have been encouraged. Reflecting the strong growth prospects of the Indian economy, the country has received large investment inflows, both direct and portfolio, since 1993–4 as compared with negligible levels till the early 1990s. Total foreign investment flows (direct and portfolio) increased from US$ 111 million in 1990–1 to

US$ 17,496 million in 2005–6 (April–February). Over the same period, CADs remained modest—averaging 1 per cent of GDP since 1991–2 and in fact recorded small surpluses during 2001–4. With capital flows remaining in excess of the current financing requirements, the overall BoP recorded persistent surpluses leading to an increase in reserves. Despite such large accretion to reserves, inflation could be contained reflecting appropriate policy responses by the Reserve Bank and the government.

The emergence of foreign exchange surplus lending to continuing and large accretion to reserves since the mid-1990s has been a novel experience for India after experiencing chronic BoP problems for almost four decades. These surpluses began to arise after the opening of the current account, reduction in trade protection, and partial opening of the capital account from the early to the mid-1990s. The exchange rate flexibility practised since 1992–3 has been an important part of the policy response needed to manage capital flows.

The composition of India's BoP has undergone a significant change since the mid-1990s. In the current account, the growth of software exports and, more recently, of business process outsourcing has increased the share of service exports on a continuing basis. Even more significant is the growth in remittances from NRIs, now amounting to about 3 per cent of GDP. The latter exhibit a great deal of stability. The remittances appear to consist mainly of maintenance flows that do not seem to be affected by exchange rate, inflation, or growth rate changes. Thus, the Indian current account exhibits only a small deficit, or a surplus, despite the existence of merchandise trade deficit that has grown from 3.2 per cent of GDP in the mid-1990s to 5.3 per cent in 2004–5. On the capital account, unlike other emerging markets, portfolio flows have far exceeded FDI in India in recent years. Coupled with other capital flows consisting of official and commercial debt, NRI deposits, and other banking capital, net capital flows now amount to about 4.4 per cent of GDP.

The downturn in the Indian business cycle during the early part of this decade led to the emergence of a current account surplus, particularly because the existence of the relative exchange rate insensitive remittance flows. Consequently, foreign exchange reserves grew by more than US$ 120 billion between April 2000 and April 2006.

The management of these flows involved a mix of policy responses that had to keep an eye on the level of reserves, monetary policy objectives related to the interest rate, liquidity management, and maintenance of healthy financial market conditions with financial stability. Decisions to do with sterilization involve judgements on the character of the excess forex flows: are they durable, semi-durable, or transitory. This judgement itself depends on assessments about both the real economy and of financial sector developments. Moreover, at any given time, some flows could be of an enduring nature whereas others could be of short term, and hence reversible.

On an operational basis, sterilization operations through OMOs should take care of durable flows, whereas transitory flows can be managed through the normal daily operations of the LAF.

By 2003–4, sterilization operations, however, started appearing to be constrained by the finite stock of government securities held by the Reserve Bank. The legal restrictions on the Reserve Bank on issuing its own paper also placed constraints on future sterilization operations. Accordingly, an innovative scheme in the form of MSS was introduced in April 2004 wherein the Government of India dated securities/Treasury Bills are being issued to absorb enduring surplus liquidity. These dated securities/Treasury Bills are the same as those issued for normal market borrowings and this avoids segmentation of the market. Moreover, the MSS scheme brings transparency in regard to costs associated with sterilization operations. Hitherto, the costs of sterilization were fully borne by the Reserve Bank in the first instance and its impact was transmitted to the government in the form of lower profit transfers. With the introduction of the MSS, the cost in terms of interest payments would be borne by the government itself in a transparent manner.

It is relevant to note that the MSS has provided the Reserve Bank the flexibility to not only absorb liquidity but also to inject liquidity in case of need. This was evident during the second half of 2005–6 when liquidity conditions became tight in view of strong credit demand, increase in the government's surplus with the Reserve Bank and outflows on account of bullet redemption of India Millennium Deposits (IMDs) (about US$ 7 billion). In view of these circumstances, fresh issuances under the MSS were suspended between November 2005 and April 2006. Redemptions of securities/Treasury Bills issued earlier—along with active management of liquidity through repo/reverse repo operations under LAF—provided liquidity to the market and imparted stability to financial markets (Figure 7.2). With liquidity conditions improving, it was decided to again start issuing securities under the MSS from May 2006 onwards. The issuance of securities under the MSS has thus enabled the Reserve Bank to improve liquidity management in the system, to maintain stability in the foreign exchange market, and to conduct monetary policy in accordance with the stated objectives.

The Indian experience highlights the need for EMEs to allow greater flexibility in exchange rates but the authorities can also benefit from having the capacity to intervene in foreign exchange markets in view of the volatility observed in international capital flows. A key lesson is that flexibility and pragmatism are required in the management of the exchange rate and

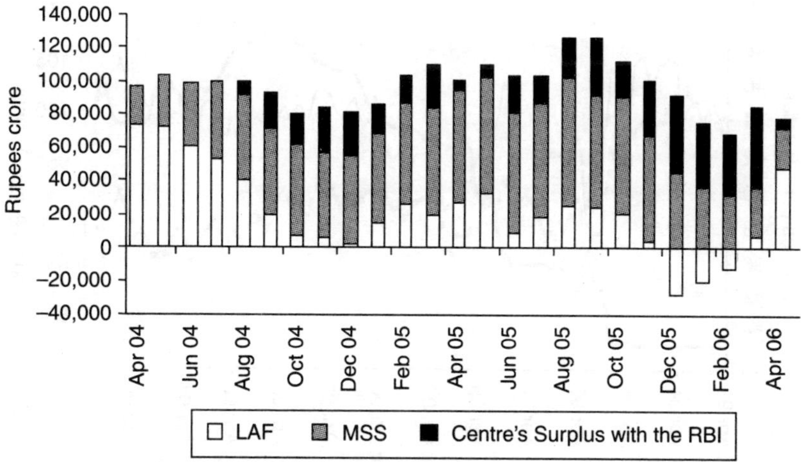

Figure 7.2 Liquidity Management

Source: RBI.

monetary policy in developing countries, rather than adherence to strict theoretical rules.

Three overarching features marked the transition of India to an open economy. First, the administered exchange rate became market determined and ensuring orderly conditions in the foreign exchange market became an objective of exchange rate management. Second, as already indicated, vicissitudes in capital flows came to influence the conduct of monetary policy. Third, lessons of the BoP crisis highlighted the need to maintain an adequate level of foreign exchange reserves and this in turn both enabled and constrained the conduct of monetary policy. From hindsight, it appears that the strategy paid off with the exchange rate exhibiting reasonable two-way movement (Figure 7.3).

Credit Delivery

Given that the Indian financial system is still predominantly bank-based, bank credit continues to be of great importance for funding different sectors of the economy. Consequent to deregulation of interest rates and substantial reduction in statutory pre-emptions, there was an expectation that credit flow would be correspondingly enhanced. In the event, banks continued to show a marked preference for investments in government securities with no reduction in the proportion of their assets being held in investments in government securities, until recently, when credit growth picked up in 2003–4. With the shift in approach from micro management of credit through

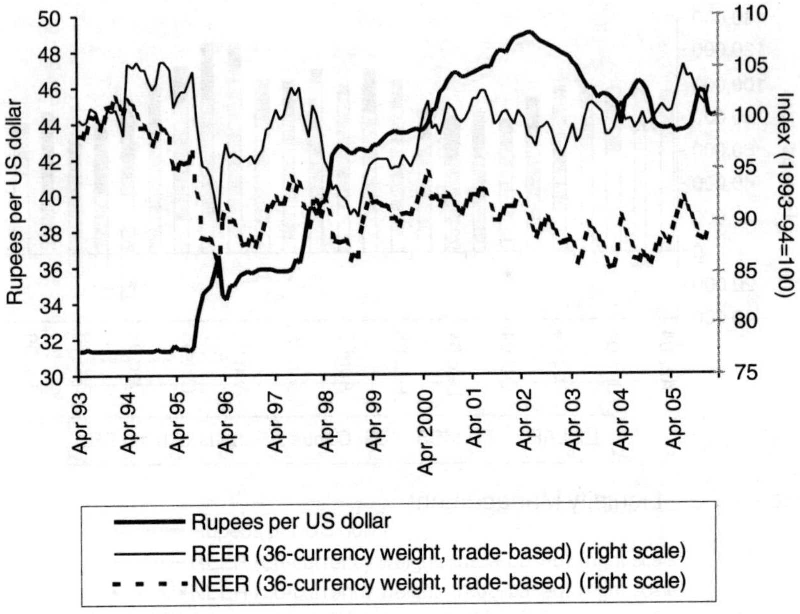

Figure 7.3 Exchange Rate

Note: REER—Real Effective Exchange Rate; NEER—Nomial Effective Exchange Rate.

Source: RBI.

various regulations, credit allocation targets, and administered interest rates, to a risk-based system of lending and market-determined interest rates, banks have to develop appropriate credit risk assessment techniques. Apart from promoting healthy credit growth, this is also critical for the efficiency of monetary management in view of the move to use of indirect instruments in monetary management.

The stagnation in credit flow observed during the late 1990s, in retrospect, was partly caused by reduction in demand on account of increase in real interest rates, turn down in the business cycle, and the significant business restructuring that occurred during that period. A sharp recovery has now taken place.

The stagnation during the 1990s has seen a sharp recovery in the past few years. The credit–GDP ratio, after moving in a narrow range of around 30 per cent between the mid-1980s and late 1990s, started increasing from 2000–01 onwards (Figure 7.4). It increased from 30 per cent during 1999–2000 to 41 per cent during 2004–5 and further to 48 per cent during 2005–6. However, sharp growth of credit in the past couple of years has also led to some areas of policy concern and dilemmas, as discussed later.

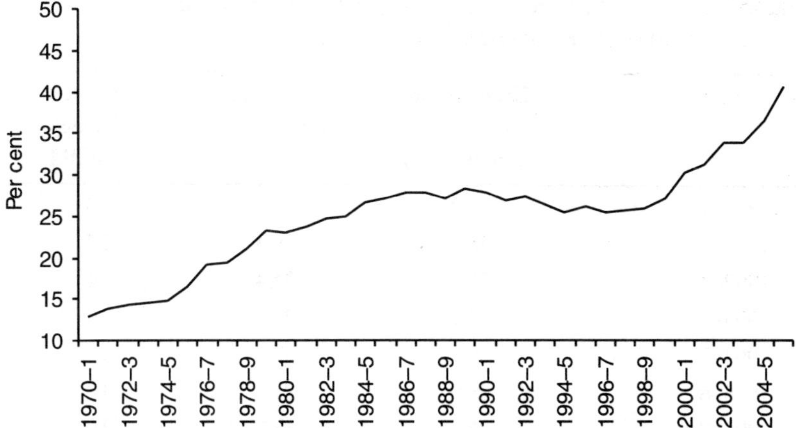

Figure 7.4 Credit–GDP Ratio

Source: RBI.

How did the monetary policy support the growth momentum in the economy? As inflation, along with inflation expectations, fell during the earlier period of this decade, policy interest rates were also brought down. Consequently, both nominal and real interest rates fell. The growth rate in interest expenses of the corporates declined consistently since 1995–6, from 25.0 per cent to a negative of 11.5 per cent in 2003–4 (Table 7.8). Such decline in interest costs has significant implications for the improvement in bottom lines of the corporates. Various indicators pertaining to interest costs, which can throw light on the impact of interest costs on corporate sector profits have turned positive in recent years.

SOME EMERGING ISSUES

This review of financial sector reforms and monetary policy has documented the calibrated and coordinated reforms that have been undertaken in India since the 1990s. In terms of outcomes, this strategy has achieved the broad objectives of price stability along with reduced medium- and long-term inflation expectations; the installation of an institutional framework and policy reform promoting relatively efficient price discovery of interest rates and the exchange rate; phased introduction of competition in banking along with corresponding improvements in regulation and supervision approaching international best practice, which has led to notable improvement in banking performance and financials. The implementation of these reforms has also involved the setting up or improvement of key financial infrastructure such as payment and settlement systems, and clearing and settlement systems for

Table 7.8 Monetary Policy and Corporate Performance: Interest Rate–Related Indicators

Year	Growth rate in interest expenses (%)	Debt service to total uses of funds	Interest coverage ratio (ICR)[a]
1990–1	16.2	22.4	2.8
1991–2	28.7	28.3	2.7
1992–3	21.6	24.4	2.4
1993–4	3.1	20.9	2.9
1994–5	8.1	27.2	3.5
1995–6	25.0	21.5	3.6
1996–7	25.7	18.7	2.9
1997–8	12.5	8.1	2.8
1998–9	11.1	17.6	2.6
1999–2000	6.7	17.6	2.8
2000–1	7.1	14.0	2.8
2001–2	–2.7	19.4	2.7
2002–3	–11.2	8.9	3.7
2003–4	–11.5	14.1	4.9

Note: [a] ICR is defined as earnings before interest, taxes, and depreciation (EBITD) over interest expenses. This is based on a sample of non-government non-financial public limited companies collected by the RBI.

debt and forex market functioning. All of this financial development has been achieved with the maintenance of a great degree of financial stability, along with overall movement of the economy towards a higher growth path.

With increased deregulation of financial markets and increased integration of the global economy, the 1990s were turbulent for global financial markets: Sixty-three countries suffered from systemic banking crises in that decade, much higher than forty-five in the 1980s. Among countries that experienced such crises, the direct cost of reconstructing the financial system was typically very high: for example, recapitalization of banks had cost 55 per cent of GDP in Argentina, 42 per cent in Thailand, 35 per cent in Korea, and 10 per cent in Turkey. There were high indirect costs of lost opportunities and slow economic growth in addition (McKinsey & Company, 2005). It is therefore particularly noteworthy that India could pursue its process of financial deregulation and opening of the economy without suffering financial crises during this turbulent period in world financial markets. The cost of recapitalization of PSBs at less than 1 per cent of GDP is therefore low in comparison. Whereas we can be legitimately gratified with this performance record, we now need to focus on the new issues that need to be addressed for the next phase of financial development.

That current annual GDP growth of around 8 per cent can be achieved in India at about 30 per cent rate of gross domestic investment suggests that the economy is functioning quite efficiently. We need to ensure that we maintain this level of efficiency and attempt to improve on it further. As the Indian economy continues on such a growth path and attempts to accelerate it, new demands are being placed on the financial system.

Growth Challenges for the Financial Sector

Higher sustained growth is contributing to the movement of large numbers of households into ever higher income categories, and hence higher consumption categories, along with enhanced demand for financial savings opportunities. In rural areas in particular, there also appears to be increasing diversification of productive opportunities. Thus, the banking system has to extend itself and innovate to respond to these new demands for both consumption and production purposes. This is particularly important since banking penetration is still low in India: there are only about ten to twelve automated teller machines (ATMs) in India per million population, as compared with over 50 in China, 170 in Thailand, and 500 in Korea. Moreover, the deposit to GDP ratio or the loans/GDP ratio is also low compared to other Asian countries (McKinsey & Company, 2005).

On the production side, industrial expansion has accelerated; merchandise trade growth is high; and there are vast demands for infrastructure investment, from the public sector, private sector, and through public–private partnerships. Furthermore, it is the service sector that has exhibited consistently high growth rates: the hospitality industry, shopping malls, entertainment industry, medical facilities, and the like, are all expanding fast. Thus a great degree of diversification is taking place in the economy and the banking system has to respond adequately to these new challenges, opportunities, and risks.

In dealing with these new consumer demands and production demands of rural enterprises and of SMEs in urban areas, banks have to innovate and look for new delivery mechanisms that economize on transaction costs and provide better access to the currently under-served. Innovative channels for credit delivery for serving these new rural credit needs, encompassing full supply chain financing, covering storage, warehousing, processing, and transportation from farm to market will have to be found. The budding expansion of non-agriculture service enterprises in rural areas will have to be financed to generate new income and employment opportunities. Greater efforts will need to be made on IT for record keeping, service delivery, reduction in transactions costs, risk assessment, and risk management. Banks will have to invest in new skills through new recruitment and through intensive training of existing personnel.

It is the PSBs that have the large and widespread reach, and hence have the potential for contributing effectively to achieve financial inclusion. But it is also they who face the most difficult challenges in human resource development. They will have to invest very heavily in skill enhancement at all levels: at the top level for new strategic goal setting; at the middle level for implementing these goals; and at the cutting edge lower levels for delivering the new service modes. Given the current age composition of employees in these banks, they will also face new recruitment challenges in the face of adverse compensation structures in comparison with the freer private sector. Meanwhile, the new private sector banks will themselves have to innovate and accelerate their reach into the emerging low income and rural market segments. They have the independence and flexibility to find the new business models necessary for serving these segments.

A number of policy initiatives are underway to aid this overall process of financial inclusion and increase in banking penetration. The Parliament has passed the Credit Information Bureau Act that will enable the setting up of CIBs through the mandatory sharing of information by banks. The Reserve Bank is in the process of issuing guidelines for the formation of these bureaus. As this process gathers force, it should contribute greatly in reducing the costs of credit quality assessment. Second, considerable work is in process for promoting micro-finance in the country, including the consideration of possible legislation for regulation of micro-finance institutions. Third, the Reserve Bank has issued guidelines to banks enabling the outsourcing of certain functions including the use of agencies such as post offices for achieving better outreach. These are all efforts in the right direction, but much more needs to be done to really achieve financial inclusion in India.

The challenges that are emerging are right across the size spectrum of business activities. On the one hand, the largest firms are attaining economic sizes such that they are reaching the prudential exposure limits of banks, even though they are still small relative to the large global multi-national companies. On the other hand, with changes in technology, there is new activity at the small and medium level in all spheres of activity. To cope with the former, the largest Indian banks have to be encouraged to expand fast, both through organic growth and through consolidation; and the corporate debt market has to be developed to enable further direct recourse to financial markets for the largest firms. For serving and contributing to the growth of firms at the lower end, banks have to strengthen their risk assessment systems, along with better risk management. Funding new entrepreneurs and activities is a fundamentally risky business because of the lack of a previous record and inadequate availability of collateral, but it is the job of banks to take such risk, but in a measured fashion. Given the history of PSBs outlined earlier, such a change in approach requires a change in mind set, but also focused training in risk assessment, risk management, and marketing.

Various policy measures are in process to help this transition along. The Reserve Bank issued new guidelines in 2004 on 'Ownership and Governance in Private Sector Banks'. These guidelines have increased the minimum capital for private sector banks to Rs 3 billion; provided enhanced guidance on the fit and proper nature of owners, board members, and top management of these banks; and placed limitations on the extent of dominant shareholdings. These measures are designed to promote the healthy growth of private sector banks along with better corporate governance as they assume greater weight in the economy. An issue of relevance here is that of financial stability. To a certain extent, the predominance of government-owned banks has contributed to financial stability in the country. Experience has shown that even the deterioration in bank financials does not lead to erosion of consumer confidence in such banks. This kind of consumer confidence does not extend to private sector banks. Hence, as they gain in size and share, capital enhancement and sound corporate governance become essential for financial stability. Second, the lending ability of banks has been potentially constrained by the existing provisions for statutory pre-emption of funds for investment in government securities. A bill has been introduced in Parliament to amend the existing Banking Regulation Act to eliminate the minimum 25 per cent limit of investment in government securities. As the fiscal situation improves consistent with the FRBM Act, it will then be possible to reduce the statutory pre-emption, enabling greater fund flow to the private sector for growth. Third, the bill also provides for raising of capital through Basel II consistent innovative instruments, enabling the capital expansion of banks needed for their growth.

Greater Capital Market Openness: Some Issues

An important feature of the Indian financial reform process has been the calibrated opening of the capital account along with current account convertibility. The government and the Reserve Bank have already appointed a committee to advise on a roadmap for fuller capital account convertibility. Decisions on further steps will be taken after that committee submits its report. Meanwhile, we can note some of the issues that will need attention as we achieve fuller capital account openness.

A key component of Indian capital account management has been the management of volatility in the forex market, and of its consequential impact on the money market and hence on monetary operations guided by the extant monetary policy objectives. This has been done, as outlined, through a combination of forex market intervention, domestic liquidity management, and administrative instructions on regulating external debt in different forms. Correspondingly, progress has been made on the functioning of the government securities market, forex market, and money market and their progressive integration. Particular attention has been given to the exposure of financial intermediaries to foreign exchange liabilities, and of the government in their borrowing programme. So far, some degree of success has been achieved in that the exchange rate responds to the supply demand conditions in the market and exhibits two way flexibility; the interest rate is similarly flexible and market-determined; healthy growth has taken place in trade in both goods and services; and inward capital flows have been healthy.

We have to recognize that fuller capital account openness will lead to a confrontation with the impossible trinity of simultaneous attainment of independent monetary policy, open capital account, and managed exchange rate. At best, only two out of the three would be feasible. With a more open capital account as given and if a choice is made of an 'anchor' role for monetary policy, exchange rate management will be affected. A freely floating exchange rate should, in fact, engender the independence of monetary policy. It needs to be recognized, however, that the impact of exchange rate changes on the real sector is significantly different for reserve currency countries and for developing countries like India. For the former which specialize in technology-intensive products the degree of exchange rate pass through is low, enabling exporters and importers to ignore temporary shocks and set stable product prices to maintain monopolistic positions, despite large currency fluctuations. Moreover, mature and well-developed financial markets in these countries have absorbed the risk associated with exchange rate fluctuations with negligible spillover on the real activity. On the other hand, for the majority of developing countries which specialize in labour-intensive and low and intermediate technology products, profit margins in the intensely competitive markets for these products are very thin and vulnerable to pricing power by large retail chains. Consequently, exchange rate volatility has significant employment, output, and distributional consequences (Mohan, 2004a, 2005). In this context, managing exchange rate volatility would continue to be an issue requiring attention.

A further challenge for policy in the context of fuller capital account opennes will be to preserve the financial stability of different markets as greater deregulation is done on capital outflows and on debt inflows. The vulnerability of financial intermediaries can perhaps be addressed through prudential regulations and their supervision; risk management of non-financial entities will have to be through further developments in both the corporate debt market and the forex market, which enable them to manage their risks through the use of newer market instruments. This will require market development, enhancement of regulatory capacity in these areas, as well as human resource development in both financial intermediaries and non-financial entities. Given the volatility of capital flows, it remains to be seen whether financial market development in a country like India can be such that this volatility does not result in unacceptable disruption in exchange rate determination with inevitable real sector consequences, and in domestic monetary conditions. If not, what will be the kind of market interventions that will continue to be needed and how effective will they be?

Another aspect of greater capital market openness concerns the presence of foreign banks in India. The government and Reserve Bank outlined a roadmap on foreign investment in banks in India in February 2005, which provides guidelines on the extent of their presence until 2009. This roadmap is consistent with the overall guidelines issued simultaneously on ownership and governance in private sector banks in India. The presence of foreign banks in the country has been very useful in bringing greater competition in certain segments in the market. They are significant participants in investment banking and in development of the forex market. With the changes that have taken place in the United States and other countries, where the traditional barriers between banking, insurance, and securities companies have been removed, the size of the largest financial conglomerates has become extremely large. Between 1995 and 2004, the size of the largest bank in the world has grown three-fold by asset size, from about US$ 0.5 trillion to US$ 1.5 trillion, almost double the size of Indian GDP. This has happened through a great degree of merger activity: for example, J.P. Morgan Chase is the result of mergers among 550 banks and financial institutions. The ten biggest commercial banks in the United States now control almost half of that country's banking assets, up from 29 per cent just ten years ago (*The Economist*, 2006). Hence, with fuller capital account convertibility and greater presence of foreign banks over time, a number of issues will arise. First, if these large global banks have emerged as a result of real economies of scale and scope, how will smaller national banks compete in countries like India, and will they themselves need to generate a larger international presence? Second, there is considerable discussion today on overlaps and potential conflicts between home country regulators of foreign banks and host country regulators: how will these be addressed and resolved in the years to come? Third, given that operations in one country such as India are typically small relative to the global operations of these large banks, the attention of top management devoted to any particular country is typically low. Consequently, any market or regulatory transgressions committed in one country by such a bank, which may have a significant impact on banking or financial market of that country, is likely to have negligible impact on the bank's global operations. It has been seen in recent years that even relatively strong regulatory action taken by regulators against such global banks has had negligible market or reputational impact on them in terms of their stock price or similar metrics. Thus, there is loss of regulatory effectiveness as a result of the presence of such financial conglomerates. Hence there is inevitable tension between the benefits that such global conglomerates bring and some regulatory and market structure and competition issues that may arise.

Along with the emergence of international financial conglomerates, we are also witnessing similar growth of Indian conglomerates. As in most countries, the banking, insurance, and securities companies each come under the jurisdiction of their respective regulators. A beginning has been made in organized cooperation between the regulators on the regulation of such conglomerates, with agreement on who would be the lead regulator in each case. In the United States, it is a financial holding company (FHC) that is at the core of each conglomerate, with each company being its subsidiary. There is, as yet, no commonality in the financial structure of each conglomerate in India: in some the parent company is the banking company, whereas in others there is a mix of structure. For Indian conglomerates to be competitive, and for them to grow to a semblance of international size, they will need continued improvement in clarity in regulatory approach.

As the country's financial system faces each of these challenges in the coming years, we will also need to adapt monetary policy to the imperatives brought by higher growth and greater openness of the economy.

High Credit Growth and Monetary Policy

High and sustained growth of the economy in conjunction with low inflation is the central concern of monetary policy in India. As noted above, we have been reasonably successful in meeting these objectives. In this context, one issue still remains: whether monetary policy should have only price stability as its sole objective, as suggested by proponents of inflation targeting. Several central banks, such as Bank of Canada, Bank of England, and the Reserve Bank of New Zealand, have adopted explicit inflation targets. Others, whose credibility in fighting inflation is long established (notably, the US Federal Reserve), do not set explicit annual inflation targets. Central banks are thus clearly divided on the advisability of setting explicit inflation targets. In view of the difficulties encountered with monetary targeting and exchange rate pegged regimes, a number of central banks including some in emerging economies have adopted inflation targeting frameworks.[3]

The simple principle of inflation targeting thus is also not so simple and poses problems for monetary policy making in developing countries. Moreover, concentrating only on numerical inflation objectives may reduce the flexibility of monetary policy, especially with respect to other policy goals, particularly that of growth.

Although price stability is an important objective of monetary policy, we have not favoured the adoption of the inflation targeting framework for a variety of reasons. First, supply shocks emanating from food and oil remain a key source of inflationary pressures in the Indian economy. Thus, in the short-run, headline inflation can deviate significantly from the inflation target accepted under the IT framework. In view of these factors, deviation of headline inflation from the target could be quite common and could undermine the credibility of the target. Furthermore, like other EMEs, food and oil carry large weights in the major price indices in India—as high as 50–70 per cent in the various consumer price indices. In such an environment, core measures of inflation may not carry much weight and acceptance with the general public. While such core—or other underlying—measures of inflation are useful inputs for monetary policy, they are not of much use in explaining the conduct of monetary policy to the public. Second, although there has been significant development of the various segments of the financial market, the effective transmission of monetary impulses continues to be impeded by certain rigidities such as the administered interest rate mechanism in the case of small savings. The Government ownership of public sector banks and the concomitant directions also create wedges in the effective transmission of monetary measures. These rigidities can blunt the intended impact of monetary measures and hence constrain the adoption of inflation targeting. Finally, it may be noted that the Indian record in terms of actual inflation outcome is rather satisfactory and is indeed better than many EMEs. Ultimately, it is the commitment to ensuring price stability that matters rather than the inflation targeting framework per se. The current framework of monetary policy provides the necessary flexibility to deal with large exogenous shocks, while also anchoring inflation expectations.

A contemporary issue in central banking is the appropriate response of monetary policy to sharp asset price movements that may accompany high corporate growth. In an era of price stability and well-anchored inflation expectations, imbalances in the economy need not show up immediately in overt inflation. Increased central bank credibility is a double-edged sword as it makes it more likely that unsustainable booms could take longer to show up in overt inflation. For instance, unsustainable asset prices artificially boost accounting profits of corporates and thereby mitigate the need for price increases; similarly, large financial gains by employees can partly substitute for higher wage claims. In an upturn of the business cycle, self-reinforcing processes develop, characterized by rising asset prices and loosening external financial constraints. 'Irrational exuberance' can drive asset prices to unrealistic levels, even as the prices of currently traded goods and services exhibit few signs of inflation (Crockett, 2001). These forces operate in reverse in the contraction phase. In the upswing of the business cycle, financial imbalances, therefore, get built-up. There is, thus, a 'paradox of credibility' (Borio and White, 2003). In view of these developments, it is felt that credit and monetary aggregates—which are being ignored by many central banks in view of the perceived instability of money demand—need to be monitored closely since sharp growth in these aggregates is a useful indicator of future instability.

In India, like other countries, we have also seen large rallies in asset prices. Concomitantly, credit to the private sector has exhibited sharp growth in the past two years—averaging almost 30 per cent per annum. While the credit growth has been broad-based, credit to the retail sector is emerging as a new avenue of deployment for the banking sector led by individual housing loans. To illustrate, the share of housing in outstanding bank credit has increased from 2.4 per cent in March 1990 to 12.0 per cent by March 2006, while that of other retail segments (other than housing) has risen from 4.0 per cent to 11.3 per cent. Over the same period, the share of industry went down from 48.7 per cent to 37.4 per cent.

Nonetheless, in the light of high credit growth, there is a need to ensure that asset quality is maintained. Since growth in credit was relatively higher in a few sectors such as retail credit and real commercial estate, monetary policy faces a dilemma in terms of instruments. An increase in policy rate across the board could adversely affect even the productive sectors of the economy such as industry and agriculture. While policy rates have indeed been raised, they have been mainly aimed at reining in inflation expectations in view of continuing pressures from high and volatile crude oil prices. Therefore, while ensuring that credit demand for the productive sectors of the economy is met, the Reserve Bank has resorted to prudential measures in order to engineer a 'calibrated' deceleration in the overall growth of credit to the commercial sector. Accordingly, the Reserve Bank has raised risk weights on loans to these sectors. It also more than doubled provisioning requirements on standard loans for the specific sectors from 0.4 per cent to 1.0 per cent. Thus, the basic objective has been to ensure that the growth process is facilitated while ensuring price and financial stability in the economy.

It is in this context, and consistent with the multiple-indicator approach adopted by the Reserve Bank, that monetary policy in India has consistently emphasized the need to be watchful about indications of rising aggregate demand embedded in consumer and business confidence, asset prices, corporate performance, the sizeable growth of reserve money and money supply, the rising trade and current account deficits, and, in particular, the quality of credit growth. In retrospect, this risk-sensitive approach has served us well in containing aggregate demand pressures and second round effects to an extent. It has also ensured that constant vigil is maintained on threats to financial stability through a period when inflation was on the upturn and asset prices, especially in housing and real estate, are emerging as a challenge to monetary authorities worldwide. Significantly, it has also reinforced the growth momentum in the economy. It is noteworthy that the cyclical expansion in bank credit has extended over an unprecedented thirty months without encountering any destabilizing volatility but this situation warrants enhanced vigilance.

SUMMARY

The financial system in India, through a measured, gradual, cautious, and steady process, has undergone substantial transformation. It has been transformed into a reasonably sophisticated, diverse, and resilient system through well-sequenced and coordinated policy measures aimed at making the Indian financial sector more competitive, efficient, and stable. Concomitantly, effective monetary management has enabled price stability while ensuring availability of credit to support investment demand and growth in the economy. Finally, the multi-pronged approach towards managing capital account in conjunction with prudential and cautious approach to financial liberalization has ensured financial stability in contrast to the experience of many developing and emerging economies. This is despite the fact that we faced a large number of shocks, both global and domestic. Monetary policy and financial sector reforms in India had to be fine-tuned to meet the challenges emanating from all these shocks. Viewed in this light, the success in maintaining price and financial stability is all the more creditworthy.

As the economy ascends a higher growth path and as it is subjected to greater opening and financial integration with the rest of the world, the financial sector in all its aspects will need further considerable development, along with corresponding measures to continue regulatory modernization and strengthening. The overall objective of maintaining price stability in the context of economic growth and financial stability will remain.

AFTERWORD

The important updates to this chapter 7 (since June 2006 when it was written) include greater flexibility to the RBI in the prescription of CRR and SLR following the removal of (a) the floor of 3 per cent and the ceiling of 15 per cent on the CRR following amendments to the RBI Act and (b) the floor of 25 per cent on the SLR following amendments to the BR Act. The prescribed SLR has since then been cut to 24 per cent. The CRR has been varied over time as warranted by the evolving macroeconomic and financial conditions. Thus, CRR was initially reduced from 15 per cent in the early 1990s to 4.5 per cent by March 2004 as a part of the financial sector reform process. However, in view of large and growing volume of net capital inflows, and in order to maintain macroeconomic and financial stability, the CRR was, since September 2004, raised in stages to 9 per cent by end August 2008. It was cut to 5.5 per cent by November 2008 in response to the impact of the global financial crisis on domestic liquidity conditions. The CRR continues to remain one of the monetary policy tools. While the medium-term policy objective of reducing the CRR to 3 per cent remains, the Reserve Bank retains the flexibility to change the CRR in either direction depending on the prevailing macroeconomic and monetary conditions.

The width of the LAF corridor has also varied in response to the evolving macroeconomic conditions and the volume of uncertainty. The width was initially reduced from 150 basis points in March 2004 to 100 basis points by April 2005, but was increased in stages to 300 basis points by July 2008. The width came down to 150 basis points in November 2008 following the cut in the repo rate to 7.5 per cent. The process of deepening and widening of financial markets has continued with the introduction of short-selling and 'when isssued' market in the government securities market and phased liberalization of capital outflows in the foreign exchange market.

Finally, since 1 April 2008, Indian banks having presence outside and all foreign banks operating in India have migrated to the standardized approach for credit risk and the basic indicator approach for operational risk under Basel II. All other scheduled commercial banks are encouraged to migrate to Basel II, but in any case not later than 1 April 2009.

Notes

[1] Reddy (2002) noted that the approach towards financial sector reforms in India has been based on five principles: (a) cautious and appropriate sequencing of reform measures; (b) introduction of mutually reinforcing norms; (c) introduction of complementary reforms across monetary, fiscal, and external sectors; (d) development of financial institutions; and (e) development of financial markets.

[2] The Reserve Bank has raised its key policy rate—the reverse repo rate in phases—by 100 basis points since October 2004.

[3] Although these inflation targeting countries were able to reduce inflation or maintain low inflation during the 1990s, stylized evidence shows that even non-IT countries were successful in this endeavour.

References

Ahluwalia, M.S. (2002), 'Economic Reforms in India since 1991: Has Gradualism Worked?' *Journal of Economic Perspectives*, 16 (3), pp. 67–88.

Borio, C. and W. White (2003), 'Whither Monetary and Financial Stability? The Implications of Evolving Policy Regimes', BIS Working Paper No. 147.

Crockett, A. (2001), 'Monetary Policy and Financial Stability', lecture Delivered at the HKMA Distinguished Lecture, February.

Mohan, R. (2004a), 'Challenges to Monetary Policy in a Globalising Context', *Reserve Bank of India Bulletin*, January.

_____ (2004b), 'Financial Sector Reforms in India: Policies and Performance Analysis', *Reserve Bank of India Bulletin*, October.

_____ (2005), 'Some Apparent Puzzles for Contemporary Monetary Policy', *Reserve Bank of India Bulletin*, December.

_____ (2006a), 'Reforms, Productivity and Efficiency in Banking: The Indian Experience", *Reserve Bank of India Bulletin*, March.

_____ (2006b), 'Coping with Liquidity Management in India: A Practitioner's View', *Reserve Bank of India Bulletin*, April.

_____ (2006c), 'Recent Trends in the Indian Debt Market and Current Initiatives', *Reserve Bank of India Bulletin*, April.

_____ (2006d), *Evolution of Central Banking in India*, available at *www.rbi.org.in*.

Reddy, Y.V. (2002), 'Monetary and Financial Sector Reforms in India: A Practitioner's Perspective', *Reserve Bank of India Bulletin*, May.

_____ (2006a), *Challenges and Implications of Basel II for Asia*, available at *www.rbi.org.in*.

RBI (2004), *Report on Currency and Finance*, 2003–04.

The Economist (2006), *Special Report on International Banking*, 20–26 May.

McKinsey & Company (2005), *Indian Banking 2010: Towards a High Performing Sector*, New Delhi.

8 Challenges to Monetary Policy in a Globalizing World*

Recent global developments have transformed the environment in which monetary policy operates, throwing up opportunities as well as challenges. Globalization has expanded economic interdependence and interaction of countries greatly. This has created the need for greater coordination in terms of the design of appropriate institutional architecture as well as standardization reflected in the adoption of similar monetary policy approaches. It has also been associated with a dramatic lowering of inflation worldwide. Central banks have seized these opportunities to bring about institutional reforms to enhance their own accountability and credibility of monetary policy making. Moreover, they have had to hone their technical and specialist management skills to acquire adequate competence to deal with the emerging complexities of financial markets.

The more recent evolution of the global economy has accentuated the challenges that face monetary authorities. Increasingly, monetary policy decisions have to be made in an environment of heightened uncertainty. Structural changes associated with globalization have increased the uncertainty in interpreting macroeconomic indicators regarding the state of the economy. Another form of uncertainty stems from the strategic interaction between private agents and monetary policy authorities and, in particular, the role of expectations in the monetary transmission mechanism. Financial markets, driven by massive cross-border capital flows and the IT revolution, immediately transfer the valuation of risks associated with uncertainty across the globe and this can lead to contagion. Indeed, global interdependence is marked by common shocks and a 'confidence channel' rapidly transmits these shocks to various parts of the world.

All this has rendered the conduct of monetary policy extremely complex in such an environment of interdependent risks. Therefore, even though

* Lecture delivered on the occasion of 22nd Anniversary of the Centre for Banking Studies at Central Bank of Sri Lanka, Colombo, on 21 November 2003.

monetary policy is conducted towards achieving domestic objectives, central banks have to follow developments across the world carefully. More than ever before, the choice of monetary arrangements depends on the choices that other countries make (Meltzer, 1997).

In this chapter, I propose to dwell upon the uncertainties that characterize the monetary policy environment, the underlying macroeconomic conditions in which monetary policy has to be set, the process of inflation and the changing institutional response to the commitment to price stability, the role of capital flows, and what the future holds in store. Against this backdrop, I hope to shed some light on the emerging discussion among central bankers about the course of monetary policy that is of greater relevance to developing countries such as ours.

THE CURRENT GLOBAL ECONOMIC SCENARIO

The growing internationalization of monetary policy has been brought into sharp focus by the synchronized global downturn since the late 1990s. In response, monetary authorities all over the world have made concerted efforts to ease their policy stance significantly. The United States has powered the world economy during the last seven to eight years and has been responsible for about 60 per cent of world growth. Despite bursting of the stock market bubble, a rash of corporate governance problems, and the IT bubble, the United States has been the main engine of world growth in recent years and has been partly responsible for the recovery of Asian countries after the 1997 crisis. In the bargain, the United States has accumulated twin deficits—CAD of 5 per cent and fiscal deficit of 6 per cent (a sharp turnaround from a surplus of 1.2 per cent in 2000) (Figure 8.1). With the emergence of such an imbalance in the United States, other regions in the world have to exhibit an equal and opposite imbalance of their own. Ironically, it is the developing countries of Asia who are funding the CAD of the United States and exhibiting surplus. The central banks of Asia are financing roughly 3–3.5 per cent of the CAD of the United States and most of its fiscal deficit, as compared to the earlier situation where it was private sector flows that were funding these deficits. In view of the difficulties in monetary management that the situation entails, this situation is clearly not sustainable indefinitely. There are no short-cut solutions since the problems are deep, structural, and interdependent: hence these cannot be solved through independent or unilateral action. For example, difficult structural reforms are necessary in the Euro area; more structural reforms are needed in Japan, particularly in the financial sector; India has a large fiscal deficit problem; and China cannot afford a major appreciation. Hence, relatively coordinated medium-term action is called for among the major economies of the world. Unilateral action by any country is unlikely to solve its own problems.

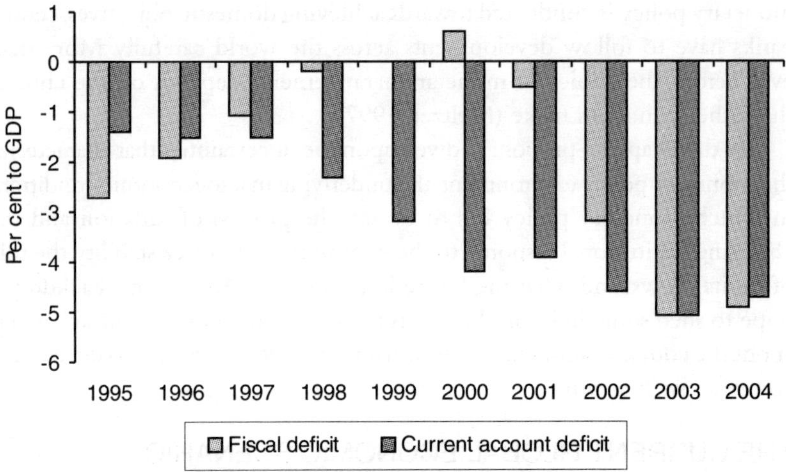

Figure 8.1 United States—Macroeconomic Imbalances

Source: *World Economic Outlook* (*WEO*), IMF, September 2003.

Recent months have seen the emerging signs of a recovery in economic activity, particularly in the United States, Japan, and emerging Asia. In the United States, the pace of growth has picked up, assisted by expansionary macroeconomic policies and supportive financial conditions. Equity and bond markets have responded with optimism to prospects of recovery with investor interest returning to technology stocks more rapidly than to other sectors. In Japan, there are stronger signs in the third quarter that a cyclical upswing is underway, led by industrial activity and exports. In the United Kingdom and Australia, signs of recovery are clearly evident with rising household spending reflected in retail price inflation, prompting monetary authorities in these two countries to raise key policy interest rates against inflation surprises. China continues to grow at a remarkably strong pace while activity in other parts of Asia is bouncing back from the effects of Severe Acute Respiratory Syndrome (SARS). There is nevertheless considerable uncertainty regarding the durability of the pick-up. In the United States, labour markets remain sluggish and significant excess capacity persists. Moreover, the substantial support provided to consumption by tax cuts is unlikely to be sustained. Despite the prospects of stronger growth, Japan continues to experience deflation. The ongoing concerns relating to structural weaknesses in the financial system remain. In contrast to the rest of the world, the Euro area remains conspicuously weak although there are tentative signs of a modest recovery in recent months. Household demand remains sluggish and the unemployment rate for the area as a whole has risen.

The burden of adjustment to the global slowdown has been highly asymmetric and this raises the risks associated with sustaining the recovery. The United States has been virtually alone among the Organisation for Economic Co-operation and Development (OECD) countries in pursuing an aggressive and flexible countercyclical monetary and fiscal policy—cuts in policy interest rates have been the largest and the swing in structural government balance from a surplus of 0.6 per cent of GDP in 2000 to a deficit of 5.1 per cent in 2003 is the largest in three decades. Global growth will continue to be led by the United States, but significant downside risks could emanate from the emergence of the record current account and fiscal deficits of the United States. While the depreciation of the US dollar has so far been relatively orderly, further and substantial depreciation remains a danger to global recovery in the shadow of the twin deficits. History suggests that even an orderly adjustment in key exchange rates is likely to be associated with a slowdown in the US growth—and, if growth in the rest of the world remains weak, in global growth as well (IMF, 2003). The continuing dependence of the world on the United States heightens the risks of disorderly adjustment, particularly if it translates into an off-setting appreciation of the Euro. In contrast to the mid-1980s, when the United States ran CADs of similar order as in 2003, neither Europe nor Japan is in a position today to pick up the slack. Looking ahead, it is unlikely that the United States can provide the degree of support to the global economy that it has in the past. In particular, high fiscal deficits would offset the longer-term benefits of tax cuts and rising debt service burdens in the household sector will curb future consumption spending.

In the Euro area, whereas monetary policy can be adjudged to have been successful in an inflation targeting framework (Figure 8.2), the economic slowdown has been deep and prolonged, with the GDP declining in the second quarter of 2003. The largest economies—Germany, France, the Netherlands, and Italy—are in recession with high levels of unemployment. The unemployment rate is 8.8 per cent for the Euro area as a whole and even higher in some individual countries: 13.2 per cent in Belgium, 9.7 per cent in France, 10.5 per cent in Germany, 8.5 per cent in Italy, and 11.4 per cent in Spain (Figure 8.3). Despite some recent improvement in expectations, household and business confidence remains depressed. The poor performance of Germany, in particular, threatens to hold back the region's recovery. Corporate balance sheets are still adjusting to the bursting of the asset price bubble of the late 1990s and this is holding down investment spending. Exports have been adversely affected by weak external demand as well as the substantial appreciation of the Euro over the past two years. Monetary policy has been accommodative but different inflation and unemployment rates in different countries blur the effectiveness of the common monetary policy. A more activist approach is warranted especially when downside risks to individual countries have potentially area-wide spillovers. Although Germany and France are expected to post fiscal deficits above 4 per cent of GDP in 2003, the scope for countercyclical fiscal policy is limited by the Stability and Growth Pact. Structural reforms hold the key to improving Europe's economic performance, including further liberalization of labour and product markets, pension reforms, and offsetting measures to deal with the ageing of population.

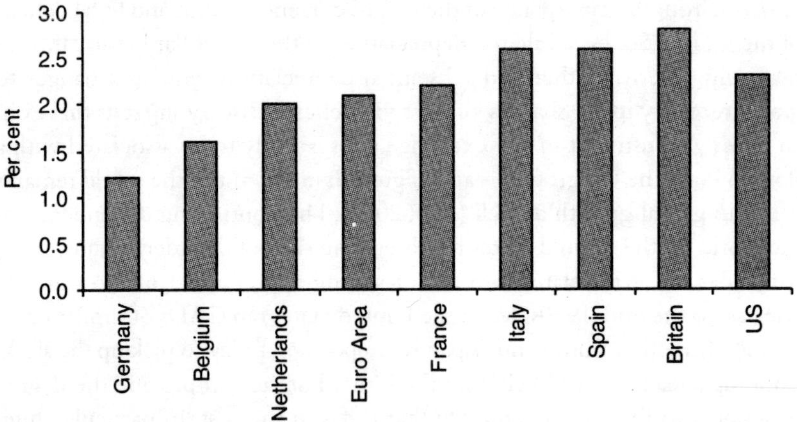

Figure 8.2 Inflation in Advanced Economies

Source: *The Economist*.

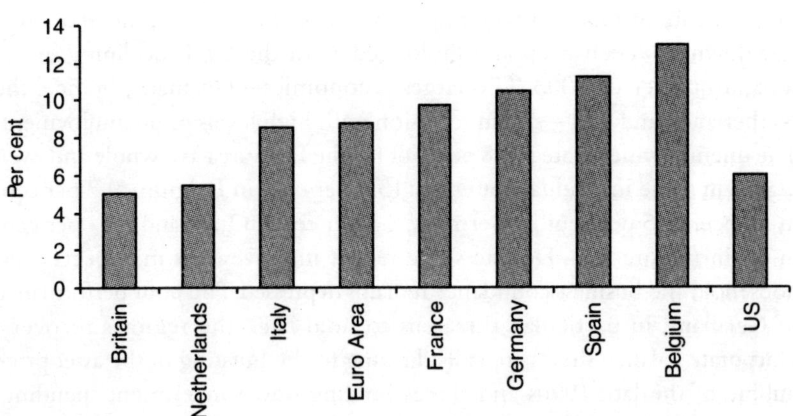

Figure 8.3 Unemployment in Advanced Economies

Source: *The Economist*.

In Japan, macroeconomic performance during 2003 has exceeded expectations alongside an improved external environment and upturn in equity markets. The outlook remains overcast with deflationary pressures and persistent weakness in the financial sector. The possibility of declines in equity or bond prices, a sustained appreciation of the Yen, and rising public debt remain dangers to a durable recovery. More rapid and bolder reforms in the financial sector are needed to address the large overhang of NPLs and the poor quality of capital in the banking sector. Financial sector measures need to be complemented by corporate restructuring. Quantitative easing of monetary policy has kept short-term interest rates at zero, but has not been aggressive enough to end deflation. The build-up of public debt and pressures from population ageing necessitate a medium-term strategy to impart sustainability to fiscal policy.

Overall, global macroeconomic imbalances and the associated misalignment of the G-3 currencies remain the most serious threat to a broad-based and robust recovery. This has implications for the pattern of capital flows. In contrast to preceding years, the US CAD has been financed primarily by sale of government and corporate paper rather than equity inflows. The bulk of these investments has been by central banks, particularly those in Asia. This is clearly unsustainable and adjustments will be needed to achieve medium-term stability. An eventual narrowing of the US CAD will require emerging economies to share in the adjustment to prevent an undue burden on the Euro area. A current issue of concern is the practice of greater flexibility in the exchange rate regimes of these countries and the resulting efforts on the real economy. Studies have shown that greater volatility in developing countries' real exchange rates has been associated with greater misalignment in G-3 countries with disruptive effect on both trade and finance channels. This emerges as a major source of uncertainty for the conduct of monetary policy.

The current imbalances in the world where Asian countries are financing Western countries, particularly the United States, could have their roots in long-term demographic imbalances. The long-term demographics facing the world, which have an effect on the savings rate, are not encouraging. The demographics in Europe, Japan, and the United States are against high saving rates. The median ages in Japan, Europe, and the United States are forty-one, forty, and thirty-five years, respectively. Current trends indicate that the median age in Japan will increase to fifty by 2025. The situation in the United States may not turn adverse due to its flexible immigration policies. Within Asia, India and China can expect their savings rate to increase further, given that the private savings of these two countries are among the highest in the world, and in view of their favourable demographics over the next twenty years. Countries like India and China, which account for a large proportion of world population, also have low urbanization levels of 30–35 per cent and will be moving to 50–55 per cent in the next twenty to thirty years. This would necessitate higher infrastructure investment requiring higher capital inflows and a higher CAD. Thus, if the Asian countries are to run large capital account surpluses and CADs, the situation in the United States and Europe would meet reversal. The issue is to try to comprehend what would be required for this macro reversal to occur. The current demographic trends in Europe and Japan are not sustainable. In the future, they may not be able to afford the pension system and social security as they exist now. The only solution in Europe seems to be US-type of immigration policies towards labour market reforms. Currently, this is not possible because of high unemployment.

INFLATION: WHAT IS GOING ON

In this brief overview of the global economic situation today, I have tried to indicate that global imbalances are inter-related and how monetary policy-making in countries like ours has become that much more difficult on a day-to-day basis. The most notable achievement in recent years has been the substantial success in almost all countries in reducing inflation to the lowest level in several decades. Sustained inflation is a relatively modern phenomenon. Until World War I, the international experience was one of long-run price stability. Following the turbulence of the inter-war period, World War II, and the Korean War of the early 1950s, the Vietnam war of the 1960s and early 1970s, inflation gradually increased from the late 1960s, partly as a result of expansionary fiscal and monetary policies. The massive oil price hike of 1973 stepped up global inflation to double digits in the United States and western Europe. There was a huge transfer of resources to the Middle East from the rest of the world including Asia. The lasting consequence of this development of the 1970s has been the migration of workers from countries like ours who are now remitting back large sums of money on a sustained basis. Although inflation abated in 1978, it rose to double-digit levels again by the end of 1979 following the second oil shock. Inflation finally broke in 1982 under the impact of aggressive disinflationary policies.

The 1980s were marked by strong and widespread efforts to restore reasonable price stability through a combination of tight monetary policy, fiscal consolidation, and structural reforms. The reduction in inflation, facilitated by a significant decline in oil prices, set the stage for a robust economic recovery that continued till the end of the 1980s. Another inflation episode in 1989–90 due to the hardening of oil prices was met with aggressive monetary policy action which enabled a cooling-off by 1991 at the cost of a much shallower recession than the early 1980s.

Since then, the world has been going through one of the longest phases of low inflation in post-World War II history. The decline in inflation is evident across countries at different stages of development (Figure 8.4). It has been most spectacular in developing countries where inflation fell from 31 per cent in early 1980s to under 6 per cent in 2000–3. In Latin America and the countries in transition where inflation averaged 230 per cent and 360 per cent, respectively, during 1990–4, it is projected at around 10 per cent in 2003. Out of 184 members of the IMF, forty-four countries had inflation greater than 40 per cent in 1992. In 2003, this number had fallen to three. For industrial countries, inflation, currently at around 2 per cent, has fallen below the lows of the 1950s. Arguably, deflation threatens more countries today than does high inflation.

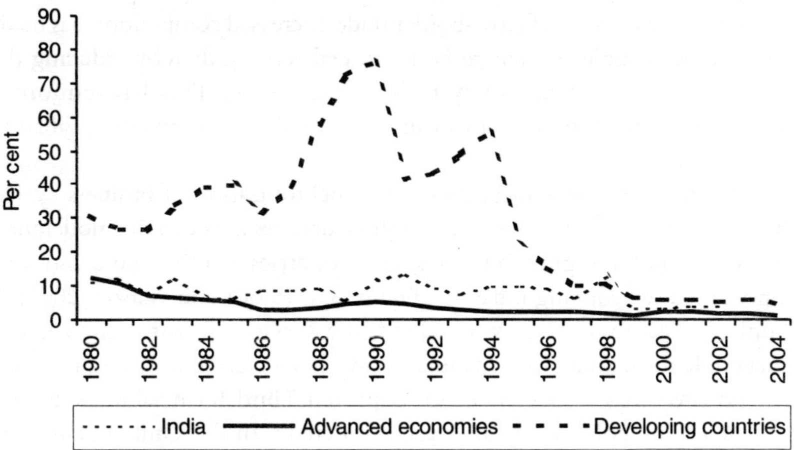

Figure 8.4 Inflation Rates

Source: *WEO*, IMF, September, 2003.

What has brought about this significant decline in inflation globally? A significant strand in the literature points to institutional changes in the conduct of monetary policy—independent central banks, increased transparency, greater accountability through contractual frameworks, and greater coordination between monetary and fiscal authorities—which have enhanced the reputation of monetary authorities and increased public credibility in their ability to deliver low inflation. An equally influential body of work, however, suggests that monetary authorities have just been lucky and that there are other factors at work such as increased level of competition due to the forces of globalization, successful fiscal consolidation in developed countries, particularly in the context of the Maastricht Treaty, and structural changes in the global economy in which productivity has a major role to play and the rising prominence of the new economy. Have central banks been lucky or good? Perhaps a bit of both (Rogoff, 2003). While the evidence on either side is still evolving, the current assessment is that it is unlikely that there will be a reversal of the current trend in inflation. It is important, however, to introspect a little further in order to understand the dynamics of low inflation and its future compatibility with monetary policy in an international setting.

An important factor that might have contributed to the lowering of inflation is productivity growth. Although productivity growth in Europe may not have been as high as it has been in the United States, the disinflationary effects of such productivity growth in one region get transmitted across borders through increased competition in a globalized world, operating through lowering of price mark-ups and erosion of monopoly pricing power through the expansion of cross-border trade. Increased competition has made prices more flexible in their response to real activity, thereby reducing the incentive for monetary policy to be expansionary. This has reinforced credibility in the commitment of monetary policy to containing inflation (Rogoff, 2003).

Despite growing globalization and synchronization of business cycles, the most striking change over the past three decades has been the moderation of volatility in GDP growth in most G-7 countries and this could also have contributed to reducing inflation (Figure 8.5) (Stock and Watson, 2003). A number of factors are at work. First, the services sector, which is less susceptible to volatility than manufacturing, has increased its share in output. Second, inventory management has improved. Third, financial markets have provided households with easier access to credit. In the United States, the sector that witnessed greatest reduction in volatility is housing. Moreover, there have been fewer oil supply and price disruptions as well as smaller productivity shocks in the 1980s and 1990s than during the 1960s and 1970s. Although only a small part of the moderation in output volatility is attributed to monetary policy, this is hotly debated. For instance, it is widely believed that monetary policy in the United States has been successful in implementing anticipatory non-inflationary policies and has focused on sustainable long-term real rates of interest. A significant increase in the flexibility of the US economy to smoothen shocks as a result of deregulation, technology, better inventory management, and flexible labour markets has enabled it to absorb shocks. The manner in which a shock is defined is critical. The perception of a smaller shock is really 'net shock', that is, gross shock minus what has been absorbed. Thus, events like September 11 can be measured only in a net sense. Moreover, in an integrated world, it would be difficult to distinguish between exogenity and endogenity; for instance, an increase in oil prices could very well be treated as endogenous.

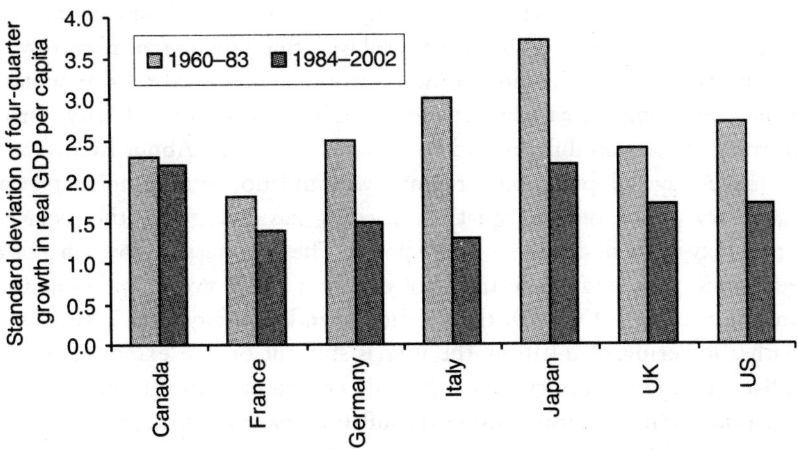

Figure 8.5 Volatility of Output Growth in G-7

Source: Stock and Watson (2003).

Yet another set of forces operating on inflation emanates from technological change. Advances in architecture and engineering as well as development of lighter but stronger materials have resulted in 'downsized' output, requiring more technology-sophisticated inputs rather than material-intensive inputs. This process has accelerated in the recent decades with the advent of the semi-conductor, the micro-processor, the computer, and the satellite. The impact of technological change is evident in the huge expansion of the money value of output and trade but not in tonnage. As a consequence, material intensity of production has declined reflecting, as Fed Chairman Alan Greenspan (1998) noted, 'the substitution, in effect, of ideas for physical matter in the creation of economic value'. This has contributed to the secular decline in commodity prices. In fact, a long-run trend decline in commodity prices over the last 140 years shows little evidence of reversal. Concerns over increasing commodity price volatility around this declining trend have, however, increasingly engaged monetary policy attention in the short run.

A significant strand in the literature credits changes in the institutional and operating framework of monetary policy with the success in achieving low inflation. After the experience of sustained inflation of the 1960s and the 1970s, the objective of inflation control became stronger and the movement of inflation targeting emerged. Massive cross-border capital flows, globalization of financial markets, and the IT revolution have combined to alter significantly the choice of instruments of monetary policy, operational settings, lag structures, and transmission mechanisms. In particular, these forces have led to the progressive erosion of the traditional anchors of monetary policy. In general, there has been a waning of the importance of intermediate targets. Even as monetary authorities deal with this difficult transition, several countries have radically altered the institutional architecture of monetary policy, including increased independence of the monetary authority, clarity of rules and responsibilities, and constrained discretion. About twenty-two countries have adopted policy regimes with inflation as the single target of monetary policy. Indeed, inflation targeting has emerged as the received orthodoxy in the design of monetary policy. The ongoing slowdown in global economic activity and the threat of deflation has, however, weakened its analytical edifice. Although the practice of inflation targeting is associated with a lowering of inflation, the jury is still out on the extent to which inflation targeting policies have actually contributed to the reduction in inflation that has occurred. Moreover, inflation that is too low, which is being observed today, is not just a disincentive for production decisions, it also delays consumer spending at a time when it could have been critical for triggering the upturn. It imparts inflexibility to labour markets, causing unemployment and deepening the slowdown. Signals from financial prices get blurred and this leads to misallocation of resources. In this context, the recent experience with inflation targeting as a framework for monetary policy warrants a close and hard scrutiny.

The fixation with short-run price stability or 'inflation nutting', to borrow a term from Mervyn King, Governor, Bank of England, can easily lead to neglect of important signs of macroeconomic and financial imbalances. Moreover, there is no available empirical evidence to suggest that inflation targeting improves economic performance. In the Euro area, for instance, setting the inflation target at close to 2 per cent is associated with weakening economic activity. This got pronounced in the second quarter of 2003 when real GDP declined, accompanied by large-scale unemployment and the threat of deflation in the larger constituents. Furthermore, the relevance of a single inflation target for a large economy, in particular, can be debated. The inflation target for the Euro area suffers from the problems of a 'one size fits all' monetary policy. Regional disparities warrant different short-run monetary policy approaches to its objectives. A certain amount of target flexibility and balancing of conflicting objectives are unavoidable in the real world, particularly that of EMEs (Eichengreen, 2002). Indeed, there is a growing sense that by the time the current phase of the global business cycle has run itself out, inflation targeting may not be seen to have stood the test of time.

High and sustained growth of the economy in conjunction with low inflation is the central concern of monetary policy. The rate of inflation chosen as the policy objective has to be consistent with the desired rate of output and employment growth. An inappropriate choice can lead to losses of macroeconomic welfare. Monetary authorities have to continually contend with the short-run trade-off between growth and inflation. The problem is compounded by the fact that the association between growth and inflation is non-linear. At some low rates, inflation could operate in a manner that assists in bringing back unemployed resources into the economy and be beneficial or, at worst, neutral to growth. At higher levels, inflation is inimical to growth. There are also very low levels of inflation that are associated with no growth or even deflation. At what level should the policy choice of inflation be or what is the threshold rate of inflation, if there is one, which is associated with the absence of harmful effects of growth? There have been various studies that have attempted to estimate threshold inflation rates. They suggest that the threshold inflation rate depends upon a number of factors such as the structure of the economy, past inflation history, the degree of indexation, and inflation expectations. Some studies suggest that the threshold inflation for developed and developing countries falls in the ranges of 1–3 per cent and 7–11 per cent, respectively (Khan and Senhadji, 2000). An abiding problem with cross-country studies, however, is the risk of being influenced by extreme values since samples include countries with inflation as low as one per cent and as high as 200 per cent and even higher. The estimation of such inflation threshold rates, therefore, needs to be done for each country separately (Rangarajan, 1998), in order to understand the behaviour of the economy in relation to inflation.

A major source of uncertainty in conducting monetary policy is the lack of a clear understanding of the inflationary process as it has unfolded in recent years. This has obscured a proper assessment of the nature of shocks impacting on the economy and the resulting risks to price stability. Variations in the timeliness and reliability of inflation indicators, uncertainty surrounding unobservable indicators like potential output and gaps in the intrinsic knowledge of the central banks about the state of the economy complicate the making of monetary policy. In countries like ours, there are other rigidities related to administered prices, wage setting procedures, and weather-induced supply shocks that influence prices. Knowledge of the relationship between inflation and its determinants remains limited (ECB, 2001). Even if there were a consensus on a suitable model, considerable uncertainty would remain regarding the strength of the structural relationships within the model. An even more fundamental problem is that parameters may vary over time as a result of structural changes in the economy. This presumably explains why no central bank uses a formal model to derive its actual policies; for the foreseeable future, models will be an aid to judgement rather than a substitute for judgement (Feldstein, 2003). The simple principle of inflation targeting thus is also not so simple and poses problems for monetary policymaking in developing countries.

THE PRIME MOVER: INTERNATIONAL CAPITAL FLOWS

Global capital flows impact the conduct of monetary policy on a daily basis. The problem, however, is that capital flows typically follow a boom–bust pattern. Net capital flows are currently limping back from the severe retrenchment imposed by the Asian financial crisis, which brought to an end the most dramatic surge of capital flows in post-World War II history. It is only in the recent period, particularly in 2003, that conditions for the rejuvenation of capital flows are emerging.

Large swings in capital flows are observed not only in the short-term patterns but there have been long-term patterns as well. A major surge in capital flows started around the 1870s and continued till World War I. The flows were mainly between the so-called developed countries—from the core countries of Western Europe to peripheral Europe and overseas European settlements—and in the form of foreign investment, with more than two-thirds comprising portfolio inflows. This era, which coincided with the operation of the classical gold standard, is widely regarded as the high watermark of capital mobility. The boom ended with World War I. A brief restoration of the gold standard was shattered by the Great Depression and the ensuing period up to the early 1940s was characterized by modest flows to the then EMEs for development finance. Capital controls were widespread in the attempt to maintain gold parities and international finance became fragmented by bilateral trade agreements. In the post–World War II period up to the 1970s, controls spread and intensified. International capital flows were primarily among industrial economies. The United States removed restrictions on capital outflows in 1974–5 while Germany retained controls over inflows until the late 1970s. The UK maintained controls until 1979 and Japan completed liberalization of the capital account in 1980. Developing countries persevered with controls with some Latin American countries embarking on flawed liberalization as part of exchange rate-based stabilization programmes in the mid-1970s.

In the period since 1973, dramatic changes set in. Private capital flows to developing countries were renewed as commercial banks furiously recycled oil surpluses. Asia and Latin America received the maximum share. Developing country debt exploded, rising at a compound annual rate of 24 per cent (World Bank, 2003) until the debt crisis of 1982 burst the bubble. Capital flows to developing countries slowed down substantially but did not dry up. Between 1983 and 1989, they fell to less than a third of their level in 1977–82. A generalized risk aversion to developing country debt dominated international financial markets and developed countries turned into attractive destinations. By the end of the 1980s, direct investment inflows to developing countries were only one-eighth of flows to developed countries; portfolio flows to developing countries were virtually non-existent. During the 1980s and the 1990s, several developing countries in Asia undertook capital account liberalization as part of unilateral financial deregulation, often in the face of large external surpluses. In general, the period from the mid-1980s to mid-1990s was characterized by removal of official restrictions on financial markets and wider market-oriented reforms in both mature and EMEs. The most dramatic move towards capital account liberalization occurred among the continental members of the EU.

Investor confidence returned to the developing world in the early 1990s in the aftermath of the Brady Plan. Net capital flows surged to pre-1914 levels by 1996, temporarily slowed by the European Monetary System (EMS) crisis of 1992. The impact of the Mexican crisis of 1994 was absorbed by the large mobilization of official financing which acted as a buffer. The composition of flows altered significantly, with private flows exceeding the official flows by the end of the 1980s. Whereas in the 1970s bank lending was the dominant component of capital flows to emerging markets, starting in the early 1990s, equity and bond investors became dominant. Over the last decade, portfolio investment exceeded bank lending in eight years. The range of investors purchasing emerging market securities broadened. Specialized investors such as hedge funds and mutual funds accounted for the bulk of portfolio inflows up to mid-1990s. In the subsequent years, pension funds, insurance companies, and other institutional investors increased their presence in emerging markets. Although portfolio flows became important, it was FDI which accounted for the bulk of private capital flows to EMEs, going through a six-fold jump between 1990 and 1997. International bank lending to developing countries increased sharply in this period, and was most pronounced in Asia, followed by Eastern Europe and Latin America. Much of the increase in bank lending was in the form of short-term claims, particularly on Asia.

In the late 1990s, capital flows to developing countries received severe shocks—first from the Asian crisis of 1997–8, then by the turmoil in global fixed income markets, and more recently by the collapse of the Argentine currency board peg in 2001 and the spate of corporate failures and accounting irregularities in 2002. Net flows to developing countries declined almost continuously after 1997 (Figures 8.6–8.8). The fall was particularly sharp in the form of bank lending and bonds, reflecting uncertainty and risk aversion. In 2002, net capital flows fell again, remaining far below the 1997 peak. Flows to Latin America reached their lowest level in a decade. Flows to Asia began a hesitant recovery with new bank lending exceeding repayments for the first time in five years. Global FDI inflows, down by 41 per cent in 2001, fell by another 21 per cent in 2002, attributable to weak economic growth, large sell-offs in equity markets, and a plunge in cross-border mergers and acquisitions. The United States and the United Kingdom accounted for more than half of the fall. The flows to Asia were held up by China.

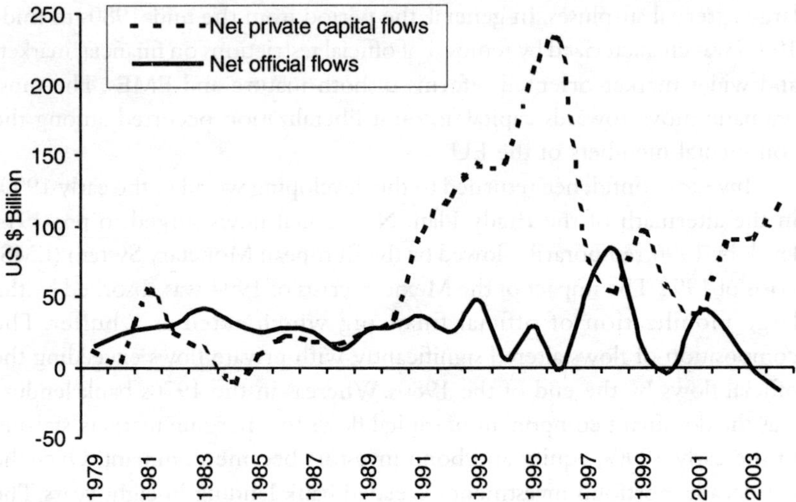

Figure 8.6 Net Capital Flows to Emerging Market Economies

Source: *WEO*, IMF, September 2003.

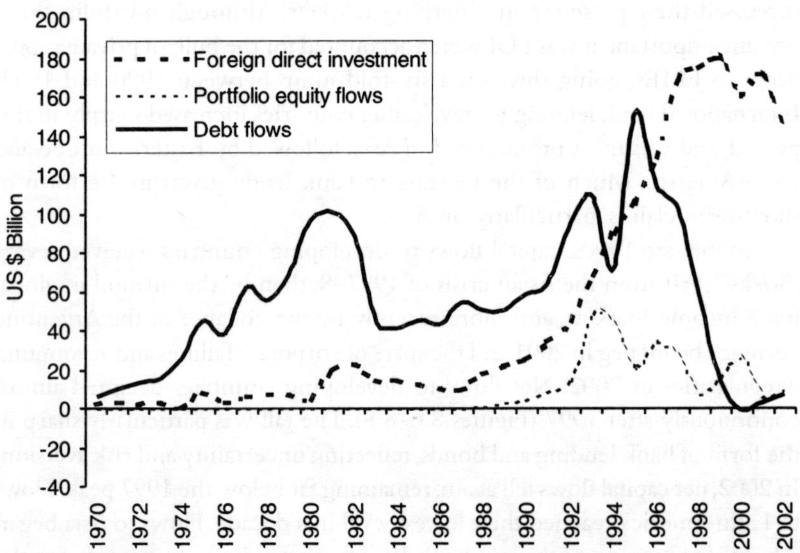

Figure 8.7 Net Capital Flows to Developing Countries

Source: *Global Development Finance*, World Bank.

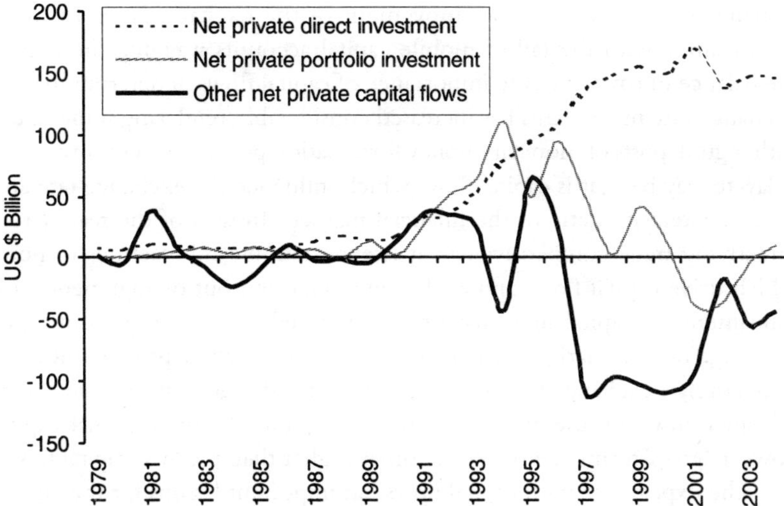

Figure 8.8 Private Capital Flows to EMEs: Component-wise

Source: *WEO*, IMF, September, 2003.

Despite the global uncertainties, conditions for capital flows have improved in 2003. Sell-offs in international bond markets in June and July reflected upward revisions in investors' expectations about growth prospects. Spillovers to credit and equity markets were limited. Emerging markets, in general, outperformed the mature markets. Some positive aspects of the roller-coaster of the last decade are: a steady consolidation of external debt by developing countries cushioned by the resilience of FDI and the growth of local-currency bond markets as an innovation to manage credit risk.

The overall experience, however, is that capital flows are characteristically volatile, both in terms of long-term waves and even more so in the short-term waves. The long-term waves influence monetary policy thinking during each era, whereas the short-term volatility has to be met through day-to-day monetary policy operations.

The experience of living with capital flows since the 1970s has fundamentally altered the context of development finance. It has also brought about a drastic revision in the manner in which monetary policy is conducted. In particular, there is a dramatic shift in the still unsettled debate on the determinants of the exchange rate and the choice of the appropriate exchange rate regime, although the weight of opinion is clearly in favour of a flexible regime. According to conventional wisdom, it was trade flows which were the key determinants of exchange rate movements. Consequently, the degree of openness to international trade, price and non-price competitiveness, and factors which determined market shares abroad were thought to have a crucial bearing on the level and the movement of the exchange rate. In more recent times, with the tail of mobile capital accounts wagging the dog of the balance of payments, the importance of capital flows in determining the exchange rate movements has increased considerably, rendering some of the earlier guideposts of monetary policy formulation possibly anachronistic. On a day-to-day basis, it is capital flows which influence the exchange rate and interest rate arithmetic of the financial markets. Instead of the real factors underlying trade competitiveness, it is expectations and reactions to news which drive capital flows and exchange rates, often out of alignment with fundamentals. Capital flows have been observed to cause overshooting of exchange rates as market participants act in concert while pricing information. Foreign exchange markets are prone to bandwagon effects. The effects of capital flows on the exchange rate are amplified by the fact that capital flows in 'gross' terms can be several times higher than the 'net' capital flows.

The experience with capital flows has important lessons for the choice of the exchange rate regime. The advocacy for corner solutions—a fixed peg *à la* the currency board without monetary policy independence or a freely floating exchange rate retaining discretionary conduct of monetary policy—is distinctly on the decline. The weight of experience seems to be tilting in favour of intermediate regimes with country-specific features, without targets for the level of the exchange rate, the conduct of exchange market interventions to ensure orderly rate movements, and a combination of interest rates and exchange rate interventions to fight extreme market turbulence. In general, EMEs have accumulated massive foreign exchange reserves as a circuit-breaker for situations where unidirectional expectations become self-fulfilling. It is a combination of these strategies which will guide monetary authorities through the impossible trinity of a fixed exchange rate, open capital account, and an independent monetary policy.

Capital movements have rendered exchange rates significantly more volatile than before. For the majority of developing countries which continue to depend on export performance as a key to the health of the balance of payments, exchange rate volatility has had significant real effects in terms of fluctuations in employment and output and the distribution of activity between tradables and non-tradables. In the fiercely competitive trading environment where countries seek to expand market shares aggressively by paring down margins, even a small change in exchange rates can develop into significant and persistent real effects. For labour-intensive export producers, volatility in exchange rate movements can easily translate into large losses of economic welfare. In the final analysis, the heightened exchange rate volatility of the era of capital flows has had adverse implications for all countries except the reserve currency economies. The latter have been experiencing exchange rate movements which are not in alignment with their macro imbalances and the danger of persisting currency misalignments looms large over all non-reserve currency economies.

The issue dominating the conduct of monetary policy and exchange rate policy today in countries such as India and China is that of excess of capital inflows. Are these flows resulting from temporary global imbalances emanating from current economic policies and problems of the G-3 countries or do they reflect global changes of a more lasting nature? It is to the consideration of this issue that I now turn.

LOOKING AHEAD: ECONOMIC DEMOGRAPHICS

Some recent research has focussed on the macroeconomic effects of demographic patterns (Joshi and Sanyal, 2003; UN, 2003). Over the next half-century, the population of the world will age faster than during the past half-century as fertility rates decline and life expectancy rises. The proportion of children (from 0–14 years) is expected to decline from 30 per cent in 2000 to 20 per cent in 2050 whereas the proportion of the aged (60+ years) will double, reaching 21 per cent of the total population by 2050. The phenomenon of global ageing is likely to be associated with a progressive decline in saving rates and growth. In the interregnum, regional patterns of global population ageing are expected to bring about fundamental alterations in saving-investment balances which would be reflected in the magnitude and direction of international capital flows with implications for the conduct of future monetary policy.

In general, economies pass through three stages of demographic transition—(a) high youth dependency (large proportion of population in the 0–14 years group), (b) rise in working age population (from 15–59 years) relative to youth dependency, and (c) rise in elderly dependency (60+ years) relative to working age population. The second stage is regarded as the most productive stage from the point of view of secular growth because it is associated with the highest rate of saving and work force growth relative to the other stages. So far, the more developed regions have been leading the process of population ageing and are likely to be deep into the third stage of demographic transition. In Europe, population ageing is most advanced and by 2050, this is projected to accelerate. Japan is currently the country with the oldest population; by 2050, it is expected to have the highest proportion of elderly people among industrialized nations (Government of Japan, 2003) (Figures 8.9–8.11). Projections suggest a turning point between 2010 and 2030 when the EU, North America, and Japan will experience a substantial decline in saving rate relative to investment which would be reflected in CADs. These regions will switch to importing capital.

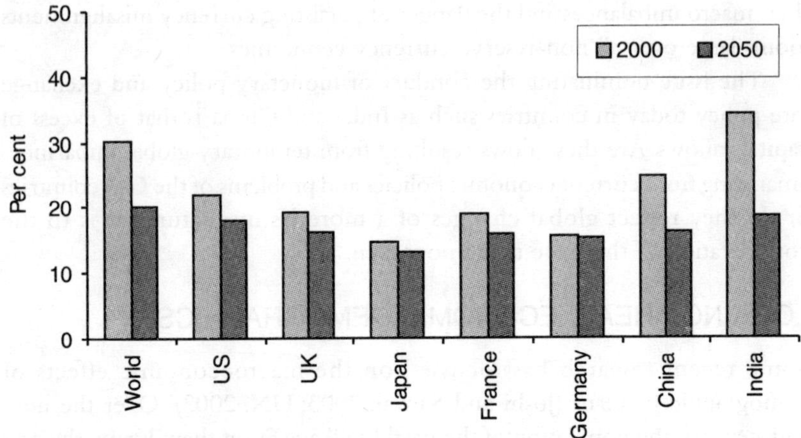

Figure 8.9 Share of Age 0–14 Years in Total Population

Source: United Nations, 2003.

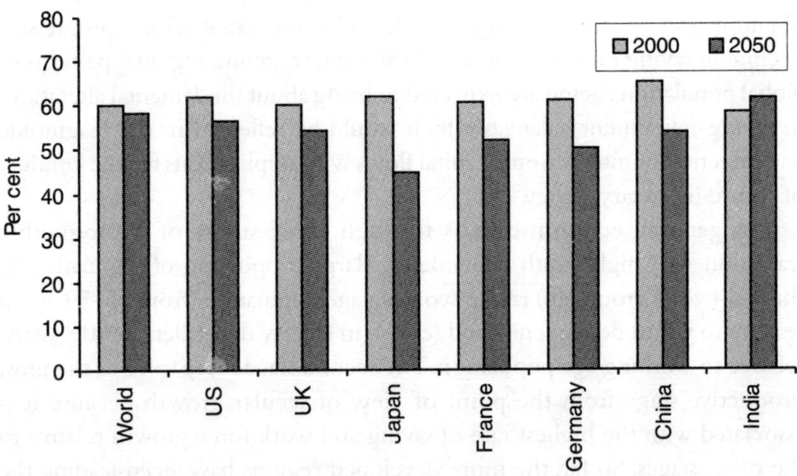

Figure 8.10 Share of Working Age in Total Population

Source: United Nations, 2003.

Most of the high performers of East Asia and China are in the second stage of the demographic cycle. Elderly dependency is expected to double by 2025. Their working age populations will increase modestly and then shrink. These projections suggest that East Asia could increasingly become an important supplier of global savings up to 2025; however, rapid population ageing thereafter would reinforce rather than mitigate the inexorable

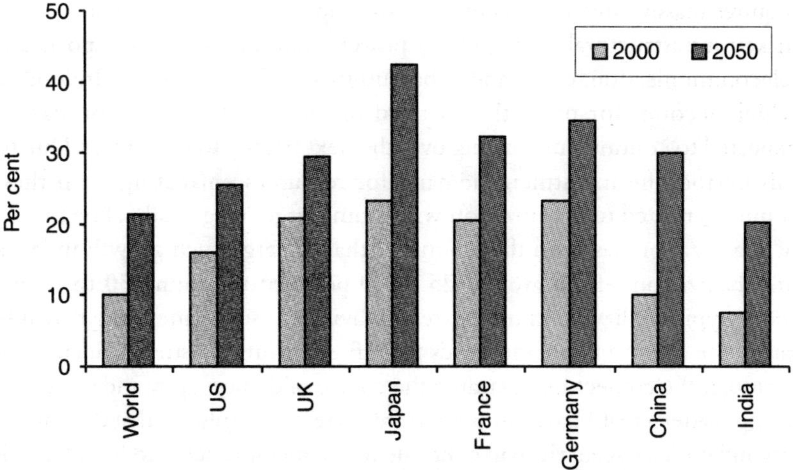

Figure 8.11 Share of People of Age 60+ Years in Total Population

Source: United Nations, 2003.

decline of global saving. Increasingly it would be the moderate and the low performers among the developing countries which would emerge as exporters of international capital. India is entering the second stage of demographic transition and over the next half-century, a significant increase in both saving rates and share of working age population is expected. The share of the labour force in population is expected to overtake the rest of Asia, including China, by 2030.

In this scenario, the current phenomenon of overall surpluses in the BoP being run by several EMEs, including India, may not be a temporary one. The largest reserve holding countries (excluding gold) in the world are EMEs. Monetary authorities in these countries are grappling with the expansionary effects of net foreign assets on domestic monetary conditions. Faced with the loss of control over the monetary aggregates, interest rates, and exchange rates, almost all of these countries are engaged in devising innovative methods of sterilization to delay the inevitable sacrifice of discretion in the conduct of monetary policy and its globalization. The emerging patterns of demography indicate that this source of uncertainty for monetary authorities could become more significant than before.

The key challenge for macroeconomic policies would be to ensure that the anticipated expansion in saving in developing countries is productively utilized within the economy and not exported abroad. Accordingly, it is vital to ensure that the investment rate rises in close co-movement with the saving rate. Sustainable growth hinges around the existence of a critical minimum in terms of physical infrastructure. The acceleration of growth in the future requires massive investments to close the gaps between demand and supply in key infrastructural areas such as power, roads and highways, ports and telecommunication, cities, and urban utilities. India, China, and Indonesia, which account for more than a third of the world's population can be expected to continue urbanizing over the next twenty to forty years. During this period, the investment demand for resources emanating from these countries related to urbanization will assume larger magnitudes. The history of urbanization has been that countries that undergo such growth in levels of urbanization—from around 25 to 30 per cent to around 50 to 60 per cent—typically have to attract external savings to supplement their own to satisfy the massive financing needs for infrastructure investment during this period. If the conjecture regarding the course of demography and associated savings pattern that I have just posited are correct, it is unlikely that the current low inflationary scenario will continue in the medium term to long term. It is also possible that the current phenomenon of increasing savings rates in Asian countries such as India and China does not continue to be valid over the next medium-to-long term. If that happens, there could again be a reversal of capital flows. There would then be tightening of liquidity in world capital markets with increased competition for resources. Thus, there is no assurance that the current trends of excess liquidity accompanied by low inflation will necessarily continue in the world. Recent experience tells us that such reversals can occur very rapidly.

This will pose significant problems in the conduct of monetary policy for our countries in the years to come. The future growth strategy will also need to be more labour absorbing to accommodate the projected expansion in the work force. Reforms in the labour market, educational systems, pensions, and medical care would gather importance within the overall intensification of structural reforms. Monetary policy would have to play an important role in bringing these forces together by ensuring appropriate real interest rates and low and stable inflation.

THE EMERGING CHALLENGES TO MONETARY POLICY

There are many issues that are of relevance to emerging economies, like India and Sri Lanka, that are opening up. It would be useful to summarize some of these here.

In a world of generalized uncertainty, monetary policy has lost its traditional moorings. As a consequence, the conduct of monetary policy has become increasingly complex. The determinants of exchange-rate behaviour have altered dramatically. Earlier, factors affecting merchandise trade flows and the behaviour of goods market provided proximate guides for operating monetary policy. In this environment, a monetary policy principally targeting low inflation was relevant and commodity purchasing power parities seemed to offer a satisfactory explanation of exchange-rate changes. Since the 1980s, vicissitudes of capital movements have shown up in volatility in exchange-rate movements with major currencies moving far out of alignment of underlying purchasing power parities. On a day-to-day basis, it is capital flows which move exchange rates and account for much of their volatility.

The impact of greater exchange rate volatility has been significantly different for reserve currency countries and for developing countries. For the former, mature and well-developed financial markets have absorbed the risks associated with large exchange-rate fluctuations with negligible spillover on to real activity. Consequently, the central bank does not have to take care of these risks through its monetary policy operations. On the other hand, for the majority of developing countries, which are labour-intensive exporters, exchange rate volatility has had significant employment, output, and distributional consequences, which can be large and persistent.

All this has made the operation of monetary policy more difficult and complicated. For developing countries, in particular, considerations relating to maximizing output and employment weigh equally upon monetary authorities as price stability. A crucial objective of the development strategy is to stabilize the fluctuations of output and employment. Accordingly, in developing countries, it is difficult to design future monetary policy frameworks with only inflation as a single-minded objective. Thus the operation of monetary policy has to take into account the risks that greater interest rate or exchange rate volatility entails for a wide range of participants in the economy. Both the fiscal and monetary authorities inevitably bear these risks. The choice of the exchange-rate regimes in developing countries, therefore, reveals a preference for flexible exchange rates along with interventions to ensure orderly market activity, but without targeting any level of the exchange rate. There is interest in maintaining adequate international reserves and a readiness to move interest rates flexibly in the event of disorderly market conditions. It needs to be recognized that most developing countries are engaged in the process of development and integration of financial markets. Consequently, signals from the market get blurred by the degree of management which is unavoidable in this transition.

The actual experience over the last two decades has been that with greater liberalization of the financial system, inflation has fallen and output volatility has moderated. Monetary policy has played an important role in taming inflation in the last two decades. A valuable lesson for an economy in the process of opening up is that increased globalization and competition have contributed predominantly towards containment of inflation. Thus countries' perspective on inflation needs to be informed increasingly by world price trends, particularly in commodities of interest to them. With continued deregulation and globalization, it is unlikely that there will be a reversal of the current trends in inflation. However, this is not to suggest that globalization is a solution for all problems. Any widespread relapses in the relatively favourable trends in globalization and deregulation, or relatively benign fiscal policies, could reverse the achievement of recent years. An important consideration for reining inflationary expectations relates to the need to have clarity on price stability, effective communication, consistency in conduct of policy, and transparency in explaining actions. Central banks should speak clearly to markets and listen to markets more carefully to ensure the intended objectives of policy.

There have been some negatives from the process of globalization in the form of greater prominence of credit and asset price booms and increasing incidence of financial crisis. The wave of financial liberalization has raised the risks in the financial system. The key policy challenge for an emerging economy would be to put in place mutually supportive safeguards to ensure both monetary and financial stabilities. The most important lesson for us is that financial imbalances can build up even when inflation is low and hence monetary policy should have a slightly longer time horizon in terms of inflation. Apart from the above, there are merits to all countries in greater transparency, combining simple rules with discretion, and effective communication. Orderly development of financial markets can make a big difference regarding the manner in which risks and shocks make an impact on the economy. A flexible exchange-rate regime imparts greater flexibility in monetary policy to deal with shocks more efficiently. On the prudential side, it would imply strengthening further the macro-prudential orientation. Monetary policy and prudential regulation should, therefore, co-exist. Greater transparency and cooperation between monetary policy and supervision has been increasingly recognized the world over and has resulted in many central banks publishing financial stability reports.

Although there is uncertainty about how economies operate and about monetary policy itself, uncertainty is no excuse for not pursuing price stability. In the pursuit of monetary goals, monetary policy authorities could adopt formal models and policy rules, informal target rules, or case-by-case decision making. In practice, no central bank relies exclusively on formal models to derive final policy. Models assist central banks to take judgements. Furthermore, as Alan Greenspan recently commented, most of the formal models are vastly simplistic and despite efforts to quantify and capture more variables, they are inadequate. Their knowledge base is barely able to keep pace with the complexities of the world. The problem is not of the models but of the complexities of the world economy. An explicit numerical target is good for anchoring inflation but it comes at a cost. If the explicit inflation target cannot be achieved, it weakens the credibility of the central bank. Thus it may not be appropriate to formulate monetary policy based on a simplistic inflation target or a single point inflexible point target as argued by many. The risks to the system can emanate from any variable, both exogenous and endogenous and policymakers' response should be dynamic and contextual. Rules can, therefore, only be viewed as thoughtful adjuncts of policy but cannot be a substitute for risk paradigms. A case-by-case approach provides a simplistic framework for analysis. Ultimately, a central bank has to judge the outcome of the policy choices it makes and also take account of and anticipate market expectations, which have become increasingly important for the attainment of desirable outcomes.

To conclude, in a globalized world it is not possible to formulate monetary policy independent of international developments. Monetary policy formulation has become more complex and interdependent. Continuous monitoring of financial markets, upgradation of technical skills at the central bank, flexibility, and eternal watchfulness hold the key to making monetary policy matter in the evolving global environment. A key factor that guides the conduct of monetary policy is how to achieve the benefits of market integration while minimizing the risks of market instability. An integral component of central bank work is the development of financial markets that can increasingly shift the burden of risk mitigation and costs from the authorities to the markets. The adverse implications of excess volatility leading to financial crises are more severe for low-income countries. They can ill-afford the downside risks inherent in a financial sector collapse. Central banks need to take into account, among others, developments in the global economic situation, the international inflationary situation, interest rate situation, exchange-rate movements, and capital movements while formulating monetary policy.

References

Eichengreen, B. (2002), 'Can Emerging Markets Float? Should they Inflation Target?', paper presented to a seminar at the Central Bank of Brazil, February.

European Central Bank (ECB) (2001), 'Monetary policy-making under uncertainty', *Monthly Bulletin*, January, pp. 43–55.

Feldstein, M. (2003), 'Monetary Policy in an Uncertain Economy', NBER Working Paper, 9969, September.

Government of Japan (2003), *Annual Report on the Japanese Economy and Public Finance*, October.

Greenspan, A. (1998), 'The Implications of Technological Changes', remarks at the Charlotte Chamber of Commerce, 10 July.

_____ (2003), 'Monetary Policy Under Uncertainty', remarks at a Conference on 'Monetary Policy and Uncertainty: Adapting to a Changing Economy' at Jackson Hole, WY, 29 August.

International Monetary Fund (2003), *WEO*, September.

Joshi, V. and S. Sanyal (2003), 'India's Opportunity', *Business Standard*, Mumbai, 9 September.

Khan, M. S. and A.S. Senhadji. (2000), 'Threshold Effects in the Relationship between Inflation and Growth', IMF Working Paper, WP/00/110, June.

Meltzer, A.H. (1997), 'On Making Monetary Policy More Effective Domestically and Internationally', in Iwao Kuroda (ed.), '*Towards More Effective Monetary Policy*', MacMillan Press Limited, London.

Rangarajan, C. (1998), *Indian Economy: Essays on Money and Finance*, UBS Publishers Ltd., New Delhi.

Rogoff, K. (2003), 'Globalisation and Global Disinflation', paper presented at a conference on 'Monetary Policy and Uncertainty: Adapting to a Changing Economy' at Jackson Hole, WY, 29 August.

Stock, J.H. and M.W. Watson (2003), 'Has the Business Cycle Changed? Evidence and Explanations', paper presented at a conference on 'Monetary Policy and Uncertainty: Adapting to a Changing Economy' at Jackson Hole, WY, 29 August.

United Nations (2003), *World Population Prospects:The 2002 Revision. Highlights*, United Nations, Population Division of the Department of Economic and Social Affairs of the United National Secretariat, New York.

World Bank (2003), *Global Development Finance*, Washington, DC.

9 Some Apparent Puzzles for Contemporary Monetary Policy*

We are living through interesting times. Oil prices have been rising at a fast pace over the last two years. The IMF in September last year had used an implicit projection of oil prices at US$ 37.25 per barrel in 2004. Now, however, the forecast for international crude prices—the biggest risk to global growth—has been revised upwards by 20.5 per cent from the April 2005 projections and world trade growth projections has been cut by 50 basis points. Unlike earlier expectations, when this price rise was expected to be relatively temporary, international opinion now is that it is more permanent than temporary. Yet, the IMF's September 2005 *World Economic Outlook* (*WEO*) has retained the global output growth forecast at 4.3 per cent, a level higher than average world output growth through the 1990s and until 2004, though it admits that risks are still slanted to the downside. In India and China there is, as yet, no sign of a slowdown: in fact, just earlier this week, we at the RBI, revised our growth forecast for 2005–6 (that is, April 2005–March 2006) for policy purposes from 'around 7 per cent' in April 2005 to '7.0 per cent–7.5 per cent' now. And we are among the countries that are said to be more energy inefficient and dependent on oil imports.

One also sees little impact of the current oil price episode on global financial markets. Undisturbed by the somewhat slowing global growth scenario, financial markets have remained generally benign with low interest rates and healthy stock markets. Moreover, corporate balance sheets in most countries have been exhibiting continuous improvement with no pause in the determined efforts observed towards restructuring and productivity promoting cost cutting activities. This is certainly true in India and presumably in China as well. In fact this financial strengthening of the real corporate

* Keynote address at the conference 'China's and India's Changing Economic Structures: Domestic and Regional Implications', organized by the IMF, the China Society of Finance and Banking, and the Stanford Center for International Development in Beijing during 27–8 October 2005.

sector is perhaps underpinning the continued health of the financial system and is emerging as a cushion against medium-term risks and uncertainties. I am saying all this against the backdrop of the difficulties that we all went through in the previous oil price shock episodes of 1973–4, 1979–80, and 1989–90.

Besides, the macroeconomic imbalances—a key risk to global growth—have actually increased with the CAD of the United States poised to cross 6 per cent of GDP and its fiscal deficit 3.7 per cent of GDP in 2005; surpluses are correspondingly set to rise in Japan, China, oil exporters in the Middle East, emerging Asia (excluding India where CADs have returned), and the Commonwealth of Independent States countries. Yet financial conditions have enabled a smooth financing of these imbalances with growth and interest rate differentials continuing to fuel investors' appetite for the United States.

At the same time, the same favourable financial developments have caused large imbalances to grow inwards, particularly in the form of household debt and increases in housing prices and this is seen as heightening risks for the future. Low bond yields and flat yield curves have triggered an ever-widening search for yields, aided by the compression of credit risk spreads. This has, perhaps, increased the risks embedded in the financial system and financial markets could become vulnerable to corrections. Questions regarding the sustainability of current global growth, overall credit quality, and the state of the household sector's finances have begun to arise. The same set of factors, however, have improved the access of EMEs to financial markets, with the low spreads of their bond yields enabling financing of strong growth with moderate inflation, strengthening of fiscal and balance-of-payments positions, and the accumulation of foreign exchange reserves.

Perhaps the greatest puzzle in current global developments is the co-existence of abundant liquidity and low consumer inflation, though there are now some incipient signs of oil price induced increases in most countries. Despite the prolonged period over which monetary policy all over the world has remained accommodative, inflation has been unusually benign, relatively impervious to soaring crude prices and the elevated levels of prices of non-fuel commodities. This phenomenon is unique in recent history.

These are not out-of-the-earth paradoxes and many explanations have been offered. Yet, taken together these stylized facts give an indication that conventional wisdom often fails to explain them. It is in this context that I shall focus on some of these apparent puzzles and their explanations in the present chapter. I am particularly concerned with possible erosion of the efficacy of traditional price-related policy measures, namely, the exchange rate and interest rate mechanisms in restoring macroeconomic balances.

The rest of the chapter is organized as follows. The second section presents some stylized facts, puzzling as they are in terms of the conventional understanding and wisdom. This is followed by a discussion on the proximate explanations in the third section. The last section has taken up an appraisal of the way ahead in terms of possible policy responses keeping in view the shifting balance of risks and the muted pricing signals.

SOME APPARENT PUZZLES

From the various puzzles that the monetary policy makers routinely face, let me focus on six issues, namely, (a) the US dollar appreciating despite increasing US twin deficits, (b) soaring oil prices accompanied by strong global growth, (c) long-term bond yields falling in the presence of Fed Fund rate hikes, (d) low consumer inflation in the presence of abundant liquidity and increasing asset prices, (e) strong global growth accompanied by slowdown in global saving and investment rates, and (f) the phenomenon of low inflation despite currency depreciation.

Increasing US Twin Deficits and the Appreciating US Dollar

Over the past two decades, the United States has transformed itself from the world's largest creditor into the world's largest debtor nation. At the end of 2004, its debt to the rest of the world exceeded its assets by about US$ 2.5 trillion, that is, 21 per cent of its GDP. Driving this massive mismatch is the quantum jump in the CAD during 2000–4 from the level during 1995–9, largely resulting from the mounting fiscal deficit and falling private savings. The US macro imbalances are set to accentuate following the disaster brought upon by Hurricanes Katrina and Rita. The IMF's September 2005 *WEO* projects the US CAD to rise to over 6 per cent of GDP in 2005, driven by higher oil prices and strong domestic demand (Table 9.1).

What is the solution to these persistent and mounting imbalances? Conventional wisdom would suggest that the existence of these twin deficits and little expectations of improvement at present would have led to a market-led sizeable adjustment of the US dollar against other major currencies. The US dollar, which did encounter depreciation in terms of Nominal Effective Exchange Rate (NEER), in the first half of 1990s, appreciated in the second half of 1990s and even in terms of Real Effective Exchange Rate (REER) during 2000–4. The process has also continued during the first eight months of 2005 despite the sustained rise in the US CAD, offset primarily by a depreciation of the Euro, pound sterling, and yen. The weakening of the Euro against the US dollar in recent months possibly reflects the increasingly unfavourable short-term interest rate differentials and growing political uncertainties in Europe following the rejection of the EU's constitution in France and the Netherlands, and post-election problems in Germany. Except

Table 9.1 US Twin Deficits, NEER and REER

Period/ Year	Current account balance/GDP (per cent per annum)	General government fiscal balance/GDP (per cent per annum)	NEER (2000=100)	REER (2000=100)
1990–4	–1.00	–4.88	85.80	87.80
1995–9	–2.06	–1.24	89.78	86.33
2000–4	–4.63	–2.39	97.13	98.09
2005	> –6.0[a]	–3.7[a]	83.13[b]	87.73[b]

Notes: [a] WEO's Projection; [b] Pertains to August 2005.

Source: *WEO*, IMF; *IFS*, IMF; and World Development Indicators Online, World Bank.

in the ASEAN-4, the trade-weighted exchange rates of the United States have generally appreciated in emerging markets, particularly in Latin America. Following the Chinese exchange rate reform on 21 July 2005—including a 2.1 per cent revaluation, the adoption of a reference basket of currencies, and a 0.3 per cent daily fluctuation range against the US dollar—the renminbi has remained broadly unchanged against the US dollar. Clearly, the steady appreciation of US dollar despite the rising CAD constitutes a daunting paradox of the day.

Strong Global Growth despite Soaring Oil Prices

After the oil shocks of the 1970s, the first half of the 1990s witnessed deflationary pressures in terms of real oil prices. However, the lull in oil prices turned out to be short-lived. Soaring oil prices have since characterized the period 2000–4 when the West Texas Intermediate (WTI) prices increased sharply from the level in the second half of the 1990s. While the IMF's real oil price index at 277 in 2005 so far remains below the peak of 452 witnessed in 1980, oil prices are scaling new heights every day driven mainly by growing or unchanged demand, low inventories, lack of spare capacity, and geopolitical tensions and uncertainties. While the accommodating global monetary conditions have placed oil futures in the class of sought-after financial assets, the persisting high levels of oil prices increasingly indicate that a large part of the oil price hike has attained a permanent character (Table 9.2).

The worrisome news on oil continues to project the image of a world besieged with higher oil prices, bringing the painful memories of the oil shocks of the 1970s to the fore. Yet, global growth remains remarkably on track. Indeed, the growth momentum has only improved from the second half of the 1990s to the first half of this decade. The growth in world trade volume (goods and services) has also recovered after some slowdown in 2001 and 2002. The September *WEO* has thus retained its April estimate for 2005 global growth at 4.30 per cent. What is all the more surprising is the increasing business confidence (for example, in the United States) coupled with high corporate profit growth during 2002–5, much higher than in the roaring 1990s.

Table 9.2 Global Growth, Business Confidence, Corporate Profit Growth, and Oil Prices Inflation

Period/ Year	World growth (per cent per annum)	Growth in world trade volume (goods and services) (per cent per annum)	US business confidence index	US corporate profit growth (per cent per annum)	WTI oil prices (US$ per barrel)
1990–4	2.62	5.57	–	7.15	20.44 (–1.86)
1995–9	3.69	7.46	54.63[a]	7.57	18.95 (4.67)
2000–4	3.84	6.34	60.50[a]	6.88	30.97 (19.36)
2000	4.71	12.44	51.66	–3.91	30.32 (58.17)
2001	2.44	0.08	43.91	–6.19	25.87 (–14.67)
2002	2.95	3.41	52.37	15.49	26.12 (0.95)
2003	3.97	5.44	53.31	16.42	31.10 (19.07)
2004	5.13	10.33	60.50	12.57	41.45 (33.29)
2005	4.30[b]	7.00[b]	54.45[c]	16.00[d]	56.01 (35.14)[b]

Notes: [a] pertains to the years 1999 and 2004 respectively; [b] IMF's WEO projection; [c] August 2005; figures in bracket are annual percentage changes; [d] 2005 Q2 YoY. The overall US Business Confidence index, referred to as the US Business Conditions Index, ranges between 0 and 100. An index greater than 50 indicates an expansionary economy over the course of the next three to six months. (Taken from *WEO*, originally compiled by the Institute for Supply Management, US.)

Source: *WEO* and *IFS*, IMF; Federal Reserve, US, and Bureau of Economic Analysis, US.

Falling Long-term Bond Yields in the Presence of Fed Fund Rate Hikes

With the economic expansion continuing strongly and risks shifting towards possible inflationary pressures, the US Fed has started reducing the degree of policy accommodation and raised the policy rate eleven times since June 2004 by a 'measured' 25 basis points each time, with indications of further such hikes. While the PLR of banks in the United States has responded to every hike in the target federal fund rate, the long-term interest rates that are set by financial markets continue to remain unusually low—what Federal Reserve Chairman Greenspan has referred to as a 'conundrum'. The best way to summarize this issue is to quote from Chairman Greenspan (Greenspan, 2005a):

> In this environment, long-term interest rates have trended lower in recent months even as the Federal Reserve has raised the level of the target federal funds rate by 150 basis points. This development contrasts with most experience, which suggests that, other things being equal, increasing short-term interest rates are normally accompanied by a rise in longer-term yields...For the moment, the broadly unanticipated behavior of world bond markets remains a conundrum. Bond price movements may be a short-term aberration, but it will be some time before we are able to better judge the forces underlying recent experience.

Given the understanding that the long-term yield tracks the behaviour of current and expected inflation (Fama, 1986) along with expected growth performance of the economy in terms of productivity of capital (Mishkin, 1991), the current behaviour of yield defies conventional wisdom (Table 9.3).

A host of hypotheses have been put forward as an explanation of the conundrum, inter alia: easy liquidity conditions, glut in global savings over investment (Bernanke, 2005), forex reserves build-up in the Asian economies, gradual expected pace of US tightening made possible by a high level of monetary credibility, low expected inflation, low term/risk premia, and flight to quality after the dot com crash in 2000. Meanwhile, the low bond yields and flat yield curves have triggered an ever-widening search for yields, aided by the compression of credit risk spreads. The behaviour of long-term rates to the short-term policy rates is, thus, posing a threat to the traditional transmission channels of monetary policy, looming large on the efficacy of monetary management the world over.

Low Consumer Inflation in the Presence of Abundant Liquidity and Increasing Asset Prices

The global economy is currently awash with liquidity. Exactly seven years ago, the US Fed responded to the 'low probability but highly adverse events' (Blinder and Reis, 2005) leading up to the Russian debt default and the long-term capital management (LTCM) collapse by an emergency cut in interest rates in September, October, and November 1998. Even though the reduction was just 25 basis points each month, it shifted the monetary policy stance to accommodation. Once again, prompted by a deflation scare, the fed fund

Table 9.3 Federal Funds Rate, PLR, and US Government. Securities Yield

(per cent)

Period		Federal fund rate	US PLR	Ten-year government securities yield
2004	May	1.00	4.00	4.72
	Jun	1.03	4.01	4.73
	Jul	1.26	4.25	4.50
	Aug	1.43	4.43	4.28
	Sep	1.61	4.58	4.13
	Oct	1.76	4.75	4.10
	Nov	1.93	4.93	4.19
	Dec	2.16	5.15	4.23
2005	Jan	2.28	5.25	4.22
	Feb	2.50	5.49	4.17
	Mar	2.63	5.58	4.50
	Apr	2.79	5.75	4.34
	May	3.00	5.98	4.14
	Jun	3.04	6.01	4.00
	Jul	3.26	6.25	4.18
	Aug	3.50	6.44	4.26
	Sep	3.62	6.59	4.20

Note: US PLR is the rate posted by a majority of top 25 (by assets in domestic offices) insured US–chartered commercial banks. It is one of several base rates used by banks to price short-term business loans.

Source: US Fed.

rate was cut over a forty-two month stretch from December 2000 to June 2003 to a forty-five year low of 1 per cent, taking the real federal funds rate into negative territory. Thus, real policy rates were effectively zero or negative until very recently in the United States and remain below the 'Wicksellian' long-term neutral rate. Real policy rates in the United Kingdom and Euro area are also generally hovering around zero. Coupled with the benign policy rates, money supply growth, which increased in the second half of the 1990s in the United Kingdom, continued at the elevated level during 2000–4. Similarly, money supply growth went up in Euro area in 2000–4 from a lower level in 1995–9. Even in the United States where money supply has lost much of its charm as an information variable, there has been accelerated growth during 1995–9 which has largely been sustained during 2000–4 (Table 9.4).

Table 9.4 Policy Rates and Growth in Money Supply, Credit, Asset Prices, Consumer Prices, and Producer Prices[1]

(per cent)

Country/ Area	Variable	1990–4	1995–9	2000–4
US	Policy rate	4.9	5.4	2.8
	Money supply	1.4	8.5	7.6
	Reserve money	7.8	8.6	3.7
	Credit	3.0	7.5	7.0
	Equity prices (Dow Jones)	7.2	24.7	–0.3
	Housing prices	–1.9	1.9	5.8
	Producer prices	1.4	0.8	3.2
	Consumer prices	3.6	2.4	2.6
UK	Policy rate	9.1	6.3	4.6
	Money supply	5.9	7.6	7.6
	Reserve money	4.1	4.6	5.3
	Credit	5.7	7.4	10.3
	Equity prices (FTSE 100)	5.8	17.8	–5.9
	Housing prices	–1.8	4.3	15.3
	Producer prices	4.2	1.6	1.1
	Consumer prices	4.6	2.8	2.4
Euro area	Policy rate		2.8 (1999)	3.0
	Money supply	7.1	4.7	6.9
	Credit		7.9 (1998–9)	5.9
	Equity prices (Xetra Dax)	12.6 (1991–4)	27.8	–5.4
	Housing prices	4.0 (1991–5)	3.5 (1996–2000)	6.8 (2001–4)
	Producer prices	2.3 (1991–5)	1.1 (1996–2000)	1.4 (2001–4)
	Consumer prices	3.2 (1991–5)	1.6 (1996–2000)	2.2 (2001–4)

Contd

Table 9.4 Contd

Country/ Area	Variable	1990–4	1995–9	2000–4
World	Consumer prices	22.3	8.3	3.8
	Consumer prices—advanced countries	3.8	2.0	1.9
	Consumer prices—emerging markets	12.9	7.6	4.3
	Non-Oil commodity prices	–6.1	–4.0	1.9

Note: Policy rates are in per cent and growth rates are annual average growth (in per cent).

Source: *IFS*, *WEO*, IMF, and relevant central banks' websites.

The policy accommodation pursued until recently by the United States has had a global impact, flooding the rest of the world with an abundance of liquidity (Table 9.5). Low interest rates in the United States have encouraged capital to flow into EMEs. For the countries that prefer some form of managed parity against the US dollar, this has resulted in a large build-up of foreign exchange reserves and excessive domestic liquidity, amplifying the Fed's policy stance. Yet, the global supply of dollars reflected in the so-called 'super money' (that is, the sum of cash and banks' reserve holdings at the Fed plus foreign reserves held by central banks around the world) is estimated to have grown by around 25 per cent per annum in the last couple of years (*The Economist*, 30 September 2004).

Table 9.5 Policy Rates, Money Supply Growth, Producer and Consumer Inflation in Select Emerging Asian Countries

(per cent per annum)

Country	Variable	1990–4	1995–9	2000–4
China	Bank rate	8.5	7.2	3.0
	Money supply	27.6	19.1	16.2
	Reserve money	28.8	15.5	12.4
	Consumer prices	10.4	5.2	1.0
	Credit	26.5	20.0	16.5
India	Policy rate	11.4	10.6	5.9
	Money supply	18.0	13.3	14.0
	Reserve money	16.9	11.4	11.5

Contd

Table 9.5 Contd

Country	Variable	1990–4	1995–9	2000–4
	Producer prices	10.5	5.5	5.2
	Consumer prices	10.2	8.9	3.9
	Credit	13.3	14.9	14.3
Thailand	Discount rate	10.5	10.0	3.5
	Money supply	20.4	9.1	4.6
	Reserve money	16.1	20.4	8.1
	Producer prices	2.8	4.5	3.8
	Consumer prices	4.8	5.1	1.7
	Credit	24.2	8.5	0.8
Malaysia	Money market rate	6.5	6.4	2.7
	Money supply	17.9	14.6	7.3
	Reserve money	21.9	10.9	2.1
	Producer prices	2.5	3.6	3.5
	Consumer Prices	3.8	3.5	1.5
	Credit	12.7	16.4	5.9
		(1993–4)		
Korea	Discount rate	6.2	4.2	2.5
	Money supply	18.2	7.2	9.2
	Reserve money	14.7	4.2	6.7
	Producer prices	3.1	4.4	1.9
	Consumer prices	7.0	4.4	3.2
	Credit	18.1	17.3	12.0
Philippines	Discount rate	12.0	11.5	8.0
	Money supply	14.6	20.3	7.8
	Reserve money	13.8	15.5	1.6
	Producer prices	4.1	6.0	9.6
		(1994)		
	Consumer prices	11.1	7.0	4.6
	Credit	40.2	19.8	6.5
Indonesia	Discount rate	14.4	19.6	12.2
	Money supply	16.0	22.5	17.0
	Reserve money	16.9	41.7	15.3
	Producer prices	5.9	28.1	8.0
	Consumer prices	8.6	20.5	8.0
	Credit	27.4	29.0	10.6

Note: Policy rates are in per cent, and growth rates are annual average growth (in per cent).

Source: *IFS*, IMF.

The global glut of liquidity has facilitated highly leveraged positions, debt financed consumption, and booming credit growth, raising financial stability concerns. While the equity prices shot up in the second half of the 1990s, they came down subsequently in the wake of the dot com crash. Facilitated by the policy accommodation in the United States and the subsequent easing in the rest of the world, the housing prices have now witnessed a boom during 2000–4 all over the world.

Perhaps the greatest puzzle in current global developments is the co-existence of abundant liquidity and low consumer inflation. Despite the prolonged period over which monetary policy all over the world has remained accommodative, inflation has been unusually benign, impervious to soaring oil prices and the elevated prices of non-fuel commodities particularly ferrous and non-ferrous metals. While the industrial countries have maintained the inflation pressures at low and stable levels both during 1995–9 and 2000–4, there has been noticeable decline in inflation during 2000–4 in EMEs. Such low levels of inflation have not been witnessed since the pre-World War period when the discipline of the fixed exchange rates under the gold standard ensured that prices were roughly stable and episodes of deflation were not uncommon. The current phenomenon is unique in recent history, prompting some to visualize the death of inflation though there are signs of its resurrection in recent weeks.

Slowdown in Global Saving and Investment vs Strong Global Growth

Global saving and investment rates have declined in recent years. Global saving increased by a fraction in 1995–9 from the level in 1990–4 before declining in 2000-4 (Table 9.6). While saving as per cent of GDP declined in the United States, the United Kingdom, and European Monetary Union (EMU) in 2000–4 from the level in 1995–9, the same in China and India witnessed an increase. The declining savings in the industrial countries could have its demographic roots with ageing population weighted against higher saving (Mohan, 2004c).

Alongside, the world investment rate declined steadily during the period, ignoring the signals of softening interest rates. Investment in the United States, the United Kingdom, and EMU fell during 2000–4 with increasing risk aversion on the part of the corporates in the wake of the dot com and other financial crises in 1990s. Investment rate has improved in China during 2000–4 while it has declined in India during 2000–3.

Notwithstanding the declining saving and investment rates, global growth has continued its surge from period to period. While consumption has arguably played a critical role in the industrial countries' growth momentum, exports might have played a similar role in the emerging markets. The sustenance of consumption as opposed to investment-led growth has thus given rise to new controversies on present versus future allocation of resources as also on the relevance of overlapping generation outlooks.

Table 9.6 Global Savings and Investment

Country/Area	1990–4	1995–9	2000–4
	GDP Growth (per cent)		
World	2.6	3.7	3.8
EMU	1.9	2.4	1.7
US	2.4	3.9	2.8
UK	1.3	3.0	2.6
India	4.9	6.5	5.7
China	10.7	8.8	8.5
	Saving (per cent of GDP)		
World	22.0	22.3	21.4
EMU	22.5	22.8	22.5 (up to 2003)
US	16.2	17.6	15.2 (up to 2002)
UK	15.8	16.6	14.2 (up to 2003)
India	22.4	21.7	22.2
China	39.7	42.1	43.6
	Investment (per cent of GDP)		
World	23.0	22.7	21.6
EMU	22.0	20.8	20.7 (up to 2003)
US	17.1	19.3	19.1 (up to 2002)
UK	17.1	17.3	16.9 (up to 2003)
India	22.9	23.2	22.7 (up to 2003)
China	38.0	38.8	40.8

Source: *WEO*, IMF and World Development Indicators Online, World Bank.

Low Inflation despite Currency Depreciations

Traditionally, the degree of exchange rate pass-through, that is, the speed and extent of transmission of exchange rate movements into domestic prices, used to be an important consideration for the conduct of monetary policy, leading to the alleged 'fear of floating' on the part of the emerging economies (Calvo and Reinhart, 2002). However, there is now increasing evidence that exchange rate pass-through to domestic inflation has tended to decline from the 1990s across a number of countries. Inflation has turned out to be largely immune and insensitive, barring the sole exception of Indonesia, to the wild volatility and currency depreciation witnessed in Korea, Thailand, the Philippines, and Malaysia in the aftermath of the Asian financial crisis (Table 9.7).

Similarly, the US dollar's substantial depreciation against the Euro during 2002–4 has not led to inflationary pressures in the United States. With inflation standing rock steady even in the face of exchange rate volatility, the traditional channels of current account adjustment have failed to work towards restoring the external balances in a sustainable manner. Further, the weakening of the US dollar against the Euro has not brought about substantial changes in the trade pattern between the United States and the Euro area. On the contrary, the US imports from the Euro area surged ahead during the phase of US dollar's depreciation against the Euro while the US exports to the Euro area did not increase, at least initially (Table 9.8).

POSSIBLE EXPLANATIONS

What factors explain these seeming puzzles and counter-intuitive relationships across a large set of variables? What really explains the divergence between the Producer Price Index (PPI) and CPI and the imperviousness of consumer prices to liquidity conditions? Is the received wisdom on the relationship between money, output, and prices undergoing yet another paradigm shift? Has the inflation process changed at its core? Country experiences present a wide diversity of circumstances, producing a variety of outcomes. This makes generalizations difficult and even adventurous.

As a central banker, I would like to subscribe to the objective of low and stable inflation in the conduct of monetary policy. Reforms in the manner in which monetary policy is set currently and the institutional changes that have occurred in the 1990s have undoubtedly enhanced the reputation of monetary authorities in terms of delivering price stability. The current trend of increasingly independent central banks, enhanced transparency, and greater accountability has, in fact, improved public credibility in these institutions. The institutional strengthening of central banks has coincided with the

Table 9.7 Exchange Rates and Consumer Prices Inflation—Select Asian Countries during the Crisis

Country	Year	1996	1997	1998	1999	2000
Korea	Exchange rate	805	951	1401	1189	1131
		(4.3)	(18.3)	(47.3)	(–15.2)	(–4.9)
	CPI inflation	4.98	4.40	7.54	0.83	2.25
Thailand	Exchange rate	25.0	31.0	41.0	38.0	40.0
		(1.7)	(23.8)	(31.9)	(–8.6)	(6.1)
	CPI inflation	5.83	5.60	8.07	0.30	1.57
Philippines	Exchange rate	26.0	29.0	41.0	39.0	44.0
		(1.9)	(12.4)	(38.8)	(–4.4)	(13.1)
	CPI inflation	7.51	5.59	9.27	5.95	3.95
Malaysia	Exchange rate	2.52	2.81	3.92	3.80	3.80
		(0.5)	(11.8)	(39.5)	(–3.2)	(0.0)
	CPI inflation	3.49	2.66	5.27	2.75	1.54
Indonesia	Exchange rate	2342	2909	10014	7855	8422
		(4.2)	(24.2)	(244.2)	(–21.6)	(7.2)
	CPI inflation	7.97	6.23	58.39	20.49	3.72

Notes: 1. Exchange rates are national currencies per US dollar.
2. Figures in bracket are the percentage changes over the previous year.
3. CPI inflation rates are annual percentage changes.

Source: *WEO* and *IFS*, IMF.

Table 9.8 Exchange Rate, Trade, and Consumer Prices Inflation—Recent Trends in the United States

Item	2000	2001	2002	2003	2004
NEER (2000=100)	100.0	105.94	104.28	91.46	83.97
REER (2000=100)	100.0	103.61	105.18	95.56	86.1
Exchange rate	0.924	0.896	0.944	1.131	1.243
(US$ per Euro)	(–13.4)	(–3.0)	(5.4)	(19.8)	(9.9)
CPI inflation (per cent)	3.38	2.83	1.59	2.27	2.68
Imports from Euro area	226,901.0	226,568.0	232,313.0	253,042.0	281,959.0
(US$ million)	(13.42)	(-0.15)	(2.54)	(8.92)	(11.43)
Exports to Euro area	168,181.0	161,931.0	146,621.0	155,170.0	172,622.0
(US$ million)	(8.63)	(–3.72)	(–9.45)	(5.83)	(11.25)

Note: Figures in bracket are the percentage changes over the previous year.

Source: *WEO* and *IFS*, IMF, and US Census Bureau.

worldwide thrust on fiscal consolidation and structural reforms in the labour and product markets, which have also worked towards attaining price stability. Specified fiscal rules such as those under the Maastricht Treaty and the Stability and Growth Pact in the Euro area have been emulated the world over, charting out explicit road maps for fiscal consolidation. Thus, fiscal deficits in EMEs are now less than half of their levels in 1970s and 1980s. It has been estimated that inflation could have declined by five to fifteen percentage points on account of lower fiscal deficits in EMEs (IMF, 2002). So there are some broad structural fiscal reasons for the worldwide decline in inflation.

Globalization has arguably unleashed the most significant anti-inflationary forces. Lower trade barriers, increased deregulation, innovation, and competition all over the world have led to exponential growth in cross-border trade with world trade racing ahead of output. With the rapid expansion in tradables, domestic economies are, therefore, increasingly exposed to the rigours of international competition and comparative advantage, reducing unwarranted price mark-ups (Greenspan, 2004b). The competition among nations to attract and retain factors of production has also induced governments to reduce entry barriers for new productive activities. Intensified competition in the domestic economy, which has now become part of the global marketplace has rendered prices more flexible, containing the impact of unanticipated inflation on output. This has reduced the incentive for monetary authorities to raise output above the potential (Rogoff, 2003). Increasingly, a firm or country that can produce for global markets, with the greatest cost efficiency, sets global prices. Currently, China is perhaps in such a position but other competitors are not far behind. It, however, needs to be recognized that globalization may not continue to maintain its tempo indefinitely into the future.[1]

An important contributor to low inflation has also been the productivity growth in a number of sectors, partly due to IT investments combined with restructuring. Even the services sector, which was otherwise believed to lag in productivity vis-à-vis industry in view of its 'cost disease' syndrome, *à la* Baumol, has witnessed impressive productivity growth with increased penetration of IT in most services activities. Productivity growth has been particularly discernible in the United States from the mid-1990s with continuing signs of sustenance in the next decade (Oliner and Sichel, 2002). While productivity growth in the Euro area may not have been as high as in the United States, the disinflationary effects of productivity growth in one region get transmitted across borders through increased competition in a globalized world (Table 9.9).

Table 9.9 Productivity in Manufacturing*

(annual percentage change)

Country/Area	1987–96	1997–9	2000–4
Advanced economies	3.1	3.37	3.76
US	2.8	3.97	4.96
UK	3.4	3.47	4.42
Euro area	–	4.13	2.88
Japan	2.7	1.57	3.62

Note: * Refers to labour productivity, measured as the ratio of hourly compensation to unit labour costs.

Source: *WEO*, IMF.

The impact of cross-country integration is also at work in the labour market. An economy which is open to migrant labour exhibits a different inflationary process from one that is not. An increase in spending raises the pressure of demand on supply and leads to upward pressure on wages and prices. But if the increased demand for labour generates its own supply in the form of migrant labour then the link between demand and prices is broken, or at least altered. Indeed, in an economy that can call on unlimited supplies of migrant labour or can go for outsourcing, the concept of output gap may not be that meaningful (King, 2005). The inflow of migrant labour both in the United States and the United Kingdom has arguably led to a diminution of inflationary pressure in the labour market in these countries (Table 9.10).

Table 9.10 Net Migration to the United States and the United Kingdom*

Country	1985–90	1990–5	1995–2000
US	3,775,000	5,200,000	6,200,000
UK	104,310	380,840	574,470

Note: * Number of immigrants *less* the number of emigrants, including both citizens and non-citizens.

Source: World Development Indicators Online, World Bank.

The expanding canvas of knowledge has also had its impact in the form of low and stable inflation. The technological advances in architecture and engineering as well as development of lighter but stronger materials has resulted in 'downsized' output, evident in the huge expansion of the money value of output and trade but not in tonnage. As a consequence, material intensity of production has declined reflecting, 'the substitution, in effect, of ideas for physical matter in the creation of economic value' (Greenspan, 1998). This has contributed to the secular decline in commodity prices, notwithstanding short spells of spikes in these prices. The increasing commodity price volatility around the declining trend has, however, engaged the monetary policy attention in the short run (Mohan, 2004a). The declining share of commodity prices in final goods prices has been an important factor, leading to a divergence between PPI and CPI. Thus even substantial increases in input prices no longer lead to corresponding increases in output prices and are further muted by the forces of global competition.

Thus the persistence of low and stable inflation worldwide despite considerable monetary accommodation in recent years can be explained by invoking these new economic developments in the real economy. The role of central banks in the recent containment of inflation can, at best, be seen to have limited applicability.

For industrial countries, the exchange rate pass-through to consumer price inflation has been found to have almost halved in the 1990s compared to the pre-1990s period (Faruqee, 2004; Gagnon and Ihrig, 2001; McCarthy, 2000). Furthermore, the pass-through has reportedly declined more in developing countries in the 1990s than in the advanced economies (Frankel, Parsley, and Wei, 2004). Financial innovations such as the availability of hedging products have also lowered the degree of pass-through by enabling exporters and importers to ignore temporary shocks and set stable product prices despite large currency fluctuations: Witness the lack of price change in BMWs, Mercedes, and Porsches in the United States despite substantial dollar depreciation with respect to the Euro. The import composition of the industrial countries is found to have shifted in favour of sectors with low pass-through such as the manufacturing sector. There is also a view that, in some cases, the low observed pass-through might be due to disappearance of expensive goods from consumption and their replacement by inferior local substitutes (Burstein, Eichenbaum, and Rebelo, 2003). That is, no more Mercedes and BMWs!

The increasing share of non-tradables in GDP has also worked towards containing the exchange rate pass-through. Non-tradables generally approximated by services have increased their share in all major industrial countries as also in China and India. As populations age, demand moves more in favour of services than for goods. Thus, the ageing population in industrial countries has provided much of the growth impetus for services. With the shift in demand composition in favour of services, no wonder, the extent of exchange rate pass-through, which works primarily through tradables has been limited (Table 9.11).

Table 9.11 Share of Services in GDP

(per cent)

Country	1990–4	1995–9	2000–4
US	71.71	72.89	74.65 (up to 2001)
UK	65.55	67.91	71.62 (up to 2003)
Japan	60.26	64.92	67.45 (up to 2002)
Euro area	64.25	67.24	69.21 (up to 2003)
China	32.74	31.36	33.72
India	42.16	45.14	50.44

Source: World Development Indicators Online, World Bank.

The role of exchange rate movements or policy-induced adjustments in influencing behaviour of economic agents through the domestic price mechanism appears to have been significantly truncated. If an exchange rate depreciation (appreciation) does not appreciably increase (decrease) domestic prices of imported goods, there would be little reason to expect a reduction (increase) in demand for imported products. Hence small exchange rate changes can scarcely be expected to help significantly in effecting changes in the current account.

There has been reduced volatility of GDP growth in most G-7 countries over the past three decades, coinciding with growing integration and synchronization of business cycles (Mohan, 2004a). The standard deviation of US GDP growth during 1984–2002 was two-thirds of that during 1960–83. This could have also contributed to lowering inflation (Stock and Watson, 2003). The growing share of services—a sector less susceptible to volatility—better inventory management, and easy access to credit with financial deepening have also brought down the volatility of GDP growth and, therefore, expectations of future inflation.

The global financial landscape has undergone a sea change over the last couple of decades, characterized by increasing liberalization and growing completeness of markets and institutions. The pursuit of flexible exchange rates for the major currencies from the 1970s has made the spot and forward foreign exchange markets strikingly efficient in tracking the expectations of economic agents. Alongside, the broadening and deepening of the secondary and derivatives markets for government and other fixed income securities has added to the flows of market information. With the onset of de-mystification and decomposition of risks, there has been a deluge of new financial products, enabling economic agents to manage, hedge, or lay off risks. Simultaneously, there has been discernible improvement in the institutional infrastructure—legal or informational—providing a durable basis for efficient functioning of the financial markets. With the arrival of options pricing in the early 1970s, more and more complex financial products are hitting the market every day. Financial markets—at least in the industrial countries—have thus transformed themselves into super-efficient vehicles for allocating resources and spreading risks across sectors, time, and space. The lower costs of financial intermediation, the greater scope for risk spreading, and the reduced reliance on any individual institution or market channel for the intermediation of savings and investment have had a spurring effect on financial activities undertaken by households, businesses, and governments. Thus, the global financial system appears to be more robust and resilient to financial shocks emanating from individual countries. Certainly, the increasing confidence of the financial system has its reflection in the sustained global growth and taming of inflation all over world (Blinder and Reis, 2005). The growing sophistication of financial markets has therefore, paradoxically, reduced the power of the price mechanism in bringing about changes in a desired policy direction.

It is, therefore, possible that such developments in financial markets have had the effect of reducing risks across the board, both spatially and temporally. Such developments have received further support from the increased focus of central banks on inflation containment and stability, along with overall financial stability. The accompanying institutional changes, mainly the increased acceptance of central bank autonomy, have probably contributed to enhancement of their credibility. Thus there could be a secular decline in risk perception and in medium- and long-term inflationary expectations, thereby reducing the neutral real interest rate. If these conjectures have some element of validity, the effect of changes in short-term policy rates on long-term yields would be muted, as seems to have happened in the United States. Paradoxically then, the central banks' own success could have blunted the efficacy of their most powerful policy instrument: the short-term interest rate.

As regards the muted impact of soaring oil prices on the general price level and economic activities, it needs to be recognized that unlike in the past when oil price surges were driven by supply shocks, the current bull market in oil is mainly the result of a perceived secular increase in demand emanating from accelerated growth in our countries, which, moreover, is expected to continue in the foreseeable future. The sharp rise in oil prices is perceived to have been triggered by sustained global growth, particularly in the United States among developed countries, and from increasing contributions from the EMEs that tend to demand relatively more oil than the developed world for a similar expansion in output. The higher oil prices of the 1970s brought to an abrupt end the extraordinary period of growth in the United States oil consumption. Between 1945 and 1973, consumption of petroleum products in the United States rose at a startling 4.5 per cent average annual rate, well in excess of real GDP growth. However, between 1973 and 2004, oil consumption in the United States grew, on an average, only 0.5 per cent per annum, far short of the rise in real GDP (Greenspan, 2005b). The mandated fuel-efficiency standards for cars and light trucks coupled with the imports of small, fuel-efficient Japanese cars and the increasing share of services sector in GDP induced slower growth of gasoline demand in the United States. Thus, while the oil intensity of output has fallen in the industrial countries, for example, from the peak of 0.19 kg per real US dollar in the United States in 1970 to 0.09 kg per real US dollar in 2000, the relatively slower decline for developing countries such as China and India has been neutralized by the pace of rise in incomes (Table 9.12).

Table 9.12 Oil Intensity in Select Countries (using Constant US$ GDP)

(kilogram of oil per real US$)

Country/Area	1970	1980	1990	2000	2003
World	0.18	0.17	0.13	0.11	0.11
US	0.19	0.15	0.11	0.09	0.09
UK	0.14	0.09	0.07	0.05	0.05
Japan	0.11	0.09	0.06	0.05	0.05
France	0.15	0.13	0.08	0.07	0.07
Germany	0.15	0.12	0.08	0.07	0.07
India	0.17	0.21	0.22	0.23	0.21
China	0.30	0.52	0.27	0.21	0.19
Malaysia	0.24	0.32	0.29	0.23	0.22
Indonesia	0.27	0.37	0.30	0.33	0.32
Philippines	0.27	0.23	0.20	0.22	0.18
South Korea	0.14	0.20	0.17	0.20	0.18
Thailand	0.27	0.31	0.25	0.28	0.28
Brazil	0.14	0.14	0.13	0.14	0.13
Mexico	0.11	0.14	0.16	0.15	0.14

Source: British Petroleum's *Statistical Review of World Energy* and World Development Indicators Online, World Bank.

Unlike the oil shocks of the 1970s, when the oil surplus with the oil exporting countries mainly found its way out into conspicuous consumption, this time around, the oil exporting countries seem to be doing a much better job of recycling the oil surpluses into the global economy. For example, the OPEC countries are running only a marginal trade surplus with China as they are importing a range of goods from China, which is using more oil to manufacture those goods. Oil exporting countries have also been active in the international investment arena, using their export revenue to buy stocks and bonds in various countries, thereby keeping the global cost of capital low.

Furthermore, the self-equilibrating demand–supply mechanism in the face of the rising oil prices has been kept in abeyance in a number of countries. While the current oil cycle has witnessed a doubling in the price of oil over the past three years, on average only a third of the price increase has been passed on to end users. While Europe and Japan have cut down high taxes on oil consumption to cushion the impact of higher oil prices, governments in many developing countries are subsiding oil prices in recognition of the lower resilience of low-income people to sudden price shocks. 'But if history is any guide, should higher prices persist, energy use will over time continue to decline, relative to GDP. Long-term demand elasticities have proved noticeably higher than those that are evident in the short term' (Greenspan, 2005b). Nevertheless, since oil use is only two-thirds as important an input into world GDP as it was three decades ago, the effect of the current surge in oil prices, though noticeable, is likely to prove significantly less than in 1970s.

The entry into the world economy of the erstwhile centrally planned economies, in general, and China, in particular, has arguably constituted a massive positive supply shock, raising the world's potential growth, holding down inflation and triggering changes in the relative prices of labour, capital, goods, and assets (BIS, 2005). In this context, the desirability of positive inflation rates has been questioned in certain circles. In other words, are central banks targeting too high a rate of inflation now that China has joined the global market economy?

During the era of rapid globalization in the late nineteenth century, falling average prices were quite common. This 'good deflation', which was accompanied by robust growth, was very different from the bad deflation experienced in the 1930s depression. Today, we could have been in yet another phase of 'good deflation' but central banks have favoured low but positive interest rates while setting and meeting their inflation targets. Furthermore, China's entry into the global economy has raised the worldwide return on capital. That, in turn, should imply an increase in the equilibrium level of real interest rates. But, central banks are holding real rates at historically low levels and one finds scenarios of excessive credit growth, mortgage borrowing and housing investment. In this context, however, some estimates suggest that the impact of Chinese exports on global inflation has been fairly modest. China's exports could have reduced (a) global inflation by 30 basis points per annum; (b) US import price inflation by 80 basis points (but in view of the United States being a relatively closed economy, the impact on producer and consumer prices has likely been quite small); and (c) import unit values inflation by 10–25 basis points in the OECD countries (Kamin, Marazzi, and Schindler, 2004). These estimates should be treated as upper bounds since they ignore the fact that China's rapid export growth has also been associated with equally rapid import growth and China is, therefore, contributing not only to global supply but also global demand. This is also reflected in the sharp rise in global commodity prices beginning early 2003.

THE WAY AHEAD

Measured by the growth in global credit or property prices, some parts of the world are currently experiencing strong asset price inflation. As with traditional inflation, the surging asset prices distort relative prices and cause a misallocation of resources. For instance, since households think they are wealthier, they spend more and save and invest less. The risk is that as interest rates rise, the fragility of the economic recovery would be exposed and decisions based on cheap credit would look less than wise.

Whereas there is no question about the desirability of maintaining financial stability, monetary policy is often considered to be too blunt an instrument to achieve financial stability, especially to counter threats from asset price misalignments. Indeed, it is often difficult to adjudge ex ante as to whether asset price misalignments are bubbles or not. Second, even if the bubble is identified on a real time basis, the typical monetary tightening measures such as increase in interest rates may not be effective in deflating asset price bubbles.

In view of such limitations of monetary policy actions as also the fact that inflationary pressures take more than the usual time to surface in conditions of low inflation, central banks need to take cognizance of emerging financial imbalances by lengthening their monetary policy horizons beyond the usual two-year framework. More importantly, in view of the possibility of the role of prices becoming muted as an equilibrating mechanism, whether in terms of changes in exchange rates, interest rates or commodity prices, central banks will have to contribute to financial stability more through prudential regulation and supervision to address the emergence of financial sector excesses or imbalances arising from excess liquidity or other economic imbalances. Indeed, greater transparency and cooperation between monetary policy and supervision is being increasingly recognized and many central banks are exploring alternatives as opposed to the traditional monetary policy instruments.

Given the fact that the defining characteristic of the monetary policy landscape is 'uncertainty', no simple rule could possibly describe the policy action to be taken in every contingency (Greenspan, 2004a). As a consequence, the conduct of monetary policy has come to involve, at its core, crucial elements of risk management. This conceptual framework emphasizes understanding as much as possible the many sources of risk and uncertainty that policymakers face, quantifying those risks when possible, and assessing the costs associated with each of the risks.

Under these conditions, the separation of the function of financial regulation and supervision from central banking has come up for critical reappraisal. Even though a formal separation of functions may have become more common than in the past, there remains a question whether that change would make much difference to the practical realities (Goodhart, 1995). In their quest for financial stability, central banks worldwide have exhibited a variety of responses. On the one hand, several central banks have been given an explicit mandate to promote financial stability. Another broad category of response has been the constitution of independent departments to oversee financial stability. Illustratively, at the Reserve Bank of New Zealand, the banking supervision department and financial markets department were merged into a Financial Stability Department, headed by a Deputy Governor. In the Netherlands, the newly established Financial Stability Division concentrates experienced staff members from monetary policy, supervision, financial markets, oversight and research departments. At the European Central Bank (ECB), the area concerned with financial stability matters (Prudential Supervision Division) was upgraded to a Directorate (Financial Stability and Supervision), which reports to a member of the Executive Board, and plays a coordination role for Euro area/EU financial stability monitoring. Finally, the Bank of England has recently constituted a dedicated Financial Stability Department for oversight of financial stability matters. The transfer of supervisory responsibilities outside the central bank in several countries has also led central banks to focus their attention on systemic issues as reflected in a reorientation of organizational arrangements.

The traditional signals such as inflation, interest rates, and exchange rates are today overly anchored while the global economy is on a long leash supported by easy finance. However, the increasing potential for sharp corrections in the medium term needs to be contained by following a two-fold strategy: consumption needs to give way smoothly to investment with the withdrawal of policy accommodation in industrial countries, and the locus of domestic demand needs to shift from countries running deficits to ones with surpluses so as to reduce the current account imbalances. Obviously, coordinated policy initiatives have to be high on the agenda of the global community for ensuring a smooth transition.

If it is indeed true that the efficacy of price-based indirect monetary policy instruments has become blunted because of central banks' own success in containing inflation and muting expectations, along with the increasing sophistication of financial markets, what alternatives do we now have to address the emerging global imbalances? Ironically, the answer perhaps is that we may need to return to more quantity based instruments, either through micro actions by central banks or structural actions by the fiscal authorities. Central banks would perhaps have to again resort to activating more detailed prudential, regulatory, and supervisory roles aimed at disciplining different segments of the financial markets. Similarly, if external imbalances are perceived to arise because of fiscal imbalances, they will have to be attacked directly, rather than through increasingly ineffective exchange rate signals.

This finally gives me an opportunity to provide some illustrations from recent monetary management actions in China and India.

The People's Bank of China (PBC) has been trying to contain the possible downside risks by way of a range of direct and indirect instruments. Required reserve ratios have been lifted several times, within the context of a newly differentiated reserve requirement system aimed at better aligning the degree of restraint with the degree of excess credit expansion, institution by institution. Moral suasion has been used with 'window guidance' and 'credit policy advice' in relation to credit allocation including warnings on the riskiness of increasing exposures to certain overheated sectors. Benchmark interest rates were increased by about 0.3 percentage points in October 2004. At the same time, the upper limit on interest rates charged by commercial banks was abolished, and the limits for urban and rural cooperatives was increased to 2.3 times the benchmark rate. The interest rates that the PBC charges for providing short-term liquidity support were increased by between 0.3 and 0.6 percentage points, and the PBC was given additional room to adjust these rates according to economic and financial conditions. The PBC has also continued its sterilization operations by way of changes in reserve ratios, OMOs and issuance of central bank bills in the wake of strong forex inflows. China has also revalued its currency and the yuan now floats against a basket of currencies. This policy of having greater flexibility in the exchange rate would allow monetary authorities to guard against the risk of any further increase in inflation in both product and asset markets. Thus, as I understand it, China has used a judicious mix of traditional monetary instruments, along with a selection of detailed prudential and regulatory instruments to deal with the possibility of overheating in the economy.

In India, monetary management has had to contend with testing challenges on several fronts—an increase in domestic prices in the first half of 2004 driven largely by a sustained increase in international commodity prices including fuel, a large overhang of domestic liquidity generated by capital inflows, and the upturn in the international interest rate cycle. The RBI has, therefore, had to strike a fine balance between reining in inflationary expectations, encouraging the impulses of growth, and ensuring financial stability. In early 2004, it was recognized that the finite stock of government paper with the Reserve Bank could potentially circumscribe the scope of outright OMOs for sterilizing capital flows which were last carried out in January 2004. The Reserve Bank cannot issue its own paper under the extant provisions of the RBI Act, 1934 and such an option has generally not been favoured in India. Central bank bills/bonds would impose the entire cost of sterilization on the Reserve Bank's balance sheet. Besides, the existence of two sets of risk-free paper—gilts and central bank securities—tends to fragment the market. Accordingly, the LAF, which operates through repos of government paper to create a corridor for overnight interest rates and thereby functions as an instrument of day-to-day liquidity management, had to be relied upon for sterilization as well. Under these circumstances, the MSS was introduced in April 2004 to provide the monetary authority an additional instrument of liquidity management and sterilization. Under the MSS, the government issues Treasury Bills and dated government securities to mop up domestic liquidity and parks the proceeds in a ring-fenced deposit account with the RBI. The funds can be appropriated only for redemption and/or buyback of paper issued under the MSS. Besides an increase in the MSS ceiling, raising of the CRR, lowering the rate of remuneration on the eligible CRR balances, hikes in the reverse repo rate by 25 basis points each in October 2004, April 2005, and October 2005, several measures were also initiated to maintain asset quality of the banking system at a time of rapid credit growth.

The runaway oil prices riding on the back of growing demand in a cyclical upturn are currently looming large on the pace and pattern of the growth performance in both the economies. While the economies have so far absorbed the oil shocks in their stride and with surprising resilience, continuing uncertainties on the oil front, however, pose a question mark on their sustained performance. Paradoxically, the reserves build-up with the Asian central banks, with its attendant cost implications has started slowing down of late with the soaring oil prices cutting into the oil importers' trade and current account surpluses. However, the growing transfer on account of oil portends yet another risk in terms of the sustenance of current accounts. Besides, FDI and portfolio inflows are also showing signs of fatigue in several Asian countries with the hardening of the rates in the United States. With sudden reversals of expectations, the Asian economies, thus, run the risk of disruption in their financial and real markets.

Several countries in Asia have followed a relatively flexible exchange rate policy to ensure smooth adjustment along with corrections in the world economy. Such flexibility has served these countries well. However, the world has to guard against any new risks arising out of any large corrections in the exchange rates of the world's major currencies accompanied by rising inflation and interest rates (Mohan, 2004b). First, the protectionist tendencies need to be curbed in keeping with the multilateral spirit of trade negotiations. Second, we need to work collectively towards developing a sound international financial architecture, the lack of which, it may be recalled, has led to excessive caution on the part of developing countries in building large reserves. Third, given the need for financial stability alongside monetary stability, central banks need to be cautious before joining the recent trend of separating the monetary and supervisory authorities, particularly in view of the muted responses to the pricing channels of monetary policy. In the recent past, faced with an unprecedented rise in housing credit, the RBI has raised the risk weight of housing loans as a counter cyclical action for the purpose of maintenance of CRAR. It is felt that availability of prudential instruments at the disposal of a central bank facilitates its twin task of monetary and financial stability.

AFTERWORD

In late 2005, when I first drafted Chapter 9, the global economy exhibited certain characteristics, which appeared to defy the basic principles of economics. Three years later, some of these puzzles appear to be unravelling in ways consistent with the basic tenets of economics. First, the US dollar depreciated substantially between October 2005 and July 2008, attributable to the concerns over the sustainability of the expanding US current account deficit (CAD), slowing down of the US economy, rising inflation and lower interest rates in the US. The depreciation has been associated with accelerated export growth leading to some improvement in the US CAD (from 6.0 per cent of GDP in 2006 to 4.6 per cent in 2008). However, the US CAD still remains substantial, and factors other than currency depreciation—such as slowing domestic growth—also appear to be at work.

Second, the sharp rise in oil prices in 2005 had surprised many observers. But, the rise in oil prices in the subsequent period and especially in the first half of 2008—oil prices almost approached a record US$ 150 a barrel—was even more surprising. While there are no convincing explanations for such an exponential rise, it led to large increase in headline inflation in most countries—almost at two decades high in many countries. Interestingly, oil prices surged in the first half of 2008, even as global growth was slowing down on the back of the sub-prime crisis led turmoil in global financial markets—the severest turmoil, according to some observers, since the Great Depression of the 1930s. Monetary authorities faced a complex combination—slowing growth and rising inflation—in the first half of 2008. After cutting the policy rates aggressively between August 2007 and April 2008, the US Fed remained on hold till September 2008. Other major central banks such as the ECB tightened further to anchor inflation expectations. However, with the intensification of the global financial markets crisis in September–October 2008, downside risks to financial stability and economic activity were accentuated, and almost all the major advanced countries were facing the threat of a severe protracted recession by the last quarter of 2008. Accordingly, central banks of almost all advanced economies loosened monetary policy, including through an unprecedented coordinated cut in policy rates in October 2008, while continuing with their unconventional efforts to increase the availability of market liquidity. The EMEs, which had exhibited a great deal of resilience up to mid 2008, were also adversely affected by the sudden deterioration in global financial market developments. With downside risks to financial stability and economic growth, major EMEs were also forced to relax monetary policy, while providing additional liquidity. In response to these developments, international crude oil prices witnessed a sudden collapse, reaching around US$ 50 levels by November 2008.

Third, it now appears that abundant global liquidity was initially reflected in elevated asset prices (mainly housing and stock prices). As housing and stock markets corrected beginning the second half of 2007, investors seemed to have moved in a herd-like fashion to the commodities market as an asset class in the first half of 2008. The sharp surge in global commodity prices got mirrored in headline inflation. Thus, abundant global liquidity initially fuelled housing and stock markets, then boosted commodities and finally, was reflected in consumer price inflation. Thus, the puzzle of low consumer price inflation in the presence of enhanced global liquidity appears to have been resolved. These developments have important implications for monetary authorities worldwide: above average growth in credit and monetary aggregates is still a useful leading indicator of future inflationary pressures, although the transmission lags could be much longer than in the past. Thus, the benign neglect of credit and monetary aggregates—in both the state-of-the-art models as well as in actual monetary policy making in most central banks—can be costly.

Finally, the puzzle of falling long term bond yields in the presence of Fed Fund rate hikes is currently unravelling in a rather unexpected manner. Low long-term yields encouraged excessive search for yield and extreme risk appetite. The search for yield led to financial engineering and development of extremely complex financial products. Risky sub-prime mortgages were bundled as AAA-rated securities, partly encouraged by the 'originate and distribute' model. As some withdrawal of monetary accommodation commenced in response to perceived or visible inflationary pressures, the sub-prime crisis revealed these vulnerabilities starkly as confidence plunged, markets froze and triggered off panic among investors and lenders regarding their inability to value complex risky assets and structured derivative products. With the deterioration in credit confidence, banks have been forced to advance loans to their off-balance sheet 'special investment vehicles' (SIVs) which used up their capital, thereby rendering other borrowers credit constrained. Thus, it can be argued that the sub-prime is a symptom rather than a cause.[2]

The ongoing turmoil in the global financial markets has raised a range of issues. A key question that has emerged from the current developments in financial markets relates to the role of monetary authorities in the context of such a crisis. Over the last decade or two, it would appear that the focus of central banks has been narrowing—such as adoption of single-minded inflation target oriented monetary policy—relative to the more complex responsibilities that they have traditionally shouldered. Thus, the separation of financial regulation and supervision from monetary policy could have contributed to ineffective and inadequate surveillance in the context of the current crisis. There is a view that problems of information asymmetry might have got further aggravated with banks reporting both to the monetary authority and the regulatory body in charge of banking supervision. When it comes to the crunch, in their roles as lenders of last resort (LOLR), and in discharging their responsibilities as the guardians of financial stability, central banks do need to perform functions that are more complex. In our case, the RBI is also the banking regulator and supervisor. We receive continuing information on the banking activities; moreover, in times such as the current turmoil, we can also obtain information quickly from leading systemically important institutions on exposures of relevance. Thus, prompt corrective action can be taken on a timely basis. In view of the recent turmoil in the global financial markets, it would be apposite for central bankers and academia alike to revisit the issue of the objectives of monetary policy: should the central banks have narrow objectives such as responsibility only for price stability or they ought to have broader objectives?

Notes

[1] It is instructive to turn to Chairman Greenspan, who said, 'We have not experienced a sufficient number of economic turning points to judge the causal linkages among increased globalization, improved monetary policy, significant disinflation and greater economic stability' (Greenspan, 2004b).

[2] See Rakesh Mohan (2007), 'India's Financial Sector Reforms: Fostering Growth While Containing Risk', *Reserve Bank of India Bulletin*, December.

References

Bank for International Settlements (BIS) (2005), *Annual Report, 2004-05*, BIS, Basel.

Bernanke, B.S. (2005), 'The Global Saving Glut and the U.S. Current Account Deficit', At the Sandridge Lecture, Virginia Association of Economics, Richmond, Virginia, 10 March.

Blinder, A.S. and R. Reis (2005), 'Understanding the Greenspan Standard', Federal Reserve Bank of Kansas City Symposium, Jackson Hole, Wyoming, 12 September.

Burstein, A., M. Eichenbaum, and S. Rebelo (2003), *Why Is Inflation So Low After Large Devaluations?, Mimeo,* Northwestern University.

Calvo, G.A. and C.M. Reinhart (2002), 'Fear of Floating', *The Quarterly Journal of Economics*, 117(2), May.

Fama, E.F. (1986), 'Term Structure Forecasts of Interest Rates, Inflation, and Real Returns', *Journal of Monetary Economics*, 25, pp. 59–76.

Faruqee, H. (2004), 'Exchange Rate Pass-through in the Euro Area: The Role of Asymmetric Pricing Behaviour', IMF Working Paper No. 04/14.

Frankel, J., D. Parsley, and S.J. Wei, (2004), *Slow Pass-through around the World: A New Import for Developing Countries?, Mimeo*, Harvard University.

Gagnon, J.E. and J. Ihrig (2001), 'Monetary Policy and Exchange Rate Pass-through', *International Finance Discussion Papers*, Number 704, Board of Governors of the Federal Reserve System, July.

Goodhart, C. (1995), *The Central Bank and the Financial System,* Macmillan.

Greenspan, A. (1998), 'The Implications of Technological Changes', remarks at the Charlotte Chamber of Commerce.

_____ (2004a), 'Risk and Uncertainty in Monetary Policy', remarks at the Meetings of the American Economic Association, San Diego, California.

_____ (2004b), 'Current Account', remarks before the Economic Club of New York.

_____ (2005a), Testimony before the Committee on Banking, Housing, and Urban Affairs, US Senate, 16 February.

_____ (2005b), 'Energy', remarks before the Japanese Business Federation in Tokyo.

International Monetary Fund (2002), *WEO*, IMF, Washington, DC.

_____ (2005), *WEO*, IMF, Washington, DC.

Kamin, S.B., M. Marazzi, and J.W. Schindler (2004), 'Is China Exporting Deflation?', *International Finance Discussion Papers*, No. 791, Board of Governors of the Federal Reserve System.

King, M. (2005), Speech delivered at Salts Mill, Bradford, Yorkshire, 13 June.

McCarthy, J. (2000), 'Pass-through of Exchange Rates and Import Prices to Domestic Inflation in Some Industrialised Economies', *Federal Reserve Bank of New York Staff Reports*, No. 111.

Mishkin, F.S. (1991), 'A Multi-Country Study of the Information in the Shorter Maturity Term Structure about Future Inflation', *Journal of International Money and Finance*, 10, pp. 2–22.

Mohan, R. (2004a), 'Challenges to Monetary Policy in A Globalising Context', *RBI Bulletin*, January.

_____ (2004b), 'Orderly Global Economic Recovery: Are Exchange Rate Adjustments Effective Any More?', intervention at the G-20 Deputies Meeting at Leipzig, Germany, 3–4 March.

_____ (2004c), 'Fiscal Challenges of Population Ageing: The Asian Experience', in Gordon Seller (ed.), *Global Demographic Change: Economic Impacts and Policy Challenges*, proceedings of a Symposium sponsored by the Federal Reserve Bank of Kansas City, at Jackson Hole, Wyoming.

Oliner, S. and D. Sichel (2002), 'Information Technology and Productivity: Where Are We Now and Where Are We Going?' *FRB Atlanta Economic Review* (Summer), pp. 15–44.

Rogoff, K. (2003), 'Globalization and Global Disinflation', *Federal Reserve Bank of Kansas City Economic Review*, Fourth Quarter, pp. 45–79.

Stock, J.H. and M.W. Watson (2003), 'Has the Business Cycle Changed? Evidence and Explanations', paper presented at a Conference on 'Monetary Policy and Uncertainty: Adapting to a Changing Economy', sponsored by the Federal Reserve Bank of Kansas City, at Jackson Hole, Wyoming, August.

10 Evolution of Central Banking in India*

I have great pleasure in mentioning that the theme of the *Report on Currency and Finance: 2004–05*, prepared by the staff of the RBI, is also that of evolution of Central Banking in India (RBI, 2005a). In going through the process of compilation of the Report, I have found the evolutionary process of central banking all over the world and also that in India to be very interesting and informative. The most striking feature of central bank functioning both across time and over countries in a contemporaneous manner, is not how similar their functions are or have been, but how heterogeneous they are and how their functions have constantly evolved over the changing times. My interest in tracking the evolution of central banking in India has also been triggered by the recent publication of the history of the RBI in three volumes, covering the period 1935–81 (RBI, 2005b).

GLOBAL EVOLUTION OF CENTRAL BANKING

Evolution of central banking is essentially a twentieth century phenomenon as there were only about a dozen central banks in the world at the turn of the twentieth century. In contrast, at present, there are nearly 160 central banks. This is not surprising since the need for central banks obviously emerged as banking became more complex, while becoming an increasingly important part of the economy over time. The many vicissitudes experienced by banks and their depositors inevitably led to cries for their regulation. Second, the central banks are essentially a nation state phenomenon, and hence proliferated as nation states themselves emerged and multiplied: again a twentieth century phenomenon. Third, it is useful to recall some of the reasons for the origin of central banks: to issue currency; to be a banker and

* Based on the lecture delivered at the seminar organized by the London School of Economics and the National Institute of Bank Management at Mumbai on 24 January 2006. Reprinted from *Prajnan*, Vol. XXXV, No. 2, July–September (2006).

lender to the government; to regulate and supervise the banks and financial entities; and to serve as a lender-of-last-resort.

This is ironic since much of the current professional thinking is that a central bank should be independent of the government, should no longer be a debt manager of the government, and should not regulate or supervise commercial banks. The new objective function assigned to the central bank is to focus on price stability, with financial stability as an additional objective in some cases. This is perhaps not surprising since price stability was historically achieved, along with preservation of currency value, through the gold standard and later through the dollar anchor and its relation to gold. The world lost its monetary anchor on 15 August 1971 when the United States decided to delink the dollar from gold, and has been floundering ever since in search of a new anchor.

After the convulsions of the 1960s and 1970s, mainly related to the financing of the Vietnam war, the expansion of world liquidity, and the ensuing somewhat enduring inflation, along with Latin American fiscal and monetary expansion, the new holy grail is independence of the central bank, a concept that is becoming almost synonymous with inflation targeting. And here, though I am too new to central banking to really offer a definitive view, I have to admit to a certain scepticism related to the current fashion among central bankers. Two pertinent questions are natural to be asked. First, why is it so obvious that central banks should abandon their 'parents', the sovereign government? One quick explanation could be that the central banks have 'come-of-age' in recent years. But then, some instances like the case of two currencies in Iraq in the 1990s and that of the Bank of Japan in recent years provide a contrary view to the 'come-of-age' hypothesis (King, 2004). Second, is it really the case that supervision and regulation of banks by the central bank leads to conflict of interest? In consideration of this conflict, the Financial Services Authority (FSA) was established in the United Kingdom in 2000, and a number of countries have followed suit. What I would like to do today is to explore some of these issues as they relate to India at the present time.

THE HISTORICAL ANTECEDENTS OF CENTRAL BANKING IN INDIA

In India, the efforts to establish a banking institution with central banking character dates back to the late eighteenth century. The Governor of Bengal in British India recommended the establishment of a General Bank in Bengal and Bihar. The Bank was set up in 1773 but it was short-lived. It was in the early twentieth century that, consequent to the recommendations of the Chamberlain Commission (1914) proposing the amalgamation of the three Presidency Banks, the Imperial Bank of India was formed in 1921 to additionally carry out the functions of central banking along with commercial banking. In 1926, the Royal Commission on Indian Currency and Finance (Hilton Young Commission) recommended that the dichotomy of functions and divisions of responsibilities for control of currency and credit should be ended. The Commission suggested the establishment of a central bank to be called the RBI whose separate existence was considered necessary for augmenting banking facilities throughout the country. The Bill to establish the RBI was introduced in January 1927 in the Legislative Assembly, but it was dropped due to differences in views regarding ownership, constitution, and composition of its Board of Directors. Finally, a fresh Bill was introduced in 1933 and passed in 1934. The RBI Act came into force on 1 January 1935. The RBI was inaugurated on 1 April 1935 as a shareholders' institution and the Act provided for the appointment by the Central Government of the Governor and two Deputy Governors. The RBI was nationalized on 1 January 1949 in terms of the RBI (Transfer to Public Ownership) Act, 1948 (RBI, 2005b).

The main functions of the RBI, as laid down in the statutes are (a) issue of currency, (b) banker to the government, including the function of debt management, and (c) banker to other banks. The Preamble to the RBI Act laid out the objectives as 'to regulate the issue of bank notes and the keeping of reserves with a view to securing monetary stability in India and generally to operate the currency and credit system of the country to its advantage'. Unusually, and unlike most central banks, the RBI was specifically entrusted with an important promotional role since its inception to finance agricultural operations and marketing of crops. In fact, the Agricultural Credit Department was created simultaneously with the establishment of the RBI in 1935.

The RBI, as a central bank, has always performed the function of maintaining the external value of the rupee. Historically, the rupee was linked with the pound sterling, which continued even after the establishment of the RBI. It was only in late September 1975 that the rupee was delinked from pound sterling and the value was determined with reference to a basket of currencies until 1991. The exchange rate regime, soon thereafter, transited from a basket-linked managed float to a market-based system in March 1993, after a short experiment with a dual exchange rate regime between March 1992 and February 1993. Prior to World War II, India was a net debtor country and the British introduced exchange controls to conserve foreign exchange. Exchange control was introduced in India on 3 September 1939 on the outbreak of World War II by virtue of the emergency powers derived under the financial provisions of the Defence of India Rules, mainly to conserve the non-sterling area currencies and utilize them for essential purposes. Even after the War, the controls continued mainly to ensure the most prudent use of the foreign exchange resources. However, the vast accumulation of sterling balances during World War II provided an opportunity for repatriation of the sterling debt, an initiative which came at the behest of the RBI.

The RBI's responsibility as bankers' bank was essentially two-fold. First, it acted as a source of reserves to the banking system and served as the lender of last resort in an emergency. The second, and more important responsibility, was to ensure that the banks were established and run on sound lines with the emphasis on protection of depositors' interest. A banking crisis in 1913 revealed major weaknesses in the banking system, such as maintenance of low reserves and large volumes of unsecured advances. Thus, regulation of the banking system was considered essential to maintain stability in the economy. In the initial years, banks were governed by the Indian Companies Act, 1913 followed by ad hoc enactments, such as the Banking Companies (Inspection) Ordinance, 1946 and the Banking Companies (Restriction of Branches) Act, 1946. As dissatisfaction with bank failures increased, the need for a statutory bank regulator became more pressing. Consequently, a special legislation called the Banking Companies Act was passed in March 1949, which was renamed as the Banking Regulation Act in March 1966.

DEVELOPMENT ROLE OF THE RBI

As in many developing countries, the central bank is seen as a key institution in bringing about development and growth in the economy. In the initial years of the RBI before independence, the banking network was thinly spread and segmented. Foreign banks served foreign firms, the British army, and the civil service. Domestic/Indian banks were linked to domestic business groups and managing agencies, and primarily did business with their own groups. The coverage of institutional lending in rural areas was poor despite the cooperative movement. Overall financial intermediation was weak. In an agrarian economy, where more than three-fourth of the population lived in the rural areas and contributed more than half of GDP, a constant and natural concern was agricultural credit. Therefore, almost every few years a committee was constituted to examine the rural credit mechanism. There has perhaps been one committee every two or three years for over a hundred years.

A clear objective of the development role of the RBI was to raise the savings ratio to enable the higher investment necessary for growth, in the absence of efficient financial intermediation and of a well-developed capital market. The view was that the poor were not capable of saving and, given the small proportion of the population that was well off, the only way to kick start the savings and investment process in the country was for the government to perform both functions. Thus the RBI was seen to have a legitimate role to assist the government in starting up several specialized financial institutions in the agricultural and industrial sectors, and to widen the facilities for term finance and for facilitating the institutionalization of savings. A special need was felt for accelerating industrial investment, particularly with the launching of the Second Five Year Plan in 1956. Over time, various term-lending industrial finance institutions were established with varying degrees of RBI involvement: the IFCI, State Financial Corporations (SFCs), IDBI, and ICICI.

The traditional concern with agricultural credit continued and the Agriculture Finance Corporation was established in 1963, followed by its transformation into the NABARD in 1982 for extending refinance for short-, medium-, and long-term finance for agriculture. The UTI was established in 1964 to mobilize resources from the wider public and to provide an opportunity for retail investors to invest in the capital market, thereby also aiding capital market development. The National Housing Bank was set up in the late 1980s to develop housing finance and the IDFC was set up in the late 1990s for infrastructure finance. The Reserve Bank also actively promoted financial institutions to help in developing the government securities market. The Discount and Finance House of India (DFHI) was set up in 1988; PDs were promoted in the late 1990s; and the CCIL was incorporated in 2001 to upgrade the financial infrastructure in respect of clearing and settlement of debt instruments and foreign exchange transactions. More recently, the Board for Regulation and Supervision of Payment and Settlement System has been constituted in 2005, and the Banking Codes and Standards Board of India in 2006 to develop a comprehensive code of conduct for fair treatment of bank customers. The RBI has been continuously involved in setting up or supporting these institutions with varying degrees of involvement, including equity contributions and extension of lines of credit.

Thus, the developmental role of the RBI has spanned all the decades since independence and is quite different from central banks in developed countries. Although the Reserve Bank was actively involved in setting up many of these institutions, the general practice has been to hive them off as they came of age or if a perception arose of potential conflict of interest. There can be little doubt that the establishment of these institutions has helped financial development in the country greatly, even though some of them have been less than successful in their functioning. It can be argued, of course, that similar institutional development could have taken place through private sector efforts or by the government. The availability of financial sector expertise in the Reserve Bank, however, was instrumental in these tasks being performed over time by the Reserve Bank.

Expansion of Banking

In the initial years of the RBI, considerable progress was made in extending the banking system but there was continuing concern about the overall accessibility of banking to the needy. In terms of coverage, many rural and semi-urban areas were yet to be covered by banking services. The transformation of the Imperial Bank of India into the State Bank of India in July 1955 was mainly motivated by the desire to extend branches across the country to stimulate banking activity. It was in continuation of the same policy to serve the needs of the developing economy that fourteen large banks were nationalized in 1969 followed by six more in 1980. The nationalization of banks mainly attempted to align banking activities with national concerns and norms, as it was perceived that the private banks neither understood social responsibilities nor observed social obligations. The general inclination in the 1950s, 1960s, and 1970s was essentially to get the government to become active in economic activities where it was felt that the private sector was not able or willing to perform actively. As a result of nationalization, the total number of branches rose from 8262 in 1969 to 60,220 in 1991 and those in rural areas from 1833 to 35,206. The increased network of branches certainly led to a large expansion of rural credit. This dimension of nationalization and expansion had its impact on the functioning and working of the RBI. Despite such vast expansion, it is interesting that we are still concerned with financial inclusion today.

Development of the Payments System

The development of a payments system is one development role that is common to most central banks. It is well recognized that an efficient payment and settlement system is essential for a well-functioning modern financial system. Therefore, in recent years, banks have been making efforts to upgrade payments and settlement systems utilizing the latest technology. One of the characteristic features of the Indian economy, historically, has been the widespread use of cash in the settlement of most financial transactions. While this has been the trend for several years, it is noteworthy that India had pioneered the use of non-cash-based payment systems long ago, which had established themselves as strong instruments for the conduct of trade and business. The most important form of credit instrument that evolved in India was termed as 'Hundis' and their use was reportedly known since the twelfth century. Hundis were used as instruments of remittance, credit, and trade transactions.

In modern times, with the development of the banking system and higher turnover in the volume of cheques, the need for an organized cheque clearing system emerged. In India, clearing associations were formed in the Presidency towns in the nineteenth century and the final settlement between member banks was effected by means of cheques drawn on the Presidency Banks. With the setting up of the Imperial Bank in 1921, settlement was done through cheques drawn on that bank. After the establishment of the RBI in 1935, the Clearing Houses in the Presidency towns were taken over by the RBI, and continued for more than five decades.

In recognition of the importance of payment and settlement systems, the RBI had taken upon itself the task of setting up a safe, efficient, and robust payment and settlement system for the country for more than a decade now. In the recent past, the RBI has been placing emphasis on reforms in the area of payment and settlement system. It was with this objective that the RTGS system was planned, which has been operationalized in March 2004. The system, once fully operational, in its present form, would take care of all inter-bank transactions and other features would be added soon.

In view of the positive response to reforms in the financial sector and the banking segment also coming of age, the RBI has now taken the policy perspective of migrating away from the actual management of retail payment and settlement systems. Thus, for a few years now, the task of setting up new Magnetic Ink Character Recognition (MICR)-based cheque processing centres has been delegated to the commercial banks. This approach has yielded good results and the RBI now envisions the normal processing functions to be managed and operated by professional organizations, which could be constituted through participation of commercial banks. This would be applicable to the clearing houses as well, which will perform the clearing activities, but the settlement function will continue to rest with the RBI. A beginning has been made in the form of the operations performed by the CCIL for effecting the clearing processes related to money, government securities, and foreign exchange markets. Under this arrangement, the RBI will continue to have regulatory oversight over such functions without actually acting as the service provider. The RTGS, which provide for funds transfers across participants in electronic mode with reduced risk, will continue to be operated by the RBI.

RELATIONSHIP OF THE RBI WITH THE GOVERNMENT

The RBI is a banker to the Central Government statutorily and to the state governments by virtue of specific agreements with each of them. The loss of autonomy of the RBI that took place in early decades was not because of any conscious decision based on the currently prevalent thinking on the relationship between central banks and the government, but rather as a consequence of overall economic policy then prevailing regarding the appropriate dominant role of the government in the economy as a whole.

Thus, it is useful to review the relationship of the Reserve Bank with the government as it has evolved over time.

The Monetary Fiscal Interface

It is common for central banks in developing countries to act as debt managers of their respective governments. Central banks have typically financed governments through monetization as and when the need arose for expansionary fiscal policy which has been often in developing countries. War financing through monetization has also been the norm for developed countries. Such financing has normally had predictable inflationary consequences for the economy. The Indian experience has been no different and expansionary fiscal policy was indeed financed by resort to automatic monetization, accompanied by financial repression and effective loss of central bank autonomy with respect to monetary policy.

In 1951, with the onset of economic planning, the functions of the RBI became more diversified. As the central bank of a typical developing country emancipated from centuries old colonial rule, the RBI had to participate in the nation-building process. Fiscal policy assumed the responsibility of triggering a process of economic growth through large public investment, facilitated by accommodative monetary and conducive debt management policies. The RBI played a crucial role in bridging the resource gap of the government in plan financing by monetizing government debt and maintaining interest rates at artificially low levels for government securities to reduce the cost of government borrowing.

The provisions of the RBI Act, 1934 authorize the RBI to grant advances to the government, repayable not later than three months from the date of advance. These advances, in principle, are to bridge the temporary mismatches in the government's receipt and expenditure and are mainly intended as tools for the government's cash management. However, in practice, the tool of short-term financing became a permanent source of funds for the government through automatic creation of ad hoc Treasury Bills whenever the government's balances with the RBI fell below the minimum stipulated balance. This automatic monetization led to the RBI's loss of control over creation of reserve money. In addition, the RBI also created additional ad hoc Treasury Bills whenever funds were required by the government. As there was unbridled expansion of fiscal deficits and the government was not in a position to redeem the ad hoc Treasury Bills, the RBI was saddled with a large volume of these bills constituting a substantial component of monetized deficit. This process continued from the 1950s to the 1990s.

By the end of the 1980s a fiscal-monetary-inflation nexus was increasingly becoming evident whereby excessive monetary expansion on account of monetization of fiscal deficit fuelled inflation. The RBI endeavoured to restrict the monetary impact of budgetary imbalances by raising the required reserve ratios to be maintained by banks. As the growth of pre-empted resources was inadequate to meet the government's requirement, it had to perforce borrow funds from outside the captive market through postal savings and provident funds, by offering substantial fiscal incentives and at administered low rates of interest. Thus, the economy was pushed into the throes of financial repression.

The logical question that follows is whether the experience of fiscal dominance over monetary policy would have been different if there had been separation of debt management from monetary management in India? Or, were we served better with both the functions residing in the Reserve Bank? What has really happened is that there was a significant change in thinking regarding overall economic policy during the early 1990s, arguing for a reduced direct role of the government in the economy. A conscious view emerged in favour of fiscal stabilization and reduction of fiscal deficits aimed at eliminating the dominance of fiscal policy over monetary policy through the prior practice of fiscal deficits being financed by automatic monetization. It is this overall economic policy transformation that has provided greater autonomy to monetary policy making in the 1990s.

In pursuance of the financial sector reforms undertaken in 1991, despite the proactive fiscal compression and efforts made by the RBI in moderating money supply during the early part of the 1990s, the continuance of the ad hoc Treasury Bills implied that there could not be an immediate check on the monetized deficit. In order to check this unbridled automatic monetization of fiscal deficits, the First Supplemental Agreement between the RBI and the Government of India on 9 September 1994 set out a system of limits for creation of ad hoc Treasury Bills during the three-year period ending March 1997. In pursuance of the Second Supplemental Agreement between the RBI and the Government of India on 6 March 1997, the ad hoc Treasury Bills were completely phased out by converting the outstanding amount into special undated securities and were replaced by a system of Way and Means Advances. The participation by the RBI in primary auctions of the government has also been discontinued with effect from 1 April 2006 under the provisions of FRBM Act, 2003. Other related measures that have been initiated since 1991 are deregulation of interest rates and lowering of statutory ratios.

The Indian economy has made considerable progress in developing its financial markets, especially the government securities market since 1991. Furthermore, fiscal dominance in monetary policy formulation has significantly reduced in recent years. With the onset of a fiscal consolidation process, withdrawal of the RBI from the primary market of government securities and expected legislative changes permitting a reduction in the statutory minimum SLR, fiscal dominance would be further diluted.

All of these changes took place despite the continuation of debt management by the Reserve Bank. Thus, one can argue that effective separation of monetary policy from debt management is more a consequence of overall economic policy thinking rather than adherence to a particular view on institutional arrangements.

The core issue of the conflict of interest between monetary policy and public debt management lies in the fact that while the objective of minimizing market borrowing cost for the government generates pressures for keeping interest rates low, compulsions of monetary policy amidst rising inflation expectations may necessitate a tighter monetary policy stance. Therefore, the argument in favour of separating debt management from monetary policy rests on the availability of effective autonomy of the central bank, so that it is able to conduct a completely independent monetary policy even in the face of an expansionary fiscal stance of the government.

But is this a realistic possibility? If there is an understanding amongst policymakers that expansionary fiscal policy that is financed by monetization leads to undesirable results, would such a policy be pursued? The Indian experience has itself shown that as such realization took place in the 1990s, the policy response was to arrive at policy conventions between the government and the Reserve Bank that enabled the practice of independent monetary policy, despite debt management continuing to be housed in the RBI.

In theory, separation between the two functions would perhaps enhance the efficiency in monetary policy formulation and debt management, but the debate in the Indian context needs to recognize certain key dynamics of the fiscal–monetary nexus. First, in India, the joint policy initiatives by the government and the RBI have facilitated good coordination between public debt management and monetary policy formulation. Whereas commitment to fiscal discipline and reduction in monetized deficit have imparted considerable autonomy to the operation of monetary policy, the proactive debt management by the RBI also facilitated the conduct of monetary policy, especially through the use of indirect instruments. In fact, the substantial stock of government securities held by the RBI enabled it to sterilize the monetary impact of capital flows through OMOs since the late 1990s. In recent years, with the reversal in the interest rate cycle, the RBI was able to prescribe higher risk weights on assets to protect the balance sheet of the banks. This step certainly ensured financial stability for the economy. Second, the RBI's experience in managing public debt over the years has equipped it with the requisite technical capacity for efficiently fulfilling the twin responsibilities of debt and monetary management in tune with requirements of the government and market conditions. The RBI has been making efforts to develop the money and government securities market since 1988 and has gained valuable experience and knowledge about related markets. This may have been difficult to accomplish if the debt management function had been effectively separate. Third, in the next five years, significant changes are slated to unfold in the Indian fiscal system: operationalization of the recommendations of the Twelfth Finance Commission, whereby the Centre ceases to operate as an intermediary for mobilizing resources for the states with the latter having to raise funds directly from the market; the RBI's withdrawal from the primary market of government paper from 1 April 2006 has implications for the management of interest rate expectations; and implementation of the proposed amendment to the Banking Regulation Act permitting flexibility to the RBI for lowering the SLR below 25 per cent of net demand and time liabilities of banks will reduce the captive subscription to government securities.

With all of these changes taking place in the monetary fiscal environment in the near future, there will be great need for a continued high degree of coordination in debt management between the RBI and the government. In fact, in the United States, even though debt management is formally done by the Treasury, the close cooperation that actually exists between the Federal Reserve Bank of New York and the Treasury is not very different in function from the relationship between the RBI and the government in its debt management function.

The evaluation of our experience therefore supports the position that a pragmatic view needs to be taken on this issue keeping in mind the specific institutional context of a particular country in mind.

Regulation and Supervision

Normally, there would be little discussion of regulation and supervision of banks in the context of the relationship between a central bank and the government. This issue arises in India because of the predominant government ownership of banks after nationalization of banks in 1969 and 1980. By the 1990s, more than 90 per cent of banking assets were in banks owned by the government. In this institutional setting there was a perception given that banks cannot fail and that depositors are effectively fully protected.

Moreover, all management appointments in public sector banks, and hence the norms of corporate governance, rested with the government. Furthermore, in the presence of administered deposit and lending rates, credit allocation and other banking decisions that rested with the government, regulation and supervision of banks also effectively became subservient to the government during the 1970s and 1980s.

Once again, it was only after the change in banking policy in 1991, emphasizing competition along with interest rate deregulation and elimination of credit allocation, that banking regulation and supervision by the Reserve Bank could become effective.

It is the introduction of competition through the entry of new private sector banks and expansion of foreign banks, along with the idea of equal regulatory treatment of private and public sector banks, that has necessitated the practice of modern regulation and supervision. The promotion of safety and soundness of the banking system and protection of depositors have again become relevant.

The primary justification for financial regulation and supervision by regulatory authorities is to prevent systemic risk, avoid financial crises, protect depositors' interest, and reduce asymmetry of information between depositors and financial institutions. The business of banking has a number of attributes that have the potential to generate instability as banks are much more leveraged than other firms due to their capacity to garner public deposits. Therefore, the need for establishing an agency to regulate and supervise the banking activity arose from frequent bank failures in various countries with ramifications for the whole economy. The central banks had started to focus their attention on ensuring financial stability and avoiding a financial crisis, since the late nineteenth century. The experience of the Great Depression had a profound effect on banking regulation in several countries and commercial banks since then have progressively been brought under the regulation of central banks.

The basic objective of bank supervision is to ensure that banks are financially sound, are well managed, and that they do not pose a threat to the interest of their depositors. The emphasis of supervision has been shifting in the recent period from the traditional CAMELS approach to a more risk-based approach. Basel II, which encompasses the risk analysis, uses a 'three-pillar' concept—minimum capital requirements, supervisory review, and market discipline—to ensure financial stability.

Central banks have traditionally regulated and supervised financial institutions, including commercial banks. However, since central banks are also regulators and influence the behaviour of market participants, supervision conducted by central banks may pose a moral hazard problem. Therefore, the idea of a separate supervisory authority has gathered some momentum in recent years. In addition, as a practising central banker, I can envisage situations of conflict between monetary policy and regulation and supervision, especially in situations of economic and financial stress. To illustrate a case of conflict, the mounting inflationary pressures in a country may require interest rates to rise sharply but then banks would be potentially exposed to write-downs of their asset valuations.

The role of the RBI, in the changing environment, recognizes the differences among various segments of the Indian banking system and accommodates appropriate flexibility in the regulatory treatment. The changing role of financial regulation and supervision of the RBI can be characterized by less accent on 'micro' regulation but more focus on 'prudential' supervision and on risk assessment and containment. The Indian approach to banking sector reforms has been gradual and different from many other EMEs, where financial sector reforms resulted in privatization of erstwhile public sector financial intermediaries. As the commercial banks are scheduled to start implementing Basel II with effect from end-March 2007, the RBI will continue to focus on supervisory capacity-building measures to identify the gaps and to assess as well as quantify the extent of additional capital, which may have to be maintained by such banks, due to operational and market risk. Finally, while recognizing the importance of consolidation, competition, and risk management to the future of banking, the RBI will continue to lay stress on corporate governance, ownership pattern of private banks, expansion of foreign banks, and financial inclusion.

Monetary Policy

The operation of monetary policy in India before 1991 has to be analyzed in the context of nationalization of banks, the then prevalent financial repression, and the closed economy. The banks were nationalized to exercise social control over their activities. In terms of outcome, nationalization succeeded in spreading the network of banks in rural areas and mobilizing private savings. The savings so mobilized were used for supporting public borrowing as well as for meeting hitherto neglected genuine credit needs in the rural areas. This called for significant changes in the institutional arrangements, and more stringent control and supervision of the banking system. To accommodate the fiscal requirements at low rates of interest, interest rates were administered and credit was directed in specific socially preferred sectors. The economy was closed, exchange rates were fixed, and exchange controls were strictly observed. In this situation of nationalized banks, fiscal dominance, and financial repression, operation of the monetary policy was severely constrained. Monetary policy resumed its operational efficiency with increasing liberalization of the economy only after 1991. Once again independence of monetary policy is more related to change in the overall economic policy framework and not from a purist stance of separating the central bank from the government.

As the financial system got liberalized up and monetary policy became more autonomous after the reversal of the previous mechanisms, the corresponding development of the money market, the government securities market, and the foreign exchange market became necessary. Appropriate monetary transmission cannot take place without efficient price discovery of interest rates and exchange rates in overall functioning financial markets.

Earlier, various factors such as administered interest rates, directed credit programmes, weak banking structure, lack of proper accounting and risk management systems, and lack of transparency in operations of major financial market participants had hindered market development. The RBI, like other central banks, has taken a keen interest in the development of financial markets, especially the money, government securities, and forex markets in view of their critical role in the transmission mechanism of monetary policy. The money market is the focal point for intervention by the RBI to equilibrate short-term liquidity flows on account of its linkages with the foreign exchange market. Similarly, the government securities market has become important for the entire debt market as it serves as a benchmark to price other debt market instruments.

The RBI had been making efforts since 1986 to develop institutions and infrastructure for these markets to facilitate price discovery. The conscious efforts by the RBI to develop efficient, stable, and healthy financial markets gained importance after 1991. The RBI followed a gradual and well-calibrated policy to facilitate the development of markets through institutional and financial infrastructure development through improvements in market microstructure. The pace of the reform was contingent upon putting in place appropriate systems and procedures, technologies, and market practices.

There has been close coordination between the Central Government and the RBI, as also between different regulators, which helped in orderly and smooth development of the financial markets in India. Following the reforms, the markets have now grown in size, depth, and activity paving the way for flexible use of indirect instruments by the RBI to pursue its objectives. In the context of the integration of Indian financial markets, with global markets, the RBI has been constantly refining the operating procedures and instruments as also various aspects of financial institutions, markets, and financial infrastructure such as risk management systems, income recognition and provisioning norms, disclosure norms, accounting standards, and insolvency in line with international best practices (Mohan, 2006).

AUTONOMY OF THE RBI

The trend towards central bank independence is not of recent origin. In the process of evolution, globally, while the spectrum of activities of the central banks has widened, the stance regarding the independence of central banks has taken an interesting turn. Before World War I, the central banks in most cases were private institutions and were formally independent of their governments. Interestingly, some central banks were established to serve as banker and debt manager to the government. The position changed around World War II—central banks in a number of countries (for example, Germany, France, England, Japan, Italy, and Sweden) were made subordinate to their governments. In recent years again, there has been a reversal in the trend. Governments have started granting more autonomy to their central banks: on the argument that a country is more likely to have low inflation if the central bank is independent. This argument has its roots in the breakdown of gold standard in early 1970s and the phase of high inflation that followed during the 1970s and 1980s. To achieve price stability, increasingly, central banks were granted autonomy along with an inflation target to meet, implying that independence was saddled with accountability. To illustrate, the Bank of England, which had substantial independence for much of the eighteenth and nineteenth centuries, but was later made subservient to the government, was legally granted independence in June 1998 but with an inflation target to achieve. The recent trend towards central bank independence has been influenced greatly by the experience of the Bundesbank and Reserve Bank of New Zealand.

In the Indian context, central bank autonomy has to be examined in a different context. Initially, since the launch of the Five Year Plans, monetary policy was expected to accommodate the expansionary fiscal policy, as I have discussed, to meet the requirements of the government. Later, to meet social obligations, the commercial banks were nationalized and statutory ratios raised, interest rates were administered, credit was rationed and channelled into priority sector, exchange rate was fixed/managed, the economy was closed, and movement of foreign exchange was strictly controlled. In such an arrangement, there was no scope for autonomy of monetary policy. Since 1991, due to reforms, the situation has changed. The reforms have led to disinvestment in PSBs, encouragement given to private sector banks, deregulation of interest rates, lowering of statutory ratios, cessation of automatic monetization, and implementation of current account convertibility. In recent years, short-term liquidity in the market is being managed successfully by the operation of an LAF on a daily basis, while longer-term liquidity has been addressed through traditional OMOs in government security auctions. As excess foreign exchange inflows intensified in 2003–4, co-operation between the Reserve Bank and the Central Government resulted in a rare innovation designed to empower the RBI with new instruments for sterlization. The government agreed to permit the RBI to issue additional government securities for sterlization purposes upto a specified limit. Thus the government/RBI cooperation resulted in a new instrument that strengthened the Reserve Bank in pursuing its monetary policy objectives. Monetary policy operation has also been constrained by the existence of minimum limits, on the CRR of 3 per cent and on the SLR of 25 per cent. In order to provide greater monetary policy flexibility to the RBI, the government has agreed to eliminate these minimum limits through introduction of amendments to the relevant acts in Parliament. Thus, monetary policy has moved from using direct instruments to market-based indirect instruments, with the development of the money and government securities market. These developments since 1991 indicate that the RBI already enjoys substantial autonomy in formulation of monetary policy.

INFLATION TARGETING

Central banks are divided on the advisability of setting explicit inflation targets. Several central banks, such as Bank of Canada, Bank of England, and the Reserve Bank of New Zealand, have adopted explicit inflation targets. Others, whose credibility in fighting inflation is long established [for example, the Bundesbank (earlier) and the Swiss National Bank], do not set explicit annual inflation targets. However, concentrating only on numerical inflation objectives may reduce the flexibility of monetary policy, especially with respect to other policy goals (see Chapters 7 and 8 in this volume).

High and sustained growth of the economy in conjunction with low inflation is the central concern of monetary policy in India. The rate of inflation chosen as the policy objective has to be consistent with the desired rate of output and employment growth. An inappropriate choice can lead to losses of macroeconomic welfare. Therefore, it is important to find the inflation rate—the 'threshold' inflation rate—which maximizes the growth rate of the economy. Such a threshold rate of inflation depends upon a number of factors such as the structure of the economy, past inflation history, the degree of indexation, and inflation expectations. Cross-country studies suggest that the threshold inflation for developed and developing countries falls in the ranges of 1–3 per cent and 7–11 per cent, respectively. Cross-country studies, however, run the risk of being influenced by extreme values. The estimation of such inflation threshold rates, therefore, needs to be done for each country separately, in order to understand the behaviour of the economy in relation to inflation. It may, however, be added that the estimated threshold inflation for any country should not be seen as fixed for all times. Countries with high threshold inflation at a given point of time can move to a lower threshold inflation level over time, although such a move may involve some cost in terms of output losses for some periods.

A major source of uncertainty in conducting monetary policy is the lack of a clear understanding of the inflationary process as it has unfolded in recent years. Variations in the timeliness and reliability of inflation indicators, uncertainty surrounding unobservable indicators like potential output and gaps in the intrinsic knowledge of the central banks about the state of the economy complicate the making of monetary policy, even when it is informed by analysis that uses macroeconomic models. The model parameters may vary over time as a result of structural changes in the economy. These problems are accentuated in countries like ours due to rigidities related to administered prices, wage setting procedures, and weather induced supply shocks that influence prices, and the less than perfect functioning of financial and credit markets inhibiting monetary policy transmission. All these complexities pose problems for monetary policy making in developing countries and can complicate the conduct of inflation targeting.

In India, we have not favoured the adoption of inflation targeting, while keeping the attainment of low inflation as a central objective of monetary policy, along with that of high and sustained growth that is so important for a developing economy. Apart from the legitimate concern regarding growth as a key objective, there are other factors that suggest that inflation targeting may not be appropriate for India. First, unlike many other developing countries we have had a record of moderate inflation, with double-digit inflation being the exception and largely socially unacceptable. Second, adoption of inflation targeting requires the existence of an efficient monetary transmission mechanism through the operation of efficient financial markets and absence of interest rate distortions. In India, although the money market, government debt, and forex market have indeed developed in recent years, they still have some way to go, whereas the corporate debt market is still to develop. Though interest rate deregulation has largely been accomplished, some administered interest rates still persist. Third, inflationary pressures still often emanate from significant supply shocks related to the effect of the monsoon on agriculture, where monetary policy action may have little role. Finally, in an economy as large as that of India, with various regional differences and continued existence of market imperfections in factor and product markets between regions, the choice of a universally acceptable measure of inflation is also difficult.

THE WAY AHEAD

The RBI has, over the years, transformed itself continuously, both functionally and structurally, in response to the changing needs of the economy and government policies. Since 1991, a special period of reforms and change has been ushered in the economy and the RBI has participated in this change very actively. The RBI continues to pursue the development role but now with some difference. In recent years, it has made consistent efforts to develop financial markets, build institutions, and encourage use of technology in the financial system.

The economy is passing through a new phase due to the enactment of the FRBM Bill, encouraging participation of private and foreign banks, increasing globalization, and continued liberalization of the capital account. The gross savings rate is nearly 30 per cent of GDP and the economy is recording a growth rate of about 8 per cent annually, in recent years. In this situation, a substantial increase in household financial savings is expected as well as the need for higher credit disbursement in the economy. The emphasis on financial inclusion will also lead to enhanced need for financial intermediation. The financial institutions would therefore have to prepare for higher volume of transactions. In view of the expected increase in competition, banking institutions would need to integrate various services like banking, e-commerce, mutual funds, insurance, and money market operations.

The new challenges facing the RBI are many. First, if the Indian banking system is to attain international excellence, it will require action on several fronts like introduction of greater competition; convergence of activities and supervision of financial conglomerates; induction of new technology; improvement in credit risk appraisal; encouragement of financial innovation; improvement in internal controls; and establishment of an appropriate legal framework. The role of the RBI in this context amounts to promoting safety and soundness while allowing the banking system to compete and innovate. Second, as a central bank, the RBI would further need to develop the financial markets, especially the money, government securities, and foreign exchange markets to enhance the efficiency of the transmission mechanism, along with the corporate debt market. Third, price stability and financial stability would continue to be of concern with expected increase in credit expansion and global integration. Fourth, concerns regarding social security and investment of pension and insurance funds would need to be addressed.

I would like to finish on an optimistic note. As the RBI has successfully faced challenges in the past, it can be expected to continue to adapt to the changing economic environment in future. We need to be mindful of the extant objectives of overall economic policy, within which monetary policy has to be placed, and the realities of economic management in India, as we contemplate the further evolution of central banking and financial regulation in India.

References

King, M. (2004), 'The Institutions of Monetary Policy', *American Economic Review*, 94, May, pp. 1–13.

Mohan, R. (2006), 'Coping With Liquidity Management in India: A Practitioner's View', *RBI Bulletin*, April.

RBI (2005a), *Report on Currency and Finance: 2004–05*, RBI, Mumbai

____ (2005b), *History of Reserve Bank of India* (Volumes I to III), RBI, Mumbai.

11 Coping with Liquidity Management in India

A Practitioner's View*

Liquidity management is a subject that is not widely discussed but is the bread and butter of daily monetary management. Whereas I was not a monetary specialist prior to coming to the Reserve Bank, I have been able to gather some insights through on-the-job training. It is also an issue of current relevance and appeal.

Conduct of monetary policy and management in the context of large and volatile capital flows has proved to be difficult for many countries. As India became convertible on the current account and liberalized its capital account in a carefully sequenced manner since the BoP crisis of 1991, it too has been faced with similar problems. The evolving policy mix involved careful calibration that took into account diverse objectives of central banking, changes in the monetary policy framework and operating procedures, and widening of the set of instruments for liquidity management.

Before the opening of the economy through the 1990s, both the current and capital accounts were controlled. However, despite trade restrictions the current account was in constant deficit, which had to be financed mostly by debt, both official aid flows and private debt. Portfolio flows were not permitted and FDI was negligible. The only largely 'uncontrolled' flows were NRI deposits, which waxed and waned according to macroeconomic conditions. The exchange rate was also controlled: it was linked to a basket of currencies and moved as a crawling peg. Consequently, monetary policy management, such as it was, did not pose serious problems, particularly since most interest rates were fixed administratively.

* Based on the addresses at the 36th Gujarat Economic Association at N.S. Arts College, Anand, on 28 January 2006 and at the 8th Annual Conference on Money and Finance in the Indian Economy at Indira Gandhi Institute of Development Research on 27 March 2006.

It is only after substantial opening of the economy and deregulation of interest rates that price discovery of the rate of interest has become important. Consequently, the Reserve Bank has had to experiment on a continuous basis. It has had to operate simultaneously on the external account in the foreign exchange market to contain volatility in the exchange rate and in the domestic market to contain volatility in interest rates. Since both the exchange rate and the interest rate are the key prices reflecting the cost of money, it is particularly important for the efficient functioning of the economy that they be market-determined and be easily observed. Excessive fluctuation and volatility masks the underlying value and gives rise to confusing signals. The task of liquidity management then is to provide a framework for the facilitation of forex and money market transactions that result in price discovery sans excessive volatility.

LIQUIDITY MANAGEMENT AND MANAGEMENT OF CAPITAL FLOWS

Let me begin with some general remarks on liquidity management and management of capital flows.

While in the macroeconomic context, liquidity management refers to overall monetary conditions, reflecting the extent of mismatch between demand and supply of overall monetary resources, for a central bank, the concept of liquidity management typically refers to the framework and set of instruments that the central bank follows in steering the amount of *bank reserves* in order to control its price, consistent with the ultimate goals of monetary policy (Bindseil, 2000). What is the price of bank reserves? The price of bank reserves is fixed in terms of short-term interest rates. This is set in terms of overnight inter-bank borrowing and lending rates either secured or unsecured which affect the reserves that the banks keep. As markets do not clear often on their own, the central bank itself steps in by influencing the short-term interest rates by affecting short-term repurchase obligations with banks (Borio, 1997).

The need for liquidity management arises from central banks' concept of liquidity measured in terms of the monetary base, of which it is the monopoly supplier. The supply of monetary base by the central bank depends on (a) the public's demand for currency, as determined by the size of monetary transactions and the opportunity cost of holding money and (b) the banking system's need for reserves to settle or discharge payment obligations. In fulfilling these needs, central banks also attempt to control and modulate liquidity conditions by varying the supply of bank reserves to meet their macroeconomic objectives subject to the constraint of financial stability. Bank reserves are, therefore, influenced through reserve requirements or OMOs. In so doing, central banks attempt to affect the level of short-term interest rates in a manner in which market movements of these interest rate movements are smoothened out as volatility of any monetary or non-monetary asset prices can be costly in terms of real output and investment decisions. It is from this standpoint that a central bank decides to modulate its market operations over a chosen time horizon to reflect its policy stance.

The importance of central bank liquidity management lies in its ability to exercise considerable influence and control over short-term interest rates by small money market operations. This ability is determined by the credibility of the central bank itself. The interventions that the central bank makes have a pronounced signalling affect. Consequently, central banks of developed countries typically aim at a target overnight interest rate, which acts as a powerful economy-wide signal. As a result, the impact of these transactions is fundamentally different from those undertaken by private market participants. The liquidity management function of a central bank involves a larger economy-wide perspective. Central bank liquidity management has short-term effects in financial markets. However, the long-term implications for the real sector are more important.

By operating on the current account balances that the commercial banks maintain with the central bank or by directly operating on the short-term money market rate, central banks attempt to influence money market liquidity in order to exercise control over the short-term interest rate. The central bank may directly set at least one of the short-term interest rates that acts as its policy rate. By controlling the short-term interest rate while letting markets determine the rest of the yield curve, the central bank attempts to transmit monetary policy impulses across the yield curve. The sovereign yield curve in turn influences the lending and deposit rates in the economy. Mortgage rates are found to be particularly sensitive to the policy rate changes through the interest rate as well as the credit channel. Once bank lending gets affected, interest rates impact real variables such as consumption and investment, which in turn impact output and inflation levels. So while active liquidity management has a localized objective of keeping short-term interest rates range bound, it also has a long-term meta objective of implementing monetary policy goals of inflation and output.

The difficulty is that monetary policy is formulated and implemented under considerable uncertainty. Injections or absorptions made over extended periods as an intended part of policy have implications on output and prices through changes in interest rates and aggregate demand. Typically, the transmission effects tend to differ across countries depending on country specific factors and institutional and regulatory frameworks. As transmission occurs with long and variable lags in all countries, the long-run impact is often unpredictable.

While liquidity management in the central banks of most advanced countries is conducted in a setting where daily demand for money typically exceeds its supply, liquidity management in emerging markets is more varied, with surplus and shortage conditions alternating and with perhaps greater fluctuations in their external accounts (Saggar, 2006). In recent years, capital flows have been a major factor affecting liquidity management in a large number of countries, particularly in Asia, which have faced large and volatile capital flows. Capital flows have little effect on liquidity in the presence of equivalent CADs that result in the absorption of capital flows in the economy and they help to accelerate growth in investment, employment and technology imports, contributing to productivity growth. In situations where they exceed the CAD, they result in a build up of foreign exchange reserves, which themselves act as a positive signalling device indicating financial stability.

But unsterilized capital inflows can result in inflation, currency appreciation, loss of competitiveness, and attenuation of monetary control. The loss of monetary control could be steep if such flows are large. Even when these flows are sterilized through OMOs, the costs could be large when sterilization operations raise domestic interest rates and result in the trap of even greater capital flows. The fiscal impact of sterilization also requires to be factored in, especially when a large stock of securities is required to be issued for the purpose.

Clearly, macroeconomic policy options for managing capital flows are difficult. The options also require taking into account the high volatility often associated with such capital flows. These flows are marked by sudden surges and reversals which, in some cases, could occur in a week's time or less. In other cases, surges could be followed by stoppages in a short span of time. Stoppages could also give way to reversals at slight triggers. There are also cases where capital flows are sustained over a long period of time or a drought in flows occurs over a medium term. In sum, these flows are somewhat unpredictable and it is very difficult to assess the liquidity scenario even over a quarter, far less over a year. At the same time, monetary policy operates with transmission lags that could run three to four quarters or longer and these lags are often unpredictable.

Typically, countries that are in the quest for capital flows fall under the impossible trinity problem, referred to earlier. Notwithstanding the theoretical basis, history is replete with examples of countries falling under the temptation to achieve all these goals when faced with opportunities for benefiting from global asset portfolio allocations (Obstfeld, Shambaugh, and Taylor, 2004). Generally, countries seek to retain their monetary policy independence as they face asymmetric shocks and common currency area conditions are not pervasive. They are also tempted to keep their exchange rates stable for financial stability or for inflation containment objectives. In most cases countries end up making a costly exit from a hard peg. With greater financial openness, many countries have to move towards greater exchange rate flexibility or accept the subordination of monetary policy goals to goals of global capital market integration. The latter, however, could be costly.

Let me now turn to our own situation and how we have coped with the evolving circumstances in India.

CAPITAL FLOWS IN INDIA

The far-reaching economic reforms in India in the 1990s, witnessed a sharp increase in capital inflows as a result of capital account liberalization in India and a gradual decrease in home bias in asset allocation in advanced economies. During 1990–1, it was clear that the country was heading for a balance-of-payment crisis caused by increased absorption due to deficit financed fiscal expansion of the 1980s and the trigger of oil price spike caused by the Gulf War. As foreign exchange reserves dwindled to less than a month's import financing requirements in 1991, global capital taps got switched off and the country faced a real possibility of a first ever sovereign default. Crisis managers got active and averted the default, leaving the country still with a default-free history. The survival stimuli it kindled, unleashed massive economic reforms. The reform story has been told several times in many different fora and I do not intend to repeat it here.

Foreign investment flows mainly in the form of foreign direct investments averaged US$ 118 million during 1990–1 and 1991–2. A significant change in our capital account took place when portfolio investments by FIIs were permitted in 1992. With the exception of 1998–9 when, in the aftermath of contagion from East Asian financial crisis, portfolio flows turned negative, total foreign investment in the form of direct and portfolio investment was US$ 4–8 billion a year till 2002–3. Excluding 1998–9, it has averaged nearly US$ 5.8 billion over a nine-year period starting 1993–4. There was another quantum leap in the following two years—2003–4 and 2004–5—with direct investment averaging US$ 5.1 billion and portfolio investment averaging US$ 10.1 billion, taking total foreign investment exceeding US$ 15 billion. As it happened, this increase in capital flows coincided with a slowdown in the economy, particularly the industrial economy after 1997–8, and instead of CADs we had current account surpluses. Consequently, even ignoring the non-resident deposit flows, equity investment flows in themselves posed a considerable challenge for monetary management.

While the year-to-year foreign investment flows provide some idea of the magnitude of the capital flows that may be required to be sterilized, the month-to-month or intra-month variations in these flows provide a better idea of the volatility of these flows which central bank liquidity management has to cope and these variations have been sizeable. They have been dominated by portfolio flows. While these flows appeared to be mean reverting till October 2002, there appears to have been a strong trend with wider oscillations subsequently. This means that the monetary authorities now have to cope with larger and more volatile capital flows than they had been faced with in about a decade from the onset of reforms.

Faced with these large capital flows, there has been a steep accretion to foreign exchange reserves starting October 2000. Over US$ 100 billion have been added in foreign exchange reserves since then, taking them from US$ 34.9 billion to US$ 143.6 billion in October 2005 before the IMD redemptions saw the reserves temporarily dropping to US$ 135 billion at end-December 2005 but the reserves were back at US$ 146.2 billion by 17 March 2006 (Figure 11.1). The reserve accretion of this large magnitude has been largely the result of massive capital flows. The capital flows are adding to absorption directly as well as indirectly through increased domestic credit growth and have resulted in a steep rise in trade deficit and till at least recently substantial excess liquidity in the economy. The problem of scarcity of 1991 is now seen as a problem of plenty by many.

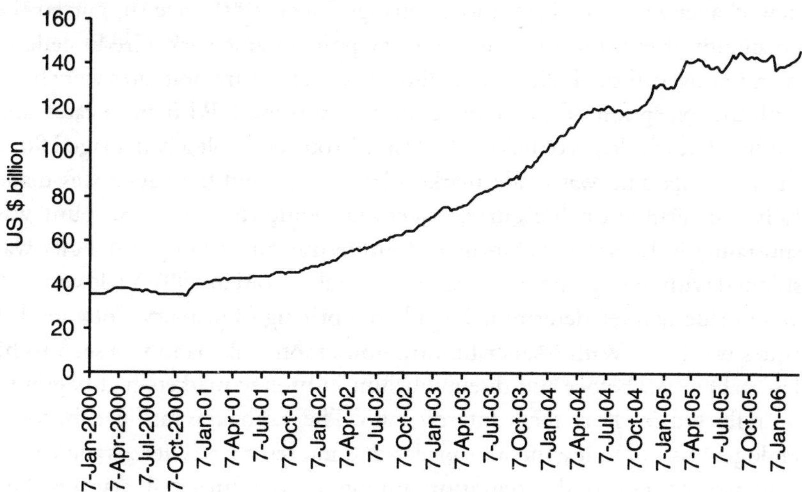

Figure 11.1 Foreign Exchange Reserves

In these circumstances, the problem for monetary management was two-fold. First, it had to distinguish implicitly between durable flows and transient flows. If capital flows are deemed to be durable and indefinite, questions arise regarding foreign exchange management. If the flows are deemed to be semi-durable, essentially reflecting the business cycle, the task of monetary and liquidity management is to smoothen out their impact on the domestic economy, finding means to absorb liquidity in times of surplus and to inject it in times of deficit. Second, in the short term, daily, weekly, or monthly volatility in flows needs to be smoothened to minimize the effect on domestic overnight interest rates. In practice, ex ante, it is difficult to distinguish what is durable, what is semi-durable, and what is transient. Hence policy and practice effectively operates in an environment of uncertainty and a variety of instruments have to be used to manage liquidity in this fluid scenario.

SHIFT FROM DIRECT TO INDIRECT INSTRUMENTS

There has been a world-wide trend for shifting from direct instruments of monetary control to indirect instruments (Alexander, Balino, and Enoch, 1995). India is one of the EMEs, where such a change has distinctly occurred. A major transformation has occurred in the monetary policy framework in the 1990s. In response to the changing financial landscape, the Reserve Bank adopted several policy changes which transformed the monetary policy framework.

Monetary policy had to respond to the challenge posed by the problem of plenty which required liquidity management to be honed up to meet the new challenge. Major institutional changes since 1991 have supported the possibility of transition in the monetary policy framework. Credit ceilings were removed, though directed lending was retained. Interest rates were freed with the exception of the saving deposit rate, some NRI deposit rates, and lending rates for loans of below Rs 2 lakh. From a completely managed float, the exchange rate was made market-determined and the rupee was made fully convertible on the current account, while the capital account was substantially liberalized. Automatic monetization of budget deficits was stopped with the signing of the Supplemental Accord in 1997. Yields on gilts were made market-determined, while the pricing of primary stock market issues was freed. With financial innovations, money demand was seen to be less stable than before and disequilibrium in money markets had begun to be reflected in short-term interest rates. The exchange rate had become endogenous to money, income, prices, and interest rates. There is increasing evidence of increased integration among various financial markets. The money market has integrated substantially with the foreign exchange market at the short-end. Furthermore, foreign exchange market efficiency was found to hold at the short-ends. The term structure was still somewhat segmented but some transmission across the yield curve was in evidence.

In response to the changing financial landscape, the Reserve Bank adopted several policy changes that transformed the monetary policy framework. Reserve requirements in the form of CRR were brought down from statutory maximum of 15 per cent of net demand and time liabilities during July 1989 to April 1993 to 4.5 per cent in June 2003 which was raised subsequently to 5.0 per cent in two stages in October 2004. The SLR, which directs banks to maintain liquid investments, mainly in the form of government securities, was reduced from an all-time high of 38.5 per cent in January 1993 to the statutory minimum of 25 per cent by October 1997. Legislation has now been introduced in the Parliament to remove both the statutory minimum for SLR and CRR in order to provide for greater monetary policy flexibility.

From the point of monetary policy framework, the significant development was the move to a 'multiple indicator approach' in 1998. Prior to the mid-1980s, monetary policy was based predominantly on direct instruments of monetary control with credit budgets for the banks being framed in synchronization with monetary budgeting. In view of the institutional changes stated in this section and the subsequent one, the Reserve Bank formally shifted its policy framework from monetary targeting to the multiple indicator approach in 1998–9. As part of this approach, it started using the information content in interest rates and rates of return in different markets along with currency, credit, fiscal position, trade, capital flows, inflation rate, exchange rate, refinancing, and transactions in foreign exchange, juxtaposing it with output data for drawing policy perspectives.

LIQUIDITY MANAGEMENT THROUGH INDIRECT INSTRUMENTS: EARLY TRENDS

Before the advent of repurchase transactions (repos), market operations by the RBI were almost invariably conducted through outright transactions in government securities. The scope of OMOs in the earlier period was limited as yields were repressed by an administered interest rate regime, including auctions of Treasury Bills on tap at fixed coupon of 4.6 per cent. The move towards a market-determined system of interest rates began by increasing coupons and decreasing maturity of government debt so as to develop the secondary markets.[1] The yields were made substantially market determined by introduction of auctions beginning the mid-1980s.[2] The Reserve Bank introduced reverse repos for absorption from December 1992. With the objective of improving short-term management of liquidity in the system and to smoothen out interest rates in the call/notice money market, it began absorbing excess liquidity through auctions of reverse repos (then called repos).[3] The development of repos into a full fledged monetary instrument in the form of LAF has been a fascinating case study of what it takes to undertake changes in operating framework. The chronology of these developments is provided in Box 11.1. Till 2003–4 market operations were primarily conducted in the form of outright sales and purchases of government securities (Figure 11.2). Since then, LAF volumes have increased considerably (Figure 11.3). The important contribution of LAF has been in keeping overnight interest rates by and large range bound. With the activation of bank rate as a policy instrument, reverse repos also helped in creating an

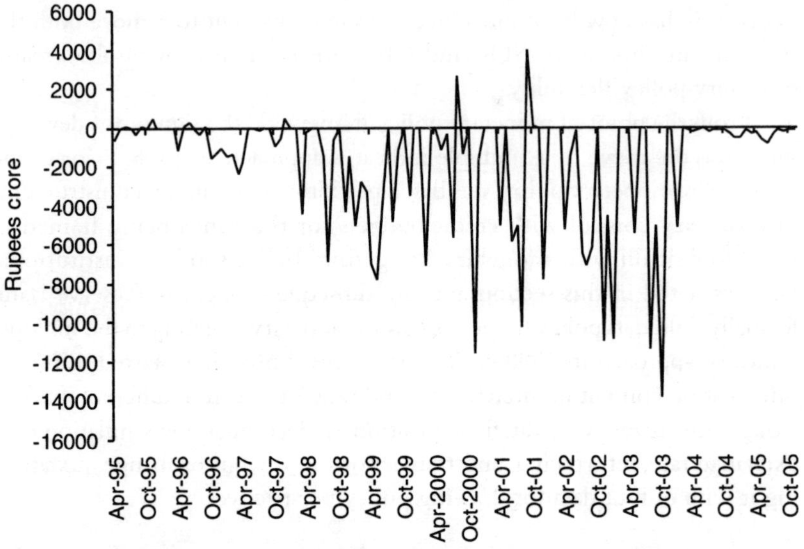

Figure 11.2 Net Purchase (+)/Sale (–) of Dated Securities

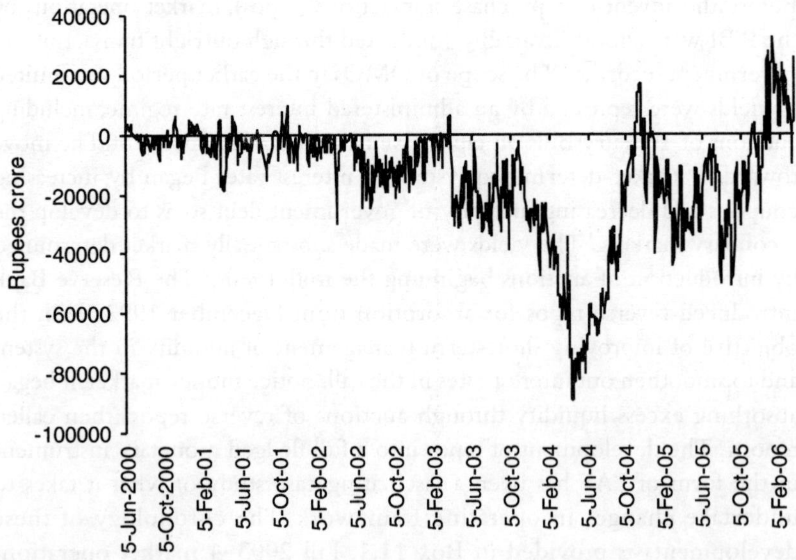

Figure 11.3 Net Injection (+)/Absorption (–) of Liquidity through LAF

informal corridor in the money market, with the reverse repo rate as floor and the bank rate as the ceiling. The use of these two instruments enabled RBI to keep the call rate by and large within this informal corridor.

Although repo auctions were conducted at variable rates when the LAF was introduced, with a view to providing quick interest rate signals, RBI did have the additional option to switch over to fixed rate repos on overnight basis, in order to meet unexpected domestic or external developments. The LAF was introduced on the basis of uniform price auctions, but the auction system was switched to multiple price auctions from 5 May 2001.

Box 11.1: Liquidity Adjustment Facility

The choice of operating framework and operating procedures in any economy is always a difficult one and depends on the stage of macroeconomic and financial sector development and is somewhat of an evolutionary process. As part of the financial sector reforms launched in mid-1991, India began to move away from direct instruments of monetary control to indirect ones. The transition of this kind involves considerable efforts to develop markets, institutions, and practices. In order to facilitate such transition, India developed a Liquidity Adjustment Facility (LAF) in phases considering country-specific features of the Indian financial system. LAF is based on repo/reverse repo operations by the central bank.

In 1998, the Committee on Banking Sector Reforms (Narasimham Committee II) recommended the introduction of LAF under which the Reserve Bank would conduct auctions periodically, if not necessarily daily. The Reserve Bank could reset its repo and reverse repo rates which would in a sense provide a reasonable corridor for the call money market. In pursuance of these recommendations, a major change in the operating procedure became possible in April 1999 through the introduction of an Interim Liquidity Adjustment Facility (ILAF) under which repos and reverse repos were formalized. With the introduction of ILAF, the general refinance facility was withdrawn and replaced by a collateralized lending facility (CLF) up to 0.25 per cent of the fortnightly average outstanding of aggregate deposits in 1997–8 for two weeks at the bank rate. Additional collateralized lending facility (ACLF) for an equivalent amount of CLF was made available at the bank rate plus 2 per cent. CLF and ACLF availed for periods beyond two weeks were subjected to a penal rate of 2 per cent for an additional two-week period. Export credit refinance for scheduled commercial banks was retained and continued to be provided at the bank rate. Liquidity support to PDs against collateral of government securities at the bank rate was also provided for. ILAF was expected to promote stability of money market and ensure that the interest rates move within a reasonable range.

The transition from ILAF to a full-fledged LAF began in June 2000 and was undertaken in three stages. In the first stage, beginning 5 June 2000, LAF was formally introduced and the ACLF and level II support to PDs was replaced by variable rate repo auctions with same day settlement. In the second stage, beginning

Contd

Box 11.1 Contd

May 2001 CLF and level I liquidity support for banks and PDs was also replaced by variable rate repo auctions. Some minimum liquidity support to PDs was continued but at interest rate linked to variable rate in the daily repos auctions as determined by RBI from time to time. In April 2003, the multiplicity of rates at which liquidity was being absorbed/injected under back-stop facility was rationalized and the back-stop interest rate was fixed at the reverse repo cut-off rate at the regular LAF auctions on that day. In case of no reverse repo in the LAF auctions, back-stop rate was fixed at 2.0 percentage point above the repo cut-off rate. It was also announced that on days when no repo/reverse repo bids are received/accepted, back-stop rate would be decided by the Reserve Bank on an *ad hoc* basis. A revised LAF scheme was operationalized effective 29 March 2004 under which the reverse repo rate was reduced to 6.0 per cent and aligned with bank rate. Normal facility and backstop facility was merged into a single facility and made available at a single rate. The third stage of full-fledged LAF had begun with the full computerization of Public Debt Office (PDO) and introduction of RTGS marked a big step forward in this phase. Repo operations today are mainly through electronic transfers. Fixed rate auctions have been reintroduced since April 2004. The possibility of operating LAF at different times of the same day is now close to getting materialized. In that sense we have very nearly completed the transition to operating a full-fledged LAF.

With the introduction of Second LAF (SLAF) from 28 November 2005 market participants now have a second window to fine-tune the management of liquidity. In past, LAF operations were conducted in the forenoon between 9.30 am and 10.30 am. SLAF is conducted by receiving bids between 3.00 pm and 3.45 pm. The salient features of SLAF are the same as those of LAF and the settlement for both is conducted separately and on gross basis.

The introduction of LAF has been a process and the Indian experience shows that phased rather than a big bang approach is required for reforms in the financial sector and in monetary management.

Sources: RBI, 1999; RBI, 2003a.

The introduction of LAF had several advantages.

1. Foremost, it helped the transition from direct instruments of monetary control to indirect and in the process certain dead weight loss for the system was saved.
2. It has provided monetary authorities with greater flexibility in determining both the quantum of adjustment as well as the rates by responding to the needs of the system on a daily basis.
3. It enabled the Reserve Bank to modulate the supply of funds on a daily basis to meet day-to-day liquidity mismatches.
4. It enabled the central bank to affect demand for funds through policy rate changes.

5. And most important, it helped stabilize short-term money market rates.

The call rate has been largely within a corridor set by the repo and reverse repo rates, imparting greater stability in the financial markets. As has been mentioned, the emergence of corridor was gradual. The transition is not a menu choice as is sometimes viewed in text books.

LAF has now emerged as the principal operating instrument of monetary policy. Although there is no formal targeting of overnight interest rates, the LAF is designed to nudge overnight interest rates within a specified corridor, the difference between the fixed repo and reverse repo rates. The LAF has enabled the Reserve Bank to de-emphasize targeting of bank reserves and focus increasingly on interest rates. This has helped in reducing the CRR without loss of monetary control.

LIQUIDITY MANAGEMENT IN THE MORE RECENT PERIOD

Let me now focus on my experience in liquidity management in recent years. After the introduction of the second stage of LAF in May 2001, liquidity has generally been in surplus mode with the increase in levels of capital flows. With the continuing accretion to foreign exchange reserves, there was corresponding injection of liquidity that had to be sterilized. At the same time, the reverse repo policy interest rate was reduced in successive steps from 6 per cent in March 2002 to 4.5 per cent by August 2003 before raising it to 5.5 per cent by January 2006 in four increases of 25 basis points each. Thus, the aim of monetary policy was to keep overnight call money market rates in the system within the informal interest rate corridor.

On the whole, LAF has had a pronounced favourable impact of lowering volatility of short-term money market rates. Monthly average call rates, which were volatile in a 5–35 per cent band during 1990–8, have clearly stabilized subsequently and have generally ranged between 5–10 per cent (Figure 11.4). Call rates have become largely bounded by the informal interest rate corridor after the introduction of LAF (Figure 11.5). The corridor between repo and reverse repo rates which was set at 200 basis points initially and was widened to 250 basis points in August 2003 was lowered to 150 basis points in March 2004, to 125 basis points in October 2004, and further to 100 basis points, in April 2005. The call rates have remained anchored around the lower corridor since June 2002, except for a brief period during February–April 2003 and between October 2004 and January 2005. Again since October 2005, the system appears to have clearly moved from enduring surplus to marginal deficits.

Monetary management since mid-2002 has clearly focused on managing surplus liquidity. This was accomplished by the simultaneous operation of the LAF and open market operations.

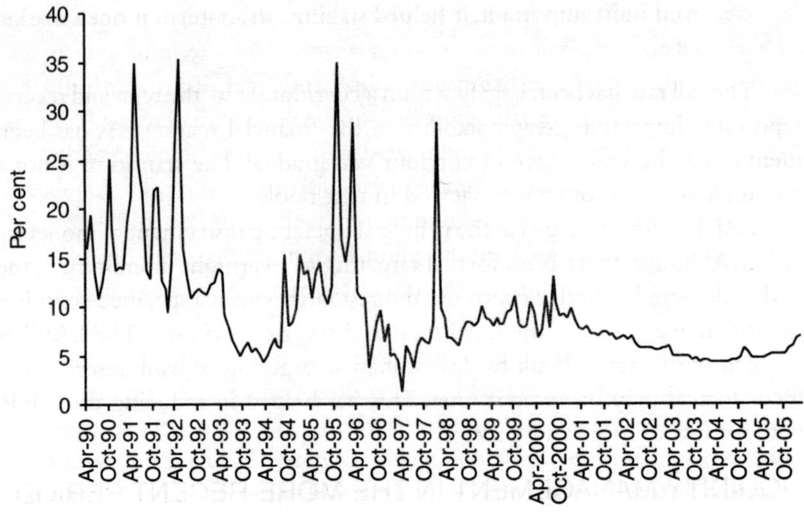

Figure 11.4 Call Money Rate

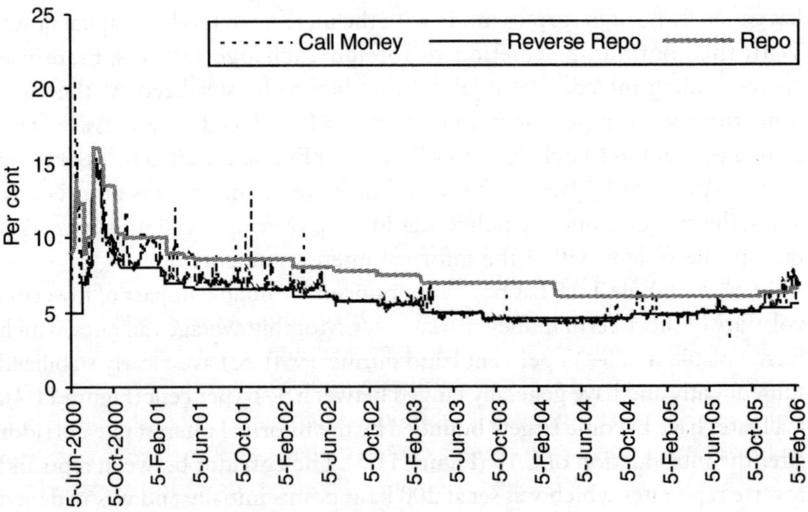

Figure 11.5 Call Money Rate and LAF Corridor

Given that RBI had a finite stock of government securities, its ability to mop up large capital inflows indefinitely was therefore limited, and LAF operations began to bear the burden of stabilization disproportionately. Moreover, the LAF is essentially designed to take care of fictional liquidity on a day-to-day basis; hence its function was itself beginning to get distorted by such a sterilization function.

In order to address these issues, the Reserve Bank appointed a Working Group (Chairperson: Usha Thorat) on Instruments of Sterilization. After considerable discussion, the consequence was that the Reserve Bank signed a Memorandum of Understanding (MoU) with the Government of India for the issuance of Treasury Bills and dated government securities under MSS on 25 March 2004 (Box 11.2). The new instrument empowered the Reserve Bank to undertake liquidity absorption on a more enduring but still temporary basis. The objective is to keep LAF for fine-tuning on a day-to-day basis, while using MSS to manage sterlization operations, along with the use of more conventional OMOs for the absorption or injection of liquidity on an even more enduring basis.

Box 11.2: Market Stabilization Scheme (MSS)

The money markets operated in liquidity surplus mode since 2002 due to large capital inflows and current account surplus. The initial burden of sterilization was borne by the outright transaction of dated securities and T-bills. However, due to the depletion in stock of government securities, the burden of liquidity adjustment shifted on LAF, which is essentially a tool of adjusting for marginal liquidity. Keeping in view the objective of absorbing the liquidity of enduring nature using instruments other than LAF, the Reserve Bank appointed a Working Group on Instruments of Sterilization (Chairperson: Usha Thorat). The Group recommended issue of T-bills and dated securities under MSS where the proceeds of MSS were to be held by the government in a separate identifiable cash account maintained and operated by RBI. The amounts credited into the MSS Account would be appropriated only for the purpose of redemption and/or buy back of the Treasury Bills and/or dated securities issued under the MSS. In pursuance of the recommendation the Government of India and RBI signed a Memorandum of Understanding (MoU) on 25 March 2004. As part of the MoU, the scheme was made operational in April 2004. It was agreed that the government would issue Treasury Bills and/or dated securities under the MSS in addition to the normal borrowing requirements, for absorbing liquidity from the system. These securities would be issued by way of auctions by the Reserve Bank and the instruments would have all the attributes of existing T-bills and dated securities. They were to be serviced like any other marketable government securities. MSS securities are being treated as eligible securities for Statutory Liquidity Ratio (SLR), repo, and LAF.

The payments for interest and discount on MSS securities are not made from the MSS Account. The receipts due to premium and/or accrued interest are also not credited to the MSS Account. Such receipts and payments towards interest, premium and discount are shown in the budget and other related documents as distinct components under separate sub-heads. The T-bills and dated securities issued for the purpose of the MSS are matched by an equivalent cash balance held by the government with the Reserve Bank. Thus, they have only a marginal

Contd

Box 11.2 Contd

impact on revenue and fiscal balances of the government to the extent of interest payment on the outstanding under the MSS.

For mopping up enduring surplus liquidity, policy choice exists between central bank issuing its own securities or government issuing additional securities. A large number of countries, such as Chile, China, Colombia, Indonesia, Korea, Malaysia, Peru, Philippines, Russia, Sri Lanka, Taiwan, and Thailand have issued central bank securities. However, central banks of many of these countries faced deterioration in their balance sheets. As such, there are merits in issuing sterilization bonds on government account. This is more so, in case of an already well established government debt market, where issuing of new central bank bills of overlapping maturity could cause considerable confusion and possible market segmentation which could obfuscate the yield curve, reduce liquidity of the instruments and make operations that much more difficult.

MSS has considerably strengthened the Reserve Bank's ability to conduct exchange rate and monetary management operations. It has allowed absorption of surplus liquidity by instruments of short term (91-day, 182-day, and 364-day T-bills) and the medium-term (dated government securities) maturity. Generally, the preference has been for the short-term instruments. This has given the monetary authorities a greater degree of freedom in liquidity management during transitions in liquidity situation.

Source: RBI, 2003b.

The proceeds of the MSS are held by the government in a separate identifiable cash account maintained and operated by the Reserve Bank. The amount held in this account is appropriated only for the purpose of redemption and/or buyback of the Treasury Bills and/or dated securities issued under the MSS. The ceiling on the outstanding amount under MSS was fixed initially at Rs 60,000 crore but in accordance with the MoU provisions was enhanced to Rs 80,000 crore on 14 October 2004 and has now been reduced to Rs 70,000 crore. The total outstanding amount absorbed under MSS had increased to over Rs 78,906 crore as on September 2005 but has been unwinding since then and the outstanding have currently dropped to Rs 30,000 crore. Nearly Rs 50,000 crore of liquidity has been released through MSS unwinding, even while overall marginal liquidity has transited from surplus to deficit.

The introduction of MSS has succeeded in restoring LAF to its intended function of daily liquidity management. With MSS levels averaging about Rs 54,000 crore in November 2004, total surplus liquidity averaged around the levels seen before the introduction of MSS as excess capital flows continued. LAF operations returned to surplus mode thereafter and by March 2005 averaged around Rs 30,000 crore with total surplus liquidity as reflected in LAF, MSS, and government cash balances in the vicinity of Rs 1,15,000 crore. By September 2005, total surplus liquidity had surpassed Rs 1,20,000 crore. However, the liquidity situation has changed significantly since then. With the change in stance of monetary policy, hiking of the policy rate four times by 25 basis points each since October 2004, high credit growth and bulk redemptions of IMD liability of US$ 7.1 billion, LAF levels again turned to neutral levels in December 2005 and there have been liquidity injections through LAF thereafter (Figure 11.6).

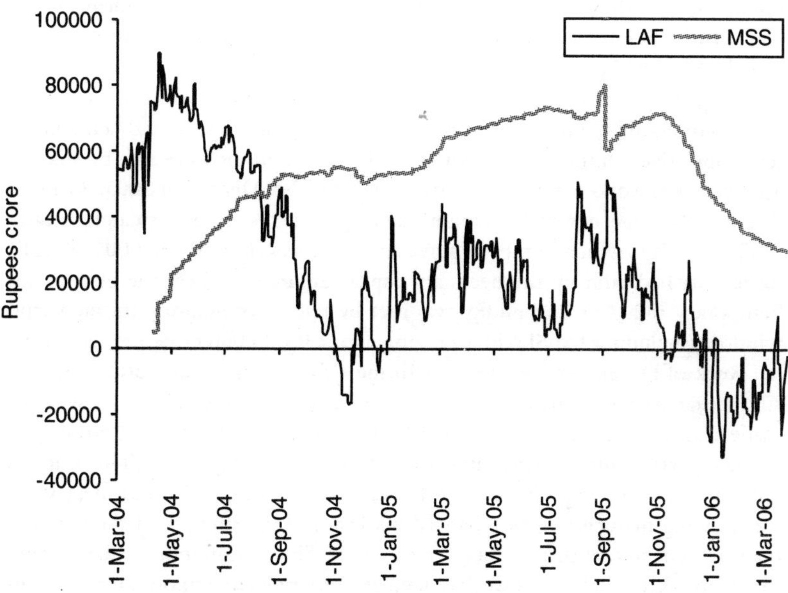

Figure 11.6 RBI's Liquidity Management (Absorption +/Injection –) through LAF and MSS

Credit growth has witnessed a sea change since mid-2004. Thus, the growth in non-food credit in 2004–5 was over 30 per cent, the highest in thirty-five years. In recent years, the banks had been subscribing to government securities much higher than the minimum SLR requirements. Making a forward looking assessment, the Reserve Bank began to unwind MSS from September 2005 and the MSS part in the weekly auctions was discontinued from 9 November 2005. This helped in the orderly withdrawal of liquidity equivalent to US$ 7.1 billion involved in the redemption of IMD. Managing bunched withdrawal of liquidity of such a large size is expected to pose a big challenge for monetary operations. Box 11.3 explains the measures taken proactively by the Reserve Bank, which helped in limiting

Box 11.3: Liquidity Management during IMD Redemption

The IMDs were foreign currency denominated deposits issued by State Bank of India (SBI) in 2000, on advice of the Government of India. It mobilized a sum of US$ 5.5 billion for a tenor of five years. IMD carried coupons of 8.50 per cent, 7.85 per cent, and 6.85 per cent on US dollar, Pound Sterling, and Euro denominated deposits respectively. IMD subscription was limited to non-resident Indians, persons of Indian origin, and overseas corporate bodies. The interest income earned on IMD was exempted from tax and there was provision of premature encashment after six months only in non-repatriable Indian rupees. These IMDs matured on 28–9 December 2005 and the large sums involved threw a challenge for liquidity management.

Liquidity management in face of IMD redemptions was carried out to contain disequilibrium while retaining monetary policy stance with a medium-term objective. Outflows on account of the redemptions were met by smooth arrangements worked out in this regard. During 27–9 December 2005, RBI sold foreign exchange out of its foreign exchange reserves to SBI totalling nearly US$ 7.1 billion, which in rupee equivalent terms was about Rs 32,000 crore. SBI on its part had built up the necessary rupee resources to meet the obligations. Temporary tightness in liquidity was met by release of liquidity through repo window (including the SLAF) averaging about Rs 23,000 crore per day in the last week of December coinciding with the IMD redemptions, outflows due to advance tax payments and the continued surge in credit offtake. The SLAF window made available since 28 November 2005 provided an additional opportunity to market participants to fine tune their liquidity management. The smooth redemption of the IMD liability of this size, bunched at a point of time, reflects the growing maturity of the financial markets and the strength of the liquidity management system that has been put in place. Short-term money market rates eased remarkably in the first week of January 2006 reflecting smooth redemptions of IMDs but again firmed up in the second week reflecting pressures emanating from scheduled auctions of government securities.

the liquidity mismatch to a large extent. Coupled with the high demand for credit (31.1 per cent growth year-on-year as on 17 March 2006) that has emerged the liquidity situation has nevertheless changed radically relative to the situation prevailing in most of 2005. The availability of LAF and MSS has enabled the RBI to manage these changed in an orderly manner.

The evidence of this efficient liquidity management may be seen in the relatively orderly movement in both exchange rates and interest rates. During times of excess visible liquidity, the call rates have essentially hugged the reverse repo rate, as might be expected, whereas they are near or slightly higher than the repo rate in times of tighter visible liquidity.

Preparing the Markets

An important element in coping with the liquidity management has been the smoothening behaviour of the central bank and the communication strategy. In August 2004, the headline inflation rate shot up to 8.7 per cent, partly on account of rising global oil prices and partly due to resurgence in manufacturing inflation. The turning of the interest rate cycle looked imminent. The issue was addressed through burden sharing by appropriate monetary and fiscal coordination and by preparing markets for a possible interest rate reversal. In measured and calibrated steps the monetary policy stance was changed and measures such as those on CRR and reverse repo were taken in a phased manner. Also, banks were allowed to transfer Held for Trading (HFT) and Available for Sale (AFS) securities to Held to Maturity (HTM) category, thereby affording them some cushion against the possible interest rate shock. Markets were prepared with a careful communication on the stance of the monetary policy by explaining that the central bank would strive for provision of appropriate liquidity and would place equal emphasis on price stability. It would consider measures in a calibrated manner. Monetary management succeeded in building credibility and keeping inflation expectations low. Headline inflation receded with the year ending with 5.1 per cent inflation. Inflation again surged temporarily early this year, but has been kept under leash even while the central bank moved to mop up excess liquidity. Markets were again told in October 2005 that the central bank is prepared to take measures in a calibrated and prompt manner and while genuine credit needs would be ensured, emphasis would be on price stability. Policy communications have been backed by credible actions in accordance with stance to keep inflation in tight leash.

In the more recent period, the IMD redemptions were carried out successfully with temporary volatility in money markets accompanied by liquidity shortages during December 2005. However, monetary policy operations were carried out to contain disequilibrium in line with the monetary policy stance with a medium-term objective. At the same time necessary liquidity has been provided in recent months to address the tighter liquidity due to frictional factors. It may be added that the Reserve Bank has enough instruments to manage liquidity.

LESSONS FROM THE INDIAN EXPERIENCE AND COPING AHEAD

What has been the lesson from the Indian experience of coping with liquidity management under large and volatile capital flows?

First, by putting reforms on a more stable footing by adopting gradualism but avoiding reversals, it has been able to sustain capital inflows on a more stable basis with lower volatility than has been seen in some other emerging markets. This has helped central banks in smoothening out interest rates under cyclical transition.

Second, in cases where money and debt markets have depth, development of OMOs through repo operations is particularly important for building up microeconomic capacities for macroeconomic objective of liquidity management. In India, the emergence of LAF was the single biggest factor which helped to manage liquidity amidst large and volatile capital flows and to keep short-term interest rates stable in this environment. It widened the range of instruments for monetary policy and enabled the Reserve Bank to operate on shorter range of interest rates. Restricting the maturities of interest rates at which the central bank operates to a smaller range at the short-end has reinforced market functioning.

Third, in the face of constraints on sterilization arising from paucity of instruments, the monetary authorities in India adopted a careful strategy which preserved the strength of the central bank balance sheet and the credibility of the central bank, while causing minimal frictions in the debt markets. MSS was not contemplated of initially even while capital flows had distinctly increased since 1993–4. However, in face of large surplus liquidity since 2000, MSS was evolved as a very useful instrument of monetary policy to sustain open market operations. MSS has marginal costs, but it has helped the monetary authorities manage business and liquidity cycles through the surpluses and the deficits. With MSS, the monetary authorities now have the option of assigning LAF for day-to-day liquidity management, using MSS for addressing semi-durable liquidity mismatches, while using outright sales/purchases of dated securities for truly long-term liquidity surpluses or deficits. The MSS experience tells us that operating framework and procedures undergo changes and one needs to keep innovating to calibrate market operations to the evolving liquidity conditions.

Fourth, by focusing on the microstructure of the markets and by facilitating development of a wider range of instruments such as CBLO, market repo, IRS, CDs, and CPs, in a manner that avoided market segmentation while meeting demand for various products, liquidity management could be placed on a much firmer footing. Market and central bank practices evolved to institutional developments. Payment and settlement system proved to be the most difficult area, but one which delivered the enabling environment for micro and macro developments supportive of the liquidity management procedures now in place. The focus on micro-aspects reinforced the central bank's ability to signal and transmit policy changes.

Fifth, with efforts to build up indirect instruments for liquidity management, the transmission of monetary policy has improved. The link between overnight interest rates and yields on Treasury Bills and liquid dated securities has become far stronger. While the lending rates and even more so deposit rates have been taking considerable time to adjust, the strength of the transmission has been in evidence in recent periods. It is important to note that in a situation of large surplus liquidity, the transmission is understandably weaker. However, in the more recent period, as considerable amount of excess liquidity was mopped up by the central bank, the rate signal efficacy has gone up substantially.

Sixth, the monetary policy setting through signalling improves as the central bank's liquidity management is able to establish its control over short-term interest rate. By reducing volatility in these rates by removing working balance constraints for the banks, it can influence the term structure of interest rates as reflected in money market rates of various maturities and the sovereign yield curve.

Lastly, while temporary mismatches in liquidity conditions do pose a problem for maintaining immediate goals of monetary operations, the overall objective of liquidity management needs to accorded primacy. In India, in spite of difficulties posed by sudden transitions in liquidity conditions, macroeconomic success of overall policies are reflected in delivering low inflation, which at 4.7 per cent, has averaged below 5.0 per cent over last five years in terms of the headline rate. Consumer price inflation has averaged still lower at around 4.0 per cent on a point-to-point basis and 3.9 per cent on an average basis.

In spite of relative success in liquidity management in India, several challenges remain ahead.

First, notwithstanding the large size of the debt markets, absence of a vibrant term market, the illiquidity of a large set of securities, and limitations of corporate debt market continue to come in way of further contemplated changes.

Second, while the Reserve Bank now enables market participants to meet their marginal liquidity demand twice a day on each working day, there is a moral hazard that passive operations by central bank in the market may be resulting in some market players who may not be doing enough for their own liquidity management.

Third, as the system moves to maintenance of SLR securities at statutory minimum levels, liquidity provision would become more difficult unless the instrument set is widened to facilitate market players to even out their liquidity mismatches.

Fourth, as RBI withdraws from the primary market in accordance with the FRBM Act, 2003, there is an urgent need to bridge the institutional gap with minimal necessary changes so that the market operations retain their efficiency, both from the view point of the central bank and the market participants.

Finally, further improvements in liquidity management would substantially depend on our abilities to improve forecasting of liquidity in the system. The short span within which liquidity conditions have been changing by a large amount has been the biggest constraint in targeting short-term interest rates. More effort for understanding the fiscal position and the government cash balances, as also the timing of foreign capital flows are of paramount importance in this context.

Notes

[1] During 1985–6 to 1997–8, the maximum coupon rate was increased from 6.5 per cent to 11.5 per cent. The maximum maturity was brought down from thirty to twenty years.

[2] Treasury Bills auctions introduced included 182-days Treasury Bills in November 1986, 364-days Treasury Bills in April 1992, and 91-days Treasury Bills in January 1993.

[3] Only banks and institutions having current account and Subsidiary General Ledger account with RBI at Mumbai were eligible to participate in these auctions. Initially, repos were conducted for one to three days but later they were replaced by a 14-day cycle covering reserves maintenance period.

References

Alexander, W.E., T.J.T. Balino, and C. Enoch (1995), 'The Adoption of Indirect Instruments of Monetary Policy', *IMF Occasional Paper*, No. 126, Washington, DC.

Bindseil, U. (2000), 'Central Bank Liquidity Management: Theory and Practice', April, European Central Bank, available at *https://www.ecb.int/events/conferences/html/opf.en.htm.*

Borio, C. (1997), 'The Implementation of Monetary Policy in Industrial Countries', *BIS Economic Papers No. 47*, Bank of International Settlements.

Obstfeld, M., Shambaugh, J.C., and A.M. Taylor (2004), 'The Trilemma in History: Tradeoffs Among Exchange Rates, Monetary Policies and Capital Mobility', *NBER Working Paper No. 10396.*

RBI (1999), *Repurchase Agreements (Repos): Report of the Sub-group of the Technical Advisory Committee on Government Securities Market*, April, Reserve Bank of India, Mumbai.

_____ (2003a), *Report of the Internal Group on Liquidity Adjustment Facility*, December, Reserve Bank of India, Mumbai.

_____ (2003b), *Report of the Working Group on Instruments of Sterilisation*, December, Reserve Bank of India, Mumbai.

Saggar, M. (2006), 'Monetary Policy and Operations in Countries with Surplus Liquidity', *Economic and Political Weekly*, Vol. 41, No. 11, 18 March, pp. 1041–52.

12 Central Banks and Risk Management

Pursuing Financial Stability*

I have chosen to discuss 'Financial Stability' for a number of reasons. Although financial stability has always been of concern to central banks, it is a relatively new concept in terms of the widespread attention being given to it in recent years. I thought it would be useful to discuss why it has become so important to central banks. Achieving this understanding would also help in explaining some of the behaviour of central banks. I will also try to explain why it is important for us.

FINANCIAL STABILITY: WHAT IS IT?

What is financial stability? Despite widespread usage of the term, there is no widespread agreement on a useful working definition of the term. Some define financial stability in terms of what it is not—the absence of financial instability. Others take a more macro-prudential view and specify financial stability in terms of limitation of risks of significant real output losses in the presence of episodes of system-wide financial distress.

In the absence of a widely accepted definition it is useful to discuss what we expect a financial system to do.

The primary function of the financial system is to smoothly and efficiently facilitate inter-temporal allocation of resources from savers to the ultimate users. This process of intermediation of funds enables the utilization of available resources to their most productive uses. Such a process implies management of financial risk on an inter-temporal basis. In doing so, however, the financial system is expected to absorb real economic surprises and shocks. If for some reason this is not done well, it could impair the

* Address at the 4th Annual Conference on Cash, Treasury, and Risk Management in India on 21 November 2006 at New Delhi.

efficient functioning of the financial system as a whole and engender financial instability.

But we need to be careful in thinking about financial instability. Disturbances in financial markets or at individual financial institutions need not constitute financial instability if they do not impair overall economic functioning. Illustratively, a closure of a small financial institution, or for that matter, movement in asset prices within certain limits or even minor corrections in financial markets need not necessarily hamper stability. On the contrary, fluctuations in asset and other prices in financial markets may actually be good for overall financial stability as adjustment mechanisms. Such market adjustments also help to keep authorities alert and sensitive to incipient developments and can enable them to identify and monitor newer risks. What are important from the macroeconomic standpoint are issues related to contagion and systemic risk, which can lead to economy-wide upheavals and would, therefore, need to be monitored on an on-going basis.

The point of making these observations is that unlike price stability, which can be easily quantified, financial stability cannot be easily summarized into a single measure. As a consequence, monitoring financial stability needs to encompass not only financial institutions and markets, but also the state of financial infrastructure: a stable financial system depends as much on the health of financial institutions as it does on the complex inter-linkages between those institutions and the interplay between the financial system, the financial markets, and the associated financial infrastructure. The integrity of the payment system is at the core of the financial system, and confidence in the use of money as a unit of account is essential to the maintenance of financial stability. While central bankers have always been concerned with addressing these aforesaid aspects, the issue therefore remains: why is there an overt concern with financial stability in modern-day financial systems?

HISTORICAL BACKGROUND

To understand the current outbreak of concerns, let us review a little bit of history. It would be useful to start with salient developments in the world economy since the early 1900s in order to understand the relevance of financial stability in modern day financial systems.

Until World War I, the international experience had broadly been of long-run price and monetary stability. A great degree of turbulence followed after the conclusion of World War I: the German hyper-inflation, the Great Depression, World War II itself, the Korean war, and later the Vietnam war. It is not surprising that in the presence of such economic and political dislocation, price and financial stability also suffered during this period. The financing of wars led to fiscal expansionism usually financed by money creation. Thus, a period of relatively high inflation ensued in the 1960s and 1970s, culminating in double-digit inflation in the United States and western Europe in the late 1970s, spiked by severe oil shocks of the 1970s. Thus, after this long tumultuous period of fluctuating inflation during the 1960s and 1970s, aggressive disinflationary policies of the early 1980s brought international inflation down to tolerable levels.

Prior to World War I, the gold standard was, in some sense, the anchor of monetary, price, and financial stability. Central banks' commitment to ensuring the convertibility of their currency into gold at fixed prices did much to engender confidence in the system. There was also a significant degree of cooperation among the central banks and governments of major economies, which helped to lubricate the system in its functions in times of financial imbalances (Eichengreen, 1992). The gold standard, however, came under severe strain after World War I in the wake of the breakdown in cooperation between the countries. The consequence was the Depression, competitive devaluations, beggar thy neighbour policies, decline in world trade, and high unemployment, at different times in different countries during the inter-war period. Overall, there was a great degree of instability during this period.

The quest for a new international economic order that would restore economic and financial stability in the world gave rise to the Bretton Woods institutions and the Bretton Woods Currency System. It was not until 1958 that most European currencies became convertible and many currency adjustments took place after the end of World War II. The anchor now was essentially the US dollar as the reserve currency and the commitment to its convertibility to gold at a fixed rate of $ 35 per ounce. The IMF was to act the lender of last resort in case of BoP crises. But even this fixed exchange rate system lasted only till 1971. The over-financing of exports, the economic pick up in hitherto war torn countries leading to the glut of the dollars; and the American inflation of the 1960s, all contributed to the cessation of dollar convertibility to gold. The fixed exchange rate system got abandoned after the Smithsonian Agreement. The floating exchange rates that then followed meant that the world was left without an easily understood, credible monetary anchor. Hence the increasing quest for methodologies promoting financial stability.

The other major feature of global financial markets has been the trends in capital flows. A major surge in capital flows started around the 1870s and continued till World War I. This era, which coincided with the operation of the gold standard, has been regarded until recently as the golden era of capital mobility. Open trade and open labour markets also characterized this period. In retrospect, there was an effective system shutdown after World War I, almost until the 1970s. During the inter-war period, the world economic system got characterized by increasing trade restrictions, high tariffs, curbs on capital flows, fixed exchange rates, and other rigidities. Post-World War II, it has taken a long time to open up international trade through the successive GATT Rounds and now through the WTO.

The period after 1973 has been characterized by floating exchange rates and gradually increasing international capital flows, along with increasing volumes of international trade. The geographical demarcation of national borders gradually became less of a constraint for both trade and capital flows. By the 1990s, open trade and open capital accounts led to a phenomenal growth of cross-border flows, including in developing countries and the emerging economies in Eastern Europe.

All this entailed a phenomenal expansion of financial activity. This was partly in response to the demographically driven increase in the amount of investible wealth, but it also reflected the increased need for markets and institutions to channel funds between an increasingly active and diverse range of borrowers and lenders.

At the same time, domestic financial liberalization led to the removal of constraints on the activities of financial institutions of different kinds within a given national market in many countries. The liberalization of cross-border capital movements and rights of market access meant that a broader range of domestic and foreign institutions were able to provide banking and other financial services in a given market. The range of services on offer also expanded and an increasing number of both markets and institutions became active across national boundaries. While this entailed lower costs of products and services for consumers, this also entailed the possibility of contagion with ramifications extending well beyond national borders particularly in the context of inadequate development of financial markets in some countries.

On the flip side, however, this transformation of the financial marketplace extended and tightened linkages across markets and institutions, increasing the uniformity of the information sets available to economic agents and encouraging greater similarity in the assessment of information, driven to a large extent by advances in IT and communications networking. This, in effect, meant that weaknesses in the financial system could engender serious and far more disruptive economic consequences than was previously the case, and could increasingly engender contagion effects extending well beyond national boundaries. The Mexican crisis of 1994–5, the East Asian crisis of 1997–8, and the more recent crises in Argentina and Turkey bear ample testimony to this fact. At the national level, the banking crises in Nordic countries in the 1980s and 1990s, the problems in the Philippines and Korean banking systems in the 1990s (and the near panic at the time of the LTCM affair), and the financial bubble in Japan whose costs are felt even at present, deserve mention.

During the 1980s and 1990s, nearly one hundred national banking systems collapsed, many more than in any comparable previous period. The range of movements in exchange rates and the extent of deviations in market exchange rates from real exchange rates—the magnitude of undershooting and overshooting—were larger than in any previous period. There were also massive asset price bubbles in some countries: Japan, Sweden, Thailand, South-East Asian countries such as Malaysia, and finally in the United States.

All this meant that the sources of crises, which were earlier traced primarily to weaknesses in banking systems, became manifold, and could emanate from any segment of the financial sector with possibilities of spillovers to other sectors and countries. More importantly, as the Asian crises amply demonstrated, such crises could even affect economies with sound real sector fundamentals. The deficiencies in the international financial architecture meant that the IMF was no longer large enough to take care of the crises. The earlier concerns on banking stability therefore become much larger in scope and content, to assume the term 'financial stability'.

These developments have had several consequences for the institutional and systemic structure. Among the most important of these from the point of view of systemic significance has been disintermediation. Credit worthy firms are relying increasingly on capital markets, rather than bank loans, to finance investment projects. This has led to the deepening of capital markets of various kinds, as well as to a more important role for the institutions that deal in traded securities.

A second important structural change is the emergence of markets for risks of different kinds, in which exposures to specific market or credit risk can be bought and sold separately from financial assets. This has provided economic agents the leeway to reduce or increase their exposure to specific categories of risk.

A third key trend has been changes in the business profile of financial institutions. In many countries, services traditionally associated with 'banking' are now offered by institutions not legally characterized as banks, while banks are increasingly engaged in para-banking activities.

These fundamental changes—deregulation, liberalization, and disintermediation—have, not surprisingly, made financial systems far more interconnected, with possible ramifications for contagion in the event of an exigency in any country. As a consequence, central banks, which were traditionally focused on monetary and banking stability, have increasingly come to focus on financial stability as a key concern in the conduct of monetary policy.

HOW ARE CENTRAL BANKS RESPONDING TO THIS DEVELOPMENT?

Avoiding crises becomes ultimately a national responsibility. The impact of instability in times of crisis typically tends to be borne by domestic taxpayers rather than the global private entities. The burden of such an asymmetric adjustment means that there is a need to institute domestic mechanisms that could focus on the aspect of financial stability on an ongoing basis. As institutions traditionally mandated with the task of price stability, central banks became the natural choice for the governments to be entrusted with oversight of financial stability.

Given that financial stability has become a paramount focus of the central banks, the key question therefore arises is: how are central banks responding to the challenge? Interestingly, new legislations explicitly provide mandates for financial stability; illustratively, Hungary passed such legislation in 2001, the Netherlands in 1993, Spain in 1994, and the United Kingdom in 1997.

So, the question is why have the central banks become interested in financial stability? Central banks are clearly responsible for issue of currency, maintaining its value as a means of exchange and unit of account. They are also responsible for maintaining the efficiency and integrity of payment systems. Ultimately, they are the lenders of last resort. Notwithstanding the complexity involved, evidence suggests that involvement in financial stability can be broadly categorized into five types of activities. Being a key fulcrum of the policy apparatus responsible for financial stability, the central banks might be involved in several of these tasks.

First, oversight of the financial infrastructure: This involves the operation as well as oversight of the payments and settlement systems and securities clearing system. It might also involve oversight of financial disclosures, market conduct, and the like. It is important to note that all at the markets need the payment system, including the capital market.

Second, regulation and supervision of financial entities: This involves the formulation of prudential guidelines (capital adequacy and reserve requirements, provisioning norms, risk management standards), the monitoring of compliance with those rules (on-site inspection and off-site surveillance), and the imposition of sanctions in case of non-compliance.

Third, safety net provisions: This involves decisions to restructure troubled banks as well as 'honest brokering'. It also involves the operation of financial safety net in the form of DI.

Fourth, liquidity: The response to a crisis may necessitate judicious use of the emergency liquidity assistance facilities in order to avoid disruptions from disorderly failures and to contain contagious strain. Only the central banks can inject liquidity.

Fifth, market surveillance: Central banks are often involved in the regulation and surveillance of markets. The three markets that are primarily the focus of surveillance by central banks are the money, bond, and foreign exchange markets.

In addition, central banks are typically concerned with macro financial stability. This encompasses monitoring the behaviour of all important players in the financial sector, the health of non-financial sector balance sheets as well as assessment of systemic vulnerabilities. This analysis is accompanied by communication policy on financial stability issues, either through dedicated financial stability reports or disclosure of information on financial stability as part of regular reports (Annex A). The basic motive behind such reports is to communicate to the markets and the public at large and thereby express the commitment of the central bank for achieving its objectives. This is accompanied by a process of structured communication among the various bodies involved in the pursuit of financial stability.

In their quest for financial stability, central banks worldwide have exhibited a variety of responses. On the one hand, several central banks have been given an explicit mandate to promote financial stability (Annex B). Another broad category of response has been the constitution of independent departments to oversee financial stability. Illustratively, at the Reserve Bank of New Zealand, the supervisory and financial market departments were merged into a Financial Stability Department. At the ECB, the area concerned with financial stability matters (Prudential Supervision Division) was upgraded to a Directorate (Financial Stability and Supervision) which reports to a member of the Executive Board and plays a coordination role for Euro area/EU financial stability monitoring. Finally, the Bank of England has also constituted a dedicated Financial Stability Department for oversight of financial stability matters, headed by a Deputy Governor. The transfer of supervisory responsibilities outside the central bank in several countries has also led the central banks to focus their attention on systemic issues as reflected in a reorientation of organizational arrangements.

The crux of these observations is that financial stability has been a prime locus of change in the central banks and increasingly, central banks are taking a proactive stance to address the threats posed by financial instability. For instance, the Financial Stability Forum was created in the aftermath of the Asian financial crisis, comprising members as major countries, international financial institutions such as BIS and IMF, and the international standard setters such as International Organization of Securities Commissions (IOSCO) and International Association of Insurance Supervisors (IAIS).

Having traced the broad contours of the growing importance of financial stability worldwide and the role played by the central banks in the process, let me turn to how the Reserve Bank has been responding to the challenge.

INDIAN EXPERIENCE ON FINANCIAL STABILITY—AN OVERVIEW

Till the onset of reforms in the early 1990s, India was a relatively closed economy, being largely insulated from the vicissitudes of global markets. It was not, of course, totally insulated from exogenous shocks. The severe drought from 1965 to 1967, the oil shocks of 1973, 1979, and 1989, and wars all had significant effects including the emergence of external payments crises. However, the financial system was effectively controlled, particularly in the 1970s and 1980s, and the risk of financial contagion was therefore not high.

The gradual opening up of the economy since the 1990s raised several important challenges for the central bank. The opening of the external sector meant that developments in India came to be increasingly influenced by the developments abroad. It is interesting to look at some numbers. Contrary to various perceptions, the Indian economy is now substantively open. As the Finance Minister observed in a lecture at Yale University, whereas India's GDP in 2004–5 was roughly US$ 700 billion, the gross flows on the current account and the capital account, put together, came to US$ 500 billion.[1] This is despite the fact that trade tariffs are still higher than in most other countries in the world and that capital account controls still exist. The large capital inflows, despite the cautious approach to liberalization, meant that such flows can engender volatility in exchange rate movements. The speed of capital flows, both inward and outward, is much higher than current account flows and can therefore destabilize the exchange rate, and operation of financial and capital markets, possibly in response to external events unconnected with the domestic economy (Jalan, 2003). Consequently we have to be concerned with exchange rate instability, as distinguished from mere fluctuation, for its potential to affect other markets, both goods and capital markets. Exchange rate instability arising from external events can give rise to domestic instability in the operation of the stock market, government securities markets, and the money markets, along with their attendant effects. For emerging economies such as India, it therefore becomes necessary to institute special defenses for ensuring financial stability. Furthermore, with the interest rate emerging as a key channel of monetary policy signals, the efficacy of monetary transmission is predicated on the health of the financial sector. The gradual liberalization of the financial sector has also witnessed the emergence of conglomerates, with attendant systemic implications.

More broadly however, the period since the 1990s has been testimony to several shocks impinging on the economy. Illustratively, nuclear sanctions and the border tensions in the late 1990s, the monsoon vagaries in the recent past, most recently in 2003, the crises in East Asia in 1997 and 1998, the upheaval in domestic stock markets in May 2004 coupled with the recurrent oil price fluctuations have meant that the economy has been susceptible to intermittent shocks. And unlike the shocks of earlier decades, the economy has been able to withstand these disruptions with limited impact on the financial sector. The role of central banks in such a milieu is not hard to foresee. The response of the Reserve Bank in May 2004 is a case in point.[2] Judged thus, the role of Reserve Bank in its task of monitoring financial stability can hardly be over-emphasized.

Financial stability has, therefore, emerged as a key consideration in the conduct of monetary policy. In this process, the Reserve Bank has adopted a two-track approach in the pursuit of financial stability. First, by ensuring monetary stability through lowering of inflation, it has lowered inflationary expectations, thereby fostering financial stability. Second, the Reserve Bank has adopted a multi-pronged strategy, with suitable country-specific adaptations, to promote stability of financial institutions, financial markets, and the financial infrastructure. The stable economic regime combined with the macro financial oversight of the financial system has imparted confidence to market players to conduct their business in an orderly manner.

In general, it is possible to discern two broad sets of instruments by which the Reserve Bank has been addressing the financial stability concerns: preventive instruments comprising micro and macro prudential measures and reactive instruments comprising liquidity support measures and public intervention tools aimed at safeguarding depositors' interests.

With regard to *institutions*, the Reserve Bank founded the Board of Financial Supervision in 1994 to upgrade its practice of financial supervision. A set of prudential norms for the commercial banking sector had been instituted as early as 1994 with regard to capital adequacy, IRAC, provisioning, exposure norms, and more recently, in respect of their investment portfolio. The approach adopted here was one of gradual convergence with international best practices, while internalizing it to suit country-specific requirements. In tandem with the gradual opening up of the economy, the regulatory and supervisory framework was spruced up comprising a three-pronged strategy of regular on-site inspections, technology-driven off-site surveillance, and extensive use of external auditors. As a result of improvements in the regulatory and supervisory framework, the degree of compliance with the Basel *Core Principles* has gradually improved. The supervisory framework has been further upgraded with the institution of a framework of Risk Based Supervision (RBS) for intensified monitoring of vulnerabilities. A scheme of PCA was effected in December 2002 to undertake mandatory and discretionary intervention against troubled banks based on well-defined financial/prudential parameters. In view of the growing emergence of financial conglomerates and the possibility of systemic risks arising therefrom, a system of consolidated accounting has been instituted. A half-yearly review based on financial soundness indicators is being undertaken to assess the health of individual institutions and macro-prudential indicators associated with financial system soundness. The findings arising thereof are disseminated to the public through its various Reports. In fact, in 2003 the Reserve Bank published a chapter titled 'Financial Stability' in its *Report on Currency and Finance* in that year, highlighting its challenges and problems in the pursuit of stability. Subsequently, with effect from 2004, the annual statutory *Report on Trend and Progress of Banking in India* has began to publish a dedicated chapter on financial stability. This is in addition to the periodic Monetary and Credit Policy Reviews where the Governor highlights the threats and challenges to the financial environment before announcing policy measures.

Given the multi-faceted nature of financial stability, no one body might be in a position to monitor it in its entirety. Keeping this in view, the Ministry of Finance has constituted a High-Level Coordination Committee on Financial and Capital Markets with the Governor, RBI; Chairman, Securities and Exchange Board of India (SEBI); and Chairman, Insurance Regulatory and Development Authority (IRDA) along with the Finance Secretary, Government of India as members to address policy gaps and overlaps.

An important aspect of the financial stability process has been the growing emphasis on the role of market discipline. As part of the process, the Reserve Bank has laid strong emphasis on the levels of transparency and standards of disclosure in banks' balance sheets. These disclosures, presently supplemented as 'Notes on Accounts' not only encompasses prudential ratio pertaining to capital adequacy (tier-I and tier-II separately) ratio, non-performing loans, exposure to sensitive sectors (capital market, real estate, and commodities), but also financial ratios such as interest and non-interest income as percentage of working funds, return on average assets, and net profit per employee. These disclosures have been gradually expanded over time and presently include maturity pattern of assets and liabilities (both rupee and foreign currency), movements in NPLs, issuer composition of non-SLR investment, assets subject to corporate debt restructuring as well as details of assets sold to Securitization/reconstruction company.

The performance of the non-financial sector has an important bearing on financial stability. Keeping this in view, the Reserve Bank has also been closely monitoring the stability ratios of the non-financial sector. In the corporate sector for instance, the reduction in debt liabilities following corporate restructuring and reduced interest expenses in an environment of low interest rates has improved the financial stability indicators in manufacturing. Available indications are that both consumption and investment demand are currently buoyant. Business surveys also point to high levels of both business confidence and capacity utilization. The improved investment sentiment and business confidence, as reflected in the increasing number of firms incurring capital expenditure, suggests the prospects for buoyant manufacturing growth in 2005–6.

You would all be aware that issues of governance in banks have assumed relevance worldwide in the wake of accounting irregularities in the United States and elsewhere. Problems in governance can derail even the best efforts on the part of regulators to ensure financial stability. To address this aspect, the Reserve Bank issued guidelines on ownership and governance based on well-defined principles, namely a well-diversified ownership and control, important shareholders being 'fit and proper', directors and chief executive officer (CEO) being 'fit and proper', and observation of sound corporate governance principles.

An important hallmark of the pursuit of financial stability in India has been the adoption of a consultative approach to policy formulation, taking on board the various stakeholders in the financial system. Such an approach has had the merit of providing useful lead time to market participants to adjust their behaviour in conformity to the regulatory guidelines.

Evidence suggests that no two crises are exactly alike. As a result, in addition to preventative instruments just discussed, the Reserve Bank had also resorted to reactive instruments.

One such instrument is emergency liquidity support. Thus, in very rare and unusual circumstances, when a bank faces a sudden and unforeseen liquidity problem, the Reserve Bank has, on an earlier occasion, at its discretion, extended liquidity support to the bank.

A second such instrument is the provision of safety net in the form of DI. In India, DI is mandatory and covers all banks [commercial/cooperative/RRBs/local area banks (LABs)].[3] All deposits except (a) deposits of foreign governments, (b) deposits of Central/state governments, (c) inter-bank deposits, and (d) deposits held abroad are covered by Deposit Insurance and Credit Guarantee Corporation (DICGC). The amount of coverage is presently Rs 1 lakh (Rs 1,00,000), and is provided to deposits held in the same right and in the same capacity. Given the present limit, as much as 95 per cent of deposit accounts and 66 per cent of assessable deposits are fully protected. Given the level of per capita GDP at constant prices (Rs 15,017 in 2004), this implies that the coverage limit is roughly six times the per capita GDP (Annex C). The premium is charged on a flat rate basis, which is presently 8 paise per Rs 100 of assessable deposits for the year 2004–5 and 10 paise from 2005–6 (earlier it was 5 paise per Rs 100 of assessable deposits).

A third instrument is treatment of insolvent banks (winding down). The Reserve Bank, rather than closing them down, has shown a preference for merging such banks with healthy banks. The rationale behind such an approach has been dictated by two considerations. First, given the dominance of commercial banks, their closure can raise systemic concerns. Second, given that a significant portion of bank depositors in India are small, it is imperative to safeguard their interests, while dealing with insolvent banks (Mohan, 2004).

The second broad element of strategy has been the development of financial markets. Ensuring orderly conditions in financial markets has been an important component of the Reserve Bank's approach towards financial stability. The cornerstone of the process has been to widen, deepen, and integrate various segments of financial markets to enable the price discovery process, lower transactions costs, and enhance market liquidity. Accordingly, the operating procedures of monetary policy have been continuously fine-tuned to attune it to the realities of market dynamics.

In the money market, the focus has been on developing a deep and liquid money market, supplanted by a wide array of instruments to modulate monetary conditions with a relative emphasis on indirect policy instruments to enable swift responses to changing market conditions. In the face of large capital flows, a new facility in the form of MSS was instituted in April 2004. The MSS essentially seeks to differentiate the liquidity absorption of a more enduring nature by way of sterilization from the day-to-day normal liquidity management operations.

In the foreign exchange market, the exchange rate policy adopted by India has been one of managing volatility with no fixed target, while allowing the underlying demand and supply conditions to determine the exchange rate movements over a period in an orderly way. Market players are also enabled to manage risk through various designated hedging instruments. Prudent management of the external sector coupled with a calibrated approach to capital account liberalization has been an important component of macroeconomic policy to ensure financial stability.

In the government bond market, the major objectives of reforms were to impart liquidity and depth to the market by broadening the investor base and ensuring market-clearing interest rate mechanism. The important initiatives introduced included a market-related government borrowing and consequently, a phased elimination of automatic monetization of Central Government budget deficits. This, in turn, enabled the shift from direct to indirect tools of monetary regulation—activating open market operations and the development of secondary market. The entire range of changes necessitated developments in (a) instruments, (b) institutions, and (c) technology, along with concomitant improvements in (d) transparency and (e) the legal framework. As of 1 April 2006 the FRBM Act now prohibits the Reserve Bank from subscribing to the government securities in the primary market. This has necessitated the further development of techniques and instruments to ensure stability in the government securities market.

Developing a robust and secure financial infrastructure has been a key component of financial stability. Towards this end, the Reserve Bank undertook several initiatives to upgrade the payment and settlement system in the country. Salient among these included electronic clearing service, electronic funds transfer, and the establishment of a secured private network which serves as a private gateway to the financial system. On the basis of the framework prevalent in developed financial markets, an RTGS system has been operationalized. RTGS provides for an electronic-based settlement of inter-bank and customer-based transactions with intra-day collateralized liquidity support from the Reserve Bank. Side by side, in its quest for benchmarking with international best practices, the Reserve Bank has benchmarked its conformity with the Core Principles for Systemically Important Payment Systems. The degree of compliance with these Principles is presently on par with those prevailing internationally.

CHALLENGES TO FINANCIAL STABILITY

Given the inherent dynamic nature of financial stability, its operationalization raises several challenges.

First, the changing structure of the financial system with the blurring of boundaries between financial institutions and markets raises significant policy challenges. As I remarked earlier, services traditionally associated with 'banking' are presently being offered by institutions not legally characterized as banks, while banks are increasingly engaged in para-banking activities. Such 'conglomerization' of financial activity raises the possibility of systemic risk with attendant implications for financial contagion, which lies at the very root of financial instability.

Second, in this context, coordination between the regulators assumes paramount importance. In recognition of these concerns, the Reserve Bank has taken a structured approach to their surveillance by instituting a coordinated monitoring mechanism with other domestic regulators (SEBI and IRDA) on matters of supervision of financial conglomerates. In addition, the Reserve Bank has been holding half-yearly discussions with the CEOs of the conglomerates in association with other principal regulators to address outstanding issues and supervisory concerns. This process is working well at present. However, as financial development takes place in India, we can expect further blurring of distinction between different types of financial intermediaries. We can also expect greater presence of large financial conglomerates, including foreign ones. Hence, we need to consider the development of a more organized approach to the regulation and oversight of the emerging financial conglomerates as has been done in other countries. In the United States, for example, the Federal Reserve Board has been designed as the lead umbrella supervisor of FHCs. Pending such developments, as a workable measure, there could be a need to execute general/specific MoU as part of the process of supervisory coordination towards furtherance of financial stability.

Third, another significant feature of the Indian economy post-reforms has been the greater opening up of the economy. The size of merchandise, as well as services trade, has been increasing steadily in recent years, reflecting greater integration of the economy with the rest of the world. The recent experience also suggests subtle shifts in international comparative advantage with software, business, and commercial services gaining prominence. Overall capital flows have also been buoyant, given the positive outlook on the economy. The large capital flows have, in turn, resulted in accumulation of reserves, rendering the reserve position comfortable according to various indicators of reserve adequacy. While these developments have resulted in benefits, it has also made the economy much less quarantined from global developments and the task of central bankers that much more difficult than in the erstwhile autarkic regime. As a result, central bankers have to be continuously alert and watchful not only to domestic but also global developments because, as the Asian crises testify, developments abroad can have significant domestic ramifications even for an economy with perfectly sound fundamentals.

Fourth, the spread of the financial system with growing liberalization of the economy and the increasing reach of formal finance has gradually expanded to cover larger segments of the population. The 'demographic dividend' of a larger and younger labour force has meant that banks have been able to expand their loan portfolio quite rapidly, enabling consumers to satisfy their lifestyle aspirations at a relatively young age with an optimal combination of equity and debt to finance consumption and asset creation. On the other side, such opening up has also meant that interest rates have become a much more potent tool of monetary policy, affecting consumption and investment decisions of the population in a fashion much more rapidly than was the case earlier. With a sizeable proportion of the population having limited ability to insure themselves against unforeseen contingencies, there is merit in considering the need to devise 'shock absorbers' in order to insulate the economy from contagion effects. Continuous and proactive efforts towards developing a robust financial system and instituting appropriate market surveillance mechanisms that can throw up 'early warning signals' of financial distress are important parameters of such resilience.

The fifth challenge to the maintenance of financial stability lies in the increasing growth of the economy. The traditional measure of national accounting does not take cognizance of the knowledge flows that create value in the medium to long run. This phenomenal growth of the knowledge economy and its value-enhancing effect are only recently being addressed for the US economy. Judged from this standpoint, it seems that central banks would not only need to keep track of traditional measures of consumption and investment, but, in addition, also have a hang of the knowledge flows across borders in order to assess the impact of their decisions on the real economy. This is easier said than done and moving ahead from the traditional accounting framework to a more 'realistic' one incorporating 'knowledge flows' is a challenging task that the central bankers will have to deal with sometime sooner than later.

Another challenge relates to the issue of coordination policymaking bodies. Instabilities can arise in any segment of the financial system and not necessarily in segments which are under the domain of the Reserve Bank, although through contagion effects, their effects are likely to be felt across the entire financial sector. This calls for closer and continuous coordination among the various policymaking bodies, including an even broader set of players such as accounting standard setters, legislators, and tax authorities. The multiplicity of policy actors emphasizes the need for a cooperative organization of policy efforts in this regard.

The opening of trade has meant the death of commodity inflation. The expectations of financial market participants on financial variables are different from the market expectations of commodity prices. The recent surge in the stock market is likely to engender the 'wealth effect', which through multiplier process, is likely to spillover into prices and, more particularly, into asset prices. Although such a phenomenon is widely acknowledged, attempting to precisely quantify the spillover from commodity to asset prices and the magnitude of such over-extension remains a challenge. There is a need in this context for serious analytical work that can explore the link in the movements between commodity prices and asset prices.

SUMMARY

Over the last few years, the global financial system has been buffeted by a number of pressures and some unprecedented shocks. Nonetheless, the system has continued to prove resilient and financial stability has been maintained. Potential fault lines that have emerged in the process, namely, those pertaining to corporate governance, auditing, and accounting standards, and prudential norms have been receiving close scrutiny from policymakers.

The Indian financial system is not quarantined from global developments, but our judgement is that it remains robust, underpinned by the continued expansion of the Indian economy. The task for all of us is therefore to remain alert and proactive, identify and address newer risks, eschew harmful incentives, and adjust the regulatory environment to address any unforeseen contingency in the economic environment.

Notes

[1] Chidambaram (2005).

[2] On 17 May 2004, the stock market witnessed turbulent conditions, caused mainly by political uncertainty after the general elections. External factors such as rising oil prices and apprehensions of rise in international interest rates also contributed to the sudden reversal of market sentiment. In response, the Reserve Bank initially intervened in the forex market and once it was realized that there were no spillovers to other markets, maintaining the integrity of the payment and settlement system assumed prominence. Accordingly, the Reserve Bank operated at three different levels. First, settlement banks were informed that in case of liquidity problems, they could access the 'backstop facility' under LAF from the Reserve Bank. Second, a statement was made informing market participants that there was no shortage of liquidity in the system, either in domestic or in foreign currency. Finally, this was followed by a statement that carried credibility for the system at large. A Task Force was constituted for providing clarifications and liquidity assistance. Certain prudential relaxations were provided for a temporary period to market players in the light of market conditions and the same was subsequently restored to normal levels once markets returned to normal functioning. The idea inherent in this process was to ensure no transmission of panic from equity to other markets.

[3] DI is not applicable to cooperatives where the Cooperative Societies Act under which they are registered, does not comply with the provisions of Section 2 (gg) of the DICGC Act, 1961. Deposit insurance has also not been extended to cooperative banks in certain North-eastern states (Meghalaya, Mizoram, Arunachal Pradesh, and Nagaland) and union territories (Lakshadweep, Chandigarh, and Dadra and Nagar Haveli) which do not have the legal framework in place.

References

Chidambaram, P. (2005), 'India, the US and the Evolving World Economy', lecture delivered at Yale University, September.

Eichengreen, B. (1992), *Golden Fetters: The Gold Standard and the Great Depression, 1919–1939*, Oxford University Press, New York.

Jalan, B. (2003), 'Exchange Rate Management: An Emerging Consensus?', address at the 14th National Assembly of Forex Association of India on 14 August 2003, *RBI Bulletin*, September.

Mohan, R. (2004), 'Financial Sector Reforms: Policies and Performance Analysis', *RBI Bulletin*, November.

ANNEX A

Financial Stability Reports Published by Central Banks

Central bank/ monetary authority	Name of periodical	Frequency of publication	Languages
	Dedicated financial stability reports		
Australia	*Financial Stability Review*	Bi-annual	English
Austria	*Financial Stability Report*	Once/twice a year	English, German
Belgium	*Financial Stability Review*	Annual	English (excerpts in Dutch and French)
Brazil	*Financial Stability Review*	Bi-annual	English, Portuguese
Canada	*Financial System Review*	Bi-annual	English, French
France	*Financial Stability Review*	Bi-annual	English, French
Hungary	*Report on Financial Stability*	Bi-annual	English, Hungarian
Norway	*Financial Stability Report*	Bi-annual	English, Norwegian
Spain	*Financial Stability Report*	Bi-annual	English, Spanish
Sweden	*Financial Stability Report*	Bi-annual	English, Swedish
UK	*Financial Stability Review*	Bi-annual	English
	Financial stability articles		
European Central Bank	Financial Stability and Supervision (section in *Annual Report*)	Annual	English, other EU languages
Germany	Report on the Stability of German Financial System (section in *Bundesbank Monthly Report*)		English, German
Hong Kong SAR	Half-yearly Monetary and Financial Stability Report (section in *Quarterly Bulletin*)	Bi-annual	English, Chinese

Contd

Annex A Contd

Central bank/ monetary authority	Name of periodical	Frequency of publication	Languages
India	Reinforcing Financial Stability (published as a chapter of *Report on Currency and Finance, 1999–2000*)[a]		English, Hindi
The Netherlands	Financial Stability (section of *Quarterly Bulletin*)	Quarterly	English, Dutch

Note: [a] A regular chapter titled 'Financial Stability' has been introduced in the statutory *Report on Trend and Progress of Banking in India* from the year 2003–04.

ANNEX B

LEGAL BASIS FOR FINANCIAL STABILITY FUNCTION

Central bank	Legal basis for the financial stability function
Australia	The Reserve Bank of Australia (RBA) Board should use its monetary and banking policy so as to best continue to (a) the stability of the currency, (b) the maintenance of full employment, and (c) the economic prosperity and welfare of the people of Australia.
Austria	Article 79(I) of the Austrian Banking Act 1993 (as amended in 2001) observes 'observations and findings of a fundamental nature or of particular importance in the area of banking...' should be exchanged between the Oesterreichische Nationalbank (OeNB), the Financial Market Authority, and the Federal Ministry of Finance. Moreover, Article 13(I) of the Financial Market Authority Law explicitly states that 'A Financial Market Committee shall be established at the Federal Ministry of Finance in order to promote the co-operation and exchange of opinions as a platform by the institutions jointly responsible for the stability of the financial markets'.
Belgium	The amended National Bank of Belgium Act 1988 (Article 8) states that 'the Bank contributes to the stability of the financial system'.
Canada	According to Section 19(g.I) of the Bank of Canada Act, the Bank may purchase or sell a wider than normally allowable range of securities for the 'purpose of promoting the stability of the Canadian financial system'.
European Central Bank	'The primary objective of the European System of Central Banks (ESCB) shall be to maintain price stability. Without prejudice to the objective of price stability, it shall support the general economic policies in the Community with a view to contributing to the achievement of the objectives of the Community.' *'The basic tasks to be carried out through the ESCB shall be....to promote the smooth operation of the payment systems.'* 'The ESCB shall contribute to the smooth conduct of policies pursued by the competent authorities relating to the prudential supervision of credit institutions and the stability of the financial system.'

Contd

Annex B Contd

France	According to the Banking Act of 1984, the Governor of the Banque de France chairs the Commission Bancaire, which is responsible for the supervision of credit institutions and investment firms.
Germany	The German Banking Act stipulates that the supervisory authority 'shall counteract undesirable developments in the banking and financial sector which...involve serious disadvantages for the national economy'.
Hungary	The Central Banking Act of 2001 states: 'The MNB shall promote the stability of the financial system and shall contribute to the development and smooth conduct of policies related to the prudential supervision of the financial system'.
The Netherlands	The Bank Act 1998 (Section 3) states that 'in implementation of the (EU-) Treaty, the Bank shall, within the framework of the ESCB, contribute to the smooth conduct of policies pursued by the competent authorities relating to the prudential supervision of credit institutions and the stability of the financial system'.
Norway	Section I of the Norges Bank Act states that the Bank shall... 'promote efficient payment system domestically as well as vis-à-vis other countries, and monitor developments in the money, credit and foreign exchange markets'.
Spain	The law that granted independence to the Banco de Espana (Law on Autonomy of the Banco de Espana 1994) includes as one of its objectives promotion of financial stability.
Sweden	The Riksbank Act states that it is the mission of the bank to promote a safe and efficient payment system.
UK	The Bank was formally charged with the responsibility for the 'overall stability of the financial system as a whole' by the Chancellor in a letter to the Governor in May 1997 and subsequently in the MoU between HM Treasury, the Bank of England, and the FSA, published in October 1997.

ANNEX C

FEATURES OF DEPOSIT INSURANCE SCHEME

Feature	*India*	*European Union*	*US*	*World average*
Explicit	Yes	Yes	Yes	68 countries
Coverage limit	US$ 2,288[a]	US$ 25,823[b]	US$ 1,00,000	3 times per capita GDP
Co-insurance	No	10 per cent	No	17 out of 68 countries
Coverage of foreign currency deposits	Yes	Can be excluded	Yes	48 out of 68 countries
Coverage of inter-bank deposits	No	No	Yes	18 out of 68 countries
Source of funding	Joint (public *plus* private)	Not regulated	Joint	Joint: 51 Private: 15 Public:1 Not available for 1 country
Administration	Public	Not regulated	Public	Joint: 24 Public: 33 Private: 11
Membership	Compulsory	Compulsory	Compulsory	55 out of 68 countries have compulsory membership
Premium levied (% of deposits)	0.08	Varies markedly	0.00–0.27	58 countries regularly levy premium
Risk-adjusted premium	No	Not regulated	Yes	31 out of 68 countries

Notes: [a]US$ 1 = Rs 43.7; [b]US$ 1 = Euro 0.7745.

13 Monetary and Financial Policy Responses to Global Imbalances*

The issue of 'Monetary and Financial Policy Responses to Global Imbalances' is an issue that has been among the top concerns of central bankers in the last few years. So it is the right opportunity to discuss it in this chapter.

The issue of large global imbalances has been debated at length since the beginning of this decade, both at international fora and also in regional conferences and seminars. In India, we have regularly highlighted this issue in our Annual Reports and Annual Policy Statements. Y.V. Reddy, the Governor of the RBI, has also addressed these issues in two of his recent speeches.

It is pertinent to note that whereas the existence of global imbalances is well-recognized, there are still no definite answers on its possible impact and what policy responses need to be considered. Therefore, seminars of this kind assume importance in exploring the implications of global imbalances for EMEs and developed countries alike.

In this chapter, I will first give a brief introduction to the concept of global imbalances, while highlighting some of the recent global initiatives that have been undertaken to correct these imbalances. This will be followed by discussion of the efforts that are further required in this direction. Thereafter, I would present the Indian perspective on global imbalances against the backdrop of the strength and resilience of the Indian economy exhibited in the recent years.

GLOBAL IMBALANCES: CONCEPT AND CONTRIBUTING FACTORS

CONCEPT

Conceptually, from a single country perspective, imbalances arise when the economy exhibits, on a sustained basis, large CADs or surpluses that are

* Paper presented at the Bank Indonesia Annual International Seminar, 16–17 November 2006.

essentially external manifestations of large domestic saving–investment gaps in a macroeconomic framework. From a global perspective, however, the BoP identity, in principle, should ensure that high surpluses in some countries are matched by deficits in other countries. Thus, the emergence of a large surplus or deficit in one country's external account implies the mirror image elsewhere. Hence, the global concerns are not about the existence of current account deficits or surpluses per se, but the persistence of large deficits and surpluses, particularly in large and systemically important economies.

In reality, global imbalances in the international economic system today refer to the large and increasing CAD of the United States and correspondingly large surpluses in other regions, particularly in Asia. The extent of these imbalances has become large, particularly in the aftermath of the Asian crisis and has generated issues of unsustainability of such global imbalances and chances of disorderly adjustment hampering the global economy, in general.

The Contributing Factors

Twin Deficits in the United States

The current global imbalance is largely attributed to the large and increasing CAD of the United States that has been financed by surpluses elsewhere, especially in emerging Asia, oil exporters, and Japan. The United States has been experiencing a CAD in each year since 1982. The US deficit remained below 3 per cent of GDP till the mid-1990s. Since then, however, it has risen substantially. The period following the bursting of the IT bubble in the United States was marked by highly accommodative monetary policy along with expansionary fiscal policies. On the one hand, the decline in the rate of interest led to the housing boom and increase in housing and other asset prices while, on the other hand, fiscal stimulation led to increase in consumption. While real activity in the United States did provide a stimulus to activity in the rest of the world, it has been accompanied by large and growing twin deficits—fiscal as well as CADs. In absolute terms, the CAD of the United States has seen a seven-fold increase from US$ 114 billion in 1995 to US$ 791 billion in 2005. As a percentage of GDP, the CAD of the United States has almost doubled itself every five years since the early 1990s. During 2005, the CAD to GDP ratio was close to 6.4 per cent, the highest ever for the United States (Table 13.1).

It is widely agreed that wealth effects arising from increasing asset prices, particularly of housing, have also contributed significantly to lower savings rates and higher consumption rates in the United States. The large current account and fiscal imbalances in the United States also find their reflection

Table 13.1 Macro Parameters of the United States

(per cent, annual average)

Period	GDP growth	CAD/GDP	General government fiscal balance/GDP	Savings–investment gap/GDP
1981–5	3.3	–1.3	–2.9	–1.6
1986–90	3.3	–2.4	–2.4	–2.2
1991–5	2.5	–1.1	–3.1	–0.9
1996–2000	4.1	–2.6	–0.2	–2.2
2001–5	2.4	–5.0	–3.5	–3.9

Sources: Bureau of Economic Analysis, US Department of Commerce; World Bank online database; *WEO*, IMF, various issues.

in the savings–investment mismatches that have risen substantially in the present decade. The private net savings in the United States has declined from 8 per cent of GDP in the 1980s to less than 2 per cent in 2005.

Surpluses in the Emerging Economies

Contrary to the United States that has fed the domestic demand, in Asia and other emerging economies, growth since the late 1990s has been led by external demand. The current account has recorded large surpluses since 1999, particularly for China and other East Asian EMEs (Indonesia, Malaysia, Taiwan, and Thailand). Surpluses of two island economies, namely Hong Kong and Singapore, have also increased significantly. India too registered current account surpluses between 2001 and 2004, albeit small.

In the post-Asian crisis period the savings rate in most East Asian EMEs, which has generally remained higher than the industrialized countries exhibited a modest decline. Investment rates, however, showed sharp declines resulting in the widening of the savings investment gap in the EMEs (Table 13.2).[1] India, however, remains an exception to this trend and still continues to have a negative savings investment gap.

Surpluses in Oil Exporting Countries

The large current account surplus of the oil-exporting countries has also emerged as a new source contributing to the global imbalances. The Middle East region recorded current account surpluses of 18.5 per cent of GDP in 2005. Oil revenues in the Middle East region have risen further in the first half of 2006 because of both higher prices and some expansion in production.

Table 13.2 Savings–Investment Gap in Emerging Economies

(per cent to GDP, annual average)

Country	1981–5	1986–90	1991–5	1996–2000	2001–5
China	–0.1	–0.4	1.5	3.2	2.4[a]
Hong Kong	3.9	9.8	3.2	1.1	8.6
India	–2.2	–1.5	–0.4	–1.4	–1.3[a]
Indonesia	2.0	1.5	1.5	5.5	6.7
Korea	–1.7	4.1	–1.1	3.7	2.6[a]
Malaysia	–2.7	7.6	–1.6	13.9	19.7[a]
Singapore	–2.9	4.6	11.8	16.4	23.6
Thailand	–4.4	–1.8	–5.3	6.4	4.5

Note: [a] Average for four years 2001–04.

Source: World Bank online database.

The surplus for 2006 is projected by the IMF's *WEO* (September 2006) to rise further to 23 per cent of GDP (almost US$ 280 billion). Higher net savings by oil exporters are also believed to have contributed towards the softening of global interest rates and consequent boost to demand in economies with market-based financial systems such as the United States. The depth of US financial markets together with rapid innovation of new products for effective risk management have made the United States an attractive destination for global investors' funds. Any correction of global imbalances on this account depends on what oil producers do with their surging oil revenues in terms of their domestic absorption.

MOVE TOWARDS CORRECTION

Currently, there is an emerging consensus that US consumers cannot continue to support worldwide demand indefinitely and Asian EMEs and oil-exporting countries cannot continue financing these perpetually. Yet there are differing views on the process of correction, its nature, pace, and consequences. In this context, the International Monetary and Financial Committee (IMFC) Communique, 22 April 2006 (IMF, 2006a) reiterates, 'Any action for orderly medium-term resolution of global imbalances is a shared responsibility, and will bring greater benefit to members and the international community than actions taken individually'. Key elements of an orderly global rebalancing which are generally advocated include increase in the US savings, structural reforms in the Euro area and Japan, and exchange rate flexibility in the EMEs.

Some developments observed in the recent months may contribute towards correcting global imbalances in future. These are set out in the following paragraphs.

First, in the United States, the fiscal deficit has come down to 2.0 per cent of GDP in the second quarter of 2006 mainly because of revenue buoyancy. Federal tax revenues have remained buoyant in 2005 and 2006 so far and expenditure discipline has been maintained, suggesting that the federal budget deficit in fiscal 2006 is likely to outperform initial budget estimates and fall modestly to 2.25 per cent of GDP (IMF, 2006b). The US fed funds rate has risen to reach 5.25 per cent. The US dollar in the recent period has depreciated marginally against some other major currencies.

Second, higher investment witnessed in some Asian emerging economies may contribute towards correcting imbalances. China has recently exhibited a very rapid investment growth, though concerns have been raised about the possibility of an investment boom–burst cycle (IMF, 2006c). In the first three quarters of 2006, the total investment in fixed assets in China has been 27.3 per cent higher than that in the same period last year. As has been advocated repeatedly by the Chinese policymakers, the need now is for Chinese consumption to increase faster than their investment growth.

Third, increased exchange rate flexibility has been observed in some of the Asian countries. The US dollar has seen some depreciation while the non-US currencies have appreciated. During 2005, currencies in many developing countries have also appreciated steadily against the US dollar accompanied by some movement towards more flexible exchange rate policies. This is noticed most notably in China, which has revalued its currency against the dollar by around 2.1 per cent. Malayasia has also taken similar steps. During 2006, there were significant changes in the exchange rate of Euro/US dollar (from US$ 0.84 per Euro in early 2006 to US$ 0.78 per Euro by September 2006), yet there has been little significant impact in US Euro trade patterns. In view of this, the efficacy of the exchange rate as an equilibrating mechanism needs to be investigated. Within the EMEs, the impact of exchange rate movements on trade balances varies significantly depending upon whether they are predominant exporters of manufactures, non-oil commodities or oil (Allen, 2006).

Furthermore, there are signs of a decline in the exchange rate pass-through to inflation, both in developed and developing economies. The lowering of the pass-through can be attributed to a number of factors such as low and stable inflation, well-anchored inflation expectations, increasing share of non-tradables, and availability of hedging products. These developments have enabled exporters and importers to ignore temporary shocks and set stable product prices despite large currency fluctuations. With the shift in demand composition in favour of non-tradables like services, the extent of exchange rate pass-through, which works primarily through tradables, has been limited.

As a result of all these development, there has been a significant weakening of the role of exchange rate adjustments in influencing domestic prices and external trade. Hence, small exchange rate changes can scarcely be expected to help significantly in effecting changes in the current account (Mohan, 2005).

Thus, the following issues assume importance:

1. Will the recent developments see some domestic correction in the United States, leading to a decline in its CAD?
2. Are there chances of investment increasing in the Asian countries and whether this would reduce their surplus?
3. Can exchange rate adjustments contribute significantly towards correcting current account imbalances?

Further Efforts

Notwithstanding the progress that has been made towards correcting imbalances, further efforts are desirable—with every country doing its part—to help reduce medium-term risks associated with the imbalances.

The United States will have to try to curb household and government borrowings and strengthen national savings, without hurting recovery and excessive dollar depreciation. The focus of fiscal consolidation in the United States has to remain on the expenditure side, though revenue measures aimed at broadening the revenue base and tax system with greater emphasis on consumption tax rather than income tax cannot be ruled out (*WEO*, September 2006). With the housing market slowing down in the United States, some increase in private savings is expected. This will be further helped by policy initiatives such as introduction of health savings accounts that would raise incentives for household savings and passing of pension legislation.

The Euro area needs to pursue structural reforms, especially product and labour market policies, to boost domestic demand and broad base the recovery. Japan has started recovering finally. Its current account surplus has begun to narrow down from 3.8 per cent of GDP in 2004 to 3.6 per cent of GDP in 2005 and the trend is continuing in 2006 with domestic demand strengthening. It is widely agreed that Japan should further strengthen its financial system and carry out other structured reforms to provide further flexibility in the economy.

Further flexibility in exchange-rate policies is desirable for the EMEs. Any attempt by the EMEs to intervene excessively and sterilize their forex reserves to maintain their competitiveness will further delay the adjustment process. However, as indicated earlier that unless there are substantial changes in exchange rates, it seems that one cannot expect corrections to global imbalances. Studies have shown that with unchanged growth rates in the United States and the rest of the world, the US dollar would need to depreciate by nearly 33 per cent—equivalently, the non-US currencies would have to appreciate, on average, by 50 per cent—to balance the US trade account (Obstfeld and Rogoff, 2004, 2005). Another study has pointed out that dollar should depreciate by 30 per cent in real terms to bring US CAD within 2 per cent of GDP (Mussa, 2004).

Promoting efficient absorption of higher oil revenues in oil-exporting countries with strong macroeconomic policies should also be a key element of this correction mechanism. It is suggested that these countries could boost expenditures to some extent in areas where social returns are high such as education, health, infrastructure, and social security. Given economic interlinkages, all countries and regions will have a role to play by increasing the flexibility of their economies and adapting to changing global demand patterns.

Let me quote our own *Mid-term Review of the Annual Policy Statement* announced on 31 October 2006 (RBI, 2006):

> Global imbalances have continued to widen during 2006. With some central banks actively reassessing their stance now, the potential drainage of global liquidity would test the resilience of world financial markets and weigh upon the outlook on the global economy. It is in this context that the IMF's projection of the U.S. current account deficit at about 7 per cent of GDP in 2007 with large surpluses continuing in Japan, emerging Asia and oil-exporting countries is disturbing. The sharp rise in the net foreign liability position of the US raises the risks of abrupt and disorderly adjustment of major currencies as the global imbalances unwind. However, there is an interesting lull in the serious concerns expressed both by policy makers and financial markets in regard to the global imbalances, possibly on the assumption that universal recognition of the problem would per se lead to harmonised actions that would avoid hard landing.

THE INDIAN SETTING

In recent years, the Indian economy has seen a massive transformation from a closed, controlled, slow growing economy to a more open, liberalized, and one of the fastest growing economies of the world. Economic reforms in India since July 1991 have accelerated growth, enhanced stability, and strengthened both external and financial sectors. India has remained an attractive destination for foreign investors. Despite high capital flows, India has been successful in managing liquidity. India's foreign exchange reserves are in excess of the total outstanding external debt of the country. The trade as well as financial sector is considerably integrated with the global economy. Even during difficult times, that is the East Asian crisis, the Russian crisis during 1997–8, and post-Pokhran sanctions, Indian economy has shown substantial resilience in withstanding the contagion.

Since the 1970s, India's current account has exhibited surplus only on six occasions (Table 13.3). The deficit has been modest and has remained below 2 per cent of GDP in most years. Only in 1990–1 on the brink of a BoP crisis, the CAD to GDP ratio had marginally crossed the 3 per cent mark. Thus, in so many years, India has had a balanced external account that has also been reflected in the corresponding savings-investment gap.

In the recent period, i.e., 2001–2 to 2003–4, India experienced a surplus in the current account though the magnitude was small and it was essentially the consequence of business cycle slowdown in the early part of the decade along with corporate restructuring. With a turnaround in business cycle, investment picked up in 2004–5 and India moved back to a CAD scenario. The CAD further widened during 2005–6 reflecting the cumulative impact of the high level of international crude oil prices and growth in imports emanating from strong industrial activity. The sustained rise in its invisibles surplus during 2005–6 emanating from the buoyant software exports, remittances, and various professional and business services continued to moderate the impact of a growing merchandise trade deficit. According to current projections, during the Eleventh Plan period (2007–8 to 2011–12), current account is projected to remain in deficit and the normal and stable capital flows are expected to finance the deficit comfortably.

Unlike in many of the Asian EMEs where current account surpluses have mainly contributed towards greater accumulation of reserves in these economies, in India reserve accumulation has been mainly due to large capital

Table 13.3 Range of India's Current Account Balance since 1970–1

Range of current account balance/GDP	Frequency
Current account surplus	6
Equal to 1 per cent	2
Between 1 and 2 per cent	4
Current account deficit	30
Between (–)1 and 0 per cent	15
Between (–)2 and (–)1 per cent	11
Between (–)3 and (–)2 per cent	3
Between (–)3 and (–)4 per cent	1 (in 1990–1 when CAD was 3.1 per cent)

Source: *Handbook of Statistics on Indian Economy*, RBI.

flows and the current account surplus had only a minimal role to play in this regard, for a few years. Thus, it is clear that India, as such, has not contributed towards enhancing global imbalances.

India's macro policy has clearly laid a lot of stress on maintaining financial stability. The Indian economy as a whole and the financial sector in particular is now more resilient and in a better position to absorb financial shocks. This resilience has been achieved by improving the macroeconomic fundamentals and regulatory frameworks. Besides, unlike some EMEs that have seen demand to be predominantly driven externally, the Indian economy is mostly domestic-demand driven. While India's exports constituted 11.5 per cent of GDP, its share in world trade is only 0.8 per cent. Second, India's export basket is fairly diversified (Reddy, 2005). Hence, its exposure to volatility in growth patterns across the world is limited than most EMEs. Higher GDP growth in India during last three years has also seen a rise in savings rate from 23.5 per cent in 2000–1 to 29.1 per cent in 2004–5. A significant turnaround in public sector savings has been a major cause for the increase in domestic savings. Given the reform initiatives envisaged under the FRBM Act, public savings are expected to improve further. Besides, households in India are the major contributors to savings and given the favourable Indian demographics over the next twenty years, the savings rate in India is expected to remain high. This is in sharp contrast to other East Asian countries as well as in the United States, where major contributor to savings are the corporates that largely depend on the cyclical path of the economy.

POSSIBLE IMPACT OF GLOBAL IMBALANCES ON INDIA

FISCAL

India continues to have a high fiscal deficit by international standards though it has declined significantly in recent years. In order to achieve sustainable fiscal correction and consolidation, both the Central and state governments have adopted fiscal responsibility legislations, that is, FRBM Acts. The combined fiscal deficit of the Centre and states is budgeted to come down to about 6.5 per cent by 2007 (Table 13.4). Even if it is assumed that the Centre and the states comply with their respective FRBMs, their combined fiscal deficit would continue to remain above 6 per cent by 2009–10. Generally, one would presume that India remains somewhat vulnerable to the impact of global imbalances on this account. However, the Indian case is unique as the government does not resort to external financing to finance domestic debt. This would help India in not being subject to the consequences of global imbalances.

In addition, both the RBI and the Government of India have undertaken various initiatives to develop government securities market. The earlier

Table 13.4 Combined Gross Fiscal Deficit of the Centre and the States

(average per annum, as per cent to GDP)

Period/Year	Combined deficit
1980–1 to 1984–5	7.19
1985–6 to 1989–90	8.88
1990–1 to 1994–5	7.75
1995–6 to 1999–2000	7.73
2000–1 to 2004–5	9.00
2005–6 RE	7.45
2006–7 BE	6.50

Note: RE: Revised Estimate, BE: Budget Estimate.

Source: *Handbook of Statistics on Indian Economy, 2005–06*, RBI.

features of an administered market with automatic monetization have been done away with. The Indian government securities market today is more broad-based, characterized by an efficient auction process, an active secondary market supported by an active PD system and electronic trading and settlement technology (Mohan, 2006).

The effect of global imbalances, however, could be indirect through a rise in domestic interest rates as a consequence of rise in international rates. There could be an increase in the cost of borrowings of the government. However, since most of the outstanding debt is at fixed rates and not on floating rates, the rise in the borrowing cost will be incremental. This situation also provides greater headroom for a flexible monetary policy to adjust policy rates, as and when warranted, without any excessive impact on the fiscal deficit (Reddy, 2005, 2006).

Private Corporate Sector

Private corporate external borrowing has been liberalized substantially in India. The stock of private external debt rose from about US$ 5 billion at end-March 1996 to US$ 15.6 billion at end-March 2001 and has further risen to US$ 32.4 billion as at end-March 2006 (Table 13.5). Potentially, corporates are expected to borrow more in future and hence, could be susceptible to the consequences of global imbalances. If there are sharp fluctuations in interest rates and exchange rates on account of the adjustment process, corporates that have borrowed at variable rates would be subject to both exchange rate and interest rate risk, depending on the magnitude and efficacy of the risk mitigation activities. However, without full capital account convertibility in India, the government and the RBI administer the overall incremental debt exposure and put ceilings on total external commercial borrowings. Besides, corporates in India are encouraged to hedge their foreign exchange exposure.

Table 13.5 Exposure to Foreign Capital of Private Corporates—External Debt of the Private Corporate Sector

Year	In US$ billion	As per cent to reserves
1996	5.0	23.0
2001	15.6	36.9
2006	32.4	21.4

Source: *India's External Debt: A Status Report*, Ministry of Finance, Government of India.

Financial Intermediaries

In India, exposure of the financial intermediaries to external debt is limited and regulated. Their foreign currency borrowings have been subject to the prudential limit of 25 per cent of their tier-I capital. These limits amounted to US$ 2.7 billion as of 31 March 2006. With a view to enabling banks to raise resources overseas, the latest monetary policy announcement on 31 October 2006 has enhanced this limit to 50 per cent of their tier I capital or US$ 10 million, whichever is higher. Foreign currency borrowings by the banks beyond this ceiling are linked to their net worth, exclusively for the purpose of export finance. With a move towards fuller capital account convertibility, banks are likely to access forex markets more, underscoring the need for further enhancement of the risk management capabilities of the banking system.

Banks in India have been financing investment in assets, home loans, and retail market as well as equities. Like in many EMEs, asset prices and the equity market have seen a rising trend in the recent past in India as well. Should there be any reversal of capital flows, asset prices could potentially decline as did happen in May 2006. The most significant impact on banks' balance sheet, however, could be felt through their investment portfolio. Banks in India hold substantial investments in government and other fixed income securities. To the extent a rise in international interest rates impacts the domestic interest rates, it would entail marked-to-market losses on the investment portfolios (Reddy, 2006).

To prevent any unforeseen eventualities, the Reserve Bank has been constantly monitoring the banks' exposure to risky assets and has put ceilings on their exposure to equity markets. In addition to a CRAR for the sector of 12 per cent, specific steps have been taken to meet the interest rate risk. Separate provision for capital against market risk has been introduced.

Conduct of Monetary Policy

More importantly, one needs to look at the impact on monetary policy. As indicated in a speech that I made sometime back in Colombo (Mohan, 2004), in a globalized world, it is difficult to formulate monetary policy independent of international developments. Monetary policy has become more complex and central banks will have to take into account, among other issues, developments in the global economic situation, the international inflationary situation, interest rate scenario, exchange rate movements, and capital flows while formulating monetary policy. Besides, in developing countries such as India considerations relating to maximizing output and employment weigh equally upon monetary authorities as price stability. As far as the impact of the adjustment policies on India's monetary policy is concerned, any significant readjustment of the currencies and rise in interest rates could affect global growth, in turn affecting growth prospects of several emerging economies including India. The conduct of monetary policy will have to factor in these downside risks to inflation and any kind of turbulence to financial markets due to repricing of risks while maintaining the delicate balance in terms of growth vis-à-vis price stability. A key feature of Indian monetary policy formulation in recent years has been to look at both domestic and global factors and to guard against various risks as and when they evolve. The Indian economy now is more resilient and in a better position to absorb a financial shock.

As indicated in our *Mid-Term Review on Annual Policy Statement for 2006–7* announced on 31 October 2006,

> Barring the emergence of any adverse and unexpected developments in various sectors of the economy and keeping in view the current assessment of the economy including the outlook for inflation, the overall stance of monetary policy in the period ahead will be:
>
> - To ensure a monetary and interest rate environment that supports export and investment demand in the economy so as to enable continuation of the growth momentum while reinforcing price stability with a view to anchoring inflation expectations.
> - To maintain the emphasis on macroeconomic and, in particular, financial stability.
> - To consider promptly all possible measures as appropriate to the evolving global and domestic situation.

Downside Risks

Notwithstanding these positive aspects of the Indian economy, downside risks remain as indicated in the various monetary policy statements released by the RBI.

First, moderation of demand on account of high oil prices poses the biggest challenge. The oil market remained highly volatile during 2005 and the first half of 2006 on account of geopolitical uncertainty and supply disturbances. The average international oil prices increased from about US$ 25 per barrel in 2002 to US$ 54 per barrel in 2005 and further to US$ 73 per barrel around mid-July 2006. Though oil prices have softened in the more recent period (US$ 61 per barrel during September 2006), they still continue to remain at high levels. The medium-term outlook also does not give much comfort, especially to the oil-importing developing economies, in view of the continued geopolitical tensions in the Middle East and possible disruptions in other major oil-producing regions, along with the tight global demand-supply scenario. Though pass-through of the hike in international oil prices to domestic consumers is limited in the Indian context because of the government policies, its impact on the trade deficit via increase in oil imports bill cannot be ruled out. This further worsens the global imbalances by creating higher surpluses in the oil exporting countries.

Second, as mentioned before, India has not directly contributed to the global imbalances and has built in enough stabilizers to keep it insulated from the consequences of global imbalances. Yet any disorderly unwinding of global imbalances is likely to have global ramifications and may affect the Indian economy indirectly. The speed at which the US current account ultimately returns towards balance, the triggers that drive that adjustment, and the way in which the burden of adjustment is allocated across the rest of the world have enormous implications for the global exchange rates. Private corporates and financial intermediaries are bound to get exposed to exchange rate risks if these variables exhibit substantial fluctuations, though the impact might be less than other EMEs.

Third, any reversal of global capital flows from emerging and developing economies in the case of realignment of interest rates and slow investment growth on account of higher interest rates with the tightening of monetary policy stance by major central banks remain the other downside risks.

Fourth, domestic developments exhibit strength and resilence with some downside risks. There is a pick-up in the momentum of growth which also appears to be spreading across all constituent sectors of the economy. Domestic financial markets have exhibited stable and orderly conditions. In the external sector, there are signs of abiding strength and the CAD has been well-managed so far. On the other hand, there are indications of growing demand pressures and potential risks from rapid credit growth and strains on credit quality. High levels of monetary expansion and the evolution of the liquidity situation will need to be continuously monitored for any signs of risks to inflation. The elevated levels of asset prices also represent a risk to the outlook for macroeconomic and financial stability. In brief, at the current juncture, for policy purposes, the two major issues that exert conflicting pulls are exploration of signs of overheating firming up to warrant a policy response, and, the impact of lagged effects of earlier policy action on the evolution of macroeconomic developments.

SUMMARY

To sum up, being a closed economy earlier, India had remained relatively insulated from global developments and hence, had little experience in dealing with them. During the last fifteen years, India has opened up considerably, while simultaneously reforming the financial sector, improving its fundamentals, and creating some built-in measures to ensure financial stability. The overall approach has given the Indian economy enough resilience to withstand some major global risks. Indian growth prospects remain bright and any significant correction to global imbalances via abrupt and sharp changes in exchange rates and international interest rates will be taken into account.

Note

[1] According to Barro and Lee (2003), the East Asian crisis has exerted permanent depressing effects on investment in these economies. There has been an investment drought rather than a savings glut.

References

Allen, M. (2006), 'Exchange Rates and Trade Balance Adjustment in Emerging Market Economies', IMF Staff Paper, October.

Barro, R. and J.W. Lee (2003), 'Growth and Investment in East Asia before and after the Financial Crisis', *Seoul Journal of Economics*, 16 (2).

Frankel, J., D. Parsley and S.J. Wei (2005), 'Slow Pass through around the World: A New Import for the Developing Countries?', Working Paper No. 116, Center for International Development, Harvard University.

Gagnon, J. and J. Ihrig (2001), 'Monetary Policy and Exchange Rate Pass Through', *FRB International Finance Discussion Paper*, No. 704, July.

International Monetary Fund (2006a), *Communique* issued by the International Monetary and Financial Committee (IMFC), 22 April.

_____ (2006b), Article IV Consultation with the United States, *Public Information Notice*, 28 July.

_____ (2006c), *IMF WEO*, September.

Mohan, R. (2004), 'Challenges to Monetary Policy in Globalising Context', *Reserve Bank of India Bulletin*, January.

Mohan, R. (2005), 'Some Apparent Puzzles for Contemporary Monetary Policy', *Reserve Bank of India Bulletin*, December.

_____ (2006), 'Recent Trends in the Indian Debt Market and Current Initiatives', *Reserve Bank of India Bulletin*, April.

Mussa, M. (2004), 'Exchange Rate Adjustments Needed to Reduce Global Payments Imbalances', in C.F. Bergsten and J. Williamson (eds), *Dollar Adjustment: How Far? Against What?*, Institute of International Economics, Washington, DC.

Obstfeld, M. and K.S. Rogoff (2004), 'The Unsustainable US Current Account Position Revealed', NBER Working Paper No. 10869, Washington, DC, November.

_____ (2005), '*Global Current Account Imbalances and Exchange Rate Adjustments*', The Brookings Institution.

Reddy, Y.V. (2005), 'Implications of Global Financial Imbalances for the Emerging Market Economies', *Reserve Bank of India Bulletin*, December.

_____ (2006), 'Global Imbalances–An Indian Perspective', speech delivered at the Financing for Development (FFD) Office, Department of Economic and Social Office (DESA), United Nations, New York on 11 May 2006, *Reserve Bank of India Bulletin*, June.

RBI (2006), *Mid-Term Review of Annual Policy for the Year 2006–07*, Mumbai, October.

Afterword

Global Financial Crisis and Key Risks: Impact on India and Asia*

The turmoil in the international financial markets of advanced economies, that started around mid-2007, has exacerbated substantially since August 2008. The financial market crisis has led to the collapse of major financial institutions and is now having a significant adverse impact on the real economy in the advanced economies. Major advanced economies are already in or close to recession and output in these economies, as a group, is expected to contract in 2009, the first decline in the past six decades. As this crisis is unfolding, credit markets have dried up in the developed world. With the substantive increase in financial globalization and high degree of trade integration, how much will these developments affect India and other emerging market economies (EMEs)?

In this Afterword I first briefly set out reasons for the relative resilience shown by the Indian economy to the ongoing international financial markets' crisis. This is followed by some discussion of the impact till date on the Indian economy and the likely implications in the near future. Our approach to the management of the exposures of the Indian financial sector entities to the collapse of major financial institutions in the US is discussed next. Orderly conditions have been maintained in the domestic financial markets, which is attributable to a range of instruments available with the monetary authority to manage a variety of situations. Finally, I discuss the extent of vulnerability of the EMEs, in general, to the global financial market crisis.

FINANCIAL GLOBALIZATION: THE INDIAN APPROACH

The Indian economy is now a relatively open economy, despite the capital account not being fully open. The current account, as measured by the sum

* Based on the author's remarks at IMF–FSF High-Level Meeting on the Recent Financial Turmoil and Policy Responses at Washington D.C. on 9 October 2008, and updated till end November 2008.

of current receipts and current payments, amounted to about 53 per cent of GDP in 2007–8, up from about 19 per cent of GDP in 1991. Similarly, on the capital account, the sum of gross capital inflows and outflows increased from 12 per cent of GDP in 1990–1 to around 64 per cent in 2007–8.[1] With this degree of openness, developments in international markets are bound to affect the Indian economy, and policy makers have to be vigilant in order to minimize the impact of adverse international developments on the domestic economy.

The relatively limited impact of the ongoing turmoil in financial markets of the advanced economies on the Indian financial markets, and more generally the Indian economy so far, needs to be assessed in this context. Whereas the Indian current account has been opened fully, though gradually, over the 1990s, a more calibrated approach has been followed to the opening of the capital account and to opening up of the financial sector. This approach is consistent with the weight of the available empirical evidence with regard to the benefits that may be gained from capital account liberalization for acceleration of economic growth, particularly in EMEs. The evidence suggests that the greatest gains are obtained from the opening to FDI, followed by portfolio equity investment. The benefits emanating from external debt flows have been found to be more questionable until greater domestic financial market development has taken place (Henry, 2007; Prasad et al. 2007).

Accordingly, in India, while encouraging foreign investment flows, especially direct investment inflows, a more cautious, nuanced approach has been adopted in regard to debt flows. Debt flows in the form of external commercial borrowings are subject to ceilings and some end-use restrictions, which are modulated from time to time taking into account evolving macroeconomic and monetary conditions. Similarly, portfolio investment in government securities and corporate bonds are also subject to macro ceilings, which are also modulated from time to time. Thus, prudential policies have attempted to prevent excessive recourse to foreign borrowings and dollarization of the economy. In regard to capital outflows, the policy framework has been progressively liberalized to enable the non-financial corporate sector to invest abroad and to acquire companies in the overseas market. Resident individuals are also permitted outflows subject to reasonable limits.

The financial sector, especially banks, is subject to prudential regulations, both in regard to capital and liquidity (Mohan, 2007b). As the current global financial crisis has shown, liquidity risks can rise manyfold during a crisis and can pose serious downside risks to macroeconomic and financial stability. The Reserve Bank of India (RBI) had already put in place steps to mitigate liquidity risks at the very short-end, risks at the systemic level and at the institution level as well. Some of the important measures by the RBI in this regard include, first, restricting the overnight unsecured market for funds to banks and primary dealers (PD) as well as limits on the borrowing and lending operations of these entities in the overnight inter-bank call money market. Second, large reliance by banks on borrowed funds can exacerbate vulnerability to external shocks. This has been brought out quite strikingly in the ongoing crisis in the global financial markets. Accordingly, in order to encourage greater reliance on stable sources of funding, the RBI has imposed prudential limits on banks on their purchased inter-bank liabilities and these limits are linked to their net worth. Furthermore, the incremental credit deposit ratio of banks is also monitored by the RBI since this ratio indicates the extent to which banks are funding credit with borrowings from wholesale markets (now known as purchased funds). Third, asset liability management guidelines for dealing with overall asset–liability mismatches take into account both on and off balance sheet items. Finally, guidelines on securitization of standard assets have laid down a detailed policy on provision of liquidity support to Special Purpose Vehicles (SPVs).

In order to further strengthen capital requirements, the credit conversion factors, risk weights and provisioning requirements for specific off-balance sheet items including derivatives have been reviewed. Furthermore, in India, complex structures like synthetic securitization have not been permitted so far. Introduction of such products, when found appropriate, would be guided by the risk management capabilities of the system.

The RBI has also issued detailed guidelines on implementation of the Basel II framework covering all the three pillars, with the guidelines on Pillar II being issued as recently as 27 March 2008. In tune with RBI's objective to have consistency and harmony with international standards, the Standardised Approach for credit risk and Basic Indicator Approach for operational risk have been prescribed. The minimum capital to risk-weighted assets ratio (CRAR) would be 9 per cent, but higher levels under Pillar II could be prescribed on the basis of risk profile and risk management systems. The banks have been asked to bring Tier I CRAR to at least 6 per cent before 31 March 2010. After analysing the global schedule for implementation, it was decided that all foreign banks operating in India and Indian banks having a presence outside India should migrate to Basel II by 31 March 2008 and all other scheduled commercial banks encouraged to migrate to Basel II in alignment with them but not later than 31 March 2009.

In addition to the exercise of normal prudential requirements on banks, the RBI successively imposed additional prudential measures in respect of exposures to particular sectors, akin to a policy of dynamic provisioning. For example, in view of the accelerated exposure observed to the real estate sector, banks were advised to put in place a proper risk management system to contain the risks involved. Banks were advised to formulate specific policies covering exposure limits, collaterals to be considered, margins to be kept, sanctioning authority/level and sector to be financed. In view of the rapid increase in loans to the real estate sector raising concerns about asset quality and the potential systemic risks posed by such exposure, the risk weight on banks' exposure to commercial real estate was increased from 100 per cent to 125 per cent in July 2005 and further to 150 per cent in April 2006. The risk weight on housing loans extended by banks to individuals against mortgage of housing properties and investments in mortgage backed securities (MBS) of housing finance companies (HFCs) was increased from 50 per cent to 75 per cent in December 2004, though this was later reduced to 50 per cent for lower value loans. Similarly, in light of the strong growth of consumer credit and the volatility in the capital markets, it was felt that the quality of lending could suffer during the phase of rapid expansion. Hence, as a counter cyclical measure, the RBI increased the risk weight for consumer credit and capital market exposures from 100 per cent to 125 per cent.[2]

An additional feature of recent prudential actions by the RBI relates to the tightening of regulation and supervision of Non-banking Financial Companies (NBFCs), so that regulatory arbitrage between these companies and the banking system is minimized. The overarching principle is that banks should not use an NBFC as a delivery vehicle for seeking regulatory arbitrage opportunities or to circumvent bank regulation(s) and that the activities of NBFCs do not undermine banking regulations. Thus, capital adequacy ratios and prudential limits to single/group exposures in the case of NBFCs have been progressively brought nearer to those applicable to banks. The regulatory interventions are graded: higher in deposit-taking NBFCs and lower in non-deposit-taking NBFCs. Thus, excessive leverage in this sector has been contained.

Various segments of the domestic financial market have been developed over a period of time to facilitate efficient channelling of resources from savers to investors and enable the continuation of domestic growth momentum (Mohan, 2007a). Investment has been predominantly financed domestically in India—the current account deficit has averaged between 1 and 2 per cent of GDP since the early 1990s. The government's fiscal deficit has been high by international standards but is also largely internally financed through a vibrant and well developed government securities market, and thus, despite large fiscal deficits, macroeconomic and financial stability has been maintained. Derivative instruments have been introduced cautiously in a phased manner, both for product diversity and, more importantly, as a risk management tool. All these developments have facilitated the process of price discovery in various financial market segments.

The rate of increase in foreign exchange market turnover in India between April 2004 and April 2007 was the highest amongst the 54 countries covered in the latest Triennial Central Bank Survey of Foreign Exchange and Derivatives Market Activity conducted by the Bank for International Settlements (BIS) in April 2007. According to the survey, daily average turnover in India jumped almost five-fold from US$ 7 billion in April 2004 to US$ 34 billion in April 2007; the share of India in global foreign exchange market turnover trebled from 0.3 per cent in April 2004 to 0.9 per cent in April 2007. There has been consistent development of well-functioning, relatively deep and liquid markets for government securities, currency, and derivatives in India, though much further development needs to be done. However, as large segments of economic agents in India may not have adequate resilience to withstand volatility in currency and money markets, our approach has been to be increasingly vigilant and proactive to any incipient signs of volatility in financial markets.

In brief, the Indian approach has focused on gradual, phased, and calibrated opening of the domestic financial and external sectors, taking into cognizance reforms in the other sectors of the economy. Financial markets are contributing to efficient channelling of domestic savings into productive uses and, by financing the overwhelming part of domestic investment, are supporting domestic growth. These characteristics of India's external and financial sector management coupled with ample forex reserves coverage and the growing underlying strength of the Indian economy reduce the susceptibility of the Indian economy to global turbulence.

IMPACT OF THE CRISIS ON INDIA

While the overall policy approach has been able to mitigate the potential impact of the turmoil on domestic financial markets and the economy, with the increasing integration of the Indian economy and its financial markets with rest of the world, there is recognition that the country does face some downside risks from these international developments. The risks arise mainly from the reversal of capital flows on a sustained medium-term basis from the projected slowdown of the global economy, particularly in advanced economies, and from some elements of potential financial contagion. In India, the adverse effects have so far been mainly in the equity markets because of reversal of portfolio equity flows, and the concomitant effects on the domestic forex market and liquidity conditions. The macro effects have so far been muted due to the overall strength of domestic demand, the healthy balance sheets of the Indian corporate sector, and the predominant domestic financing of investment.

As might be expected, the main impact of the global financial turmoil in India has emanated from the significant change experienced in the capital account in 2008–9 so far, relative to the previous year (Table 1).

Table 1 Trends in Capital Flows

(US$ billion)

Component	Period	2007–8	2008–9
Foreign Direct Investment to India	April–September	9.3	19.3
FIIs (net)	April–November	22.0	–12.2
External Commercial Borrowings (net)	April–June	7.0	1.6
Short-term Trade Credits (net)	April–June	1.8	2.2
Memo:			
ECB Approvals	April–November	21.7	13.5
Foreign Exchange Reserves (variation)	April–November	74.3	–63.9
Foreign Exchange Reserves (end-period)	End-November 2008	273.5	246.0

Note: Data on FIIs presented in this table represent inflows into the country and, thus, may differ from data relating to net investment in stock exchanges by FIIs.

Source: Reserve Bank of India

Total net capital flows fell from US$ 17.3 billion in April–June 2007 to US$ 13.2 billion in April–June 2008. While FDI inflows have continued to exhibit accelerated growth, portfolio investments by foreign institutional investors (FIIs) witnessed a net outflow as compared with a net inflow in the corresponding period in 2007–8.

Similarly, external commercial borrowings of the corporate sector declined from US$ 7.0 billion in April–June 2007 to US$ 1.6 billion in April–June 2008, partially in response to policy measures in the face of excess flows in 2007–8, but also due to the current turmoil in advanced economies. With the existence of a merchandise trade deficit of 7.7 per cent of GDP in 2007–8, and a current account deficit of 1.5 per cent, and change in perceptions with respect to capital flows, there has been significant pressure on the Indian exchange rate in recent months. Whereas the real exchange rate appreciated from an index of 104.9 (base 1993–94 = 100) (US$ 1 = Rs 46.12) in September 2006 to 115.0 (US$ 1 = Rs 40.34) in September 2007, it depreciated to a level of 102.0 (US$ 1 = Rs 49.0) in November 2008.

With the volatility in portfolio flows having been large during 2007 and 2008, the impact of global financial turmoil has been felt particularly in the equity market. The Bombay Stock Exchange (BSE) Sensex (1978–79 = 100) increased significantly from a level of 13,072 as at end-March 2007 to its peak of 20,873 on 8 January 2008 in the presence of heavy portfolio flows responding to the high growth performance of the Indian corporate sector. With portfolio flows reversing in 2008, partly because of the international market turmoil, the Sensex dropped to a level of 9093 by end-November 2008, in line with similar large declines in other major stock markets.

As noted earlier, domestic investment is largely financed by domestic savings. However, the corporate sector has, in recent years, mobilized significant resources from global financial markets for funding, both debt and non-debt, their ambitious investment plans. The current risk aversion in the international financial markets to EMEs could, therefore, have some impact on the Indian corporate sector's ability to raise funds from international sources and thereby impede some investment growth. Such corporates would, therefore, have to rely relatively more on domestic sources of financing, including bank credit. There has also been a tightening of funding environment for NBFCs with consequent impact on select sectors for which NBFCs are an important source of funding. This could, in turn, put some upward pressure on domestic interest rates. Moreover, domestic primary capital market issuances have suffered in the current fiscal year so far in view of the sluggish stock market conditions. Liquid money market mutual funds witnessed substantial redemption pressures during October 2008, accentuated by liquidity mismatches between their assets and liabilities. Thus, one can expect more demand for bank credit, and non-food credit growth has indeed accelerated (26.9 per cent on a year-on-year basis as on 21 November 2008 as compared with 23.7 per cent a year ago).

The financial crisis in the advanced economies and the likely slowdown in these economies could have some impact on the IT sector. According to the latest assessment by the NASSCOM, the software trade association, the current developments with respect to the US financial markets are very eventful, and may have a direct impact on the IT industry and are likely to create a downstream impact on other sectors of the US economy and worldwide markets. About 15 to 18 per cent of the business coming to Indian outsourcers includes projects from banking, insurance, and the financial services sector, which is now uncertain.

In summary, due to the combined impact of the reversal of portfolio equity flows, the reduced availability of international capital (both debt and equity), the perceived increase in the price of equity with lower equity valuations, and pressure on the exchange rate, growth in the Indian corporate sector is likely to feel some impact of the global financial turmoil. On the other hand, on a macro basis, with external savings utilization having been low traditionally, between 1 and 2 per cent of GDP, and the sustained high domestic savings rate, this impact can be expected to be at the margin.

Moreover, the continued buoyancy of FDI suggests that confidence in Indian growth prospects remains healthy.

IMPACT ON THE INDIAN BANKING SYSTEM

A detailed study undertaken by the RBI in September 2007 on the impact of the sub-prime episode on Indian banks had revealed that none of the Indian banks or the foreign banks, with whom the discussions had been held, had any direct exposure to the sub-prime markets in the US or other markets. However, a few Indian banks had invested in the collateralised debt obligations (CDOs)/bonds which had a few underlying entities with sub-prime exposures. Thus, no direct impact on account of *direct exposure* to the sub-prime market was in evidence. However, a few of these banks did suffer some losses on account of the mark-to-market losses caused by the widening of the credit spreads arising from the sub-prime episode on term liquidity in the market, even though the overnight markets remained stable.

Consequent upon filing of bankruptcy under Chapter 11 of the United States Bankruptcy Code by Lehman Brothers Holdings Inc., all banks were advised to report the details of their exposures to Lehman Brothers and related entities both in India and abroad. Out of 77 reporting banks, 14 reported exposures to Lehman Brothers and its related entities either in India or abroad. An analysis of the information reported by these banks revealed that majority of the exposures reported by the banks pertained to subsidiaries of Lehman Brothers which were not covered by the bankruptcy proceedings. Overall, these banks' exposure especially to Lehman Brothers Holding Inc. which had filed for bankruptcy was not significant and banks were reported to have made adequate provisions.

In the aftermath of the turmoil caused by bankruptcy, the RBI has announced a series of measures to facilitate orderly operation of financial markets and to ensure financial stability which predominantly includes extension of additional liquidity support to banks.

RBI RESPONSE TO THE CRISIS

The financial crisis in advanced economies on the back of sub-prime turmoil has been accompanied by near drying up of trust amongst major financial market and sector players, in view of mounting losses and elevated uncertainty about further possible losses and erosion of capital. The lack of trust amongst the major players has led to near freezing of the uncollateralized inter-bank money market, reflected in large spreads over policy rates. In response to these developments, central banks in major advanced economies have taken a number of coordinated steps to increase short-term liquidity. Central banks in some cases have substantially loosened the collateral requirements to provide the necessary short-term liquidity.

In contrast to the extreme volatility leading to freezing of money markets in major advanced economies, money markets in India have been, by and large, functioning in an orderly fashion, albeit with some pressures. Large swings in capital flows—as has been experienced between 2007–8 and 2008–9 so far—in response to the global financial market turmoil have made the conduct of monetary policy and liquidity management more complicated in the recent months. However, the RBI has been effectively able to manage domestic liquidity and monetary conditions consistent with its monetary policy stance.

This has been enabled by the appropriate use of a range of instruments available for liquidity management with the RBI such as the cash reserve ratio (CRR) and statutory liquidity ratio (SLR)[3] stipulations and open market operations (OMO) including the Market Stabilization Scheme (MSS)[4] and the Liquidity Adjustment Facility (LAF). Furthermore, money market liquidity is also impacted by our operations in the foreign exchange market, which, in turn, reflect the evolving capital flows. In 2007 and the previous years, large capital flows and their absorption by the RBI led to excessive liquidity, which was absorbed through sterilization operations involving LAF, MSS, and CRR. During 2008, in view of some reversal in capital flows, market sale of foreign exchange by the Reserve Bank led to withdrawal of liquidity from the banking system. The daily LAF repo operations emerged as the primary tool for meeting the liquidity gap in the market. In view of the reversal of capital flows, fresh MSS issuances were scaled down and there has also been some unwinding through buyback of securities issued under the MSS. The MSS operates symmetrically and has the flexibility to smoothen liquidity in the banking system both during episodes of capital inflows and outflows. The existing set of monetary instruments, thus, provided adequate flexibility to manage the evolving situation. In view of this flexibility, unlike central banks in major advanced economies, the RBI did not have to invent new instruments or to dilute the collateral requirements to inject liquidity. LAF repo operations are, however, limited by the excess SLR securities held by banks.

While LAF and MSS have been able to bear a large part of the burden, some cuts in CRR and SLR were also resorted to meet the liquidity mismatches. The CRR which had been gradually increased from 4.5 per cent in 2004 to 9 per cent by August 2008 was cut by 350 basis points during October–November 2008 on a review of the liquidity situation in the context of global and domestic developments. Similarly, SLR was cut by 100 basis points. Thus, as the very recent experience shows, changes in the prudential ratios such as CRR and SLR combined with flexible use of the MSS, could be considered as a vast pool of back-up liquidity that is available for liquidity management as the situation may warrant for relieving market pressure at any given time. The recent innovation with respect to SLR for combating temporary systemic illiquidity is particularly noteworthy. Apart from the cuts in the CRR and SLR, other measures undertaken by the Reserve Bank to improve rupee and forex liquidity included MSS buyback, special refinance upto 1 per cent of a bank's NDTL under section 17(3B) of RBI Act, re-institution of special market operations in oil bonds, increase in ceilings on non-resident deposits, relaxation of norms for accessing ECBs, and introduction of forex swaps for banks having overseas branches. These measures were supported by initiatives to improve credit delivery through extension of time period for concessional export credit and scaling back of risk weights and provisioning norms in respect of standard assets (Annex II). The relative stability in domestic financial markets, despite extreme turmoil in the global financial markets, is reflective of prudent practices, strengthened reserves, and the strong growth performance in recent years in an environment of flexibility in the conduct of policies.

Active liquidity management is a key element of the current monetary policy stance. Liquidity modulation through a flexible use of a combination of instruments has, to a significant extent, cushioned the impact of the international financial turbulence on domestic financial markets by absorbing excessive market pressures and ensuring orderly conditions. In view of the evolving environment of heightened uncertainty, volatility in global markets, and the dangers of potential spillovers to domestic equity and currency markets, liquidity management will continue to receive priority in the hierarchy of policy objectives over the period ahead.

IMPACT ON ASIAN EMEs

In contrast to the previous episodes of global turmoil, EMEs have exhibited relative resilience, though equity market and exchange rate pressures have intensified in recent days. So far, the investment sentiment is positive for the Asian EMEs, reflecting their strong economic performance and, for some countries, favourable investment opportunities associated with elevated commodity prices, though they have adjusted downwards in recent times, while being somewhat volatile. Credit policy reforms, better structuring of banking sector debt, and improved fiscal positions have also played their role making the EMEs resilient from the crisis. In addition, large foreign exchange reserves, particularly in Asia, also provide a degree of protection against possible sudden stops. Another factor that could be of relevance for this favourable situation is the relatively smaller presence of foreign banks in the Asian banking sector. This is evident from the fact that the share of banking assets held by foreign banks in these economies generally lies between 0 and 10 per cent (World Bank, 2008).

The spillovers to the EMEs from the current global financial market crisis have occurred mainly in and through financial markets, reflecting the relatively high level of integration of such markets in the global financial system. In this respect, there have been four major spillovers, viz., (i) a rise in the price of risk; (ii) a reduction in international bond issuance; (iii) a sell-off in equity markets; and (iv) some unwinding of carry-trade positions. The major EMEs in Asia have been recording surpluses on the current account in recent years, with the exception of Korea and India. Thus, the vulnerability of Asia, other than Korea and India, is relatively contained to that extent. It is in this context the foreign exchange markets in India and Korea have experienced greater pressure in recent times.

Despite the fact that no significant macroeconomic disruption has taken place in EMEs, some vulnerabilities exist. There are indications that the current crisis will have some implications in terms of higher funding costs and raising external finance, particularly, for lower rated firms. Further, countries with significant foreign bank presence, mostly East European economies, might be vulnerable to financial stress faced by a parent bank. Similarly, slowdown in advanced countries might impact the remittances to EMEs.

As regards the impact of financial turbulence on the real sector, Asian EMEs cannot be entirely immune to slowing growth in developed economies. For East Asian economies, since most of them are small and their trade sector (export plus imports) as proportion of GDP varies at a significantly higher level between over 200 per cent and 60 per cent as opposed to the weight of domestic demand as in India, it is an area of significant concern. Therefore, for these set of countries, the crises could be transmitted through the trade channel. In this context, it is relevant to note that growth in advanced economies is estimated to have decelerated from an annual average of 2.8 per cent during 2006–7 to 1.4 per cent in 2008 and the IMF forecasts the output to contract by 0.3 per cent in these economies in 2009. This will mark the first decline of output in advanced economies in the post-war period. Concomitantly, the IMF projects that growth in world trade volume (goods and services together) would record a substantial drop from an annual average of 8.3 per cent during 2006–7 to only 2 per cent by 2009. These developments are expected to have a dampening impact on the near term prospects of the EMEs. While strong regional sources of growth within EMEs may be a mitigating factor, most EMEs still retain substantial trade linkages with developed economies. In Asia, while intra-regional trade has been growing rapidly over recent years, much of this activity is still driven by developed economies as a major destination for final goods.

According to the analysis contained in the International Monetary Fund's latest *Global Financial Stability Report* (October 2008) (IMF, 2008a), both domestic and global factors are important in explaining the movement in equity prices in the EMEs. Correlation of equity markets in EMEs with those in the advanced economies has risen, suggesting a growing transmission channel for equity price movements. Amongst the three groups of EMEs (Latin America, Asia, and Emerging Europe), the spillover from global factors is found to be strongest in Latin American EMEs, followed by Emerging Europe and Asia. The wealth effect of stock market changes on consumption and investment, although statistically significant, is found to be weaker in EMEs vis-à-vis the advanced economies. Furthermore, such wealth effects tend to play out gradually.

During the early part of financial turmoil, commodity prices may have been pushed higher to some extent by increased demand for commodities as a hedge against a depreciating US dollar and possibly also as a hedge against higher inflation. However, with the emergence of stronger signs of slowdown in global economic activity, commodity prices witnessed a sharp correction in the second half of 2008. The sharp correction in commodity prices represents a downside risk to commodity-exporting EMEs, which is particularly relevant for some Latin American EMEs. In an extreme scenario, where commodity prices fall dramatically, this could have significant implications for economies that have had a heavy reliance on the performance of commodities in recent years, and might furthermore pose some risks to the financial stability in these countries. On the other hand, Asian EMEs which are commodity importers may benefit from the correction in global commodity prices. This may alleviate inflationary pressures in these economies and may provide the necessary flexibility to monetary policy in these countries. However, the beneficial impact of softening commodity prices is getting partly eroded by the depreciation pressures in some of the EMEs, thus, limiting to some extent the manoeuvrability available to the monetary policy.

The deepening and widening of the financial crisis is already getting reflected in elevated volatility in the financial markets of key EMEs and widening of spreads of the EME assets. Although a large amount of liquidity has been injected by the central banks of the major advanced economies, short-term market rates remain well above policy rates. Financing costs for the EMEs have increased over the past few months and could further deteriorate in the coming months. If the financial crisis were to linger longer and the economic activity in these regions slows down significantly, the adverse impact on the real economies in the major EMEs could turn out to be stronger than that has been observed so far. The IMF projects that growth in emerging and developing economies is likely to slow to 5.1 per cent in 2009 from the robust pace of almost 8.0 per cent each in 2006 and 2007. Thus, financial headwinds–both through reduced capital flows, widening of spreads and elevated volatility in domestic financial markets of the EMEs and through weakening of demand in major advanced economies—have increased downside risks of the major EMEs, especially for the relatively more open economies in the region.

CONCLUDING OBSERVATIONS

India has by-and-large been spared of global financial contagion due to the sub-prime turmoil for a variety of reasons. India's growth process has been largely domestic demand driven and its reliance on foreign savings has remained around 1.5 per cent in recent period. It also has a very comfortable level of forex reserves. The credit derivatives market is in an embryonic stage; the originate-to-distribute model in India is not comparable to the ones prevailing in advanced markets; there are restrictions on investments by residents in such products issued abroad; and regulatory guidelines on securitization do not permit immediate profit recognition. Financial stability in India has been achieved through perseverance of prudential policies which prevent institutions from excessive risk taking, and financial markets from becoming extremely volatile and turbulent.

However, in view of the severity of the global financial crisis and the sharp contraction in output in the advanced economies and the significant slowdown in world trade growth, some deceleration in growth in India, as in other EMEs, is expected in 2008–9 from the strong pace of the preceding four years. Illustratively, according to the latest estimates of the RBI, as set out in its Mid-term Review (October 2008), real GDP growth is likely to be 7.5–8.0 per cent in 2008–9 as compared with the average growth of 8.7 per cent in the preceding years. A host of measures have been taken by the Reserve Bank and the Government in response to the evolving situation and these measures are expected to offset, to a certain extent, the adverse impact of the global developments. Notwithstanding some short-term deceleration in the growth momentum, medium-term growth prospects remain robust. High domestic savings and investment, competitiveness and productivity gains brought out by the calibrated pace of structural reforms, strong corporate balance sheets, the remarkable resilience of the domestic financial sector and domestic demand are expected to help recovery in growth momentum during 2009–10 and the coming years.

Notes

[1] It may be noted that India is more open as compared to the US: the ratio of current receipts and current payments was 41 per cent of GDP in the US in 2007, while capital inflows and capital outflows were around 15 per cent and 10 per cent, respectively.

[2] The status in India with regard to proposals in the April 2008 Report of the Financial Stability Forum (FSF) is given in Annex I.

[3] Since 8 November 2008, banks are required to hold 24 per cent of their net demand and time liabilities (NDTL) in government (and some other approved) securities. As against this requirement, banks' holdings of SLR securities were 27.3 per cent of their NDTL at end-November 2008. Thus, banks held nearly 3.3 per cent excess SLR securities–equivalent to Rs 1300 billion–which could be used by them to avail of liquidity from the RBI under the daily LAF operations.

[4] In view of sustained large capital flows on the one hand and the finite stock of government securities with the Reserve Bank, and the absence of the option of issuing central bank securities under the RBI Act on the other hand, a new scheme, Market Stabilization Scheme (MSS), was introduced in April 2004 to manage the large capital flows. Under this scheme, the Reserve Bank has been empowered to issue government Treasury Bills and medium duration dated securities exclusively for sterilization purposes, so as to manage liquidity appropriately. The proceeds collected under MSS auctions are kept in a separate identifiable cash account with the RBI, and can be used only for redemption and/or buy back of securities issued under the MSS. The payments for interest and discount on MSS securities are not made from the MSS account, but shown in the Union budget and other related documents transparently as distinct components under separate subheads. The MSS securities are indistinguishable from normal government Treasury Bills and dated securities. The introduction of MSS has succeeded broadly in restoring LAF to its intended function of daily liquidity management (see Mohan, 2006).

References

Bank for International Settlements (2007), 'Triennial Central Bank Survey: Foreign Exchange and Derivatives Market Activity in 2007', December, Basel.

Henry, Peter Blair (2007), 'Capital Account Liberalization: Theory, Evidence, and Speculation', *Journal of Economic Literature*, Vol. XLV, December, pp. 887–935.

International Monetary Fund (2008a), *Global Financial Stability Report*, October, Washington D.C.

_____ (2008b), *World Economic Outlook*, October, Washington D.C.

Mohan, Rakesh (2006), 'Coping With Liquidity Management in India: A Practitioner's View', *Reserve Bank of India Bulletin*, April, Mumbai.

_____ (2007a), 'Development of Financial Markets in India', *Reserve Bank of India Bulletin*, June, Mumbai.

_____ (2007b), 'India's Financial Sector Reforms: Fostering Growth While Containing Risk', *Reserve Bank of India Bulletin*, December, Mumbai.

Prasad, Eswar S., Raghuram G. Rajan, and Arvind Subramanian (2007), 'Foreign Capital and Economic Growth', *Brookings Papers on Economic Activity*, 1.

Reserve Bank of India (2008), *Annual Policy Statement for the Year 2008–09*, April, Mumbai.

World Bank (2008), *Global Development Finance 2008*, June, Washington D.C.

ANNEX I

FINANCIAL STABILITY FORUM (FSF) REPORT: STATUS

In the wake of the turmoil in global financial markets, the FSF brought out a report in April 2008 identifying the underlying causes and weaknesses in the international financial markets. The Report contains, *inter alia*, proposals of the FSF for implementation by end-2008 regarding strengthening prudential oversight of capital, liquidity and risk management, enhancing transparency and valuation, changing the role and uses of credit ratings, strengthening the authorities' responsiveness to risk, and implementing robust arrangements for dealing with stress in the financial system. The Reserve Bank had put in place regulatory guidelines covering many of these aspects, while in regard to others, actions are being initiated. In many cases, actions have to be considered as work in progress. In any case, the guidelines are aligned with global best practices while tailoring them to meet country-specific requirements at the current stage of institutional developments. The proposals made by the FSF and status in regard to each in India are as follows.

Strengthened Prudential Oversight of Capital, Liquidity, and Risk Management

(i) Capital requirements—Specific proposals will be issued in 2008 to:
- raise Basel II capital requirements for certain complex structured credit products;
- introduce additional capital charges for default and event risk in the trading books of banks and securities firms;
- strengthen the capital treatment of liquidity facilities to off-balance sheet conduits.

Changes will be implemented over time to avoid exacerbating short-term stress.

(ii) Liquidity—Supervisory guidance will be issued by July 2008 for the supervision and management of liquidity risks.

(iii) Oversight of risk management—Guidance for supervisory reviews under Basel II will be developed that will:
- strengthen oversight of banks' identification and management of firm-wide risks;
- strengthen oversight of banks' stress testing practices for risk management and capital planning purposes;
- require banks to soundly manage and report off-balance sheet exposures;

Supervisors will use Basel II to ensure banks' risk management, capital buffers, and estimates of potential credit losses are appropriately forward looking.

(iv) Over-the-counter derivatives—Authorities will encourage market participants to act promptly to ensure that the settlement, legal and operational infrastructure for over-the-counter derivatives is sound.

The road-map for the implementation of Basel II in India has been designed to suit the country-specific conditions. The phased implementation process got underway with the Basel II Accord being made applicable to foreign banks operating in India and Indian banks having operational presence outside India with effect from 31 March 2008. All other commercial banks (except Local Area Banks and RRBs) are encouraged to migrate to Basel II in alignment with them but in any case not later than 31 March 2009. The process of implementation is being monitored on an on-going basis for calibration and fine-tuning.

The minimum capital to risk-weighted asset ratio (CRAR) in India is placed at 9 per cent, one percentage point above the Basel II requirement. Further, regular monitoring of banks' exposure to sensitive sectors and their liquidity position is also undertaken. In India, off-balance sheet vehicles in the form of SPVs for the purpose of securitization are in existence for which extensive guidelines, in line with the international best practices, have already been issued. Liquidity facilities to such SPVs are subject to capital charge. Banks were required to put in place appropriate stress test policies and relevant stress test frameworks for various risk factors by 31 March 2008.

In order to further strengthen capital requirements, the credit conversion factors, risk weights, and provisioning requirements for specific off-balance sheet items including derivatives have been reviewed. Further, in India, complex structures like synthetic securitization have not been permitted so far. Introduction of such products, when found appropriate, would be guided by the risk management capabilities of the system.

The Reserve Bank had issued broad guidelines for asset–liability management and banks have flexibility in devising their own risk management strategies as per board-approved policies. However, in regard to liquidity risks at the very short end, the Reserve Bank has taken steps to mitigate risks at the systemic level and at the institution level as well. The Reserve Bank has introduced greater granularity to measurement of liquidity risk by splitting the first time bucket (1–14 days, at present) into three time buckets, viz., next day, 2–7 days, and 8–14 days. The net cumulative negative mismatches in the three time buckets have been capped at 5 per cent, 10 per cent, and 15 per cent of the cumulative cash outflows.

The Reserve Bank had recognized the risks of allowing access to unsecured overnight market funds to all entities and, therefore, restricted the overnight unsecured market for funds only to banks and primary dealers (PD). Since August 2005, the overnight call market is a pure inter-bank market. Accordingly, trading volumes have shifted from the overnight unsecured market to the collateralized market.

Greater inter-linkages and excessive reliance on call money borrowings by banks could cause systemic problems. The Reserve Bank has, therefore, introduced prudential measures to address the extent to which banks can borrow and lend in the call money market. On a fortnightly average basis, call market borrowings outstanding should not exceed 100 per cent of capital funds (i.e., sum of Tier I and Tier II capital) in the latest audited balance sheet.

Recognizing the potential of 'purchased inter-bank liabilities' (IBL) to create systemic problems, the Reserve Bank had issued guidelines in March 2007 prescribing that IBL of a bank should not exceed 200 per cent of its net worth (300 per cent for banks with a CRAR more than 11.25 per cent).

Enhancing Transparency and Valuation

(i) Robust risk disclosures:
- The FSF strongly encourages financial institutions to make robust risk disclosures using leading disclosure practices at the time of their mid-year 2008 reports.
- Further guidance to strengthen disclosure requirements under Pillar 3 of Basel II will be issued by 2009.

(ii) Standards for off-balance sheet vehicles and valuations—Standard setters will take urgent action to:
- Improve and converge financial reporting standards for off-balance sheet vehicles;
- Develop guidance on valuations when markets are no longer active, establishing an expert advisory panel in 2008.

(iii) Transparency in structured products—Market participants and securities regulators will expand the information provided about securitized products and their underlying assets.

The Reserve Bank has, over the years, issued guidelines on valuation of various instruments/assets in conformity with the international best practices while keeping India-specific conditions in view. In order to encourage market discipline, the Reserve Bank has developed a set of disclosure requirements which allow the market participants to assess key pieces of information on capital adequacy, risk exposure, risk assessment processes and key business parameters which provide a consistent and understandable disclosure framework that enhances comparability. Banks are also required to comply with the Accounting Standard (AS) on Disclosure of Accounting Policies issued by the Institute of Chartered Accountants of India (ICAI).

In recognition of the fact that market discipline can contribute to a safe and sound banking environment and as part of the ongoing efforts to implement the Basel II Accord, the Reserve Bank issued guidelines on minimum capital ratio (Pillar 1) and market discipline (Pillar 3) in April 2007, and guidelines for Pillar 2 (supervisory review process) were issued in March 2008. Under these guidelines, non-compliance with the prescribed disclosure requirements would attract a penalty, including financial penalty.

Changes in the Role and Uses of Credit Ratings

Credit rating agencies should:

- Implement the revised IOSCO Code of Conduct Fundamentals for Credit Rating Agencies to manage conflicts of interest in rating structured products and improve the quality of the rating process;
- Differentiate ratings on structured credit products from those on bonds and expand the information they provide.

Regulators will review the roles given to ratings in regulations and prudential frameworks.

The Reserve Bank has undertaken a detailed process of identifying the eligible credit rating agencies whose ratings may be used by banks for assigning risk weights for credit risk. Banks should use the chosen credit rating agencies and their ratings consistently for each type of claim, for both risk weighting and risk management purposes. Banks are not allowed to 'cherry pick' the assessments provided by different credit rating agencies. If a bank has decided to use the ratings of some of the chosen credit rating agencies for a given type of claim, it can use only the ratings of those credit rating agencies, despite the fact that some of these claims may be rated by other chosen credit rating agencies whose ratings the bank has decided not to use. External assessments for one entity within a corporate group cannot be used to risk weight other entities within the same group.

Banks must disclose the names of the credit rating agencies that they use for the risk weighting of their assets, the risk weights associated with the particular rating grades as determined by the Reserve Bank through the mapping process for each eligible credit rating agency as well as the aggregated risk weighted assets as required.

In India, complex structures like synthetic securitizations have not been permitted so far. As and when such products are to be introduced, the Reserve

Bank would put in place the necessary enabling regulatory framework, including calibrating the role and capacity building of the rating agencies.

Strengthening the Authorities' Responsiveness to Risks

- A college of supervisors will be put in place by end-2008 for each of the largest global financial institutions.

In the Indian context, there has been exchange of supervisory information on specific issues between the Reserve Bank and few other overseas banking supervisors/regulators. Supervisory cooperation has been working smoothly and efficiently.

The Mid-Term Review of October 2007 had announced the constitution of a Working Group to lay down a road-map for adoption of a suitable framework for cross-border supervision and supervisory cooperation with overseas regulators, consistent with the framework envisaged in the Basel Committee on Banking Supervision (BCBS). A Working Group was constituted in March 2008 and is in the process of finalizing its report. A number of overseas regulators of countries such as the US, the UK, Canada, Hong Kong, Australia, and Singapore have been formally approached to share systems and practices, including legal positions, in the matter of supervisory cooperation and sharing of information with overseas regulators. The response from a few countries has been received and is being examined. The 'Supervisory College' arrangement for this purpose is also being examined by the Group.

Robust Arrangements for Dealing with Stress in the Financial System

- Central banks will enhance their operational frameworks and authorities will strengthen their cooperation for dealing with stress.

In the Reserve Bank, there is an institutional arrangement in place to oversee the functioning of the financial markets on a daily basis. There is a Financial Market Committee monitoring and assessing the functioning of different financial markets. Based on such an oversight, appropriate and prompt action is taken, whenever necessary.

The Reserve Bank has the necessary framework for provision of liquidity to the banking system, in terms of Sections 17 and 18 of the Reserve Bank of India Act, 1934. The regular liquidity management facilities of the Reserve Bank include the LAF, OMO and MSS besides standing facilities such as export credit refinance (ECR) and the liquidity facility for standalone PDs. The Reserve Bank can undertake purchase/sale of securities of the Central or State Governments and can purchase, sell, and rediscount bills of exchange and promissory notes drawn on and payable in India and arising out of *bona fide* commercial or trade transactions for provision/absorption of liquidity for normal day-to-day liquidity management operations as also for provision of emergency liquidity assistance to the banks under the lender of last resort function.

The Reserve Bank is empowered under the existing legal framework to deal with the resolution of weak and failing banks. The Banking Regulation Act provides the legal framework for voluntary amalgamation and compulsory merger of banks under Sections 44 (A) and 45, respectively. The Deposit Insurance and Credit Guarantee Corporation (DICGC) offers deposit insurance cover in India. The mergers of many weak private sector banks with healthy banks have improved overall stability of the system. Not a single scheduled commercial bank in the country has capital adequacy ratio which is less than the minimum regulatory requirement of 9 per cent.

Source: Annual Policy Statement for the Year 2008–09, Reserve Bank of India.

ANNEX II

Measures Taken by the Reserve Bank during September–November 2008 in Response to the Global Financial Market Developments

Rupee Liquidity

- CRR cut by 350 basis points to 5.5 per cent.
- Repo rate cut by 150 basis points to 7.5 per cent.
- SLR cut by 100 basis points to 24 per cent.
- Purely as a temporary measure, banks allowed to avail of additional liquidity support exclusively for the purpose of meeting the liquidity requirements of mutual funds, NBFCs, and housing finance companies to the extent of up to 1.5 per cent of their NDTL. Concomitantly, special 14 days' repo are being conducted every day up to a cumulative amount of Rs 60,000 crore with a view to enabling banks to meet the liquidity requirements of mutual funds and NBFCs.
- For fine-tuning the management of bank reserves on the last day of the maintenance period, a second LAF (SLAF) is being conducted on a daily basis.
- Buyback of MSS dated securities undertaken so as to provide another avenue for injecting liquidity of a more durable nature into the system. Buyback is calibrated with the market borrowing programme of the Government of India.
- A special refinance facility under Section 17(3B) of the Reserve Bank of India Act, 1934, introduced, whereby all scheduled commercial banks (excluding RRBs) can avail refinance from the Reserve Bank equivalent to up to 1.0 per cent of their NDTL as on 24 October 2008 at the LAF repo rate up to a maximum period of 90 days. During this period, refinance can be flexibly drawn and repaid.
- The mechanism of Special Market Operations (SMO) for public sector oil marketing companies reinstituted.
- Under the Agricultural Debt Waiver and Debt Relief Scheme, government had agreed to provide to commercial banks, RRBs, and co-operative credit institutions a sum of Rs 25,000 crore as the first instalment. At the request of the government, the RBI agreed to provide the sum to the lending institutions immediately.
- Under the existing guidelines, banks and FIs are not permitted to grant loans against certificates of deposits (CDs). Furthermore, they are also not permitted to buyback their own CDs before maturity. It was decided to relax these restrictions for a period of 15 days effective 14 October 2008, only in respect of the CDs held by mutual funds.

Forex Liquidity

- Interest rates on FCNR (B) Deposits and NRE(R)A deposits increased by 175 basis points each to Libor/Euribor/Swap rates plus 100 basis points and to Libor/Euribor/Swap rates plus 175 basis points, respectively.
- Banks allowed to borrow funds from their overseas branches and correspondent banks up to a limit of 50 per cent of their unimpaired Tier I capital as at the close of the previous quarter or US$ 10 million, whichever is higher, from the earlier limit of 25 per cent.
- ECB policy norms relaxed. ECBs up to US$ 500 million per borrower per financial year are permitted for rupee expenditure and/or foreign currency expenditure for permissible end-uses under the automatic route. All-in-cost ceilings enhanced to 300 basis points for ECBs of average maturity period of three years and up to five years and to 500 basis points for ECBs over five years. All-in-cost ceiling for trade credit less than three years enhanced to six months Libor plus 200 basis points.
- As a temporary measure, Systemically Important Non-Deposit taking NBFCs (NBFCs-ND-SI) permitted to raise short-term foreign currency borrowings under the approval route, subject to their complying with the prudential norms on capital adequacy and exposure norms.
- Housing finance companies (HFCs) registered with the National Housing Bank (NHB) allowed, as a temporary measure, to raise short-term foreign currency borrowings under the approval route, subject to their complying with prudential norms laid down by the NHB.
- In view of Foreign Currency Convertible Bonds (FCCBs) issued by Indian corporates trading at a discount, corporates permitted buy-back of their FCCBs at the prevailing discounted rates.
- Forex liquidity provided to Indian public and private sector banks having foreign branches or subsidiaries, through forex swaps of tenors upto three months. For funding the swaps, banks can also borrow under the LAF for the corresponding tenor at the prevailing repo rate. The Reserve Bank of India is prepared to consider any specific relaxation of SLR requirements for this purpose.
- The Reserve Bank announced that it would continue to sell foreign exchange (US dollars) through agent banks to augment supply in the domestic foreign exchange market or intervene directly to meet any demand–supply gaps.

Credit Delivery

- In view of the difficulties being faced by exporters on account of the weakening of external demand, the period of entitlement of the first slab of pre-shipment and post-shipment rupee export credit, currently available at a concessional interest rate ceiling of the benchmark prime lending rate (BPLR) minus 2.5 percentage points, extended from 180 days to 270 days and from 90 days to 180 days, respectively.

- The export credit refinance limit (ECR) limit increased from 15 per cent of the outstanding rupee export credit as at the end of the second preceding fortnight to 50 per cent of the outstanding export credit eligible for refinance.
- In order to ensure the growth momentum in the employment-intensive sectors of micro and small enterprises and housing, it was decided to allocate amounts, in advance, from scheduled commercial banks for contribution to the SIDBI and the NHB to the extent of Rs 2,000 crore and Rs 1,000 crore, respectively, against banks' estimated shortfall in priority sector lending in March 2009.These allocations will be adjusted against the banks' actual achievement of the target/sub-targets for priority sector lending as at the end of March 2009.
- During 2005–7, as a counter-cyclical prudential measure, the general provisioning requirement on standard advances for residential housing loan beyond Rs 20 lakh had been progressively increased from 0.25 per cent to 1.0 per cent, and that on standard advances in the commercial real estate sector, personal loans including outstanding credit card receivables, loans and advances qualifying as capital market exposure and non-deposit taking systemically important NBFCs from 0.25 per cent to 2.0 per cent. On a review, the provisioning requirements for all types of standard assets were reduced to a uniform level of 0.40 per cent (except in case of direct advances to agricultural and SME sector which shall continue to attract provisioning of 0.25 per cent, as hitherto). Similarly, risk weights on banks' exposures to certain sectors, which had been increased counter cyclically, were also revised downward from 150 per cent to 100 per cent for (a) unrated claims on corporates exposures above Rs 50 crore from 1 April 2008 and for exposures above Rs 10 crore from 1 April 2009; (b) claims secured by commercial real estate; (c) claims on rated as well as unrated non-deposit taking systemically important NBFCs (NBFC-ND-SI).

Index